FLESH MADE WORD

FLESH
MADE WORD

Saints' Stories and the Western Imagination

AVIAD KLEINBERG

Translated by Jane Marie Todd

The Belknap Press
OF HARVARD UNIVERSITY PRESS
CAMBRIDGE, MASSACHUSETTS
LONDON, ENGLAND
2008

To my parents, and to my sister

LIBRARY OF CONGRESS CATALOGING-IN-PUBLICATION DATA

Kleinberg, Aviad M.
[Histories de saints. English]
Flesh made word: saints' stories and the Western imagination /
Avid Kleinberg; translated by Jane Marie Todd.
p. cm.
Includes bibliographical references and index.
ISBN-13: 978-0-674-02647-6 (hardback: alk. paper)
ISBN-10: 0-674-02647-0 (hardback: alk. paper)
1. Christian saints.   2. Church history.   I. Title.
BX4655.3.K5413 2008
235'.2—dc22   2007031305

Contents

Before telling the first story of this book, he said: "The stories people tell around the world contain many mysteries and sublime things, but they have been spoiled, because much is missing from them, and now they are muddled and are not told in the proper order. And what should be at the beginning is told at the end, and vice versa, and so forth. But truly there are very lofty things in the tales of nations. And the Baal Shem Tov, blessed-be-his-righteous-and-holy-memory, was able to use such a tale to unite [with God]. And when he saw that the channels of heaven were blocked and could not be repaired through prayer, he repaired them and reconstituted them with a tale.

The Book of Tales, by Rabbi Nahman of Breslau (1772–1818)

INTRODUCTION

Some years ago I saw Mother Teresa on television. She spoke of her decision to take the veil and go to India, and how, after a time, she had found what was to be her vocation: helping the most needy—the lepers, the disabled, the many dying without a word of consolation, without shelter, without a bowl of rice. She recounted how she had taken care of her first patient, a dying leper. He had been lying in the gutter for who knows how long, his body rotting away, crawling with worms. Mother Teresa had carried him in her arms to a shelter. She had cleaned him up with a piece of cloth and had patiently fed him some gruel. At first the man was completely passive and let her handle him as she pleased. Then he seems to have come to. He looked at her and asked, "Why?" Compassion requires an explanation. At this point a change came over Mother Teresa. Until then she had spoken in a matter-of-fact, almost neutral tone, apparently taking no notice of the camera. Now she turned directly toward it and said, "I answered him: 'Because I love you.'"

This response shocked and confused me. It was not the words themselves that surprised me: How often have they been spoken in vain? "I love you." Empty words. I am a skeptic by nature, and when it comes to religious phenomena, my field of specialization, I am even more skeptical. Alas, I have heard every cliché too many times. I find wild-eyed mystics and wise gurus suspect. Mother Teresa should not have been any different. I could easily have thought that it was not *him* that she loved. He was a mere object, a rung on the ladder to the kingdom of heaven. There is nothing more selfish than the charity of the righteous. All you granted that stranger was a few moments of compassion. You were charitable for a moment, and immediately the angels dispelled all human stench with a flick of their wings. It's not him you loved, it's God. You loved your own image as a saint.

But that was *not* what I said to myself. I did not wonder how many times the story had already been told. I did not ponder the extent to which Mother Teresa's turning her eyes toward the camera could be attributed to training and experience. Not at all. I believed her. For an instant, at least, I believed that those words were the pure truth, that she had truly loved *him*, the leper dying in her arms. That love transformed the scene from a banal act of Christian charity into something truly heroic, sublime even.

What made me believe? I don't know. You had to be there. Generations have been there and believed. From time to time, perfectly normal people, skeptical and pragmatic, run into someone who causes them to lose their cynicism, who convinces them that altruism, self-sacrifice, unconditional love—make up your own list—are possible in real life and not just in homilies. Meeting such an "extraordinary" person does not generally impel us to act. We are not inclined to follow her, much less to imitate her. Sometimes such people earn smug and wan approval from us: "There are such wonderful people in this world!" Sometimes meeting such a person actually arouses antagonism. We feel that our mediocrity has been exposed. But we console ourselves by saying that goodness is just romantic drivel, that those grandiose actions and words conceal petty self-interest, that saintliness is only a pious façade. Freud forever demolished the sublime. When saintliness is not a con, it is self-deception. The sublimations of the righteous are more heroic than our own, but the internal mechanism is the same: the pursuit of psychological reward and the fear of psychological punishment. The subconscious is a cruel master. Some find their pleasure in feeding their id, some in nourishing their superego.[1] The moment of "faith" that took hold of me while watching Mother Teresa was brief. Immediately I was filled with doubts, beset by my usual cynicism. I was almost ashamed of my naïveté.

But skepticism was not always the "right" attitude. In medieval Christian society one was expected to have faith. The presence of saints, those virtuosos of goodness, was acknowledged in every aspect of life. An encounter with a saint was not a momentary puzzlement to be explained away. It was a call to action, to acts of devotion or imitation. Not that there were more saints then than now: there are never many saints. But what characterized medieval society was the desire *not* to place the existence of goodness in doubt but to have faith at any cost, almost. In the harsh and cruel world of the time, the presence of the saints bore witness not only to the possibility of doing good but also to the invisible hand of God here below. People believed that without saints, the life of ordinary mortals was unbearable. The Christian God had almost impossible moral expectations, and most people were unable (and perhaps unwilling) to live up to them. Divine justice could be terrible: it expressed itself in God's daily retributions and in the eternal horrors of hell. And yet, so long as there were people in the world who responded heroically to the moral imperatives of the Lord, so long as there were people found worthy of divine grace, all was not lost for the others.

The righteous do not have to tremble in fear before God. They are not the unfaithful servants but the beloved sons and daughters to whom God lends his ear and on whom he bestows his grace. He gives them his power, reveals a share of his hidden mysteries to them, and saves them, along with their neighbors, from the waters of his deluge. "Woe to the wicked man and to his neighbor!" goes a Hebrew proverb. "Blessed is the righteous man and blessed his neighbor!" Christian society was a community with a division of labor. The saint's role was to keep the world ethically functional. In addition, saints were living transmitters: they transmitted God's grace, knowledge, and strength to humanity, and humanity's petitions and pleas to God. Society needed them and resented their holy selfishness. Humility impelled saints to hide their virtues from those around them so as to avoid vainglory. That dangerous humility threatened to deprive society of the indispensable services the saint could render. Such irresponsibility could not be allowed. Hence when people discovered a saint, they rushed to him, devouring him with unbridled love, venerating him, flooding him with devotion and high praise, demanding in return that he give himself entirely, totally to them, that, like Mother Teresa, he really, truly love them.

The saint offered a window of hope, a consolation, and an antidote. People's need was so great that saints did not necessarily have to be "there" to function. Just learning of a saint's existence was almost as good as his or her real presence. Fantastic stories were told about saints. Powers and virtues, as great as the anxieties and sins they were supposed to heal, were attributed to them. Often a story was enough to give hope. The scrap of a garment the saint had (or had not) worn, water the saint had (or had not) touched, the saint's blood (or perhaps just red pigment) were enough. Such relics were permeated with the saint's power and, more important, with the devotees' expectations and hopes. Relics were a presence. Believers who had never seen Mother Teresa could share the same space with her. Relics were Aladdin's lamp. They could be brought to life by being rubbed with the believers' stories. And what did it matter if there was no saint at all to whom that blood, those garments, and that water had belonged? "The faith of the faithful, even if it is founded on error, brings them security," wrote the canonist Cardinal Henricus de Segusio (Hostiensis) in the thirteenth century.[2]

This book examines saints' stories from the first centuries of Christianity until the later Middle Ages. It seeks to understand the role these stories played in structuring religious systems and the tensions created by the contradictory and disturbing messages found in the different stories. It deals with the encounter between the "wild" creative energies of devotees and the suspicious prudence of the hierarchy. For the creative religious force of the community was not expressed in learned theological treatises or in canon law, not even in the church liturgy. It found expression in stories, tales about men and women. It is there, in these stories, that the faithful were engaged in a dialogue with and about their saints, with and about God.

ONE

Sanctity

"Sanctity" implies separation, demarcation. When a thing is sanctified, it is separated from others belonging to the same category. Generally, that separation also involves a "consecration," the transmission of the thing in question to someone or something. Hence in the Jewish wedding vows, the man proclaims, "You are sanctified to me," thus transforming a woman who is "permitted to every man" into a woman who is forbidden to everyone but her husband. In sanctifying the Sabbath, God proclaimed it different from the other days of the week, a day belonging to him alone. In Latin, the words *sacer* and *sanctus* have a similar meaning. *Sanctus* designates something that has been removed from the realm of the ordinary, sanctified, and is now "untouchable"; *sacer* designates what is specifically consecrated to the gods. In ancient Roman law the formula *sacer esto* (be sanctified) was used during executions. The condemned passed from the realm of human beings to the realm of the gods.[1] Sometimes these two Latin words were combined to express sanctity with a particular force, *sacrosanctus*.

In Hebrew and Latin the designation of a thing as sanctified or holy conferred a particular status on it. Since such a status generally involved religious ceremonies, over time the term "sanctity" took on an essentially religious meaning. All sacred things—temples, religious institutions, objects of worship, and individuals dedicated to the service of the faith—belonged to God and were subject to particular rules. They were more vulnerable than others to the danger of impurity, and any assault on their integrity or purity constituted the sin of sacrilege *(sacrilegium)*. Even when the ceremony was not explicitly accompanied by consecration to a god, it was surrounded with a religious aura that implied a divine presence.

The etymology of the word indicates that before anything else, the holy place, the holy object, and the holy man stand out, are an exception in the profane world. Conceptually, the idea of exceptionality precedes the notion of moral excellence that we now tend to associate with sanctity. Moral excellence is just one way of standing out. Someone who is exceptionally good sets himself off from ordinary people and indicates thereby that he belongs in some way to the kingdom of God (who is, somewhat paradoxically, consecrated to himself; by his very nature he is *sanctus sanctorum* and set apart from the created world).[2]

Sanctity, then, is intrinsically "irregular." It is also unstable. A saint needs to be "exposed" to be labeled holy. Such labeling is never beyond a reasonable doubt. Sanctity is in the eye of the beholder, and different beholders can have altogether different eyes. Attempts are made to stabilize sanctity. The authorized "experts" or the experienced authorities of a group can declare that their identification is final and that whatever doubts still remain, they must not be voiced in public. In the Catholic world from the late twelfth century on, certain individuals were granted (through the process of canonization) the status of authorized saints. This official status, however, did not necessarily give rise to intense feelings within the community. Official sanctity is a technical attribute, not a charismatic promise. Hence every priest *(sacerdos* in Latin) is "sacred" in the technical sense—he is subject to specific rules of purity, and any assault on him is sacrilege—yet the priest can be seen as utterly "worldly" in the eyes of the community. Conversely, an ascetic or mystic may be a layman lacking any formal recognition, yet the community may believe that he is close to God and serves as an agent of the supernatural world.

In any religious community there is tension between the way the authorities define sanctity and the way different groups define it in opposition to the authorities and without consulting them, at least initially. When the elite's power to make religious rules is explicitly challenged, the entire existence of the elite is put in doubt. Religious authorities always take such doubts seriously, especially if they are systematic, and take measures to suppress them. But sometimes the elite's authority is not explicitly challenged. Instead, seekers of innovation use creative misunderstanding to offer a new definition of sanctity without dismissing the old. They continue to accept in principle what they deny in practice. Devotees insist that particular places or people "fit in" with the accepted norms, that they not be exceptions to the rule but rather a legitimate interpretation of it. This produces not open war but more subtle forms of social struggle. It is to struggles of this sort that we now turn.

Charisma and Institutions

The term "charisma" is vague and takes on various meanings in everyday use and in the specialized literature. The approach taken in research on the subject is often as mystical as the notion itself. We are supposed to believe that certain people are endowed with an inner power to sway their peers. Those who have no charisma recognize that power in those who do, and their herd instinct impels them to follow the individual possessing it. I suggest that we resist any inclination to see charisma as an objective essence that a person possesses or does not possess. Charisma is a quality or an energy attributed to certain individuals by others. Without an audience there is no charisma. Charisma is redefined in every new encounter between a charisma-hungry group and a candidate (that is, an individual the group sees as an acceptable giver of orders, whether his own or those of the invisible powers). A person with an astonishing influence over one group might be the laughingstock of another. "Charisma" is the name given to the positive result of an implicit (or at times explicit) negotiation. The person to whom it is attributed has something the group wants; the group indicates in various ways what that something is and what it is willing to pay for it.

If the price is right, a charismatic situation develops. If it is not, the candidate's powers fail. Without a responsive audience that cultivates and nurtures it, the system of relations we call "charisma" would not exist. The precise content—what it is exactly that groups "see" in a candidate—varies: extraordinary courage, a self-assurance that radiates outward, a sense that the person in question is in direct contact with God (the term comes from the Greek *charis:* "divine gift," "grace"). It is difficult to come up with a definition, even for the participants in the charismatic dialogue. But in fact the definition is unimportant. What the different sorts of charisma have in common is their social repercussions: the person to whom charisma is attributed is supposed to possess qualities and powers that give him or her *authority*, whatever his or her official status.

The right to speak up and to be heeded constitutes an important privilege, which traditional societies tend to limit to the elite and its delegates. In the absence of appropriate social controls, that privilege can have a potentially devastating effect on the social order. Hence those who have authority always seek to persuade the entire community that extraordinary powers—the right to govern others, the right to intercede with the gods—reside solely with them and their delegates. In other words, "there is no power but of God." They rarely succeed. There is simply too much to gain by not going through the official channels. Religious charisma, the exceptional capacity to establish contact with God or the gods, can serve as a significant shortcut for gaining access to a share of the communal pie. The person to whom supernatural powers and divine favor are attributed is not subject to the "normal" laws governing society. A prophet can be a herdsman and simple farmer like Amos; but inasmuch as he is the mouthpiece by which the divine word is expressed, he is authorized to speak confidently and aggressively to his superiors—for example, to the priest Amaziah (Amos 7:10–17), to whom Amos directs the worst curses imaginable for attempting to silence the prophet. Charisma, then, is a boon to the lower classes. Those without power can gain access to it in a roundabout way—by using God as an intermediary. Thus visionaries, seers, dreamers, hearers of voices, and prophets again and again appear in the "wrong" places, in the margins of society, where they constantly seek detours to avoid the many roadblocks set up by the elite. Charismatics display their spiritual wares wherever they can. If they succeed in persuading at least some of the people that they have what consumers want, they become a serious problem. If the authorities completely reject such people, there is the risk that religion will "dry up." For were it not for the political and religious problems they pose, charismatic people could be quite useful. Charismatics serve as witnesses confirming in the first person what the authorities state in the third: that God exists and continues to transmit messages and powers to his faithful.

What should be done, then? Different cultures offer different solutions. In post-biblical Judaism, for example, the problem of charisma was solved in the most radical fashion: "Since the Temple was destroyed, prophecy has been taken from prophets and given to fools and children."[3] In a single sleight of hand, the rabbis solved that thorny problem once and for all. Intelligent grownups who hear voices and have visions are, a priori and by definition, false prophets. No further examination is necessary. Such a rule, which amounts to leaving prophecy to those who should not be heeded and to those whose prophetic power can be established only after the fact, may constitute a rare example of rabbinical humor.

There was a price to be paid for that decision. When people possessing noninstitutional religious charisma disappeared from Judaism, it became—theoretically at least—an entirely rational religion in which the learned elite (the "sages" and their disciples) resolved religious questions using agreed-upon rules of exegesis and syllogism. In the famous story of the controversy between Rabbi Eleazar and the other sages, Rabbi Yehoshua, the representative of the majority, responds to God's voice from heaven, which takes Rabbi Eleazar's side, by saying that the right to decide in halachic matters "is not in heaven." Revelation is over and done with. The halacha (Jewish religious law) belongs to the sages. "No one should heed [heavenly] voices anymore." Noninstitutionalized religious charisma was marginalized in Judaism. The words of various self-proclaimed prophets rarely attracted serious attention.

Coming to Grips with the Saints

In the Catholic Church, prophecy has not ceased. True, the Christian elite, like the Jewish, proclaimed the end of revelation with a capital *R*. The Montanists are wrong. God no longer reveals himself to people from the mountaintop, no longer becomes flesh and blood, no longer walks among them. God is no longer visible to all eyes or audible to all those with ears. Yet some still hear the voice of God and see his image. What was once available to all may have become the privilege of a few, but those few, those happy few—visionaries, dreamers, prophets, saints—continue to see and hear. More important, they can make the voice of God heard even by those who have lost their spiritual senses, who need eyeglasses and hearing aids. God speaks. At critical moments he reveals himself to his faithful—intermediaries between himself and the hard of hearing—and grants them what the exegetes cannot procure: a sense of presence, concrete and up-to-date information. In the Catholic Church, the central authority has continued to recruit those who possess charisma and to engage in intensive dialogue with them. A cleric could recognize the charismatic powers of a visionary and serve as his or her confessor, friend, and spiritual guide, easing the charismatic's move from the crowded margins to the center. The visionary offered visions and behaved in a way that fired up the enthusiasm of an audience. The guide explained to his protégée which of her visions were true (those the church could accept) and which were false (those the church could not). He taught her what was Christian and what was not (what is Christian is what the church defines as Christian). If that dialogue went along smoothly and the charismatic did not rebel against the authority of his or her guide on questions of faith, the guide could serve as intercessor with the church authorities (the person in question was acceptable, she could be counted on not to embarrass the authorities). The guide could help spread the fame of the charismatic by publishing a book (an authorized biography, a book of revelations) or by mentioning him or her in a sermon, for example. In short, he would serve as impresario. We must not regard these relationships cynically. In most cases the "impresario" sincerely believed in his protégée, felt that he was helping a saint reveal himself in all his splendor. Usually the guide was superior to his protégée from the institutional point of view but inferior from the moral and spiritual one. In their exchange the saint gained "translation services," publicity, and political support; the guide, better access to the kingdom of heaven and all the benefits of being the confidant of a saint. It should be noted that the church did not create its own charismatics the way it ordained its priests, for example. It preferred "ready-mades." Members of different communities were allowed to develop particular types of religious fervor, to produce the prophets and saints that suited them. Each community debated the saint's authenticity. Was he the real thing? Was the life he was leading consonant with the attribution of supernatural powers? Were the voices he heard divine voices? Were the miracles attributed to him "true"? Might he not be a false prophet or a fool? If a consensus of sorts formed within a community, then a *fama sanctitatis* emerged, and that person attracted a following. When that following was large enough to cause trouble, the authorities—local in the less important cases, central in the more important—intervened. They sent someone with authority to check who exactly this man was whom his followers considered a saint. How far was he from the established norms? Were there rumors of scandalous behavior? Was there any reason to suspect heresy or apostasy? If the authorities came to the conclusion that the public enthusiasm could serve the church's cause, or at least not damage it, they allowed the charismatic and his following to carry on and did not interfere very much in the affairs of the local community. If, however, the authorities came to believe there was a danger, they did what they could to put an end to the veneration and sometimes, in the case of a living person, to its object.

When the would-be saint had successfully passed the church's quality tests, and when a trustworthy "impresario" had made him sufficiently "presentable," the church was ready to move him from the margins to the center. The authorities gave their "imprimatur" to the messages God transmitted through this person and circulated the history of his life. Even when they became "authorized," however, charismatics were not allowed to meddle with church dogma. Theology, like halacha, was decided not by divine voices but by highly skilled professionals and by the *magisterium*, those with the *authority* to teach. But religion is not just dogma. It is also sacred narrative—a corpus of holy stories concerning God, his mother, and his agents on earth. It is also a catalogue of consecrated rules of conduct. In those spheres the contribution of charismatics to the Christian religion was enormous. Each new saint added new colors and nuances to the repertoire of acceptable behavior, simply because he or she served as a "saintly" model. Visionaries incessantly told new stories about God and the heavenly host. These stories reshaped the psychological profile of God and rewrote his biography. Without them Christianity would be a totally different religion. It is thanks to the church's policy of allowing people of all backgrounds to move into the symbolic and political center that Catholicism—its rigid image notwithstanding—became a religion in constant flux. It has persistently maintained a living dialogue between the center and the margins, between God and his faithful, between the old and the new.

We will examine this process in detail. At this point we may conclude that religious charisma is not an essence but a particular kind of social dynamic. It is not a predetermined list of qualities but a disposition on the part of a particular group to attribute exceptional qualities, generally a relationship with God, to one of its members. Charisma often arises at the margins of society and not at its center. Like any force, charisma has political implications. It involves a confrontation between the authorities and the charismatic group, that is, the person with charisma and his group of admirers. That confrontation takes place between those who hold authority but have no charisma and those who have charisma but no authority. The elite may attempt to remove those who possess dangerous charisma from the public stage (generally with only partial success). It may also attempt to translate the unruly and subversive language of charismatic people into the canonical language of the center. The Catholic Church was often willing to experiment with highly volatile social materials. In the chapters that follow, we will see why it acted in that way and what the consequences of that choice were.

TWO

The Beginnings

CHRISTIANITY BEGAN AS A PERSONALITY CULT. The first Christians considered themselves fully Jews; what differentiated them from other Jews was that they believed that Yeshua of Nazareth, Jesus, was the Messiah. When John the Baptist asked, "Are You the Coming One, or do we look for another?" Jesus replied, "Go and tell John the things which you hear and see: *The* blind see and *the* lame walk; *the* lepers are cleansed and *the* deaf hear; *the* dead are raised up and *the* poor have the gospel preached to them" (Matt. 11:3–5).[1] Jesus does not answer the question by describing his "program." He does not allege that he is of the House of David (as his disciples would later do on his behalf). His credentials are neither genetic nor ideological; they are charismatic. Jesus lists one by one the external manifestations of his power. These powers are so great that he cannot be considered a mere miracle worker or one more preacher inspired by the Holy Spirit. He must be the intercessor par excellence, the anointed of God—the Messiah. For his early disciples, the designation "Son of God" did not express a metaphysical relationship with God. The disciples did not think that God had begotten Jesus; that was a later belief. The designation indicated that Jesus had an intimate and singular relationship with God. Just as

God is the "father" of his chosen people, so is he the "father" of the Savior. He has come. One need no longer wait for another.

Jesus' singularity also found expression in some of his miracles. He drives out demons with a simple command, without the usual formulas or rites. He forgives sinners, something that, in the eyes of those around him, is the privilege of God alone (Mark 2:7–11). He interprets the Torah "as one having authority, and not as the scribes" (Mark 1:22), that is, not by comparing different verses or by *midrash* (creative interpretation). He simply speaks with authority: "You have heard that it was said . . . but *I* say unto you."

When Jesus arrives in Jerusalem, astride an ass "that it might be fulfilled what was spoken by the prophet [Zechariah]" concerning the Messiah (Matt. 13:35), he is greeted by multitudes crying, "Hosanna to the son of David!" The crowds in Jerusalem have no knowledge of the genealogy of the Galilean rabbi, but someone whose powers bear witness to the fact that he is the Messiah is, as a consequence, necessarily the "son of David."

Yet some remained skeptical. On a number of occasions Jesus is suspected of obtaining his powers not from God but from Satan. Some of those close to him fear he has quite simply gone mad: "But when His own people heard *about this*, they went out to lay hold of Him, for they said, 'He is out of His mind.' And the scribes who came down from Jerusalem said, 'He has Beelzebub,' and, 'By the ruler of the demons He casts out demons'" (Mark 3:21–22). Miracles do not in themselves attest to the moral status of a miracle worker. Satan has a disturbing tendency to disguise himself as an angel of light, and his minions can possess very impressive powers. There was also a more down-to-earth skepticism:

> And when the Sabbath had come, He began to teach in the synagogue. And many hearing *Him* were astonished, saying, "Where *did* this Man *get* these things? And what wisdom *is* this which is given to Him, that such mighty works are performed by His hands! Is this not the carpenter, the Son of Mary, and brother of James, Joses, Judas, and Simon? And are not His sisters here with us?" So they were of-

fended at Him. But Jesus said to them, "A prophet is not without honor except in his own country, among his own relatives, and in his own house." Now He could do no mighty work there except that He laid His hands on a few sick people and healed *them*. And He marveled because of their unbelief. (Mark 6:2–6)

No one is a prophet in his own country: or were there just too many prophets in that country? When the Galilean and his disciples arrived in the big city, they thought Jerusalem would fall at their feet. It did not. In Jerusalem there was never any shortage of prophets, miracle workers, and would-be messiahs. In the face of the Jerusalemites' skepticism, Jesus' tone became darker. It was not only his followers who were to suffer for his sake; he himself had to suffer. Already in the Sermon on the Mount, his most important ideological statement, Jesus had expressed profound suspicion and hostility toward the existing order of things. He declared that there was no relationship between success achieved in this world and the grace granted by God. According to his view, the suffering of the righteous was not an abnormal phenomenon, an outrage that God must justify and rectify: it was the "normal" order of things. Rather than being an outrage, it was the path leading to salvation:

Blessed *are you poor,*
For yours is the kingdom of God.
Blessed are you who hunger now,
For you shall be filled.
Blessed *are you* who weep now,
For you shall laugh.
Blessed are you when men hate you,
And when they exclude you,
And revile *you,* and cast out your name as evil,
For the Son of Man's sake.
Rejoice in that day and leap for joy!
For indeed your reward *is* great in heaven,

For in like manner their fathers did to the prophets.

But woe to you who are rich,

For you have received your consolation.

Woe to you who are full,

For you shall hunger.

Woe to you who laugh now,

For you shall mourn and weep.

Woe to you when all men speak well of you,

For so did their fathers to the false prophets.

(Luke 6:20–26)

"Blessed are you when men hate you." Material success is not a sign of divine favor but a source of moral anxiety. This world belongs to the wicked. They have benefited from it, and in making their choice have renounced the world to come. The righteous man wanders through the world, insults and invectives heaped upon him, like one exiled from his true home, the kingdom of heaven.

It appears that Jesus himself did not disdain success at first. In fact, he seems to have been surprised by the hostile attitude of the people of his own country. In any case, he acted not as if he were seeking to break away from the world but rather as if he were trying to be its leader. It was only gradually that bitterness overtook him and he came to consider himself not the uncontested leader of the "disinherited" masses to whom the kingdom of heaven belongs, but a rejected and tormented messiah. He realized that he was offering salvation to people who either did not want to be saved or did not want to be saved *his* way. In Jerusalem, Jesus attracted the animosity of members of the Jewish religious leadership, and they, following the Christian tradition, handed him over to the Roman authorities. Only a week after he entered Jerusalem, Jesus was crucified by order of the governor, Pontius Pilate. The Jerusalemites seem to have remained indifferent. It also appears that even the disciples did not get the message that earthly power was to be totally rejected. They were not exceedingly glad when the Messiah was being reviled and persecuted. Indeed, up to the last minute they expected him to use his power to stop the moral outrage of his persecution, to come down from the cross and take revenge on his tormentors. When this did not happen, they abandoned Jesus and dispersed, disappointed. The Messiah's death was a moment not of triumph but of terrible loneliness. "My God, My God, why have You forsaken Me?"

But shortly after Christ's death, for reasons that are not altogether clear to us, something happened within the group of disciples. They reached the conclusion that Jesus' death did not prove that he was *not* the Messiah—as most Jews had assumed—or that his mission was a failure. Surely he knew all along. His death was not the breaking of promises but their fulfillment. The resurgence of that belief on the part of the disciples found symbolic expression in Jesus' resurrection. The disciples let those around them know that Jesus was not dead, that he had risen and had revealed himself to their eyes. Whether or not the disciples actually "saw" the risen Christ, one thing is clear: the community that had formed around Jesus' charismatic personality and around the promises of salvation decided to continue its existence around a new Jesus, a mythic Jesus who, unlike the living Jesus, had not failed, had not been overcome by anger, and had not fallen into despair. These disciples were the heirs and agents of the resurrected Jesus.

The community, now organized not around a living charismatic leader but around a "memory," part historical and part mythical, had to reinterpret, indeed re-create, the leader in light of his tragic death. The suffering of Jesus was preordained; it was indispensable, not only so that *he* would be taken up to the kingdom of heaven but so that everyone else would be as well. He suffered and died for others, for us. That conception had a precedent in the suffering servant portrayed in Isaiah's prophecy (53:3–11):

> He is despised and rejected by men,
> A Man of sorrows and acquainted with grief.
> And we hid, as it were, *our* faces from Him;
> He was despised, and we did not esteem Him.
> Surely He has borne our griefs
> And carried our sorrows;
> Yet we esteemed Him stricken,
> Smitten by God, and afflicted.

But He *was* wounded for our transgressions,

He was bruised for our iniquities;

The chastisement for our peace *was* upon Him,

And by His stripes we are healed.

All we like sheep have gone astray;

We have turned, every one, to his own way;

And the LORD has laid on Him the iniquity of us all.

He was oppressed and He was afflicted,

Yet He opened not His mouth;

He was led as a lamb to the slaughter,

And as a sheep before its shearers is silent,

So He opened not His mouth;

He was taken from prison and from judgment,

And who will declare His generation?

For He was cut off from the land of the living;

For the transgressions of My people He was stricken.

And they made His grave with the wicked—

But with the rich at His death,

Because He had done no violence,

Nor *was any* deceit in His mouth.

Yet it pleased the LORD to bruise Him;

He has put *Him* to grief.

When You make His soul an offering for sin,

He shall see *His* seed, He shall prolong *His* days,

And the pleasure of the LORD shall prosper in His hand.

He shall see the labor of His soul, *and* be satisfied.

By His knowledge My righteous Servant shall justify many,

For He shall bear their iniquities.

For Jesus' disciples, there was no doubt that *he* was the suffering servant.[2] Yet during his lifetime he had not been despised and abandoned by men; on the contrary, he was a spiritual guide and a leader whose commands were obeyed even when not fully understood. Jesus' death on the cross gave a somber new meaning to his entire life. The unjust death of a righteous man is always a distressing sight; the death of the Messiah was a sacrilege and an outrage. Worse, there was nothing heroic about Jesus' death. He was executed as a common criminal. How can one explain a death so wretched, so ordinary? The disciples refused to accept that the messianic epic could end on such a minor chord. No, his death was common and wretched only in appearance. The cross became a battleground; the moment of desperate, solitary death was transformed into a triumph that had saved humanity. "By His stripes we are healed." The Lamb of God bore the weight of our iniquities on his shoulders. "The chastisement for our peace was upon Him."

The idea of a suffering messiah was not alien to Judaism. It appears in the Dead Sea scrolls; it exists in the Orthodox Jewish tradition in the figure of Messiah, Son of Joseph (in Hebrew, Mashiakh Ben Yosef), who will die at the hands of his enemies, preceding Messiah, son of David. But Jewish suffering messiahs were only paving the way for the Messiah proper, the triumphant Messiah. Indeed in Judaism, power is one of the surest signs of the Messiah, weakness a sure sign of a fake. "Are you the Coming One?" Jesus answered this question with a description of his power, but that was before he died. For his disciples this contradiction in (Jewish) terms—a weak, defeated messiah—was the one. He had come. There was none before him and there would be none after him.

Jesus was the Savior of mankind. Those who wanted to offer more modest salvations had to follow the path he—or his disciples—had marked out. He was the ultimate, the one true model. To follow in his footsteps, one had to despise the things of the world, to live as if at any moment one might be called upon to make the ultimate sacrifice and die for him who died for us. Dying for the Savior—and like the Savior—constituted the most reliable proof of a person's true value. If this was the critical test, it was not long before Christians were put to it.

Persecutors and the Martyrs

Put to the ultimate test, a person willing to lose his life rather than his faith bears witness to the truth of such faith. The Greek word for witness is *martyr.* Those who died for the Christian faith were "martyrs," witnesses to the truth of the Christian message. The first martyr, we are told, was a Greek Jew named Stephen. About two years after Jesus' death, Stephen was taken before the Sanhedrin and charged with blasphemy. He refused to recant. He blamed his judges for rejecting and murdering Jesus, and proclaimed that he saw the heavens opening and Jesus on the right hand of God. Stephen was then driven from the city and stoned to death. That was the beginning.

The government of the Roman Empire was usually indifferent to people's religious convictions. What people believed was their private affair. Religious practice was a different matter, especially when it moved out of the home into the public sphere. But as long as those practices did not seem to pose a direct threat to the *respublica,* they were tolerated. Christianity was not. Like Judaism, it was monotheistic. Belief in one God was seen not simply as the choice of a preferred deity; it was the denial of all other cults tolerated by the state. It threatened the harmony of the multicultural, multireligious empire. It prevented the group from being completely integrated into the life of the empire. The veneration of state gods and of the emperor, among other cults, was an important instrument for unifying the empire. Each group was free to practice its cult alongside the common cult. Jews and Christians refused to respect other gods, including the state gods. That was dangerous.

Nevertheless, Judaism was tolerated. It was ancient, and Romans respected the Jews' fidelity to their ancestral tradition.[3] In addition, the Greek experience had shown that any attack on the religion of the Jews would stir up trouble and lead to bloodshed. Jews formed a fairly significant minority in the empire. Christianity was different: it was both asocial and new.[4] The initial attempts by the Christians to pass themselves off as Jews in order to benefit from the authorities' tolerance ran up against the opposition of Jewish leaders. Jews refused to consider Christians one more stream within Judaism, like the Pharisees and Sadducees; they considered them apostates and heretics, and did everything they could to exclude them from their community. Christians found themselves stripped of all protection. They were worse than Jews and much easier to persecute.

One can always do with a good scapegoat. Christians were perfect for the role. As Tertullian wrote in the second century: "If the Tiber reaches the walls, if the Nile does not rise to the fields, if the sky doesn't move or the earth does, if there is famine, if there is plague, the cry is at once: 'The Christians to the lion!' *(Christianos ad leonem)*."[5] Christians were accused of atheism because they refused to worship the Roman gods; they were accused of murdering babies, whose blood they supposedly drank at their closed meetings and whose flesh they supposedly ate; they were accused of witchcraft and incestuous orgies. Their crimes, it was claimed, threatened to lead their innocent neighbors to ruin.[6]

The first persecutions of Christians occurred in A.D. 64.[7] Christians were accused of burning down the city of Rome in the time of Emperor Nero. The Roman historian Tacitus, who despised the Christians for other reasons, had no doubt that they were *not* guilty of setting the fire. The aim of that persecution, he observes, was to deflect suspicion away from the emperor himself; according to persistent rumors, it was Nero who had given the order to burn the city. The Christians were put to death by the cruelest methods: they were covered with animal skins and thrown to wild beasts, crucified, or burned alive. If we are to believe Tacitus, the torments they endured were so horrendous that the spectators were overcome with pity, not because the tormented did not deserve to be punished, but because the brutal violence was inflicted not "for the public good" but rather to satisfy the cruelty of a single man.[8]

The exact number of Christians put to death is not known. Given the size of the Christian community and the nature of the accusations, it must have been very small. According to an ancient tradition, among those killed were two of the most important leaders of the community: Peter, the first disciple, and Paul, a Jew of Tarsus who had never met Jesus, but who, having converted to Christianity, had become the most important ideologue and missionary of the "Jesus movement." Peter was put to death by crucifixion, a particularly degrading method of execution. Paul, as a Roman citizen, was entitled to a more honorable form of death: he was decapitated.

The first wave of persecutions ended as suddenly as it had arisen. Until the third century, persecutions of Christians were sporadic and local. The Roman authorities refused to grant Christianity legal status; officially, merely belonging to the Christian sect was a criminal offense. But they did not seek to liquidate the Christian community. Like other groups that served as scapegoats, Christians were "used" when the need arose. Between waves of persecution, when the community did not require "guilty parties," Christians were tolerated de facto if not de jure. Emperor Trajan (r. 98–117) set a policy that was to remain in force until the third century: provincial governors were not to seek out Christians on their own initiative or pay attention to anonymous denunciations. Those shown to be members of the sect should be allowed to recant and prove their loyalty to the *respublica* by making sacrifices to the gods. Only those who refused to be "social" should be executed. The policy consisted of turning an official blind eye and offering a handy escape route for Christians whose neighbors turned them in. Hence the number of "martyrs" in the first and second centuries was not large.

Nevertheless, in spite of its relative rarity, martyrdom has become the "root metaphor" of Christianity and the martyr the Christian hero par excellence.[9] That process was not a matter of course. Although it is true that every community honors those who have died out of loyalty to its norms, those heroic dead do not always have a central role in the life of the community. In the Jewish community of the time, for example, the exemplary hero was not the individual who died for his faith but rather the sage. In the second century, Judaism also went through a period of persecutions when Hadrian's decrees set off the Bar Kochba revolt. Jewish martyrs died for disobeying the imperial decrees that forbade circumcision and public study of the Torah. Yet these martyrs were not the object of any particular veneration, and the names of most of them (with the exception of important rabbis) have not been preserved.[10] Even the attitude toward martyred rabbis was ambivalent, as attested in the following dialogue between Rabbi Yose Ben Kisma and Rabbi Chanina Ben Teradyon in the *Babylonian Talmud* (*Avodah Zarah* 18a):

Chanina, my brother! [says Rabbi Yose], Do you not know that from heaven they have imposed as rulers over us this nation, which has destroyed God's house [the Temple], burned His sanctuary (the Holy of Holies), killed His pious ones and caused His noble ones to perish, and it still exists. And yet I have heard about you that you sit and engage in Torah study and convene gatherings in public with a Torah [scroll] in your lap!

[R' Chanina said to R' Yose in reply]: From heaven they will have mercy on me. [R' Yose responded to R' Chanina]: I am saying something sensible to you, and you are telling me that from heaven they will have mercy?! I would be amazed if they do not burn you and the Torah scroll in fire.

"I am saying something sensible to you, and you are telling me that from heaven they will have mercy?!" That attitude, pragmatic and at times even critical of martyrdom, is also found in a halachic rule that can probably be attributed to Rabbi Yose Ben Kisma: "In regard to whoever submits himself to death on account of words of Torah, the law is that we do not cite any halachic statement in his name" (*Babylonian Talmud, Bava Kamma* 61a). Rabbis accepted martyrdom only as the last resort. If every means for remaining alive had been exhausted, then one was obliged to die for one's faith. All the same, any sign of contempt for life or a lack of prudence raised grave doubts about the martyr's wisdom and even his moral standing.[11]

That was not the case for Christianity. The Christian community was willing to venerate the memory of martyrs even when death could have been easily avoided (by flight, by bribes, or by lies). The clearest indication of the tendency to see a particular degree of moral excellence in the martyr was the attribution of martyrdom to the apostles. The apostles were the elect of God in the most literal sense. There was no need for further proof, since Jesus had chosen them in person. He had spent his preaching career in their company and had appeared to them after his death. Nevertheless, the community felt that this was not enough. Something was lacking—a cruel voluntary death. There were more or less reliable testimonies of the martyrdom of Peter and Paul, of James the Great (martyred by the order of Herod Agrippa I), and of James the Just, who was stoned to death in A.D. 62. But tradition also attributed martyrdom to the others: Andrew, Matthias, Simon, and Philip were supposedly crucified, Bartholomew flayed, Thomas and Matthew run through with swords, and Thaddaeus (Judas) lynched by the mob. As for John the Apostle, an ancient tradition attributed a long life to him, but later traditions explained that this was not the apostle's fault. John had been immersed in a tank of boiling water and had miraculously come out safe and sound.[12] He would have been a martyr had God not intervened.

The Christian martyr's death was not always the last resort. Christian descriptions of martyrdom emphasize the deliberate act that turns the martyr from passive victim of the violence of others to master of his (and others') fate. In other words, by choosing martyrdom, the martyr—like Jesus, whom he imitates—is transformed from victim to priest: it is he who sacrifices himself, not his evil tormentors who sacrifice him.[13] An example of this attitude can be found in an ancient text from the early second century. It is the martyr himself who speaks. In A.D. 107 Ignatius, bishop of Antioch, wrote a letter to the Christian community of Rome. Sentenced to death as a Christian, Ignatius was taken to Rome under military escort, to be thrown to wild beasts in the arena. He writes:

> Let my blood be spilled in sacrifice to God, while yet there is an altar ready. . . . I die willingly for God, provided you do not interfere. I beg you, do not show me unseasonable kindness. Suffer me to be the food of wild beasts, which are the means of my making my way to God. God's wheat I am, and by the teeth of wild beasts I am to be ground that I may prove Christ's pure bread. Better still, coax the wild beasts to become my tomb. . . . Petition Christ in my behalf that through these instruments I may prove God's sacrifice. Not like Peter and Paul do I issue any orders to you. They were Apostles, I am a convict; they were free; I am until this moment slave. But once I have suffered, I shall become a freedman of Jesus Christ, and united with Him, I shall rise a free man. . . . And should [the beasts] be unwilling to attack me who am willing, I will myself compel them. . . . Permit me to be an

imitator of my suffering God. . . . And should I upon my arrival plead for your intervention, do not listen to me. Rather, give heed to what I write to you. . . . My yearning is for death.[14]

All the elements of Christian martyrdom are present here: the desire to follow in the footsteps of Jesus; death that is life, life that is death; freedom that is slavery, and slavery that is freedom.[15] The signs in this world and in the next are reversed. More significant, the site of the execution is conceived as an altar, and the tormentors (Roman officials and wild beasts) are mere instruments in the martyr's hands. Death is redemptive. "My yearning is for death."

Fear and remorse are absent from the triumphal exclamations of Saint Ignatius. They were rarely absent from those left behind, for martyrdom is often the source of severe anxiety. Public torture and execution are didactic tools. Their aim is to engrave a cautionary tale in the spectators' memory: the wicked are punished and the moral balance of the world, upset by the condemned man's crime, is reestablished. Ideally the condemned cooperate with the justice system of which they are the victims. They accept the sentence; they beg forgiveness and mercy or behave in a shameful and cowardly way which proves that they deserve their punishment. When the condemned accept their punishment, they are reintegrated into the community. They have made themselves useful again. Public executions, then, are not merely elimination but ritual theater.[16] Each of its acts was meant to enhance the dramatic effect: the exit from prison, the procession to the place of execution (a *via dolorosa* that made possible verbal exchanges between the condemned and the spectators), various ceremonies near the gallows, and finally the execution itself and the removal of the corpse. The success of the drama depended on the condemned playing their part and on the audience's being convinced that their punishment had served them right.[17]

Christian martyrs were bad actors in the Roman legal drama. They had their own script and simply refused to obey their executioners' stage directions. Not only would they not acknowledge their offenses, but they also played the villain role scandalously—refusing to beg for mercy. They acted honorably, indeed heroically. This behavior produced strong reactions among their non-Christians spectators, ranging from great anger (Why aren't you behaving as you ought?) to shock and self-doubt (Is it possible that people who conduct themselves like Stoic sages are really ordinary criminals?). "Many among you," writes Tertullian, "preach the endurance of pain and of death. [He cites the names of several philosophers.] And yet their words never find so many disciples as the Christians win, who teach by deeds. . . . For who that beholds [that obstinacy] is not stirred to inquire, what lies indeed within it?"[18]

Even those who thought the punishment served the victims right felt that something was wrong. It was not easy to feel contempt for such people. Were they really deserving of contempt? What made them act so heroically? Why did they insist on proving their moral superiority, making a travesty of justice?[19] Cognitive dissonance can be very annoying.

The reaction of Christian spectators was more complex. For Christians, it was obvious that the execution was a scandal, that this was not justice but legalized murder. For them there was no question of restoring moral justice in the world. True justice was not of *this* world. The execution was a monstrous reversal of roles: the "criminals" were innocent, the judges criminals; the Roman spectators were not a Greek chorus encouraging those carrying out a sacred duty but a murderous mob thirsty for innocent blood. The martyrs played their role well according to the Christian scenario, but that scenario was the record of the terrible injustices, the utter senselessness, of the world.[20]

The blood of the innocent cries out from the earth and disturbs the peace of the living. Innocence is relative. In comparison with the holy martyrs, no survivor is innocent. The blameless victims of injustice are endowed with terrible powers. Their blood cries out for vengeance. They must be appeased. Psychologically, the innocent are more threatening to their fellows than to their murderers. The perpetrators are protected by the conviction that their victims *are not* innocent, or that they are not truly human beings. But those who are convinced of the innocence of the dead are troubled by great guilt. The sense persists that more could have been done to save them, or better still, to join them. The living owe their lives to their moral mediocrity. They were less willing than their brethren to turn their backs on the world, to despise torture and death, to imitate the Lamb of God. The moral chasm between the perfect and the imperfect threatens to devour the latter in order to appease the former. The Babylonian Talmud tells of the Babylonian general who enters the temple in Jerusalem to find a puddle of boiling blood. When he inquires about it, he learns it belonged to the prophet Zechariah, murdered at the site by the Israelites. The blood has been boiling ever since. The Babylonian decides to appease the blood. He orders the execution of thousands of Jews on the spot. But the bloodthirsty blood will not stop boiling. Only when the exasperated general asks, "Zechariah! Zechariah! . . . Do you want me to kill them all?" is the blood's thirst finally quenched (*Sanhedrin* 96b).

Christians did not appease the blood of the martyrs with blood—either their enemies' or their own. They mollified it with veneration. They had a model, of course. The apostles' veneration grew out of Christ's broken body. It arose among those who had stood idly by as he was killed. It emerged from their guilt. The disciples brought the Lord back to life so that his boiling blood would not consume them. The resurrection gave the disciples another chance. As we have seen, they did not fail a second time.

Jesus was resurrected; the martyrs still await the day of universal resurrection. But although martyrs are not resurrected in the flesh, the flesh they leave behind does not die. It is not like other flesh. It is spiritualized flesh that can bridge the gap between the community left behind and the martyr who has taken his place on the right hand of God. A text written in A.D. 156 is the first testimony we have of the Christian attitude toward the martyr's bodily remains. It is a letter in which members of the community of Smyrna describe the martyrdom of their elderly bishop Polycarp. After the execution a dispute erupted between Christians and Jews concerning the bishop's remains. The Christians tried to take possession of the body and the Jews tried to prevent them. If they were allowed to have the body, the Jews claimed, the Christians would use it for ritual purposes; they would worship Polycarp's body instead of Jesus. In other words, the Jews accused their Christian neighbors of adopting ever lower forms of idolatry. As if worshiping a human being were not bad enough, the Christians, given the opportunity, would replace the cult of the absent Jesus with something more concrete, the body of Polycarp. The Christians rejected that accusation: they *worship* God alone; they *love and venerate* the martyrs because they are the disciples and imitators of Jesus.

But the Jewish accusation that Christians were making ritual use of the martyr's body was not without foundation. The Roman centurion confiscated the remains and burned them, hoping thereby to put an end to the affair. He failed. "We have collected his bones more precious than fine stones, and more valuable than gold," notes the letter, "and we have buried them in an appropriate place. If God allows, we will assemble there as often as possible and will celebrate his martyrdom—the anniversary of his birth[21]—in joy and happiness, to remember heroes of the past and to instruct and prepare heroes to come."[22]

Let us consider two elements of the last sentence quoted: memory and example. The veneration of the martyr and the gratitude the community feels toward him finds expression in the tremendous effort made to preserve his memory. It is significant that the graves of martyrs were called *memoriae.* By his heroic witnessing, the martyr moves from the private and familial realm to the public domain and from private to collective memory. When a community decides to integrate someone into its store of things "worthy of memory," worthy of being remembered by the entire community, it declares him or her a constitutive element in its identity formation. Because group identity must remain fairly simple to be accessible to all and available at all times, it tends to be made up of a limited number of cultural clichés—exaggerated and simplified "memorable" elements. Whenever a new element is added to this core of culture, it modifies the relative status of all other elements within it. It also demands the creation of the particular aide-mémoires necessary for fixing it on the slippery ground of collective memory. As soon as someone becomes part of the group's official history, events and persons of lesser importance are situated in relation to him or her. Hence events occur "before Christ," or "after the foundation of Rome." The "anniversary" of the saint's birth becomes a reference point in time. Any element in his image or in the account of his life that has been chosen for preservation becomes a moral and theological point of reference.[23]

The Christian community places martyrs and the accounts of their suffering in the category of "things worthy of memory" *(digna memoriae)*. In antiquity and in the Middle Ages, history was not a passive reflection of events but a moral choice. Each generation had the moral obligation to choose a list of things worthy of being included in the record of humanity and to transmit them to the next generation. Simply to record things "as they were" would have meant imposing an intolerable burden on society's memory. Most things are best forgotten. They are noise that obfuscates the music of history. But the martyrs must not be forgotten. Their memory is an act of piety toward the dead; it sets a sacred example for the living, and it is confirmation of the community's faith in the Christian message. Each life lived for Christ, and each voluntary death *for him,* is proof of the Gospel's power to give meaning to life and to death. In the ancient world every family was morally obliged to preserve the memory of its dead. The martyr is a symbolic ancestor, the collective flesh and blood of the entire community. He turns the community into a family. But martyrs are not the ordinary dead. Whereas the Greek dead in Homer's Hades depend on blood offerings to reactivate their consciousness, the martyrs' blood feeds the community and invigorates it.

In purely logical terms, martyrdom does not make a very good argument. The fact that people are prepared to die for a cause does not in itself say anything about the value of the cause. But human psychology is not an Aristotelian syllogism. The steadfastness and heroism of the martyrs are evidence of their moral fiber and, by implication, of the truth of their conviction, for are we not constantly told that falsehood begets cowardice and truth fortitude? Is it conceivable, then, that people possessing a moral fortitude far surpassing that of their tormentors would have allowed themselves to be duped by sham beliefs? Is it conceivable that they died in vain?

Having been declared worthy of memory, martyrs needed mnemonic devices to institute and maintain their memory. The community procured a more or less official version of what it believed ought to be committed to memory and then circulated it—in written or oral form—within and outside the community. Letters written by the martyrs themselves, when they existed, were copied and sent to the various Christian communities; eyewitness accounts were attached to them, accompanied by pious commentary. The martyrs' stories were told and retold, each repeating the "core tale" and adding elements that had not necessarily found expression in the "official" written version. That official account served as a measuring rod that could be used to correct weaker versions when they strayed too far from the original. But "wild" oral accounts had an enormous importance in the creation of social memory, not simply because they reached a larger public, but precisely because they had an "elasticity." Each version could express the needs of a specific group of listeners and tellers.

In "the field," versions less authentic from a historical standpoint, but more "effective" psychologically for a specific group in a specific set of circumstances, often prevailed over the authentic official version. The validity of the original version was not challenged, but since it was made to coexist side by side with very "powerful" reproductions, it lost its status as the sole true copy. Truth was not dichotomous. All pious versions were to some extent true. Only the "learned" continued to view historical authenticity as fixed, and with time only the learned had access to the source. Furthermore, since those who recounted new versions were not always content with the vague status of pious retellings and sought to gain full authority as "extensions" of the original (relying on rediscovered oral tradition, or more rarely on divine revelations), several "official" traditions sometimes arose concurrently. Social "memory" was not (and is not) fixed.[24] The only thing that mattered was the "fact" of martyrdom itself. The blood of the martyrs cleansed the community of its sins, and the martyr was its agent in the kingdom of heaven. If there was not martyrdom, the whole social structure that was built upon it collapsed. The many useful and beautiful retellings, the miracles, the religious energies of the devotees were all in vain. The taller the edifice, the less likely a community would undermine it.

In addition to narratives of the martyrs' heroism, community ceremonies were organized in memory of the martyr and served as mnemonic devices. On a fixed date the community came together at a specified place (the saint's church or tomb) and remembered him or her. The ritual interrupted the normal flow of time. The community was summoned to remember the martyr and his or her sacrifice. Sometimes mass was celebrated on the day of martyrdom; sometimes an abridged version of the *Passio* was read. Sometimes, when all details had been lost to oblivion, only one thing remained: the name of the martyr and the fact of martyrdom. The community could not reproduce a text or transmit a story; it celebrated its remembrance, its commemoration. Memory—as act, as a fulfilled moral obligation, not as specific content—was a license to fill in missing details, to complete what was lacking.

That process of transforming historical memory (lost or repressed) into social memory was of crucial importance in the cult of saints. Ritual memory was an authorization to forget. From the moment the saint's words appeared in a book and his anniversary was fixed on the calendar, it was no longer necessary to reproduce the martyr's historical image, an image that quickly became "anachronistic," dated, passé. The saint's history was gradually stripped of its historical nuances and translated into sacred formulas, which facilitated memory (the concrete martyr had become an ideal martyr, that is, a martyr like all the others) and served as a saintly syrup to which the waters of each generation could be added. That process made the saint more conventional, turned him or her into an icon—a man or a woman for all seasons. It allowed, indeed called for, creativity: the icon had to be readjusted to fit the needs of the moment.[25]

To cite the words of the Smyrna community, it was instruction and preparation for "heroes to come"—not the keeping of an accurate historical record—that was the intention of the martyrdom narrative.[26] "Heroes to come" took part in the ritual, during which the community expressed its faith in the martyr, singing his or her glory and reaffirming the act of memory. Martyrs were the new heroes; they achieved immortality not only in the kingdom of heaven but, like the ancient Greek and Roman heroes, on earth as well: they were not forgotten. The "heroes to come" heard updated and revised accounts of martyrdom. The ritual showed them the lofty symbolic status they could achieve in the eyes of their community; they too could be made worthy of memory. The narratives offered a repertoire of heroic models. They constituted a sort of training manual for future martyrs. For identification with the martyrs to be possible, the concrete historical event had to be transformed into a symbolic event. It was the role of these narratives to reenact, reinterpret, reincarnate the symbolic.

By the second century, then, the veneration of martyrs had developed, and the first signs of saints' cults had appeared in the Christian community. The community remembered its notable dead. It recalled them in its prayers and asked them to intercede in its favor with God. Clusters of graves began to form around martyrs' tombs and continued to grow. Everyone wanted to be close to the servants of God. Ceremonies on the martyr's anniversary were relatively simple. Veneration did not yet occupy the preponderant place it was destined to assume later on.

The Great Persecution and the Institutionalization of Martyrdom

Between the early second and the mid-third century, the Christian community enjoyed relative security. Christianity was tolerated de facto though not de jure. Persecutions were local and sporadic. Even where they did take place, they generally affected only a small part of the local Christian community. Only those who had been turned over to the authorities by their neighbors for one reason or another were arrested and tried. Others stayed out of harm's way to the best of their ability. They supported and encouraged the prisoners during their arrest (the authorities did not usually ask the visitors too many questions about their own religious affiliation), took care of their families, attended the public torture sessions and executions, and did their best to reclaim the martyrs' remains and offer them a Christian burial. Most of the time the Christian community was able to lead a relatively quiet life. There were Christian soldiers, merchants, and low-ranking civil servants. They openly built houses of prayer, and bishops were known to their pagan and Jewish neighbors. In those relatively peaceful years, Christians had the opportunity to consolidate their faith and the structure of their community; occasionally they even engaged in fairly amicable debates with non-Christians. Nevertheless, the absence of legal status posed a permanent danger to the peace of the community. At any moment a new wave of violence could break out and shatter the tranquillity.

The first disconcerting signs of trouble appeared in the early third century. In 202 Emperor Septimius Severus published a decree forbidding Jews and Christians from engaging in missionary activity. The sudden imperial attention was a bad omen. But once again the persecutions that erupted after the decree was published were local and short, affecting northern Africa particularly. A much more serious persecution occurred under Decius (r. 245–251). Circumstances had deteriorated in the empire: it suffered Barbarian invasions along the Danube and internal unrest. The crisis drove the emperor to attempt a reunification of the empire around the ancient values of Roman virtue *(virtus romana)*. In 250, before leaving Rome to fight the Goths in the north, Decius published a decree ordering all residents of the empire to sacrifice to the gods and to obtain a certificate attesting to that sacrifice. Anyone unable to present a certificate to the local inspectors would be forced to make a sacrifice on the spot. Those who refused were to be executed.

The Roman army was defeated, and Decius was killed in a battle with the Goths in 251. The emperors Gallus (r. 251–253) and Valerian (r. 253–260) continued the persecutions. Valerian tried to destroy the Christian community by attacking its leaders—and by confiscating its property. That persecution ended when he was defeated in battle and fell into the hands of the Persians in 260. Valerian's son Gallienus (r. 260–268) reached the conclusion that the anti-Christian policy was accomplishing nothing. In 261 he published a decree granting tolerance to all residents of the empire. During the forty-two years that followed, the Christian community experienced peace. Then came the storm.

In 285 Diocletian became emperor. That tough Illyrian general was determined to save the empire from the economic and military crisis in which it was immersed. He reorganized the imperial administration, doubled the size of the army, and named soldiers to government posts. He greatly increased the tax burden. The price of commodities and the exchange rate were fixed by imperial decrees, and any modification of them was prohibited. Unpopular civil occupations, such as that of soldier or municipal council member, were declared hereditary and could not be evaded without imperial authorization. The Roman state became more centralized and more authoritarian than it had ever been before. Finally, Diocletian chose the cult of the emperor as a symbol of the new values of order and obedience to the Roman state. The emperor was now surrounded by elaborate court ceremonies influenced by Eastern practices. His subjects prostrated themselves in his presence. Patriotism was to focus on the person of the emperor.

In the heterogeneous Roman Empire that cult of the emperor served to enhance social cohesion: whatever their religious preferences and allegiances, all residents of the empire were called upon to express their *political* fidelity through that cult. Diocletian was not a megalomaniac. He was a conservative military man who, like Decius in his time, sought to return the empire to the values of the past. By refusing to participate in the emperor's cult, Christianity and Manichaeism[27] expressed a dangerous lack of solidarity and patriotism. Christian and Manichaean soldiers refused to make sacrifices. They were forced to leave the army. The emperor ordered the persecution of the Manichaeans in 297 and that of the Christians in 303. Through a series of imperial decrees, the command was given to destroy Christian books, to demolish churches, to abolish civil rights, to compel sacrifices to the emperor's genius, and to inflict forced labor in the mines and capital punishment on those who refused to submit.

The gravity of the persecutions varied from place to place. In some provinces the imperial decrees were not applied at all. In others the governors confined themselves to destroying churches. In some provinces, executions continued for about two years; in others, they went on for ten years. But this persecution was different from the previous ones in that this time the state was attempting once and for all to get rid of Christianity as a religion and of Christians as a community. That attempt failed.

In 312 Emperor Constantine the Great ascended the throne. Without any transition period, Christianity went from being a persecuted religion struggling for its survival to a privileged religion enjoying the emperor's favor. Such shifts sometimes come about when one group manages to prevail over another in battle, or when an oppressed population rebels against its oppressors and imposes a modification of the "social contract" in effect. This was not the case here. Christianity was not imposed on the empire under duress. Unlike Jews, Christians did not represent a threat to the empire. Even when persecuted, they had not offered violent resistance. Christianity became the state religion not by an imperial act of *Realpolitik* but because of the emperor's personal decision. The full explanation eludes us. More surprising even than Constantine's strange decision was the ease with which it was accepted by the pagan population. It is not surprising that Christians saw the triumph of Christianity as a miracle.

How the persecutions ended undoubtedly influenced the way they were perceived after the fact. A sense of moral failure had accompanied their end in the 250s: too many had failed to withstand the ordeal.[28] By contrast, after the "Great Persecution" a tremendous sense of victory predominated in the church: many—thousands, perhaps tens of thousands—had faced death voluntarily. For Christians it represented the triumph of spirit over matter. The Christianization of the empire proved that the meek can indeed inherit the earth.

In the Christian community the massacre of the innocents did not constitute a theological problem. On the contrary, the innocents were massacred *because* they were innocent. "Torture us, rack us, condemn us, crush us; your cruelty only proves our innocence," wrote Tertullian.[29] The world here below is dominated by the enemies of the Messiah; they persecute and murder his faithful. Unlike Jews in similar circumstances, Christians did not feel that God had "turned away his face" from his faithful. The Great Persecution was the golden age of the church. "The blood of Christians is seed"[30]—the seed of salvation. The church did not mourn its martyrs; it rejoiced in them.

But all was not well. If the martyr is the model Christian, what is the status of those who are not martyrs? If the era of martyrdom is the golden age of the church, what is the status of the era that follows it? If the world to come is destined for those who have renounced the world here below, what will be the fate of those into whose hands the earthly world has fallen like a ripe fruit? Can one have both worlds? Christianity as state religion seemed like a contradiction in terms, a recipe for moral disaster. During the first three hundred years of its existence, Christianity had constituted itself in opposition to the authorities. "My kingdom," said Jesus, "is not of this world" (John 18:36). The Christian lived in this world as a stranger. He wanted only one thing: to be allowed to complete his period of exile on earth and come "home" to the kingdom of heaven.[31] As for the rulers of this world—render unto Caesar what is Caesar's. "Let every soul be subject to the governing authorities," writes Paul in the Epistle to the Romans (13:1–2). "For there is no authority except from God, and the authorities that exist are appointed by God. Therefore whoever resists the authority resists the ordinance of God, and those who resist will bring judgment on themselves."

If Christianity in its beginnings could be considered a movement with a potential for rebellion (Jesus was crucified as a rebel), its radicalism very quickly turned out not to be political. Christians forbade themselves the use of violence. The martyr met his tormentors with only passive resistance. He denied their right to impose on him any action that went against his conscience, but not the legitimacy of their authority. He threatened them with heavenly punishment, not with armed resistance. In fact, submission to the authorities was part of the radical rejection of the legitimacy of this world in general. Christians were obliged to obey the rulers, even if these rulers were bloodthirsty monsters or were in the service of Satan, and even if wealth and earthly power tainted and corrupted them. The hierarchy of the world was the inverted and distorted image of the true hierarchy, that of the world to come. There the last would be first and the victims would enjoy the spectacle of the eternal torments inflicted on the tormentors.[32]

The shocking political reversal in the status of the Christian community, the sudden accession to earthly power and prestige, was a prize that this community, or at least a large portion of its leaders, had difficulty turning down. Almost without realizing it, Christians found themselves up to their necks in the affairs of this world: the authorities lavished money on them, built magnificent churches, named clergy to posts as advisers and ministers, sent militias to repress their adversaries, and enforced against pagans the type of discriminatory legislation that had previously targeted Christians.[33] The waves of new converts to Christianity made practically impossible the cautious separation of the Christian community from the "profane world" and destroyed its inner cohesion. This did not come about all at once. As adherence to the Christian religion gradually offered more advantages and privileges, and as other religious groups were repressed, newcomers were attracted not to the religion of the poor and persecuted who would one day gain access to the kingdom of heaven but to the religion of those who had already inherited the earth. What was rendered unto Caesar became confused with what was rendered unto God.

Things might have been simpler had the Christian empire been a kingdom of priest-kings leading the world toward the *Parousia* (Christ's Second Coming). But the Christian Roman Empire was not holy. Like all potentates, Christian rulers got their hands dirty in the exercise of power. Like other empires, the Christian empire had recourse to moral compromises. Worldly power has a price, which is automatically deducted from our moral accounts. The Christian community tried to avoid the price, or at least ignore it. Power had brought good things: it had helped spread the good news of salvation to the four corners of the *oekumene*; it had ensured that Christ's voice would not be silenced. But Christian leaders wanted to preserve the ancient values and continue to consider themselves the moral avant-garde, a community living in this world but whose thoughts are completely focused on the next. Such conceptual acrobatics were not easy, but religions excel at doing the impossible. Church leaders fit the Roman Empire into the plan of salvation. The empire was no longer the Great Whore of Babylon gorging herself on the innocent blood of the martyrs. It was a positive force that united a significant portion of the human race under a single power and used that power to spread the Christian message. It was, as it turned out, a missionary instrument in the invisible hand of God. That instrument was not perfect—Christian emperors were not exactly Melchizedeks—but it did the job: it helped bring about a better future.

Perhaps. The problem of the past, however, was more complex. How could it be said that the triumphant fourth-century church was the direct continuation of the church of martyrs? The two displayed very little family resemblance. Two possibilities presented themselves to church leaders: modify the present or modify the past. They chose to do both. In the fourth century, we can detect two major reactions to the moral crisis caused by the Christianization of the empire: the ascetic (or eremitic) movement and the cult of saints. The ascetics sought to create artificially and deliberately what the pagan authorities had imposed in the past, namely, a way of life marked by difficulty and suffering. At the sight of the suffering and torments of the ascetic's life, no one could think that he or she was a Christian for reasons of convenience; the ascetic's pursuit of heaven was hell on earth in the eyes of ordinary people. Only total faith in the promised heavenly reward could justify such a heroic renunciation of comfort, pleasure, and physical security. Asceticism was thus a "spiritual martyrdom," and anyone practicing it showed thereby that only contingencies prevented him or her from choosing martyrdom.

The ascetics changed the present to make it more like the past. The cult of saints, for its part, changed the past to perpetuate it in the present. In a sense, the community proclaimed that the past was not gone, that it was still present in time and space. The saints were not dead. The church continued to be the church of martyrs.

Dead Saints, Living Relics

No one proclaimed an official new "policy" regarding the saints. Through their acts, Christian communities simply translated the need to express their connection to the martyrs more forcefully than in the past. Until the fourth century there was a clear division between the living and the dead:

the community of the living was *intra muros,* that of the dead, even the special dead, *extra muros.* Roman law prohibited burial inside the walls of the city. Cemeteries were located outside, along roadsides and near the city's gates. The bodies of the martyrs were therefore always "out there." On the martyr's anniversary the faithful went to his tomb, "honored his memory" with a simple and modest ceremony, and expressed their certainty that he was in heaven, since God rewarded those who suffered in his name. At the end of the ceremony, the faithful returned to the world of the living. In the fourth century, the boundaries separating the city of the living from the city of the dead began to blur. Constantine himself undertook an enormous church construction project on the site of martyrs' tombs. Hence a church was built over the tomb of Peter on Vatican Hill, another over Paul's tomb, and of course the Church of the Holy Sepulcher was constructed over Jesus' tomb in Jerusalem. But it was not always the church that came to the martyr; sometimes the martyr came to the church.

People began to open saints' tombs and disturb their rest—taking astonishing and scandalous liberties, making possible an even more radical meeting of the world of the living with the world of the dead. According to Roman law, a tomb was a "religious site" *(locus religiosus).* All contact with cadavers once they had been placed in the sarcophagus was prohibited. Judaism and Islam, in which the cult of tombs was also widespread, continued to observe that ancient taboo. Christianity did not.[34]

Tombs were opened to allow the spread of the martyrs' influence. Since it was martyrs who provided the link between the present and the past and between heaven and earth, there was suddenly a shortage of martyrs. The communities that had once rejoiced at being spared by the persecutions now felt great jealousy for their sisters whose soil had been irrigated with the blood of martyrs. Martyrs constituted a patrimony both spiritual and material. The communities to which they had accrued enjoyed spiritual power. The martyrs' remains worked miracles, healed, punished, gave hope and meaning. All of this bore witness to the fact that the martyr was alive. But the communities that hosted the living dead enjoyed not only spiritual consolations but something more earthly as well: prestige, influence, even economic gain. For visitors to the martyrs were eager to display their faith and their gratitude by means of gifts and donations, which were handled by the dead martyrs' custodians. The bishops of Rome accumulated vast material and spiritual benefits from the priceless stores of martyrs (especially the apostles Peter and Paul) under their control.

But the distribution of relics among the different communities did not reflect the status of those communities in the world after the Christianization of the Roman Empire. Thus, for example, the new capital of the East created by Constantine and bearing his name was shockingly devoid of martyrs. The Christian emperors set about remedying that state of affairs. During the 350s, the remains of the saints Timothy, Andrew, and Luke were transported to Constantinople. Christians in the generations prior to the Christianization of the empire had not granted any particular importance to the burial sites of the different saints, not even to the heroes of the New Testament. While their spirits were remembered, their bodies were not. Now the flesh too was in demand. The forgotten bodies were craving to be discovered, to amaze the faithful with their presence, with their miracles. Enterprising members of the community hastened to recover what had been lost from sight. Little by little the vanished saints of scripture were "discovered," and with them many others not mentioned in the scriptures.

The beginnings were modest. In 386 Ambrose, archbishop of Milan, inaugurated the new basilica of the city, the Ambrosian basilica. The "people" called on the archbishop to adorn the church with saints' relics. The voice of the people, when it expresses what one wishes to hear, is truly the voice of God. An intuition (or, according to other witnesses, a dream or a vision) led Ambrose to a parcel of land adjoining a church on the outskirts of the city. A dig at the site uncovered the cadavers of two decapitated martyrs, Gervase and Protase. Beside them were traces of blood. (According to other versions, fresh blood poured out of their grave.) These martyrs, it turned out, had been forgotten by the Milanese. Rediscovered, they were transported in great pomp to the new basilica and buried under its altar.[35] The city of Milan was jubilant. Its residents, filled with civic pride, could transfer their fidelity from the Roman saints Felix and Nabor to the newly rediscovered local saints. The city elders now remembered having come across these names in ancient writings that had been lost.[36] Memory is an astonishing thing.

The discoveries of the archbishop of Milan did not end there. He also exhumed the bones of the martyrs Vitalis and Agricola from the Jewish cemetery of Bologna (the people in the area recalled a tradition regarding a treasure hidden in that cemetery) and the relics of Nazarius and Celsus from a garden outside the city of Milan. "If the holy priest went to pray in a place where he had not previously been," writes Paulinus, Ambrose's faithful secretary and biographer, "it was a sign of the [imminent] discovery of a martyr's remains."[37]

Word of these discoveries spread rapidly throughout the empire. Ambrose was not some local fanatic showing initiative; he was a theologian widely admired throughout the empire and an important church leader who had a personal relationship with Emperor Theodosius. Only the Arian heretics of Milan dared place in doubt the archbishop's miraculous discovery. They claimed, writes Ambrose's biographer, that this honorable man had bribed people to act as if they were possessed by demons and to pretend that these demons were tormented by the presence of the martyrs and of the archbishop. "The demons screamed [through the mouths of the possessed]: 'We know you are martyrs,' whereas the Arians said: 'They are not martyrs.'"[38] But who would listen to the envious slander of heretics when the demons themselves were saying just the opposite? No faithful Catholic placed that discovery in doubt; and, more important, no one dared doubt the way it had come about. The path was now clear for less modest discoveries.[39] The bodies Ambrose had exhumed were of anonymous martyrs, but there were other, better-known saints waiting to be brought to light.

In 415 Gamaliel (the rabbi who secured the release of Peter and John, arrested for preaching that Jesus was the Messiah [Acts 34–41]), appeared in a dream to a humble priest by the name of Lucian from the village of Gamla near Jerusalem (traditionally identified as the village of Beit Jimal).

Gamaliel told Lucian that he and his son Abibas (Habib) had been secretly baptized. After the execution of Stephen, the first martyr, the saint's body was thrown as fodder to wild beasts and birds of prey. Gamaliel had taken care to secure an honorable burial for the holy remains in his own family plot. Buried alongside Stephen were Nicodemus, Abibas, and Gamaliel himself. In the dream, Gamaliel ordered Lucian to go at once to John, bishop of Jerusalem, and free Gamaliel and the others from the grave where they were lying abandoned.

Lucian was not quick to obey the order. According to his report, he suspected satanic delusion and decided to wait and see whether the old man would reappear at least two more times. Gamaliel did reappear, increasingly impatient and angry. On his third appearance he threatened Lucian with the harshest of fates if he did not go to John at once. It was then that Lucian rushed to Jerusalem and received authorization from the bishop to look for the remains. When the grave was opened, a wonderful fragrance filled the air. Surely these were the bodies of saints, just as Gamaliel had promised in the dream. The less important remains were transported to a church built on that very site; those of Stephen were transported in great pomp to the Church of Zion in Jerusalem.[40] Unlike Gervase and Protase, who were fairly minor local heroes, Stephen was a figure admired throughout the Christian world. The "discovery" of his remains was an event of universal import. Lucian made the announcement in a letter addressed to "the whole church." The text was immediately translated into Latin and Syriac. It gave rise to a wave of enthusiasm throughout Christendom. All of a sudden, Stephen's name was on everyone's lips. Everyone addressed prayers to the proto-martyr, every community wanted to receive him and benefit from his presence. The discoveries (aptly called *inventiones* in Latin) and transfer of remains (*translationes*) were a response to the growing demand for saints. The supply grew: the bodies of Micah, Habakkuk, Zechariah, Job, and Barnabas, among others, were discovered one after another. The transfer of bodies allowed a more balanced distribution of martyrs throughout the geopolitical region.[41]

In the end, however, there was a limited number of important saints.

Granted, certain communities "discovered" unknown saints of their own, but many communities did not have a sufficiently well-developed sense of exploration. Yet they too wanted to enjoy the presence of the major saints of Christianity, who reinforced the community's sense that it was linked to a universal brotherhood. Other means had to be found to increase the number of saints.

The Proliferation of Bodies

The solution was as simple as it was audacious. Initially, members of communities poor in saints used methods that could be called "watering down." Since the saint's remains constituted a sort of concentrate, a watered-down version of the saint could be obtained by rinsing his bones and using the water as a weakened presence. It was also possible to introduce objects into the grave, vials of oil, wine, and water, or to take a sample of the oil from lamps placed above the grave, or to scrape off stone or plaster from it. These materials were called *brandea*, *pallioa*, and *sancturia*. Since the saintly concentrate was inexhaustible, watered-down versions of the saint could be drawn off ad infinitum.[42] These materials made it possible to transfer the healing powers and, to a certain extent, the saint's presence to wherever they were needed. There was still a sense, however, that these dilutions were only pale versions of the saint. In the fourth century, therefore, people in the East began to dissect saints' cadavers and divide up the parts. In certain western areas that operation was initially perceived as shocking, even sacrilegious. When the Byzantine princess Constantina wrote Pope Gregory the Great asking for "the head of Saint Paul or another part of his body" for the chapel she had built in Paul's honor, he politely refused: he believed that the custom was an offense to the honor of the saints. The pope told Constantina that two years earlier, several Greeks had been apprehended in Rome in possession of bones stolen under cover of darkness from a cemetery near the Church of Saint Paul. When asked what they were planning to do with the bones, they confessed that they intended to transport them to Greece as saints' relics. "Following that incident," the pope wrote, "a strong suspicion arose among us [*major nobis dubietas nata est*] regarding these bones, which they claimed belonged to saints." Gregory attempted to persuade Constantina that the authentic *brandea* he was offering her were just as effective as the saint's body: "They have performed miracles in the church, just as if the saints' bodies had been especially transported there."[43]

Of course, that was easy for the pope to say. He controlled a veritable treasure trove of relics whose authenticity was not disputed by anyone, and did not need any *brandea*. People in the East, and in the less fortunate cities of the West, did not want to be satisfied with dilutions. What was required was a drop of the saint's own concentrate, which could neither perish nor weaken. Only a selfish community would keep the entire saint for itself. A piece of skull, a finger, a toenail, a bone chip, a drop of blood—the slightest bit of one of these parts was sufficient to bring to a community the saint's full and all-powerful presence.[44] Where there's a will, there's a way. In the fourth century, Victricius of Rouen offered a theory that helped make the unacceptable commonplace:

> There is nothing in relics which is not complete. . . . Flesh is held together by the glue of blood, and we affirm that the spirit also, wet with the moisture of blood, has taken on the fiery heat of the Word. This being so, it is most certain that our apostles and martyrs have come to us with their powers intact. We are taught that this is so by the benefactions even now present to us. For as we recognize the right to move them, with their good will, we understand this: they do not inflict loss upon themselves by their own dissemination, but being endowed with unity, they distribute benefactions. The flame sheds its light and bestows it, yet does not suffer the expenditure of its bounty. Thus the saints are generous without loss, full without addition, thus they have come to us without the weariness of travel. . . . We see small relics and a little blood. But truth perceives that these tiny things are brighter than the sun, for the Lord says in the gospel "My saints shall shine like the sun in the kingdom of the Father."[45]

Every relic was the saint herself. Finally, even the most humble communities of France and Spain could possess a scrap of the true cross, one of Jesus' baby teeth, a bone splinter from Saint John the Baptist, or remains of "the" woman and her seven sons mentioned in the Book of the Maccabees. Ultimately the popes yielded to the "Eastern" vogue. After all, it was the saints themselves who wanted to be transferred.[46]

If the martyrs lived on, then their biographies did not end with their bodily death. Saints went on performing miracles and expressing their will, not only in acts but also in words, which were transmitted to the communities by visionaries and dreamers always ready to serve as the saints' mouthpieces. The result of the radical fragmentation of saints' bodies was a parallel fragmentation of their biographies. The John the Baptist of Rome was different in character, and in the nature of his activities, from the John the Baptist of Paris; Saint James was one person in Jerusalem (where, according to the ancient sources, he was buried) and another in Santiago de Compostela (where, it was said, his remains had miraculously appeared). The cult of saints was understood to be a unifying act, but in fact it opened the way for religious pluralism. When it was permitted for the bodies of saints to be disassembled, their authenticity could no longer be controlled. How was it possible to know if a particular fragment or bone splinter actually came from Saint Thomas? The most common way to authenticate the relics was to examine their effectiveness: if they performed miracles, it was because they were not just bits of human tissue, bone, or hair but truly the living presence of a saint. That mode of examination had been performed even for the most sacred relic of all, the cross of Jesus. According to a tradition that originated in the mid-fourth century, Constantine's mother, Saint Helena, had gone to the Holy Land to search for relics.[47] She had excavated the hill of Golgotha and had found three crosses, which the Romans had conveniently left for future generations. Which of the three was the true cross? No one knew. But one of the crosses brought a dead man back to life, while the other two had no effect. No other proof was necessary.

Once the saint had been pulled out of the environment where a continuous historical tradition about him or her had been preserved, it became very difficult to prove the authenticity of the relics as they circulated from place to place. Miracles served as a substitute for the missing historical testimony, and sometimes even overruled it. Miracles occur when a community is seeking miracles, that is, when people are ready to declare that they have been miraculously healed, and when other people are ready to believe them without seeking alternate explanations. In the fourth century, the miraculous activity of relics became the essential thing, and relics no longer served as landmarks for the community's *historical* memory; they formed part of a parallel, imaginary history that was richer and more fruitful than its competitor. A community that managed to display a torrent of miracles could prevail over another that could present only reliable but sterile historical testimony. The Saint-Maximin community could glory in a much more active Mary Magdalene than its "authentic" (or at least more ancient) counterpart in Vézelay or than the almost entirely passive Mary of the basilica of Saint John Lateran in Rome. Where was the real Mary Magdalene located? A passive and sterile saint, however "authentic," was a useless saint. Demand for useless saints was very low.

To prove that it was truly in possession of a saint, the community needed witnesses not of faith but of power—people who had been miraculously healed. Local authorities had only very partial control over that critical group of citizens. No one could be forced to be miraculously healed. It was a buyers' market. Consumers decided to whom they would pray, which saints they preferred, what sort of contractual bond they wished to establish with the saint, when they would attribute an unexpected salvation to the saint, and when they would "waste" it (by calling it a coincidence, a natural process, or by attributing it to the direct intervention of God).

Ecclesiastical Impresarios and Their Turbulent Public

Church leaders did not remain passive when faced with that new dynamic. Bishops laid claim to important relics, transferred them to their churches, and covered them with gold and silver for the greater glory of God, for his servants in heaven, and for his humble servants (the bishops) on earth. All at once, the Western church grew richer. Some of the methods men of authority had used in ancient times, such as ostentatiously squandering money on public games and holding parades and sumptuous banquets, were now forbidden the bishop, the humble pastor of the "poor in spirit." But the new bishops were not humble men from the relatively disadvantaged classes. Many were aristocrats accustomed to giving orders and receiving honors. For them, the extravagant expenditures on the saints were an important means of displaying their status. Bishops had become the "impresarios of saints," as Peter Brown calls them. Brown assails the thesis that the cult of saints was a concession that bishops, relatively erudite and "rational," were obliged to make to the populace, who expected a less ethereal, more "earthly" religion. He shows rather that the bishops were in charge: they took the initiative and encouraged the cult of saints.[48]

Brown is right: we must not believe that the cult of saints expressed the need of only one part of the population. It expressed various needs, and the different elements of society, including the educated elite, contributed toward establishing the cult. That said, the active role of the elite "impresarios" must not keep us from seeing the other side of the coin. The emphasis on miracles and visions (the saint's *potentia*) gave great powers to the visionaries and to the beneficiaries of miracles. The reduced importance of textual memory and the increased importance of the saint's activity here and now, the desire to see him present wherever his remains were found, the enormous increase in the number of saints, which prevented any real control of their authenticity, all contributed toward a clear decentralization of the cult. Similarly, the dispersion of a given saint into a multitude of places created a de facto pluralism behind the surface unity. The council of Carthage in 401 aptly demonstrates the ambivalence in the relationship between church leaders and the believing masses:

Item, we believe that the altars erected here and there, in the fields and by the roadside, which are said to be memorials to martyrs, if it is proven that they do not contain either the body or the remains of the saint, should be destroyed, inasmuch as that is possible, by the bishops responsible for the place.

If, all the same, that is not feasible because of the protests of the masses, the bishops will instruct the people not to go to these places, to prevent righteous believers from succumbing to superstition. In no case shall the existence of a memorial raised to a martyr be acceptable unless his authenticated body and remains are found there, or a tradition with a very reliable source attests that the saint dwelt there, that the place was his property, or that he was tortured there. All the same, altars erected on the faith of the dreams or vain visions of people of every sort, wherever they may have been placed, must absolutely be rejected.[49]

The venerable church fathers of the North African church did not appreciate the liberties that the masses were taking. "People of every sort" (*quorumlibet hominum*) were claiming to have all sorts of dreams and were erecting all sorts of altars in honor of all sorts of martyrs invented from whole cloth. But doesn't that sound suspiciously like the *inventiones* we encountered earlier? Was it not the North African church itself that, less than a generation earlier, had welcomed with enormous enthusiasm the remains of Saint Stephen, discovered far from his home, away from his property, far from the place of his suffering, with no reliable tradition and solely on the faith of a dubious dream? The resemblance, said the holy fathers, was only apparent. How could one compare what was attributable to the authorities, and what they confirmed, to the wild initiatives of the masses? *Quod licet Jovis*. . . . It was preferable to destroy these altars, "if only the thing were feasible." Unfortunately, it was not feasible, because the aforementioned masses protested. The church therefore had to confine itself to protests by the bishops. Things often changed over time, and what had been a reprehensible innovation in the first generation became, a generation later, the source of local pride, a cult in which the bishop not only took part but also directed.

The usefulness of relics was definitely greater than the damage they caused. The price, it seems, was right. From the fourth century on, their great elasticity, the fact that they could be adapted to changing needs and to different communities, made relics the cutting edge, the shock troops of Christianity. Emphasis was placed on the saints' ever-useful powers against the forces competing with the church. In 351 the remains of Saint Babylas were transferred from the cemetery of Antioch, where they had been buried, to the suburbs of Daphnē. The transfer of the martyr to Daphnē was no accident. It was designed to overshadow, with the aid of the martyr's powers, the oracle of Apollo, whom people came to consult there. And in fact the saint carried out his mission well: the oracle who had spoken in Daphnē for hundreds of years fell silent.

In a world filled with anxiety and hungry for power, the Christian community offered what people wanted—an assurance that it was connected with the sources of power in the invisible world, an assurance that the future belonged to it. It also showed an implacable readiness to destroy what had existed before it. The cult of pagan deities had always been largely directed by the state; now that the state had withdrawn its support, the power of the deities was running dry. Christians assailed the ancient temples and the sacred sites of Roman antiquity, armed with miracle-working relics, and "authenticated" stories of astonishing wonders, of the paralytics whose legs itched with the desire to walk, of the blind whose sight was impatient to come forth out of dead pupils, of the deaf whose ears could already distinguish faint whispers, destined in short order to become the powerful voice of the community shouting out in chorus: "Miracle! Miracle!"

The victory of Babylas was only the start. Saints' relics arrived everywhere, and the old made way for the new: Menas took his place in the temple of Poseidon, Mary in the temple of Minerva, Cosmas and Damianus in that of Castor and Pollux. Installing a saint in a given place was an act of conquest, of spiritual and political occupation. The saint appropriated the new territory. Once a place was proclaimed holy, any pragmatic debate about private property rights became impossible. What had been given to the supreme powers could not be taken away from them. The saints "liberated" territories and blocked any attempt to restore them to their previous owners. But occupation can be a two-edged sword. The saint who had arrived to seize the place did not merely dispossess the former owner; he also appropriated all the forces attributed to that owner, and implicitly the old rules of the game.

Let us suppose that the Christian community, with the support of the imperial authorities, seized a pagan temple that had been built above a sacred fountain. The site was "purified," the temple proclaimed a church, and the remains of a martyr buried under the altar. What would happen then? Before the overthrow, "idolaters" had come there to rid themselves of their various illnesses through the curative powers the local deity had given to the water. In many cases the process of healing remained the same—with one difference: instead of being attributed to the pagan deities, or to nature, or to the site itself, the cures were now attributed to the saint.[50]

In the sixth century, the bishop of Javols had to contend with a community of peasants who worshiped a marsh located on a mountaintop. The peasants performed their libations there and made offerings of all sorts. During the wintertime it was their custom to hold at the site three days of celebrations in which rituals were combined with feasting. The bishop repeatedly threatened the peasants with divine wrath, but to no avail. In the end he understood that censure was not enough. He had to propose a substitute to his flock. He then had a church built on the banks of the marsh and deposited the relics of Saint Hilarius inside. "There is no religion in a marsh" *(nulla est religio in stagno)*, he declared. If there were powers there, they belonged to the saint. He interpreted the heavy rains that had fallen on the site during the most recent festivities as a bad omen. God was not pleased. But if the community was willing to transfer its religious energies to God and his holy servant, they would find the invisible forces favorable again. This time he succeeded. The pagan cult ended.[51]

In appearance, the victory was complete. In actuality, the bishop's triumph was less decisive. The saint had driven out the deities, who had been declared demons. But although the decor, the personnel, and the management had changed, the menu remained largely the same. The "idolaters" bowed to the new rite. They were baptized, adopted Christianity, and prayed to the saint. They were now potential beneficiaries of miracles whose private salvation would add to the glory of the saint and his impresarios. It would not have been judicious to cause them too many problems or ask too many questions. On the contrary, it was advisable to facilitate their access to the supernatural powers now attributed to the saint. In many respects, then, the new, Christian clients continued to follow the old, pagan ways. Old habits are hard to break.

The old habits were now declared "superstitions," fairly innocuous customs whose pagan character had been blurred. In fact, however, these customs continued to express the ancient values that the church was supposed to replace: the consecration of seasonal changes, solar and lunar cycles, and fertility festivals—all celebrations that sanctified the cyclical within a supposedly linear religion.[52] Christianity, an urban Judaic sect profoundly indifferent to nature, found itself in charge of a network of sites where nature was the object of worship: mountaintops (or volcanic lakes such as Javols), wells, fountains, crossroads, and caves. All of these sites had an impact on the new masters.[53] William Christian describes how, in medieval Spain, peasants "discovered" miraculous icons in nature. Every attempt to transfer the icon into an urban setting failed. The icon insisted on being worshiped where it had been found. Christian considers these phenomena a "paganization" of Christianity. The rural population of Europe "reconquered" the territory that ecclesiastical, urban Christianity had tried to seize, and reconsecrated nature.[54] But this phenomenon was not part of the specific circumstances of medieval Spain. It had been part of the inextricable tensions of Christianity ever since it became the religion of the empire. The old had never been totally rejected. It could not have been. When the whale swallowed Jonah, the prophet could disappear completely into the belly of the beast without leaving a trace. When Jonah swallows a whale, however, his entire appearance is greatly modified. The Roman Empire was a very big fish.

The ecclesiastical hierarchy was willing to pay the price of success, that is, to digest the whale, even if the church's bowels had to be turned inside out and its appearance transformed in the process. It showed an audacity and a flexibility not often attributed to supposedly narrow-minded and "reactionary" religious leaders. Bishops understood that high moral and theological standards appropriate for a small, strongly motivated community did not suit a mass movement. They had to be less fastidious about the criteria for belonging to the Christian community. A division of tasks emerged between the pastors and their flock. The demarcation line between clergy and laypeople became clearer. For the most part, ecclesiastics were expected to maintain the demanding, "authentic" form of life once expected of the entire community. They were the true heirs of the apostles and the exclusive possessors of the *arcana fidei*. They were the guardians of *orthodoxy*. Obedience had become the highest virtue of simple believers. It was better if they were not too preoccupied with complicated questions, which might confuse them and lead them off the straight and narrow. The rites of the church changed in character, making worshipers increasingly passive spectators of sacred theater. For the majority of believers, the shaping of doctrine was off-limits. Their participation in the liturgy was also severely limited. But the faithful were not excluded from aspects of religious practice not directly connected to the doctrine and liturgy of the church. The most important of these was the cult of saints.

When given the opportunity, the masses take all kinds of liberties and create all kinds of problems. What were the pastors to do with problematic manifestations of the cult of saints? What reply should be given to those who claimed that the saint replaced God in the eyes of ordinary "believers"? How should the church reply to Jews, to educated pagans, and to heretics who alleged that the veneration of saints was a thinly veiled form of idolatry? The same hallowed formulas were tirelessly repeated: "We do not regard or honor [the martyrs] as gods," explains Saint Augustine. "We do not make temples or altars or sacrifices for them. It is not to them that the priests make offerings, heaven help them! It is to God, yes, it is to God, from whom we receive everything. Even when we sacrifice on the tombs of the holy martyrs, do we not sacrifice to God? Heed this well: these holy saints occupy an honorable place there; their names appear first at the altar of Christ; but we do not worship them in place of Christ."[55] Were these explanations clear to an audience for whom theological distinctions had become less comprehensible and less important? Only in part. Most simple believers did not consider the saint a substitute for God. They recognized the existence of a supreme God, to which the saints—second-class deities, so to speak—were subordinate; but did they really make the distinction between *dulia*, the veneration due a saint, and *latria*, adoration due God alone? Did not their practices disturbingly resemble the worship of the ancient gods, as the Spanish priest Vigilantius claimed? According to Saint Jerome, that resemblance did not pose any difficulties: "The thing used to be done for the gods, hence it was despicable; now it is done for the martyrs, hence it is desirable."[56] Although this distinction was sharp and clear for Jerome, Saint Augustine had greater doubts. He was obliged to acknowledge the uneasiness that certain elements of the cult caused him: "What we teach is one thing, what we tolerate another; what it is our mission to command, one thing, what we are ordered to correct and forced to bear in the meantime, another."[57]

And in the meantime, while waiting for that correction to come about, the church was ready to tolerate a great deal. The ecclesiastical elite attempted to curb the enthusiasm of the masses for the cult of saints and to define that cult on its own terms, which it did with only partial success. The official theology was clear enough: saints are men and women like everyone else, and as such are not exempt from sin. Saints are not perfect; only God is. Saints achieve a level of moral excellence by virtue of their faith and by the grace of God, who elected them. Miracles are not proof of sainthood: sinners, demons, and witches can also perform miracles. Miracles are a possible—but not a necessary—expression of sainthood. Only the person whose faith is pure and whose acts conform to strict moral criteria is worthy of being considered a saint, whatever the miracles attributed to him or her. As for the appropriate relations to maintain with the saints, the church insisted on clearly distinguishing these relations from the cults of heroes and demons. The saint was not merely a conduit of supernatural energy but a moral paragon. A pedagogical exchange ought to exist between him and the believer. The saint of the elite set moral objectives of which he himself was an example. He punished vice and rewarded virtue.

That was the theory. A very different image emerges when we examine the saint in action—as he is described in countless encounters with his admirers. After his death the saint became public property; his character changed radically. During his lifetime he was modest, timid, and kind to his neighbors, turning the other cheek. Once dead, he became a powerful lord who behaved like any other lord, capricious, megalomaniacal, and jealous. Saints maintained relationships with their admirers that often had little to do with morality. They were overly sensitive, demanding, tyrannical, greedy, eager for gifts—gold and silver—and envious of other saints.[58] Although operating within the new context of Christian symbols and formulas, the character and conduct of saints, the types of miracles (such as those that occurred while one was sleeping on the saint's grave), and the type of relationship (such as eating and drinking on the saint's grave and establishing a contractual bond with him or her) perpetuated pagan cults of the dead and of the lower deities. That continuity was not purely pagan, just as the cult of saints was not purely Christian. It followed a logic of inclusivity (both this *and* that), whereas intellectuals, at least in their ideological declarations, employ an exclusivist logic (either this *or* that).

From the perspective of church leaders, where did the line fall between that which had to be corrected and that which could be tolerated? After all, ecclesiastical pragmatism also had its limits. Where, then, was the line between the tolerable and the intolerable? It is not easy to respond satisfactorily to that question. The term "church," as I have used it up to now (largely for reasons of convenience), is misleading. Until the twelfth century, when the pope's status as the ultimate religious authority in matters of teaching and jurisdiction took hold, there was not any actual entity that could be called "the church."[59] There were different churches, and our question would have found different, sometimes contradictory answers. Nor were the answers necessarily coherent. Yet certain tendencies can be detected. The pastors adopted a pragmatic and gradual conception of the religious instruction of the "masses." The elite grasped that a "serious" religion is a complicated and difficult matter, and that it could not be imposed all at once on someone unfamiliar with it.

The theoretical difficulty of religion (a difficulty that the elite helps perpetuate through the use of an inaccessible discourse) confers legitimacy on the authority of the "initiate." That authority is no longer perceived as an arbitrary act of domination but rather as a sort of paternalistic tutelage. At the same time, however, the difficult truth of religion allows and justifies a great deal of freedom for simple believers. In 601 Pope Gregory I sent Abbot Melitus a letter containing the following instructions, addressed to Augustine, future archbishop of Canterbury:

> It is not necessary to destroy the temples of the gods of that nation; only the idols must be destroyed. You shall sprinkle the temples with holy water; you shall build altars and deposit saints' relics in them, for if these temples have been well constructed, it is fitting to convert them from the worship of demons to that of the true God . . . and since it is the custom to sacrifice many cattle to the demons, there is reason to modify somewhat [the character of] that ceremony. On the day the churches are inaugurated, or on the anniversary of the martyred saints whose remains have been deposited there, you will build around the churches—formerly temples—huts made of boughs, where the ceremony will be observed with many religious libations. [The participants] will not sacrifice animals to Satan, but they will slaughter them for the glory of God and to serve as nourishment, and they will thank the One who provides everything for having satisfied them. . . . No doubt it is impossible to eradicate everything at once from hardened souls, and anyone who wants to scale a mountaintop also ascends one step at a time, by degrees and not by leaps.[60]

Augustine of Hippo might not have appreciated the details of the policy proposed by Gregory the Great to Augustine of Canterbury. He himself had led a protracted battle against the custom of "ritual meals" taken on the graves of the righteous, a custom much more innocent than the sacrifice of cattle. That said, there was no disagreement on the principle: applied Christianity is only a pale reflection of ideal Christianity. The Church Militant must consent to painful compromises until such time as it is reunited with the Church Triumphant.

The religious leaders were ready to make many compromises with the "masses," so long as these masses were not seeking to undermine the leaders' authority.[61] All things considered, the cult of saints was perceived as more useful than harmful. It was popular, and it allowed the clever impresario access to the hardened souls of his flock. Church authorities hoped to use it to accustom their communities gradually to more Christian ways. Gregory's "wager" proved successful. We may suppose that for several generations, the ceremonies conducted around churches were pagan ceremonies covered over by a little Christian terminology. Over time, however, the pagan content of these rites disappeared.[62] The names of the gods, the original motivation for the ceremonies, and the exact significance of their various components were forgotten. The ceremony, if it survived at all, was nothing but a sort of fossil left over from another world, just like Christmas trees or Easter eggs today. How many people are aware of their original meaning? Replacing paganism with Christianity ceased to be an option at some point. When they danced around the maypole or placed gifts at the foot of the Christmas tree, believers considered themselves altogether Christian. Similarly, the North African community, when it built its altars without the bishop's authorization, did not intend to undermine his authority.[63] Usually bishops understood that. What they truly dreaded was conscious idolatry and heresy. Superstition, by contrast, was a bother rather than an existential threat. They could live with superstitions. In fact, they could even adopt some of them.

But it is precisely in those gray zones of relatively innocuous religious practice, in the blind spots of the hierarchy, that deep structural changes began. There, where the distinction remained hazy between pagan and Christian, orthodox and heterodox, pure and impure, churchgoers con-

stantly engaged in experiments with cultural alchemy, mixing the un-
mixable, borrowing the unborrowable, putting together what should have
been put asunder. All this demanded a certain institutional inattention, a
lowering of one's guard. Profound revolutions may often go unnoticed, un-
declared, and become apparent only after the fact. Once it adopted the cult
of saints, Christianity no longer resembled the Christianity that had preceded it, and what made it different was not the decision of one ruler or
the conscious policy of its leadership. As often happens, change came as
the result of the diffuse efforts of many small agents, without a program.

It is time to move from the vast impersonal forces of history to the
individual destinies that compose them. Let us begin with the prison journal of Vibia Perpetua, an account of a Christian martyr told in the first
person.

THREE

On the Way to Heaven

Perpetua's Passion

IN A.D. 202, UNDER THE REIGN of Septimius Severus, the Christian community of northern Africa was suddenly struck with a short-term outburst of violence. It was not a "major" persecution. The authorities sought to prevent missionary activity but did not persecute longtime Christians (or Jews). Arrested were those involved in teaching the principles of Christianity and those receiving instruction before being baptized (catechumens). It is uncertain whether that persecution, which lasted about a year and claimed the lives of few victims, would have attracted much attention had it not produced an extraordinary document, the prison journal of Vibia Perpetua,[1] a young woman from a noble family who chose Christianity shortly before she was arrested (in all likelihood as a result of a denunciation). Perpetua's journal is the only autobiographical text written by a woman during antiquity that has come down to us.[2] It is also one of the rare texts to describe martyrdom from the point of view of the future martyr.

The Christian instruction given to Perpetua was rudimentary. She was a neophyte seeking to give meaning to her life; with that aim in mind, she made use of symbolic materials available to her culture, without concern for the dichotomies—paganism or Christianity, orthodoxy or Montanist heresy—to which her exegetes later sought to confine her.

Arrest in Carthage

The *Passio sanctarum Perpetuae et Felicitatis* (The Passion of Saints Perpetua and Felicity) consists of three parts, composed by three or four different authors. First there is the preface, written by an unknown author. Perpetua's prison journal follows, and includes a vision by Saturus, the saint's prison mate, as he himself dictated it. Finally, there is a statement from someone who witnessed the execution of Perpetua and her companions in Carthage in 203. That description may have also been written by the author of the preface. The document is written in faulty Latin, reflecting the North African usage of the time. The *Passio* enjoyed great popularity in northern Africa and in the western empire generally. It was quickly translated into Greek, and two abridged versions *(Acta)* have been preserved in many manuscripts. Tertullian and Augustine mention the text, and we know that it was read on Perpetua and Felicity's feast day, March 7.[3]

In the second and third centuries, most catechumens were adults. Having concluded their instruction, they were usually baptized as a group on Easter. The instruction was given by a baptized Christian, not necessarily a priest. It included a narration of sacred history and a simplified explanation of the Christian faith and of the principles of ethics.[4] The Christian community welcomed people of different classes—slaves, freemen, rich, poor. Although all members of the Christian community were brothers and sisters in Christ, each still belonged to his or her social class. Christianity did not call for revolution; it accepted the existing order. In the small city where Perpetua was born (the Greek text refers to the town of Thuburbo Minus, near Carthage), she apparently belonged to a large and prominent family originally from the capital of the province. The Roman society of the time was roughly divided into nobles (*honestiores*) and people of low condition (*humiliores*). Perpetua's family belonged to the *honestiores*. She was formally married (many couples lived together without marriage rites), and hence was entitled to be called *matrona*. She had also been educated: she knew Greek and could read and write. Her prison mates were conscious of her social status. Two of them (Felicity and Revocatus) were slaves. The status of the other three (Saturus, Saturninus, and Secundulus) is not clear, but all evidence suggests it was lower than that of Perpetua. They considered her their superior, and she seems to have found that attitude natural.

As suggested earlier, the arrest probably came after a denunciation. With the advent of Emperor Trajan's reign, the authorities no longer sought out Christians; they were arrested when their neighbors denounced them to the authorities. It is clear from the text that the procurator, Hilarianus, was not eager to shed the blood of the prisoners who were apprehended. In fact he seems to have been less eager than the accused themselves.[5] We are told that Saturus turned himself in so as to share the martyrdom of his flock. The accused were apparently arrested in Thuburbo Minus and transferred to the public prison of Carthage. The building described by Perpetua was crowded, hot, and dark. Many prisons had two levels, aboveground and underground. The small group of Christians were thrown into the lower level, where they suffered the cruelty of the guards. Nevertheless, access to the prisoners was relatively free, and widespread corruption provided ways to make life in prison less unpleasant. The prisoners, then, were not entirely isolated from their families and coreligionists. The accused were interrogated in public, in the forum, by a civil servant. The procurator Hilarianus had offered the prisoners their freedom, provided they make a sacrifice for the well-being of Emperor Septimius Severus and his sons, Caracalla and Geta (*pro salute imperatorum*). This was more a demonstration of loyalty to the authorities than an act of religious devotion. By refusing, the prisoners became guilty of rebellion—a capital offense.

The authorities had various execution methods at their disposal. The harshest and most ignominious were generally reserved for the *humiliores*, but in cases of lèse-majesté, *honestiores* lost their class privileges. Throwing victims to wild beasts was one of the three cruelest execution methods stipulated by Roman law (the others being crucifixion and burning). Unlike these other methods, execution by wild animals in the arena included a strong element of theater. Death by crucifixion could take hours, even days. Those who were burned lost consciousness fairly quickly. In both cases, the public could not expect surprises. Conversely, even unarmed prisoners could go head-to-head with the wild beasts, at least for a time (Saturus, for example, survived being dragged by a wild boar and was spared being clawed by a bear when the beast refused to attack him). In general, that type of execution was reserved for robust men who could provide a good spectacle. Death by wild beasts was a costly and complicated form of capital punishment, which the organizers were not inclined to "waste" on victims unlikely to put on a good show. Still, since Christians were often executed in cohesive groups, where emotional scenes were likely, and since they elicited great interest, they were often condemned to the most solemn and bloody forms of capital punishment. As they were not expected to put up a bold fight against the beasts, they were sometimes chained to prevent them from escaping, and the beasts had to be encouraged to attack them. Sometimes the condemned were even attached to the beasts. Every execution was accompanied by acts of humiliation. For women, the humiliation was often sexual in nature. They were stripped, or encased in a net that restricted their movement but revealed their nakedness. In some cases they were tied to a post. They were then exposed to the attacks of a raging bull.

The execution of Perpetua and her companions was particularly solemn, since it was part of the games organized in honor of Geta's birthday. The condemned were taken in procession to the prison at the garrison, near the amphitheater, and then to the arena. It seems clear that Perpetua had been to the arena before. Her visions attest to knowledge of the Pythian Games held in the provincial capital shortly before to honor the god Apollo.[6] In some cases the condemned were dressed in the garb of pagan priests, and the execution became a sacrifice of sorts to the gods.[7] Perpetua objected to that ceremony, and the authorities, displaying little religious fanaticism, relented to her wishes. Different animals were used: bulls, lions, panthers, cheetahs, bears, and boars. Some prisoners were killed and devoured, but many were only wounded. The coup de grâce was delivered by the *retiarius*, a gladiator armed with a net and trident. He slit the throats of the dying and with a sponge mopped up their blood, which was sometimes collected for magical practices. In some cases the authorities ordered the bodies burned as an additional punishment, since depriving the victim of Christian burial constituted a threat to her resurrection, according to the Christian faith, and to the peace of her soul, according to pagan belief. In this case there appears to have been no attempt to prevent burial.[8]

Perpetua's Story

If we knew that we had only a few days to live, if we knew that we were going to die a violent and painful death, what sort of text would we write? Would we attempt to retrace our life up to that moment? Would we engage in an examination of our conscience? Would we compose an indictment, an apologia? Would we write words of farewell to those we love and who love us, a letter to the child who will never know us? How does one confront imminent death, remorse, hesitation, fear? Here are the first words from the journal of Vibia Perpetua, a young mother of twenty-two, a beloved daughter whose future is about to be transformed with frightening speed into a past, whose tender life and horrible death will become proof that "divine grace did not exist solely among the ancients": "While we were still in the company of our guards," she writes, "my father sought to destroy me with his words and, out of his affection for me, persisted in desiring my fall" (3.1). The past does not exist in Perpetua's journal: everything begins with the arrest. What was there before? What kind of life did she lead? Who was she? She does not tell. Her journal is oriented toward the future: she does not engage in an examination of conscience. She writes the prologue to her martyrdom, knowing that another will have to write the epilogue. She demands that the anonymous compiler tell her story: "[In recounting her martyrdom] we are carrying out the mission, and even the mandate, with which the very holy Perpetua charged us" (16.1). Dying for the faith deserves to be remembered. But not everything about Perpetua is *dignus memoriae*, only the present, the preliminaries to martyrdom. The past belongs to an alien world: it is a pagan, profane past, where human beings are born and give birth, love one another instead of loving God—an ordinary past that must be forgotten. But that past creeps stealthily into the present of the future martyr, for Perpetua is quick to identify the villain of her tale for succeeding generations. The serpent on whose head she must step on her way to paradise belongs not to the present—the Roman procurator—but to the past. It represents not the Roman procurator but her own father.

There is something highly disconcerting about the violence expressed in Perpetua's first sentence: "My father sought to destroy me with his words and, out of his affection for me, persisted in desiring my fall." In the first paragraph Perpetua allows her father to speak directly only twice, each time with a single word: "'Father,' I said, 'do you see that jug [*vas*] on the floor, for example? It's a pitcher, isn't it?' And he said: 'I see it [*video*].' And I told him: 'Could it be called by any other name than what it is?' And he said, 'No [*non*]'" (3.1–2). Undoubtedly Perpetua's father had many other words to say—painful words, seductive words, words that express a destructive affection. Perpetua passes over them in silence. She addresses her father with all the hauteur of someone who knows she has truth and justice on her side, explaining the self-evident to an obtuse pupil. She is Christian. She is going to die. That is all there is to it. It is as obvious and as indisputable as the jug of water on the floor of her cell.

She starts with her father. If anyone can break her down, it is he. Hence she must silence his destructive words. She refuses to listen. Exasperated, he throws himself upon her as though to pluck out her eyes. But "he merely annoyed me and he went away defeated, with his devil's arguments" (3.3). He is no more than a nuisance, an impotent instrument of the devil seeking in vain to change her. Perpetua compares herself to a vessel, a Pauline image of the human being. Humans are but clay that God can mold into a vessel of honor or of dishonor.[9] She is no longer a lump of clay. She has become a vessel of honor. She does not wish to change.

Perpetua is in the hands of others. She is a prisoner about to be flung into the arena, unable to ensure even her own baby's fate. She depends in great part on the goodwill of others, who can do with her what they will. But Perpetua does not accept her status as passive victim. During the days remaining to her, she strives to redefine herself. In the world she has left behind, Perpetua was a daughter, a wife, a mother. Roman culture and law did not grant her the right to speak: she was subject to the authority of her father and of her husband, bound to her progeny by duty and tradition. Between that world and the world of the journal, Perpetua's choice forms a dividing line: she *chose* Christianity and freed herself from a world of obligations. She composes a narrative in which *she* is the heroine and depicts herself in terms of *her* actions, *her* choices, *her* strength, even *her* violence. Everything that threatens her freedom—proprieties, rules, constraints—vanishes: first her husband, whom she does not mention at all, then her father, and finally her child.

When Perpetua is baptized in prison, she wishes to have a good martyrdom, that is, to bear the suffering with dignity, to persevere. It is not easy. The prison is dark, hot, crowded, and brutal. "But worse than all this," she writes, "I was tormented by anxiety for the baby" (3.6). The baby has no name. He has no qualities. He has no identity. He cries. He suffers. He binds Perpetua to her past not by the devil's arguments but by his very being. Perpetua does not speak of her love for the child. Three times she uses the term *sollicitudo*, a term that in Late Latin indicates duty and constraint. When the child was brought to her in prison, she was "immediately relieved of the suffering and anxiety" her child was causing her (3.9: *relevata sum a labore et sollicitudine infantis*). Surely her baby's presence cheered Perpetua. She must have held him in her arms and covered him with kisses; she may have felt sorrow in her heart that she would not see him grow up. But she says nothing about such feelings or gestures. The child is a duty and a burden. When he is brought to her to breast-feed, his presence relieves her of her anxiety and allows her to concern herself with what really matters to her: the preparations for martyrdom. After the official interrogation, her father refuses to bring her the child, and she tells us that, by the grace of God, the baby has calmly given up nursing. Her breasts no longer hurt, and she is no longer anxious. From then on, she makes no more mention of the child.

We will speak again of that child, but let us first return to the father. The relationship between Perpetua and her father is completely different in the second meeting described in the journal (chapter 5). This time as well, Perpetua claims that her father is attempting to bring about her fall (5.1: *ascendit ad me ut me deiceret*), but now he does not threaten but rather begs. He repeatedly uses words that lower him and elevate her. He reminds her that he is old and that he and the other members of her family are dependent on her. He declares that he has favored her over her brothers. He wonders whether he has the right to be called her father. And finally he abases himself physically and symbolically: he throws himself at her feet in tears; he kisses her hands, and he, the paterfamilias, calls her *domina*, not daughter (5.5). If he accuses his daughter, it is the sort of accusation that inferiors direct toward superiors, that she is proud and indifferent. Like Perpetua, the father is anxiety-ridden by the suffering of his child, but unlike her he also expresses love, a desperate love. He is ready to do a great deal more than duty requires of him, to humiliate himself to a degree difficult to imagine for the time. The father's weakness and lowliness touch Perpetua's heart. She declares, "And I suffered because of my father" (5.6). But her consoling words for him remain detached. It is an impersonal counsel: "Know that we are not in our own power, but in God's" (5.6). She disappears into the plural. The pain Perpetua feels toward her father is contained in the words she addresses to her readers; it is not in the words she addresses to her father.

The father returns twice more. At the prisoners' public investigation by the procurator, the father arrives with the baby. He tries to drag his daughter down the stairs of the rostrum on which, he knows, she is getting ready once more to proclaim her indefectible Christianity (6.2). In their previous encounter he had evoked his love for her and her family obligations: her death, he warned, would bring unhappiness to the family and cast shame upon them. He understands that his words have had no impact. He has one last argument—the baby. "Have pity on your young child," he implores. The procurator Hilarianus joins the father and the child in addressing Perpetua: "Have pity on your father's white hair, have pity on your son's tender years. Sacrifice for the well-being of the emperors." "I will not" (*non facio*), she responds. "Are you a Christian?" he asks. "I am a Christian," she responds (6.3–5). One cannot call her by any other name.

When Perpetua's father persists in trying to bring about her downfall (*me deiciendam*), that is, to persuade his daughter to choose earthly life, Hilarianus orders *him* thrown down and struck in public. Defeated, the father no longer threatens Perpetua. At last she can express real empathy for him: "My father's plight hurt me, as if I were the one who had been struck" (6.5). That empathy is combined with a sense of distance: "I suffered on account of his old age." She is triumphant youth, the future; he is miserable old age, the past. In their final encounter (chapter 9), Perpetua is utterly at peace with her decision and sure of her moral superiority, which even the prison warden recognizes. The father no longer tries to talk to his daughter. He has lost all confidence in words, in his authority, and in his honor. "Consumed by sorrow, he began to pluck out the hair of his beard and throw it on the ground, and to throw himself on his face and curse his years in words that could move all creation"—all creation except Perpetua, that is. Again she writes, "I suffered on account of his unhappy old age [*infelici senecta*]" (9.2). But she has nothing to say to *him*. The devil's arguments have been silenced. Throughout the text, Perpetua says that her father is trying to destroy her. But in the end, the father's love did not destroy her; it destroyed him.

Perpetua's Four Visions

Perpetua's journal describes a series of visions (the meetings with the father appear in the text before and after them). For her readers the visions were very important. The author of the preface seems to consider them at least as important as the martyrdom itself. They prove, he writes, that divine inspiration is not a thing of the past. The Holy Spirit continues to inspire and teach even now (some scholars have suspected the editor of Montanism). But Perpetua is not trying to make sense of the Holy Spirit's action in history. She is trying to make sense of her own death.

The first vision she describes comes at the instigation of her "brother." We do not know whether this is a brother by blood or in the spirit. "Mistress Sister" *(domina soror)*, he says, "You are now worthy of great honor, so great that you may ask for a vision and you will be shown whether it is suffering [you should expect] or a commuted [sentence]." The formal address is an expression of Perpetua's status among her fellow prisoners (soon her father too will address her as "mistress"). She writes that she is already in the habit of "conversing" with the Lord *(fabulari cum domino)*, but we do not know the content of these "conversations." She is confident that she will indeed have a vision and promises a response "tomorrow." This is what she sees; she has just been baptized in prison and has had the first confrontation with her father:

> I see an extraordinarily tall brass ladder rising to heaven. It was narrow—you had to climb it one rung at a time. And all sorts of iron spikes were sticking out of the sides of the ladder. There were swords, spears, hooks, cutlasses, javelins, so that if you climbed without care or without looking up, you'd be torn to pieces and your flesh would be hanging from the iron spikes. And there was at the foot of the ladder a serpent [*draco*] of wondrous size lying in wait for the people who were climbing, trying to terrify them and keep them from climbing up. Saturus went up first—he had turned himself in afterward, on his own, because of us, because he was the one who had instructed us in the faith, and when we were arrested he was away. And he reached the top of the ladder, turned around, and told me, "Perpetua, I'm waiting for you; but be careful the serpent doesn't bite you." And I told him, "It won't harm me, in the name of Jesus Christ." And from the very

foot of the ladder, as if it were afraid of me, it slowly extended its head. And as if I were putting my foot on the first rung, I put my foot on its head and went up. And I saw the enormous expanse of a garden, and seated in the middle an imposing man with white hair, dressed as a shepherd, who was milking ewes; and standing all around him were a multitude of people dressed in white. He lifted his head, saw me, and said, "Welcome, little child." And he called me; and of the cheese that he had been milking [sic], he offered me a mouthful. And I received it with hands joined and I ate. And all in attendance said, "Amen." And at the sound of these voices, I awoke. (4.3–10)

From that vision Perpetua and her "brother" understood that "suffering" awaited them. Perpetua does not interpret the vision for her readers, as if it were only the response to the question raised by the brother who had "ordered" the vision. In certain respects the dream's meaning is clear: Perpetua leaves the earth and rises to heaven. Hence she must renounce her earthly hopes. But there is more in the vision, or rather less: the sufferings that await Perpetua are totally absent from it. Perpetua's path to heaven is strewn with dangers, but these are mere threats and do not take concrete form. Perpetua does not look back. Her vision expresses this: anyone wanting to climb the ladder to heaven must look upward. But visions reveal not what the future holds but what is concealed in the past. Perpetua's first vision does not depart from the rule. It expresses her fears and anxiety and is directly connected to what she must leave behind: life, her father's love, her child.

Christian exegetes have been quick to find a series of biblical symbols in the vision (which probably took the form of a dream): the ladder rising to heaven is Jacob's ladder; the woman who places her foot on the serpent's head is the Virgin Mary; and any shepherd is Jesus, the Good Shepherd. Different commentators have persisted in finding echoes of Christian writings (or writings adopted by Christianity) in the dream, such as the Shepherd of Hermas, the Book of Enoch, and the Old and New Testaments, from Genesis and the Song of Songs to the Epistles of Paul and Revelation.[10] Other exegetes have found echoes of the Montanist heresy, which maintained that the Holy Spirit was still revealing itself and that its authority could replace church tradition and even holy scripture. That exegesis ignores the difficulties involved in interpreting the dream along biblical lines. Not only are the specific "identifications" dubious, but there is also the simple fact that Perpetua's knowledge of the Christian canon must have been extremely limited. Perpetua was raised in a pagan family and had not even managed to complete her elementary Christian instruction when she was arrested. Although there may be some Montanist-sounding echoes in the editor's preface, it is difficult to see any in the text itself. Perpetua considered herself a Christian, as simply as a jug is a jug. In her eyes it is neither philosophical arguments nor visions that make a Christian but acts. One becomes a jug when one looks and acts like one.

But while she lacked Christian education, she was not uneducated. She was given the standard liberal instruction (*liberaliter institute*, 2.1), and she must have acquired a good knowledge of pagan culture. Her symbolic world was made of pagan, Christian, and personal images molded into a Christian narrative, in accordance with her understanding of the term "Christian."[11]

Back to the vision. Perpetua finds herself at the bottom of a brass ladder rising to heaven. "All sorts of iron spikes were sticking out of the sides of the ladder . . . swords, spears, hooks, cutlasses, javelins." In other words, the ladder is covered with weapons belonging to gladiators. Surely this is not Jacob's ladder. Jacob sees a ladder which angels are ascending and descending. God assures Jacob that he is blessed and promises him not the kingdom of heaven but "the land *on which you lie*" (Gen. 28:12–15, my emphasis). In Jacob's dream the ladder symbolizes a passage between heaven and earth used by the heavenly retinue, not by humans. Jacob does not climb the ladder. He remains a passive spectator. Perpetua's ladder is very different. Perpetua must climb the ladder herself—it is *her* ladder. She is a heroine on the path toward the treasure of eternal life. Ladders, like staircases and bridges, appear in myths and legends as symbols of the difficult and dangerous passage from this world to worlds beyond: it is the threshold the hero must cross. Perpetua must weather alone the crossing to salvation.[12] Others, such as Saturus, can guide and encourage her; they can show her the way, but the climb itself is a task she must accomplish on her own. In the first dream, "each saves his own soul."

The gladiators' weapons indicate that for Perpetua the ladder symbolizes the arena in which she will die. In the first vision the arena is evoked only indirectly and symbolically, by allusion. She still has difficulty facing the horrors of martyrdom, and focuses entirely on the reward that will come after them.[13] The road to heaven is not the *via dolorosa*. In the dream, pain cannot touch Perpetua. Death and pain strike only those who hesitate. She does not hesitate, nor does she look back. And since Perpetua acts as she does, the way becomes easy and safe: she does not mention or allude to fatigue or pain. Even the frightening serpent becomes a step on which she confidently places her foot to ascend to heaven. The forces of evil trying to prevent her from ascending cannot really harm her. Remember that the dream comes shortly after the meeting with her father. Like the father, the serpent tries to prevent Perpetua from ascending to the heavenly kingdom. It does not threaten Saturus, but it does threaten her. It is *her* serpent. The serpent, like the father, is powerless before Perpetua's resolution. He is left behind "with his devil's arguments." The act of placing her foot on the serpent's head, a widespread symbol of victory, will reappear in the fourth dream (in which Perpetua prevails over an Egyptian, a figure she also identifies with her father). Immediately after the victory over her earthly father, Perpetua meets another father figure, the heavenly shepherd.[14]

Unlike the paradise in Saturus' vision (chapter 11) with its martyrs, its elders, its angels crying *agios, agios, agios,* and its palace or temple where God sits on his throne, Perpetua's paradise suggests a vast open meadow.[15] There are no singing angels or martyrs or bishops or rites. There is a huge shepherd milking ewes whose attention is focused on Perpetua. In the background, anonymous people dressed in white (a symbol of purity) form a choir of sorts, but no one identifiable shatters the intimacy between the shepherd and Perpetua. Even Saturus, who has climbed the ladder before her, disappears once he has played his role. Shepherds, who represent providence, protection, and paternal power, were a widespread symbol of gods in antiquity—among the Jews (for example, in Psalm 23), among Christians (Matt. 18:12–13), and among pagans. When Jesus is portrayed as the Good Shepherd, he assumes the traits of pagan iconography. Christ is depicted as a young man, clean-shaven, seated like Orpheus in nature, playing his lyre to charm his flock of sheep or carrying a lamb on his shoulders like Hermes Criophorus.[16] That is not the case here. Perpetua's shepherd is not a young man carrying the lost sheep on his shoulders. He is an old man, "white-haired" (*canus*), an adjective she later uses to describe her father.[17] But the heavenly father does not argue. He is as accepting and loving as the earthly father is hostile and threatening. The words the shepherd speaks are full of affection: "Welcome, my little child [*tegnon*]." After receiving her in that way, he calls to her (*clamavit me*), even though she is already beside him. Twice, then, he expresses his love for her. Next he offers her cheese from the ewe's milk he has drawn. More than just feeding, this act evokes nursing. Perpetua can once more become her father's little girl. The father's threatening, phallic, and serpentine virility is softened by this maternal symbol of nursing. The father has been transformed. In a sense, he is also saved.

The gift of food that ends the dream moves us into the world of Christian ritual. Perpetua receives the mouthful given to her with her hands joined, and all in attendance, like the faithful in church, approve by saying "Amen." The taste she delights in brings to mind the custom of giving milk and honey to the newly baptized at the first mass following their baptism. The memory of Perpetua's first communion is undoubtedly still fresh in her mind and finds expression in the dream. But there might be another interpretation in addition to the Eucharistic reading. Perpetua is being transferred from the world of the living to the world of the dead. Certain images would naturally arise in the mind of any educated Roman considering death. These may not have been absent from Perpetua's first vision. The vision echoes mythical elements relating to Orpheus and Persephone. They blend with the other voices—personal and Christian—adding another layer of significance. As we have seen, Orpheus is directly connected to the image of the good shepherd. He is also associated with the passage to the world of the dead. Orpheus descends into Hades to retrieve his wife, Eurydice, who died of a serpent's bite (it was a "huge" serpent, according to Virgil's version in the *Georgics*).[18] Like Perpetua, Orpheus too must not look back, and like her he manages to get by a monstrous guard (Cerberus) at the entrance to the underworld. Also like her, he is destined to be torn apart (in his case by the Maenads).[19]

Orpheus is associated with images of eternal life and the idea of reward after death. In one of the rare descriptions of such a reward in classical Latin literature—the visit of Aeneas to the Elysian Fields—Orpheus finds himself in a vast green garden where men blessed by the gods dwell. He is surrounded by a host of singing and dancing people, whose foreheads are adorned with bands white as snow.[20] Perpetua was undoubtedly familiar with the *Aeneid*, like everyone who had received a Latin education. It is not unlikely that Orpheus and the pagan paradise inhabited Perpetua's imagination, for the Elysian Fields were promised to those who endured the agonies of battle for the fatherland *(ob patriam pugnendo volnera passi)*. The context is different, but the similarities are telling: for suffering the wounds inflicted while fighting for the (heavenly) fatherland (Perpetua refers to suffering in the arena as fighting—*pugnaremus*, 10.1), she earns a triumphant death and an eternal reward.

In Roman iconography Orpheus symbolizes the path taken by the soul to the underworld, and his image often appears in mortuary art, both pagan and Christian. He is depicted sitting in a meadow or garden, holding a lyre, among the wild beasts he pacifies with his music, or as a good shepherd with his flock of sheep.[21] The sheep appear in the vision; the wild beasts await Perpetua in the arena. There is more. In a short poem Martial mentions an event that occurred in a Roman arena: a criminal dressed as Orpheus was placed between sheep and wild beasts, then torn apart by a bear incited against him.[22] We do not know whether Perpetua was familiar with that poem, but it is probable that she had heard about similar theatrical executions, like those, for example, mentioned by Tertullian, her fellow citizen and contemporary. As a matter of fact, the execution of Perpetua and her companions was also supposed to have a theatrical aspect. The authorities wanted to dress up the condemned as priests and priestesses of Saturn and Ceres. It is quite likely that Perpetua heard rumors of this plan, which must have reminded her of another pagan myth about the path leading to the underworld, Ceres' journey to save her daughter, Proserpina. The mother manages to obtain Pluto's consent to have her daughter freed from the underworld, but Proserpina allows herself to be tempted by the god and eats a pomegranate seed he has offered her. She consequently becomes part of the world of the dead. Perpetua also eats the food of the dead. She awakes with its taste in her mouth, knowing that she "no longer has any hope in this world."[23]

Perpetua's second dream occurs after she has performed well at her interrogation by the procurator Hilarianus:

A few days later, as we were all praying, all of a sudden, in the middle of my prayer, my voice rose up and I pronounced the name "Dinocrates." And I stood dumbfounded, because he had never come to my mind until that moment, and it hurt me to remember his sad fate. And I immediately understood that I was worthy, and that I must pray for him. And I began to pray many prayers for him and cry out to the Lord. Consequently, that very night, this vision came to me: I see Dinocrates coming from a dark place, where there were many others. He was very hot and very thirsty, his face dirty and his complexion livid; and on his face he still had the wound he had at the time of his death. This Dinocrates was my brother according to the flesh, seven years old. He died miserably of an illness, his face eaten away by an ulcer, so that his death was horrible to everyone. It was on his behalf, then, that I prayed. We were separated from each other by a great distance, so that neither could approach the other. In the place where Dinocrates was, there stood a pool filled with water, with an edge too high for the child to reach. And Dinocrates was straining as if he wanted to drink. I was distressed, because the pool had water and yet its edge was too high and prevented him from drinking. And I

awoke and understood that my brother was in pain; but I was sure
that I would be able to relieve that pain. (7.1–8)

The vision is ostensibly about the suffering in the underworld and the
possibility of salvation through the aid of another. But again one must examine the circumstances. Immediately after the interrogation, Perpetua
tells us, she sent the deacon Pomponius to tell her father to bring her child
to the prison so that she could continue to breast-feed him. He refused.
"God willing," she writes, "[the baby] no longer craved the breasts nor
did [the sudden discontinuation of nursing] cause fever. I was no longer
tormented either by my anxiety for the baby nor by breast pain." All was
well then.

Or perhaps not. In the second vision a thirsty child appears, asking for
her help. This time Perpetua no longer needs anyone to order her to have
the dream. It practically bursts forth, along with the name of her dead
brother. In the first dream, Perpetua was the protagonist. She was the one
who needed the help and support of Saturus, of the shepherd, and even of
the serpent. In the second dream, she does not appear at all: she is a spectator. There is no longer a narrow ladder by which everyone is obliged to save
his or her own soul. Perpetua knows she has the power to save *others*. But
since she is no longer part of the world of the living, the soul she saves is
that of her dead little brother, Dinocrates. Unlike all the living members
of her family, whom she is leaving behind and forgetting, her dead brother
bears a name.

Where is Dinocrates, and why does he suffer? The standard interpretation is that Dinocrates is in a kind of purgatory, a place for dead souls who
do not deserve hell but are unable to reach paradise for one reason or another. Dinocrates is there because he was not baptized. Yet Perpetua, as a
future martyr, can gain him a symbolic baptism and end the suffering of
his soul. But is this a plausible interpretation? As Peter Dronke has rightly
remarked, Dinocrates does not want to be baptized; he wants to drink. The
description of the world he dwells in brings to mind classical descriptions
of the pagan underworld in Homer and Virgil, with which Perpetua was

quite familiar.[24] In that underworld the dead wander in darkness and in the stifling heat; they suffer an unquenchable thirst. Their bodies still bear the wounds they died from, and they are unable to see the living who watch them. The description of Dinocrates vainly standing on his tiptoes to drink water from the pool brings to mind the torments of Tantalus.

In the first dream, suffering was only a possibility, a threat; in the second, it is a presence. Perpetua is not yet directly affected by it, but it is closer to home. The description of Dinocrates' dwelling place suggests not only the pagan underworld but also Perpetua's prison: the stifling heat, the overcrowded conditions, the darkness, the feeling of powerlessness. Is the suffering protagonist really Dinocrates—Perpetua indicates that he "had never come to [her] mind until that moment"—or is it a thinly veiled Perpetua? Or is he perhaps both Perpetua and the baby—who might also be dying of thirst? It is hard to believe that the baby, whose first arrival turned Perpetua's prison cell into a palace (*factus est mihi carcer subito praetorium*, 3.9), has disappeared just as surely as the swelling has disappeared from her breasts. Her anxiety about the baby, supposedly alleviated, is clearly lurking behind the second vision, but Perpetua also indirectly expresses the anxiety she feels about the suffering that awaits her and the fear that death will not end her torments, that the dead continue to suffer. An indirect reference to Perpetua's anxiety can be found in the vision that Saturus relates to Perpetua. In his vision, when he and Perpetua arrive in heaven and are received by God, Saturus assures Perpetua that the promises have been kept and that her expectation was not in vain: "This is what the Lord has promised us: we see [the fulfillment of] his promise" (11.4), and then, "Perpetua, you have what you want" (12.7). Saturus is eager to allay Perpetua's fears that the promises will not be kept. In the vision, they are.

Images of Perpetua as a child are present in the first vision, as we saw. The shepherd calls Perpetua "my little child" (*tegnon*) and feeds her milk. In the second vision, the thirsty brother, the infant, and Perpetua herself are combined into a single person. The connection between nursing and feeding, and between Perpetua as mother and Perpetua as infant, had already appeared in a fifth-century sermon of Quodvultdeus, one of

Augustine's disciples and a fellow bishop: "Perpetua nursed until she received milk, a mouthful of milk, from the shepherd, who is also a father."[25] Quodvultdeus, commenting on the first dream, makes a mistake about the chronology. Perpetua continues to nurse after the dream. But the bishop instinctively grasped a certain inner truth more important than the chronology.

The second vision ends with a child in great distress. In the third vision the suffering ends:

> I see the place I saw before, and Dinocrates, his body clean, well dressed, feeling well; and where the wound was, I see a scar. The pool I had seen earlier had its edge lowered to the child's navel, and he drank water from it without stopping. And on the edge of the pool was a gold cup filled with water. And Dinocrates approached, began to drink from the cup. And this cup did not fail. And when he had quenched his thirst, he drew near [the pool], happy to play with water as children do.

Dinocrates is saved. Perpetua does not appear in the vision, but it is her prayers that have rescued the child. By contrast with the first dream, where the heroine must make a dangerous climb to salvation, salvation comes down to the protagonist in the third vision: the edge of the pool lowers itself not just to the child's mouth but to his navel (*ad umbilicum pueri*). This may be a reminder that umbilical cords are not easy to sever. Dinocrates/Perpetua/the baby drink. The thirst is quenched; the golden cup "did not fail." In the last scene of the third vision the child plays in a carefree way, "as children do." This convinces me that although Saturus' vision appears in the text after Perpetua's third vision, Saturus communicated it to her between her second and third visions, possibly as a therapeutic tale.[26] Saturus' final confirmation, "You have what you want," may have come as a response to Perpetua's description of her anxiety at the sight of her brother's plight. The heavenly elders' injunction to Perpetua and Saturus, "Go and play" (*ite et ludite*, 12.6), is reflected in Dinocrates' joyous play. At the end of this vision Perpetua declares that she is happy (*hilaris*), just as in the third dream the child is happy (*gaudens*). Dinocrates' salvation and Perpetua's are one and the same. Hence the third vision calms the fears expressed in the first and second visions and prepares Perpetua for her fourth and final vision. On the eve of her execution, she is prepared to confront death directly:

On the eve of the day when we were to fight, I see the deacon Pomponius come to the prison door and knock with great force. And I went to meet him and opened the door; he was dressed in a white tunic without a belt and was wearing sandals with multiple straps. And he said, "Perpetua, we are waiting for you: come." And he took me by the hand and we began to advance through difficult and winding roads. Short of breath, we reached the amphitheater with great difficulty. He led me to the middle of the arena and told me, "Have no fear: I shall stay with you and suffer with you." And he went away. And I saw an enormous crowd tense with anticipation, and since I knew I had been condemned to [die by] the beasts, I was surprised that no one set beasts upon me.

And a hideous-looking Egyptian came out to meet me, accompanied by his assistants, to do battle with me. Then handsome young men, my assistants and supporters, came toward me. I was stripped of my clothing and became a man. And my supporters began to rub oil on me, as is customary for a wrestling match; and I saw the Egyptian rolling in the dust before me. Then an extraordinarily large man came out, so tall that he stood higher than even the top of the amphitheater. He was dressed in a tunic without a belt, with two strips of crimson in the middle of his chest. He had gold and silver sandals, elaborately wrought. He was carrying a rod like a referee and a green bough with golden apples on it. And he called for silence and said: "If the Egyptian here is victorious over her, he will kill her with the sword; if she wins the victory, she will receive this bough." And he went away. And we approached each other and began to go at each other with our fists, he tried to grab my feet; I struck him in the face with my heels.

And I was lifted up into the air and began to strike him, as if not touching the ground. But when I saw that the battle was slowing down, I joined my hands together, interlacing my fingers, and grabbed his head. He fell on his face, and I put my foot on his head. And the crowd began to cheer and my supporters to sing hymns. And I approached the referee and received the bough. He kissed me and said, "My daughter, peace [be] with you." And I advanced in glory toward the gate of Safe Life. And I awoke. And I understood that it was not the beasts that I was going to fight but rather the devil; but I knew that victory was mine (10.1–14).

In the fourth vision Perpetua returns to the scene and plays the principal role. The symbols have become more realistic: the dream takes place in the arena. Perpetua is in mortal danger: if she loses the battle against the monstrous Egyptian, she will be slain. And yet in this most realistic of her visions, there is no pain, only effort. Instead of being attacked by ferocious beasts and then butchered by the *retiarius*, Perpetua fights and wins in a sort of wrestling match *(pankration)*, in which the participants usually do battle bare-handed and do not fight to the death. In the dream she is not the helpless victim. In reality, Perpetua knows, death awaits her whether she "triumphs" or is defeated.

In the fourth dream, as in the first, Perpetua has a guide. Pomponius calls her, using words that echo, in the first-person plural, the words of Saturus in the first vision: "Perpetua, we are waiting for you." On the "difficult and winding" roads where they advance, Pomponius takes her by the hand, and once in the arena, he assures her that he will stay and suffer with her. In addition to Pomponius, Perpetua has "assistants" and "supporters," who prepare her for battle and sing hymns when she defeats her adversary. She also has the referee, who addresses her as "my daughter." In the third vision Perpetua learned that salvation is not a lonely climb. She has helped Dinocrates; others can help her.

It is interesting that it is Pomponius who is her guide in the fourth vision. We might have expected Saturus to play that role—the man who had introduced her to the Christian faith, who had willingly chosen martyrdom with his and her fellows, and who has shared his vision with her in prison. But perhaps Saturus had become linked with powerlessness in Perpetua's mind. Remember the first vision: Saturus showed the way, but he could not help. Pomponius is in the outside world and is not powerless. Perhaps even more important, he is the man who brought the baby to her. He is part of the world of the living. But the Pomponius of the dream is more than a friendly and helpful figure. The words he speaks to her, "I shall stay with you and suffer with you," repeat almost word for word those spoken by Perpetua's fellow martyr, the slave girl Felicity, to the assistant jailer who asked her how she would withstand the beasts, having suffered so much in giving birth to her daughter in prison: "Now *I* suffer what I suffer, but there [in the arena], there will be someone else who will suffer for me" (15.6). Pomponius thus plays the role of Jesus in this vision. The terms Perpetua uses to describe Pomponius' tunic and his sandals identify him very clearly with another figure in the dream—the referee. Pomponius is the alter ego of the referee, an obvious symbol of God: Lord of the Last Judgment, he referees the battle for the soul's redemption waged against the devil, whom Perpetua herself identifies with the Egyptian of her dream.[27] The representation of martyrdom as a battle or an athletic competition was common in the Christian community of the time. It is not surprising, then, that God appears in the vision as a referee holding the rod of justice and the green bough bearing the golden apples of heavenly reward.

But God is not a distant judge. He is also a father. Not only is his extraordinary size reminiscent of the father-shepherd in the first vision, but so are the words he speaks to Perpetua: "My daughter, peace be with you." It seems therefore that Perpetua is making a distinction between God the father, who observes the competition and grants the reward to the winner at the end, and Jesus/Pomponius, who promises to take part in the battle and to suffer with her. That distinction allows us to understand two surprising elements in the fourth dream: the fact that Pomponius/Jesus abandons Perpetua immediately after promising to stay with her, and Perpetua's transformation into a man. It is obvious that Perpetua associates virility with spirituality, strength, and superiority, while femininity is associated with materiality, weakness, and inferiority. Her transformation into a man is linked to a separation from the earth and a victory of spirit over matter. Her adversary, the Egyptian, is hideous looking (a symbol of materiality), whereas Perpetua's retinue is beautiful and spiritual.

The Egyptian rolls in the dust before the battle; he falls at Perpetua's feet, his face to the ground, while she is lifted up into the air and ultimately places her foot on her adversary's head, as she had on the serpent's head. The Egyptian, like the serpent in the first dream, clearly symbolizes her earthly father, who, in the chapter preceding the description of the dream, threw himself, facedown, onto the ground before his daughter. But Perpetua's gender acrobatics are less clear-cut than many of those who have analyzed the dream have argued. In spite of her becoming a man, the referee continues to use feminine forms to address her. Perpetua does not simply lose her feminine identity; rather, a masculine identity, the identity of Jesus, is *added* to it. Jesus does not abandon Perpetua; he suffers with her, since he has joined her during the battle. One is reminded of the account of the martyrdom of Blandina of Lyons, exposed to the horns of a raging bull some thirty years earlier. We are told that observers "watched her do battle, and saw through the body of their sister the One who had been crucified for them, to show those who believe in Him that all who suffer for the glory of Christ have an eternal place with the living God."[28] Perpetua did not necessarily know this text, though rumors about the martyrs of Lyons may have reached her ears, and the idea of becoming one with Christ through martyrdom was commonplace. During the battle, Jesus is with Perpetua, and she is Jesus. At the end, she has won more than a contest. She is not alone: the Holy Spirit visits her with visions; the Son is with her in her hour of need, and the father hands her a bough of victory, kisses her, and reassures her: "My daughter, peace [be] with you [*pax tecum*]." Her femininity, only suggested before the battle, is fully regained. There is no need to explain how Perpetua has become a woman again. She has never stopped being one. More important, she has never stopped being a daughter to a loving father. The vision ends with intimacy and life. Perpetua is now ready for death.

Perpetua's Metamorphosis

Perpetua's journal offers the tragic testimony of a young woman in a rush. She has only a few days to assimilate the knowledge that her life is suddenly coming to an end, that she has been torn away from her family, has seen her father break down, and has been separated from her child. The religion she has only recently embraced offers her a model of interpretation that she can and must adopt. Perpetua is in the process of becoming a martyr—a role that offers a set of metaphors ready at hand, a script that is known in advance, a plotline of a Christian tragedy. Ideally, all that is left for her to do is to adapt to that model: develop the typical symptoms, say her lines properly, and exit on time. The spectators are waiting for their cue to begin applauding. But "ready-made" models like "the martyr" are not simple mechanisms of social control, a means by which a society forces individuals to act out its expectations. At least, that is not all they are. They are also psychological safety nets. When the coordinates that secure us within a certain frame of reference suddenly vanish, the great cultural clichés are there to stop us from slipping into the psychological abyss of total meaninglessness.[29] But martyrdom is a safety net made of barbed wire. On the one hand, it offers honor, a rise in status, solidarity, and the kingdom of heaven. On the other, it demands everything else. That is not easy. Perpetua is not sure whether she will play the role well—it is difficult, and one usually gets just a single chance. In addition, she must have doubts about the model's validity. What if it is all a mistake? What if she is not a jug at all? What if all the suffering has been for naught? Perpetua may have written her journal in a single sitting, on the eve of her execution. At that stage she has already accepted her fate, and her dreams have given her a self-assurance she did not previously possess. Perpetua has undoubtedly filtered out everything that is not worthy of remembering, just as she has wiped out her whole life before her arrest. If we can discern more than one internal conflict in reading that journal, it is not because Perpetua wanted to reveal such conflicts but because she did not know how to obliterate them.

Later editors believed it prudent to correct that deviation from the social model. In the account of the martyrdom itself there is no trace of hesitation, either in Perpetua or in the others. In all their actions they manifest an absolute confidence in God and in the path they are taking. The model underlying the narrative is that of ironic role reversal. The weak are really strong and the strong weak. The martyrs have a sarcastic attitude toward their tormentors and toward the onlookers, based on their moral and spiritual superiority. Twice the martyrs suggest that the public will pay dearly. On the eve of the execution, they mock the mob and threaten it with God's judgment (chapter 17). On the day they are to be put to death, the men shout at the procurator, "You are our judge, but God is your judge" (18.8). The martyrs tremble, but the editor explains that they tremble for joy, not out of fear. Even when their attitude brings them more punishment—blows, for example—the martyrs feel joy as a result. Their deaths are transformed into a demonstration not only of fortitude but also of their power of prophecy: each enjoys the death he or she has chosen (chapter 19). The editor emphasizes that Saturus held "no beast more in horror than the bear," and he gloried in the bear's refusal to leave its cage and attack him. He says nothing of the anguish Saturus and his small flock must have felt, waiting for their glorious triumph.

Despite the somewhat didactic tone of the editor, the narration of the events in the arena is impressive and touching. The martyrs acted with dignity and heroism. The tormentors' attempt to elicit the audience's scorn for the women by humiliating and stripping them failed. Instead, their fragility and dignity made the audience feel ashamed. First, the women were allowed to get dressed; then, at the mob's request, efforts to throw them to the beasts a second time were abandoned (chapter 20). Perpetua played her role perfectly, as did the others.

Nevertheless, not all the journal's readers were satisfied. The complete early text conveys ambiguous messages and leaves questions open. In two brief versions of the martyrdom of Perpetua and her companions, the *Acta*,[30] probably compiled in the fifth century, Perpetua loses the central place she occupied in the earlier document. Men, Saturus especially, take center stage, both by their words and by their acts. The dialogue with the procurator is longer, and all the Christian speakers display tenacity and insolence. Parts of the journal have disappeared altogether, and the visions have been abridged: Saturus' dream and the two dreams about Dinocrates are not mentioned at all, and only a brief description of the hideous Egyptian rolling at Perpetua's feet remains from the fourth dream.[31] In the two versions of the *Acta*, Perpetua's husband has surfaced in the text, and Perpetua's relationship with her father has lost all its complexity: even the father's love for Perpetua and his growing despair in the days between his daughter's arrest and her death are not mentioned. Only a caricature of a fanatically anti-Christian pagan remains. The resemblance between the real father and the father figures in the dreams has disappeared even from the first vision, the only vision rendered more or less in its entirety. In the first version of the *Acta*, the heavenly shepherd is described as an old man (*senem*), but since his white hair is not mentioned, the connection between him and the father is toned down. In the second version of the *Acta*, he is not even an old man anymore; he is simply described as a "shepherd."[32] In both versions there is no intimacy between that shepherd and Perpetua. He addresses everyone and gives food to everyone. In the first version, the nursing symbolism is retained: it is specified that the shepherd distributes the "fruit of his milk" (*de fructu lactis*); in the second, milk is not mentioned at all, and the shepherd offers "the fruit of his flock" (*de fructibus gregis*).[33]

All the psychological depth of Perpetua's attitude toward her child has also disappeared in the later versions: her worry and anguish have been replaced by total indifference to the baby's fate. In the longer version of the first *Acta*, her farewell scene with her family is described as follows:

> When they heard [about her trial] her family—her father and mother, her brothers, and her husband with the still-nursing baby—all arrived. . . . When the father saw her standing before the proconsul's tribunal, he fell on his face and said to her: "Daughter, no longer daughter but mistress, have pity on your father's years, if I deserve to be called father; have pity on your mother, who has raised you to full adulthood; have pity on your brothers and on this most miserable

man, or at least on this baby, who will not outlive you. Give up your idea. None of us can outlive you, for something like this has never happened in my family." But Perpetua stood motionless, and directing her gaze to heaven, said to her father: "Father, fear not. If you are not stubborn, you will have a daughter in perpetuity [*perpetuam filiam*] in your daughter Perpetua." . . . Her father then placed the baby on her neck, and he, her mother, and her husband held her hands and, in tears, kissed them, saying, "Have pity on us, daughter, and live with us." But she cast the baby from her and pushed them all away saying, "I never knew you; depart from Me, you who practice lawlessness!" [Matt. 7:23].[34]

The heartrending encounters between father and daughter from the original text have been flattened out. The growing despair of the father is gone. Gone too are Perpetua's emotional responses. She pontificates, her eyes to heaven, and when the baby is laid against her neck, she pushes him away with a grand theatrical gesture: "I never knew you; depart from Me, you who practice lawlessness!" If the real Perpetua did not quite conform to the cultural cliché, the literary Perpetua is a perfect match.

The *Acta* surpassed the original version in popularity. Some ninety medieval manuscripts of the *Acta* have come down to us, in contrast to one Greek and nine Latin manuscripts of the *Passio.* In the thirteenth century, Jacobus de Voragine, in his *Golden Legend,* included a version even more abridged than the *Acta.*[35] None of the manuscripts of the *Passio* dates from after the late twelfth century. In the battle between the historical saint (or at least the imperfect cliché of a saint) retained by contemporaries and the flawless saint prepared for cultural primetime, the living saint had no chance of prevailing. All the same, victory in this battle and in others of the same type is never total. In each generation, new saints rose up who conformed badly to the cultural models, who sent mixed, confusing signals. And until they too were condemned to oblivion or deliberately refashioned, they spread to every corner of the earth the acrid, toxic, and intoxicating odor of life.

FOUR

The Ascetics

FROM OUR EARLIEST CHILDHOOD, we are taught and conditioned to identify the deferral of pleasure with strength and the inability to defer the primary drives with weakness. Language reflects this conditioning: a person "cannot resist" good food, "has a weakness" for women, "gives in" to pleasures. By contrast, according to a Talmudic maxim, "a hero is he who conquers his urges." Asceticism consists of a readiness to deprive oneself of a primary satisfaction in exchange for a secondary one. For Freud the deferral of primary pleasures comes with the emergence of the ego. The child learns to suppress his drives to avoid punishment. Asceticism is born with the superego, when the child moves from acceptance, with no little resentment, of the "reality principle" to sublimation. The child learns to make the arbitrary rules imposed on him his own. He or she develops a conscience. The ascetic drive is thus not a phenomenon linked to a specific set of historical circumstances; it is a universal drive, the bitter fruit of the tree of knowledge of good and evil. The shift from nonculture ("nature") to culture implies the end of spontaneity: the infant, an uncivilized "savage," does not possess a filter that would tell him which desires are permitted and which forbidden. His parents, educators, and culture gradually impose a set of prohibitions and permissions—"right and wrong," "values," "norms," "articles of faith"—through which, and through which alone, he must see the world. The response to the call of desire is deferred, if only for a fraction of a second, and examined for its conformity to the moral code inculcated in us by our culture. When that process of weighing and examining desire comes about very quickly and profoundly, we call it second nature. But second nature resembles the first in name alone. Not only is it the product of conditioning and training; there is nothing natural about it.

The conflict between second nature and first is a source of frustration and bitterness, inextricably linked to violent self-coercion. In a famous allegory in the dialogue *Phaedrus*, Plato compares the soul to a charioteer whose chariot is harnessed to two horses: one (representing spirituality) is good, the other (representing materiality) bad. When a man meets his beloved, the spiritual horse and the charioteer are struck with passive admiration, whereas the corporeal horse becomes active and desires carnal contact. "And when they come near [the loved one] he takes the bit between his teeth and pulls shamelessly, with head down and tail stretched out. The driver, however[,] . . . with a still more violent backward pull, jerks the bit from between the teeth of the lustful horse, drenches his abusive tongue and jaws with blood, and forcing his legs and haunches against the ground reduces him to torment."[1] The wicked horse gradually learns to sublimate. Plato notes with regret that success is not always assured, but one must aspire to rein in—that is the right term—carnal desires and transform them into spiritual, socially acceptable desires.

Human societies create their most powerful myths to justify that most unnatural act of renunciation. In exchange for renouncing immediate satisfactions, a man will enjoy not only society's approval and admiration but also great rewards in paradise. Paradise is depicted as a sort of womb where all needs are immediately met in exchange for a renunciation of free choice. It is not surprising, then, that many mystics (from Buddha and Ibn al-ʿArabī in the East to Plotinus and Meister Eckehart in the West) identify free choice with suffering and strive to reach a state where the inner rift, the war of natures, is at an end. For those who do not have a taste for the mystic way, paradise is described as a re-legitimation of primary drives: no more fear of punishment, no need to repress. In some paradises the faithful can finally give free rein to their desires in a continuous orgy of sex and food, endless feasting by the previously repressed senses; in others they rid themselves of corporeal drives in exchange for constant spiritual ecstasies, the absence of any feeling of want, any need for restraint. There is no asceticism in paradise.

A certain measure of asceticism is necessary for any human society. Every culture is founded on the suppression of primary urges. But in most societies there are people who make an art of that necessity. They renounce satisfying not just *some* of their needs but almost all of them, and they idealize the lack of satisfaction. Asceticism is perceived not as a necessary evil but as a good, not as a compromise between individual drives and social possibilities but as an uncompromising act of self-purification, not as a pragmatic tactic but as a strategy of strength. Contrary to received opinion, the ascetic is the exact opposite of the masochist. Masochism means seeking erotic pleasure through pain. The masochist is a slave to his passions. Asceticism is a repression of desire, a technique for total liberation.

To what end? Why renounce the very things for the attainment of which most of us seek power, in exchange for a mysterious power most of us would not wish to attain? In a chapter of *The Genealogy of Morals* titled "What Is the Meaning of Ascetic Ideals?" Friedrich Nietzsche tries to explain the nature of that power. Asceticism, especially religious asceticism, he argues, is not a strategy of self-improvement. It is a technique of achieving control, first over oneself, then over others. Asceticism is a weapon of the weak, of those whose weakness deprives them of satisfying their pleasure drives. Instead of accepting their condition, they deny the legitimacy of all pleasure. Pleasure is sinful. If they succeed in imposing their ideas on the powerful, their weakness becomes a strength, for they are the guides, the masters of self-denial. For Nietzsche, asceticism is an antidote to the melancholy and inferiority that plague the weak. The ascetic wishes to suppress all feeling, to suppress the ego—everything that for him is a source of frustration. All the techniques for repressing the ego, the interminable series of absurd religious prescriptions, are meant to distract the mind and to fill the day with activity. They are, for Nietzsche, so many efforts to deny the feeling of depression gnawing at the weak. But the dull and oppressive pain does not let go of those beset by it. More powerful remedies are needed. The "ascetic priest"—a sort of mythic inventor of asceticism—offers the suffering patient a radical solution: the reason for his suffering is not his inability to get what he wants. It is not his weakness but his moral inadequacy that is to blame. His suffering is a punishment. There is finally an explanation for suffering, an explanation one can suffer with. "Sins" and flaws are extraordinarily addictive forces. But the remedy, Nietzsche maintains, is worse than the illness:

> Everywhere the *will* to misunderstand suffering made the content of life, the reinterpretation of suffering as feelings of guilt, fear, and punishment; everywhere the scourge, the hair shirt, the starving body, contrition; everywhere the sinner breaking himself on the cruel wheel of a restless, morbidly lascivious conscience; everywhere dumb torment, extreme fear, the agony of the tortured heart, convulsions of an unknown happiness, the cry for "redemption." The old depression, heaviness, and weariness were indeed *overcome* through this system of procedures; life again became *very* interesting: awake, everlastingly awake, sleepless, glowing, charred, spent and yet not weary—thus was the man, "the sinner," initiated into *this* mystery. This ancient mighty sorcerer in his struggle with displeasure, the ascetic priest, had obviously won; *his* kingdom had come: one no longer protested *against* pain, one *thirsted* for pain: "*more* pain! *more* pain!" the desire of his disciples and initiates has cried for centuries.[2]

No student of asceticism can remain unaffected by Nietzsche's brilliant insights into the aggressive aspects of asceticism and its political consequences. His description of how one overcomes suffering by increasing it, by linking it to an elaborate argument, and by giving it meaning retains its rhetorical power even now, more than a hundred years after he wrote this text. But admiration for Nietzche's rhetoric must be tempered with a certain caution.

I have chosen to begin with Nietzsche because he constitutes an influential link in the long chain of interpretive approaches, still current today, that regard religion in general, and asceticism in particular, as expressions of mental weakness. For Enlightenment thinkers, religion exemplified the tendency of the masses to believe in superstitions. For Nietzsche's contemporary Karl Marx, religion was the "opiate of the people." Enlightenment philosophers believed it was possible to unburden religion of its superstitious cargo through education and reform. Marx, Nietzsche, and Freud saw religions as deliberate conspiracies on the part of certain elites that manipulated ideas and symbols in order to dupe the naïve masses into submission. Whereas Marx considered religion a conspiracy of cynics, for Nietzsche and Freud it was an illness afflicting doctors as well as patients (though doctors consciously seek to perpetuate the disease to which they are beholden for their domination over their patients). These hypotheses have in common a certain intellectual arrogance (the "masses" are gullible and spineless), as well as a real misunderstanding of religious systems and the agents that operate within them.

Nietzsche perceived asceticism as a psychopathological phenomenon that leads to an aggravation of mental problems. But asceticism cannot be reduced to emotional disturbance, nor is it simply the monstrous expansion of a psychological disorder. It is also a social institution that people embrace for reasons totally unrelated to a personal feeling of inadequacy. Moreover, what turns ascetics from marginal individuals into central figures in certain societies is not a tactical maneuver on the part of the meek in order to inherit the earth. Rather it is *society* that needs them as intercessors with the next world rather than as experts in suffering. Asceticism is often imposed by society for political rather than psychological reasons.

Why an individual chooses asceticism as a way of life and a career, and what the social meaning of such a choice might be, are two distinct questions. We need to examine the phenomenon of asceticism both from the standpoint of the individual and from that of society.

The Ascetic's Motives and the Consequences of Asceticism

The ascetic operates on three parallel planes at once: the individual, the cultural-ideological, and the social. Asceticism meets individual psychological needs, which are partly conscious and partly unconscious. The ascetic may, for example, be motivated by a strong sense of guilt that impels him to seek suffering as a punishment or as a remedy. The torment he inflicts on himself can bring relief, even pleasure. Or the ascetic may fear "normal" social relations and may use asceticism as a pretext to avoid them. In that case the ascetic does not seek deprivation at all. It is the price he is willing to pay in exchange for breaking away from society and its rules. Thus many medieval women became nuns to liberate themselves from burdensome family relations and undesired marriages. Other motivations are also possible. But to be socially acknowledged and respected, the ascetic must generally deny his more earthly benefits and claim that what drives him is a spiritual quest, one that is part of an ideology that his community considers acceptable.

The ideological foundations of asceticism vary from one society to another. Some consider it a mechanism for cleansing individuals of the impurity of everyday exchanges, making them fit to commune with the gods without "sacrilege" or defilement. Other societies see it as a magical technique. Asceticism is conceived as the means to attract the attention of the gods, to elicit their pity, and above all to establish a new moral balance with them.[3] In a sense this was the role the church attributed to Christ's passion. As a sinless victim, Christ could use his suffering to save sinful humanity. But even if the ascetic is not free from all sin, he always punishes himself beyond what is necessary to wipe out his own sins. In the unwritten account books of the universe, the surplus of suffering is recorded as a credit for the ascetic and as a debit for the gods. The gods grant powers to the ascetic to compensate for his superfluous suffering, a phenomenon we have already observed in the discussion of martyrs. As we saw, it is not only gods who are sensitive to superfluous suffering. The ascetic's willingness to inflict horrible punishment on himself poses an implicit threat. A person capable of such cruelty to himself could easily direct his terrible powers toward others, mercilessly punishing his opponents.

Whatever the ascetic's personal motivations, he should be able to claim, by word or deed, that he is submitting to an existing ascetic tradition, in other words, that his irregular behavior is in fact governed by culturally acceptable rules and is not a personal disorder. All societies respect order, even if an extraordinary order. If the ascetic model that prevails in society is precise (if it is a canonical monastic rule, for example), the ascetic is obliged to observe at least a certain number of its prescriptions so he can be seen as conforming to that model.

The ascetic attitude manifests itself on a third plane, the social. Through his acts, if not through his words, the ascetic declares he is different. Any declaration of that sort is a social threat that requires scrutiny. Why does this individual break the rules of the game? If the community does not react, the rules of the game may cease to function. There are different possible reactions. The rule breakers may be "fools" or "madmen" (labels for people whose opinions or acts a society intends to ignore). In that case, their rejection of rules stems from their *inability* to obey the rules, not from willful disrespect. Since they do not know what they are doing, they are not challenging the accepted rules, or if they are, their challenge can be safely ignored. Societies tend to treat transgressions by such individuals as if only the transgressions, not the transgressors, were the problem. Sometimes, however, the breaker of rules is evidently neither a fool nor a madman but someone willfully refusing to be "normal." Society cannot turn a blind eye to such an infringement of its norms. Asceticism, unless it takes place within socially allocated preserves (monasteries, hermitages, Sufi houses), is such an infringement. It is perceived as a technique that, whether intentionally or unintentionally, empowers the ascetic. The forces that the ascetic attracts to himself may be spiritual or material. In either case, they destabilize the existing balance of power.

The first reaction to the new ascetic's arrival is skepticism. Skeptics try to defuse social bombs by declaring them fakes. First they may cast doubt on the facts. Detractors will claim that the ascetic eats in secret, sleeps with women, does not seriously flagellate himself. If this fails, and the asceticism is generally considered authentic, it is still possible to deny its value by questioning the ascetic's motivations. He may be an opportunist willing to trade pleasure for power, for example. He may not be motivated by personal gain, but may be a heretic, that is, a person whose asceticism is founded on ideological premises not accepted by society. And finally, the ascetic may be a masochist who *enjoys* his asceticism; in other words, appearances notwithstanding, he is not really an ascetic.

These three planes exist in conjunction with one another. No attempt to separate the different kinds of interaction—the psychopersonal, the theological, and the social—would be very useful. Every ascetic has his own reasons to choose asceticism: a whole array of contradictory drives ranging from the sublime to the ridiculous and from the purest to the most squalid. The existence of such motivations does not invalidate other motivations, ideological or religious, just as the feeling of pride or self-importance that the altruist might derive from his acts does not make him an egoist. The fact that the ascetic draws satisfaction from his status, and that he uses the power that society is inclined to grant him, does not mean that status and power are his "true" motivations. Even the staunchest idealists are not made of stone. Once they become an integral part of a social dialogue that attributes powers to them or denies them such powers, that praises or blames them, they react like anyone else.

The question of what *really* motivates the ascetic is meaningless, as is the question of whether a "true" saint really exists. If "true" means perfectly pure, the response will always be negative. Nothing in the world is pure. Does this mean that everything in the world is completely impure? There again the response will be negative. In this world we are always dealing with relative values. What interests the historian about ascetics is not the worthiness of their motivations, and certainly not their "true" motivations. Only God knows the precise combination of motivations that impels people to act. Only he may judge. Furthermore, what makes a person act at one moment is not necessarily what makes him act at another. People sometimes do things without intending to do them; sometimes honor, power, habit, or fatigue can alter the purest intentions. People rarely conform to clear and precise models, just as they rarely have feet that perfectly fit size 11 shoes. They fit, more or less. They fluctuate and shift from one model to another. At any given moment their actions reflect the balance of drives and contingencies that result from a unique situation which cannot be reproduced. The historian, whose discipline and limitations demand a great deal of modesty, will ask only those questions to which he can find meaningful answers: not what an individual's "true" and personal motives were, but rather what his social and public status was, what he said and did publicly, what people said about him and how they acted toward him.

Platonic Love, Stoic Serenity, and Christian Asceticism

In the first three centuries of its existence, Christian society gave rise to a communitarian and somewhat moderate asceticism. The community rejected ostentatious consumption, sexual excess, and competitiveness. It expected this mode of behavior from all its members. Particularly devout Christians followed a more severe regimen, rejecting physical pleasures while fully participating in life and in community responsibilities. Hence, when we speak of the emergence of an ascetic movement in the fourth century, we do not mean that there were no ascetics before then. What appeared in Christian society, after the Christianization of the Roman Empire, was a new cultural model, which encouraged more extreme forms of asceticism and made room for asceticism as a career. The movement began in Egypt and gradually spread to the Christian world as a whole. Individuals and groups turned their backs on urban and rural civilization and went to live in the desert. They made asceticism their reason for being: not just one of many ways to avoid temptations of the flesh but the *via regia* that leads to salvation. Anyone who aspired to "serious" asceticism had to pull away completely from the life of this world and devote himself, body and soul, to the exhausting exercise of asceticism.[4]

There is no obvious precedent for that model of perfection in scripture. One could consider Jesus a martyr (although, technically speaking, he was not a "witness"), but he was definitely not an ascetic. We do not know whether he had sexual relations, but he did not avoid the company of women and was not radically opposed to carnal relations. Apart from the forty days of fasting that began his mission—an act of symbolic initiation rather than self-mortification—Jesus seems not to have refused food or drink. Of John the Baptist it was said that he lived in the desert, dressed in camel hair clothing, and ate locusts and wild honey. Jesus did not follow him on that path, despite the criticism he received, as he himself attests: "For John came neither eating nor drinking, and they say, 'He has a demon.' The Son of Man came eating and drinking, and they say, 'Look, a glutton and a winebibber, a friend of tax collectors and sinners!'" (Matt. 11:18–19). Jesus dressed, ate, and drank in moderation. Judaism, to which he fully belonged, looked on asceticism with suspicion. Ascetic movements such as the Essenes operated on the margins of Judaism and were rejected by the "Pharisaical" majority,[5] to which, with all his criticism, Jesus himself belonged.[6]

Whereas Judaism in great part rejected asceticism as a career, in the pagan world that mode of life occupied a cultural niche available to Christian ascetics. Two philosophical schools dominated in the intellectual world of the fourth century, the Platonic and the Stoic. Their respective conceptions of the world had ascetic implications. Plato and his disciples saw the material world as a distorting barrier that separates human beings from the world of "ideas." Platonists turned the commonsensical conception of the world on its head. According to them, the general and the abstract are not the product of intellectual processes but, on the contrary, are the source of such processes and make them possible. Ontologically, the "idea" of the horse precedes any particular horse. Real-life horses exist only as figments, shadows of the idea of "horsehood." It is only because of our human limitations, because we are trapped within the prison cell of our body, that we confuse what is essential and primary (abstract ideas) with what is accidental, secondary, and hollow (the concrete). Thanks to reason, the wise man understands that the world of matter is an illusion and gradually detaches himself from it. According to Plato, and a fortiori his Neoplatonic disciples, this process has implications beyond the intellectual. By shedding the material, we are able to encounter not merely "truth" but also beauty and salvation. Whoever has the privilege of seeing the world of ideas achieves something more precious than understanding, something that surpasses it. He achieves happiness, a mystic madness, by means of which he completely overcomes the concrete. For Plato, that process involves not tearing oneself away but rather "coming home." The world of ideas is "natural" to us, the spiritual place we have occupied before becoming prisoners of the body: "Pure was the light and pure were we from the pollution of the walking sepulchre which we call a body, to which we are bound like an oyster to its shell."[7]

The wise man learns to act against his carnal instincts, replacing sensual pleasure with spiritual ecstasy. He learns to see beyond things, to see through the obstacles that conceal the essential from him. He learns to consider his body an enemy and a walking sepulcher. That ascetic tendency—paradoxically coexisting with the philosopher's participation in the social and political life of the commonwealth—became more pronounced within the Neoplatonic school, whose most notable representative was Plotinus. Porphyrus, Plotinus' disciple and biographer, relates that his master was ashamed of having a body. He prohibited people from drawing his portrait and neglected his body to such a point that he was covered with filth and wounds and caused horror among those who looked at him.[8]

Plotinus' behavior, it should be noted, was unusual. Socrates and Plato did not avoid wine and food, nor did they neglect their bodies. Although Platonists considered the body a walking sepulcher, they did not see the concrete body as a suitable battlefield for the fight between matter and spirit. That battle was waged entirely in the wise man's mind. The wise man learned to distinguish between the essential and the inessential, between what is worthy of love, namely, the eternal, the permanent, the abstract, and what is not worthy of it, the material and the ephemeral. Like Socrates in the *Symposium*, he knew how to hold on to his spirituality, even when he was surrounded by revelers and merrymakers.

Platonic asceticism is a form of sublimation: the wise man learns to refine himself not by renouncing desire, which can be an important elevating force, but by directing it toward the desirable object. Socrates can remain indifferent to the seduction attempts of Alcibiades, the most beautiful man in Athens, because what seduces him is beauty in itself and not the concrete beauty of one individual or another. Such a renunciation obeys a logic of exchange: in renouncing what is material, one replaces the impure and contemptible with the pure and sublime. But physical beauty is not worthless if used to rouse the mind to higher things. The road to spiritual ecstasy often begins with an attraction to beautiful boys.

Stoic asceticism is different. The Stoic wise man aspires to return to the "state of nature." The Stoics do not clearly define the state of nature toward which they aspire. Rather than a concrete entity, it is action, or better, an absence of action. Nature is an imaginary point where everything is in a state of ideal harmony and perfect equilibrium. The Stoic wise man does not seek ecstasy and does not believe in replacing base passions with sublime ones. All passions are bad. The state to which the Stoic wise man aspires is the absence of all passions, *apatheia*. Like the Platonist, the Stoic believes that the ordinary man's perception of reality is wrong. Yet the error is not metaphysical but ethical. The Platonist derides the ordinary man for not understanding that there is a world more "true" than the one he perceives; for the Stoic, what holds that man back is the fact that he does not understand that external events are morally insignificant and that, as a result, they must be accepted with indifference, without joy or sadness. As Epictetus says:

> What then should we have at hand upon such occasions? Why what
> else but—what is mine, and what not mine; what is permitted me,

and what not.—I must die: and must I die groaning too?—Be fettered. Must it be lamenting too? Exiled. And what hinders me, then, but that I may go smiling, and cheerful, and serene?—"Betray a secret"—I will not betray it; for this is in my own power. "Then I will fetter you."—What do you say, man? Fetter me? You will fetter my leg; but not Jupiter himself can get the better of my choice [*prohairesis*].[9]

Epictetus distinguishes between two kinds of self, the inner self, on which the judging person (*prohairesis*) depends, and the public self (*prosopon*), which is a mask. The inner self is an inner court, a private judge. It decides which of the stimuli to which the soul is exposed should be accepted or refused. A man need only choose to will what is good and reject what is evil—a power that is granted him without restrictions—and not even "Jupiter himself" can "get the better" of him. The public self is composed of the set of external conditions that identify the individual ("who we are and by what name we are called"). Even though functions such as father, son, spouse, sovereign, citizen, or slave are external and accidental, men must accept them without complaint and meet the moral obligations they imply: as a son, one is obliged to be loyal to one's father; as a slave, one has to obey; as a sovereign, one has to command. The aim of Stoic education is to ensure that men always do the "right" thing morally, whatever the price. When men have understood that all external events, such as success and prestige, misfortune and censure, mean nothing, they will become islands of "Stoic serenity," beyond the pleasure principle:

The doctrine of philosophers promises to procure us peace from these [misfortunes] too. And what doth it say? "If you will attend to me, O mortals, wherever you are, and whatever you are doing, you shall neither grieve nor be angry, nor be compelled nor restrained; but you shall live impassive, and free from all." Shall not he who enjoys this peace, proclaimed, not by Caesar (for how should he have it to proclaim?) but by God, through reason, be contented, when he is alone reflecting and considering: "To me there can now no ill happen;

there is no thief, no earthquake. All is full of peace, all full of tranquillity; every road, every city, every assembly. My neighbour, my companion, is unable to hurt me." Another, whose care it is, provides you with food, with clothes, with senses, with preconceptions. Whenever he doth not provide what is necessary, he sounds a retreat; he opens the door, and says to you, "Come." Whither? To nothing dreadful, but to that whence you were made; to what is friendly and congenial to the elements. What in you was fire, goes away to fire; what was earth, to earth; what air, to air; what water, to water. There is no Hades, nor Acheron, nor Cocytus, nor Pyriphlegethon; but all is full of gods and daemons.[10]

It is no easy thing to arrive at the point of being so indifferent to suffering and pleasure, in such a state of serenity (*ataraxia*) and self-control (*enkrateia*) that one is ready to welcome death without fear, but also without hope. Unfortunately, life in accordance with (Stoic) nature is contrary to "human nature." To reach the state of Stoic serenity, exercise (*askēsis*) is required. The Stoic is obliged to remain constantly on his guard: "When you let go your attention for a little while, do not fancy you may recover it whenever you please; but remember this . . . A habit arises . . . of deferring the attention, and always driving off from time to time, and procrastinating a prosperous life, a propriety of behaviour, and the thinking and acting conformably to nature."[11] But it is not enough to be aware. Unlike Platonists, Stoics do not consider the body evil. Man is composed of a body and a soul. We must accept our body—beautiful or ugly, healthy or ill—as a morally neutral given, part of our "mask." To ignore it would be harmful and dangerous. It is not enough, writes Musonius Rufus, Epictetus' teacher, to exercise the soul; one must also exercise the body, train it to withstand steadfastly the seductiveness of pleasure and the horror of suffering. Exercising the body plays a role in strengthening the soul, just as exercising the soul makes the body better able to resist.[12]

Despite the major differences between the Platonic and the Stoic schools, they share an essential trait. Both consider the "ordinary man" to be lost in error, and both urge him to escape normality by adopting a way of thinking contrary to what seems natural. This is not easy. Both Plotinus and Epictetus believe that philosophical *perfection* is beyond our reach. In order to approach the ideal even a little, a person must wage an unrelenting battle day and night. Most people have neither the strength nor the inclination for such a task. At most they can contemplate with admiration the exceptional human beings who are ready to take on the exhausting regimen of training, the *askēsis* that philosophical reason demands.

In the second and third centuries, the philosopher was expected to live outside the social norm, faithful to his true, philosophical self. Philosophy was more than an intellectual activity; it was a mode of life ruled by a specific conception of the world. The philosopher lived, or at least was supposed to live, his philosophy. He was recognizable by his clothing (his simple tunic), by his beard, and—whatever his metaphysical convictions—by his mode of life. "By the late first century," writes Patricia Cox, "the profession of philosophy and an ascetic mode of living were firmly linked in the popular mind and in the thinking of the intelligentsia as well."[13] A true philosopher (even an Epicurean) turned his back on worldly pleasures.

But if a great deal was expected of all philosophers, even more was expected of the Stoics. Not only were they expected, like all philosophers, to practice what they preached, but also, as they preached the centrality of practice, they were expected to surpass all others in contempt for the world. Since the Stoic advocated a state of mind that the majority of men considered impossible to achieve, his most important mission was to prove, by way of his own life, that what he recommended to others was shown to be possible in him.

Stoics were not the only ones to emphasize the centrality of practice and of asceticism. Philosophers from the Cynic school also shared that view. Cynics advocated self-mastery, indifference to suffering and pleasure, and mastery of the soul through intense and constant training. But the Cynic was characterized by his total contempt for "the mask." Even though he lived in the polis, he refused to "perform his duties": civic, familial, and political. He despised the proprieties, the *doxa*, and constantly provoked the public. Diogenes the Cynic slept in the street, begged for a living, relieved himself and even masturbated in public.[14] The Cynics developed a view that was individualistic in the extreme: even while fulfilling a social role as critic and as living model of the philosophical life, the philosopher did so *against* society. He used provocation to stimulate thought. The Cynics lived as beggars and were crude and scandalous in their behavior. They did not elaborate a systematic theory and did not found a school in the formal sense of the term. They drew admirers (like Epictetus), as well as detractors (like Lucian), but few fellow travelers. The Cynic was not a "serious" man. The Stoic, by contrast, was seriousness personified. He acted after mature reflection, with discernment, with dignity and responsibility. While reserving the right to refuse to do what he found contrary to morality, the Stoic living in the late Roman Empire tended to be conservative. He accepted the existing order of things, even when he was its victim.

There are resemblances between Christian asceticism and philosophical asceticism. Like the Platonist, the Christian ascetic favored the logic of exchange. He exchanged the world here below for the kingdom of heaven; he learned to see beyond the appearance of things. Like the Stoic, he believed that the path to salvation did not pass through the soul alone. Whether (like the Neoplatonists) he considered the body an enemy or (like the Stoics) a part inseparable from the spirit the Christian ascetic adopted a regimen of training that would make him an athlete of Christ *(athleta Christi)*. Despite these resemblances, the Christian asceticism of the fourth century was not a continuation but a revolution. That was not because Christians believed in a personal and moral God and in individual providence, or because the Christian kingdom of heaven was very different from Platonic ecstasy or Stoic serenity, or even because Christian asceticism found its justification in holy scripture and revelation. No, what made Christian asceticism a real cultural innovation was not the theology on which it was based but the way it was applied.[15]

In the late second century, a Christian apologist still regarded asceticism with the distance proper to a Roman gentleman. "We are not Brahmans, naked sages of India, forest-dwellers, exiles from [urban] life [*sylvicolae et exsules vitae],*" writes Tertullian.[16] The Christian asceticism of the second century, according to him, was an act of spiritual and moral discipline *within* the community, not its abandonment. Christian exile was a state of mind, not a geographical location. In the eyes of a Christian Stoic such as Tertullian, the Brahmans and the Hindu yogis were the antithesis of Christian asceticism, theatrical and antisocial. Christian thinkers of the second and third centuries tended to agree with Epictetus.[17] In a discourse devoted to "training" *(Peri askēseos),* he distinguished between the philosopher's serious, levelheaded, and responsible asceticism, whose objective was to rein in the passions systematically, and the unbridled and ostentatious asceticism of miracle workers. He believed that this second kind of asceticism made one a slave to the passions rather than their master. The ideal ascetic lives in society and avoids all actions contrary to custom or nature. He elicits respect, not astonishment. Epictetus compared those who awaken the emotions to tightrope walkers hungry for publicity. They are in search of an audience that will observe them and proclaim, "O the great man!" *(O megalou anthropou!).*[18]

During the fourth century the feeling arose in Christian society that the credits column in the divine books had become dangerously short. It had become profitable to be a Christian in the Christian empire, and worldly gain necessarily meant heavenly loss. Christ promised to reward the poor, the hungry, the persecuted, "But woe unto you that are rich! for ye have received your consolation. Woe unto you that are full! for ye shall hunger. Woe unto you that laugh now! for ye shall mourn and weep" (Luke 6:24–25). What was one to do, then? One solution was to resurrect the martyrs through the cult of relics; another was to find new sufferers to protect the community from its own laxness. In both cases the solution depended on a symbolic division of labor. In exchange for veneration by lukewarm Christians, the righteous, still burning with original zeal, allowed their brethren to share the spiritual warmth.

The asceticism of fourth-century desert anchorites was much closer to the Hindu asceticism that Tertullian rejected than to the Stoic restraint he praised. Christian asceticism was not a philosophical method. Ascetic the-

ory followed ascetic practice, whose leading practitioners were not educated Greeks but Egyptian and Syrian peasants. Christian ascetics did precisely what Epictetus had warned against: they acted contrary to nature and
to custom *(ton para phusin kai para doxon)*.[19] And they attracted admirers who
exclaimed, "O the great man!" But there was something even more serious
than their ostentation: the new ascetics railed against the city and its laws.
They acted with a holy individualism to ensure their own salvation. They
scandalously destroyed the social order and refused to bow to the demands
of their "mask." All that was more reminiscent of Cynic than of Stoic asceticism. Yet unlike Cynicism, Christian asceticism was not a marginal phenomenon. It enjoyed the admiration of large sectors of the population and
the massive support of the authorities and of the intelligentsia.

The first ascetics did not rely on a well-defined conceptual framework.[20]
They operated in a dangerous twilight zone, culturally and physically
on society's margins. It was obvious that the ascetics were stretching the
existing models to the limit. Clearly they belonged to the group of
exhibitionistic and unbridled miracle workers despised by Epictetus. The
emergence of the cult of relics and of the ascetic movement utterly
changed the Christian community's attitude toward miracles. Previously, a
good portion of the Christian intellectual elite in the West had looked on
the miraculous with skepticism. Miracles, some people thought, had been
necessary when Christianity was just beginning to spread, as a didactic
means to impress pagans, but were becoming pointless. In the early fifth
century, Saint Augustine's *City of God* evoked a world in which many of his
Christian contemporaries no longer believed in miracles.[21] But such attitudes were quickly going out of fashion. In the fourth century, when the
new ascetics were making their appearance, the elite's attitude toward "popular phenomena" changed. Christianity without a daily supply of miracles
was becoming unthinkable. This turnabout not only expressed an increasing need within the community for strong and immediate ties with the invisible world but also marked the slow disappearance of the need for external legitimation. The Christian elites of the empire were less sensitive to
the criticisms of the pagan intelligentsia. It no longer mattered what Stoics
had to say.[22]

The Church Hierarchy and the Ascetics

Bishops welcomed the new ascetics as heirs to the martyrs, although they came with a price tag. In the first place, these new, unprecedented Christian heroes had to be integrated into the existing spiritual frameworks. It is true that there was little need to worry about *pagan* criticism, but elements of Stoic thinking had become part of the Christian intelligentsia's worldview. The theorists of Christian asceticism sought to tone down the scandalous elements of this new asceticism. They sought to give it the levelheaded and dignified appearance of Stoic asceticism. From the Stoics they borrowed terms such as "indifference," "self-control," "training," and "distance."[23] But that adaptation required an interpretive acrobatics, especially since the scholars themselves combined Stoic packaging with an enthusiasm for the anti-Stoic: ostentation, miracles, excess. In the second place, asceticism represented an implicit (and sometimes explicit) criticism of the mode of life of those who did not practice it—such as most bishops, for example. Now if the ascetic was the worthy heir to the martyr, the disappearance of martyrdom could no longer be used as a pretext for not leading a perfect Christian life. The problem was particularly serious for the priests, since the ordinary layman did not claim to be leading a perfect life nor to be the successor of the apostles. As soon as it became clear that asceticism was not a marginal and short-lived phenomenon, some clergymen began to criticize the monks' tendency to demean the spiritual attainments of anyone who was not an ascetic. They asserted that non-ascetics were not failed ascetics but perfectly good Christians. Asceticism, they argued, was only one way among many to achieve salvation. Abstinence, they retorted, was not a virtue in itself; the absorption of food, performed with a pure intention, was just as valid as fasting. Ascetics and non-ascetics alike would earn their reward in heaven.[24]

In the end, a modus vivendi was achieved. Despite the difficulties it raised, the ascetic movement was accepted by the majority of church leaders. Like the cult of relics, it was dangerous and useful at the same time; and like the cult of relics, it could be domesticated and exploited. Most churchmen were willing to make a place for the new perfectionists, so long as they did not seek to overthrow the hierarchy. Men who were not themselves ascetics—at least not in the new sense of the term—acknowledged the moral superiority of the desert hermits, requiring in exchange that the hermits accept the churchmen's political authority. Thus Athanasius, patriarch of Alexandria, wrote of Antony (the "first monk"): "He honored the rule of the Church with extreme care, and he wanted every cleric to be held in higher regard than himself. He felt no shame at bowing the head to the bishops and priests; if even a deacon came to him for assistance, he discussed the things that are beneficial, and gave place to him in prayer, not being embarrassed to put himself in a position to learn."[25] The bishops took the edge off the ascetics' criticism by emphasizing the enormous difficulty of their acts. Not everyone is cut out to be an athlete of Christ; very special gifts are needed, and they should be admired, not imitated. Moreover, through their surplus of virtue, ascetics allow the less virtuous to pursue their lives despite their flaws. That, after all, is the whole point of a spiritual division of labor. Asceticism, it turned out, can be an instrument in the service of the status quo.

And yet the ecclesiastical elite did not manage to domesticate asceticism completely. Theorists of asceticism attempted both to hold it in check and to radicalize it, something that did not come about without difficulty. In addition, a fundamental and insoluble problem remained: whereas the holy relics spoke only through intermediaries, usually through members of the church elite, ascetics spoke in their own voices. Those voices were not always pleasing to the church's ears.

It was not just the hierarchy that the ascetic unnerved. By the mere fact of removing himself from the community and obeying only his own laws, the ascetic constituted a threat for society as a whole. The hermit, in isolating himself, was motivated by a selfish desire to ensure his own salvation; society, conversely, wanted to make him a civil servant.[26] While he sought to separate himself from society and its temptations, society persisted in trying to reintegrate him. The ascetic struggled with his drives, his sins, and his dreams. Society was practically indifferent to his inner conflicts. It was interested in his powers alone. He was expected to deliver. It was better to mold him to fit its image than to listen carefully to what he had to say. Such conflicts of interest led to misunderstandings and deliberate distortions. Sometimes they involved coercion and violence when the ascetic's admirers tried to compel him to be what they wanted him to be. Ascetics bore in full the price society had to pay for them.

When asceticism became a movement, when a role was found for ascetics within the cultural repertoire, the character of those who chose the ascetic path changed. Whereas ascetics of the first generation were individualists ready to play a dangerous game by breaking the rules, those of succeeding generations were conformists who took a path already traced out for them. Whereas, in the first phase, the social advantages of joining the movement were not obvious, in the following phases the hermit label offered substantial cultural and social advantages. Any new social movement, like any new cultural model, attracts neophytes who are just as avid for what the movement is likely to offer them as for the ideals it champions. Church authorities understood that a certain loss of charisma and enthusiasm was the price to be paid for the institutionalization of asceticism. But in any movement there are always members who are dissatisfied with the self-complacency that may have developed within it. What allows the religious to retain their vitality are the successive waves of reform movements that "discover" with horror that the pristine purity has been lost. Reformers call for a resharpening of the now blunted ideal. Reform always meets with the resistance of existing forces, who rightly consider it an attack on their authority and an attempt to create a new elite. Conflict, uncertainty, and danger give rise to new enthusiasm. That enthusiasm, and the sense that one is obliged to invest all efforts in the mission, make members of the group ready to radicalize their positions and to accept more demanding norms of behavior. But once victory is won, slackening, institutionalization, and opportunism are not long in coming. The cycle is apparently endless: "pristine purity" is followed by "corruption," "corruption" by "purification," "purification" by "deterioration," "deterioration" by "restoration," and so on. And so on.

Real purity is not of this world, but dreams of purity shape reform movements. Reformers refuse to take into account the heterogeneity of their movements. They think in dichotomies. There is light and there is darkness. Those who are not with us are against us. Opponents willingly participate in the creation of that fiction. The two camps have an interest in making the debate simple and superficial, in sharpening their differences, ideologizing them. Yet it is precisely that tendency to disregard nuances that allows nuances to persist in the real world. We usually perceive only slight traces of them in the black and white pictures that contemporaries (and most historians) paint. Orthodoxy and heterodoxy are black and white only in appearance. A close examination uncovers the infinite shadings of the two spheres. "Ascetic ideal"? "Ascetic movement"? We should speak rather of a multitude of ideals and forms of expression making up asceticism. But if we overload the portrait too much, it runs the risk of becoming indecipherable. The strategy common to theologians and specialists brings to mind the technique of Japanese fishermen for catching tuna: they spread out steel nets in the ocean over many kilometers. Everything they collect in their nets—dolphins, sharks, or other fish—is tuna. In what follows, we shall essentially be dealing with clichés. "The ideal hermit," "the eremitic ideal": these are the nets. Keep in mind that under the surface, trapped in the steel mesh of the net that specialists and ideologues have laid, there are dolphins, crabs, sharks—and the occasional diver.

FIVE

Antony, the First Hermit

*T*he *Life of Saint Antony*, written by Athanasius, bishop of Alexandria (296–373), is the first biography of a Christian hermit. The work, written in Greek, was translated into Latin by Evagrius Ponticus about four years later, and in these two key languages became a worldwide bestseller and a model for countless imitations. After its publication, saints' Lives were never the same.

Athanasius' *Life of Saint Antony* is really an attempt to formulate a theory of asceticism. But the bishop was seeking to broaden his potential readership, and so instead of a theological essay, he wrote a biography. Biography is a genre in which the most diverse readers and listeners can take an interest. In appearance, Athanasius tells a story; but in reality, as Gregory of Nazianzus states in a sermon delivered a few years after the biography was published, Athanasius' *Life of Saint Antony* is the rule for monks disguised as a narrative.[1] "For hermits," Athanasius writes, "Antony's life is designed to serve as a model of asceticism [*kharaktēr pros askesin*]."[2] For Athanasius, the narrative form is the price he must pay if the message is to get through. But the narrative does not fade away once the mission is accomplished.

The effectiveness of narrative as a mnemonic device was well known to memory theorists in antiquity and the Middle Ages. If you wish to convey information, you must insert it into a narrative sequence and spice it up with appealing or shocking details likely to register in the memory. The trouble is that sometimes the medium prevails over the message. The narrative of the hermit's life, with the strange and astounding events it recounts—miracles, demonic attacks and temptations, visions—is easily committed to memory. The messages that accompany it, everything not "in the guise of a narrative," are the first to be forgotten. There is a permanent tension between the dramatic narrative and the actual messages it conveys, on the one hand, and, on the other, the pedagogical intentions of the author. The saint's Life is often a creature that rises up against its creator.

Athanasius' Discovery

Athanasius probably understood what a number of his contemporaries and modern scholars have failed to grasp. The use of narrative, of biography, was a stroke of genius. The success of the ascetic movement was based entirely on the supremacy of action and experience over ideology. Abstract ideas did not arouse emotions. Most readers of the major ascetics' narratives were not theologians, nor did they seek to become theologians. No theoretical debate could have caused the emotion that the ascetics stirred in the Christian communities. What delighted the ascetics' admirers, and then the readers of their deeds, was their "athletic prowess." What moved them was that these people, against all expectations, against common sense and good taste, accomplished dangerous, extraordinary, and strange things, like acrobatic feats at the circus. It is difficult to be moved reading a book devoted to the ideology of acrobatics: acrobatics, athleticism, and Christian asceticism find their true expression in action. Athanasius offered his readership a story line, a new myth, and a new hero, whom the patriarch of Alexandria constructed in his own image. He delineated, or at least attempted to delineate, the future (the eremitic movement) by depicting the past (the mythic founder, Antony).[3]

Athanasius wrote *The Life of Saint Antony* in 356 or 357. On several occasions the bishop had met the old hermit, who died in 356, supposedly at the age of 105, but Athanasius was not one of his confidants. Before composing the biography, he writes, he had intended to do systematic research, gathering the testimonies of those who had known Antony better than he had. But to his regret, that intention was not acted on. The boat that was to take the work to his hermit friends in Italy[4] was about to raise anchor, so he hastened to write it, basing it on his personal knowledge and on conversations he had had with one of Antony's close friends (probably Saint Serapion of Thumis). Those who have a gift for writing do not have time to waste on research. Let us acknowledge, to the author's credit, that the work does not feel rushed. Athanasius describes his hero without sparing details. He even quotes, verbatim, a sermon of the saint covering no fewer than twenty-eight chapters. Obviously we may be skeptical about the authenticity of Athanasius' report, but we need to remember that the bishop did not aspire to describe "what had really happened," in Leopold von Ranke's immortal phrase. He was not a positivist but an "expressionist," someone who captures the "soul" of his subject, not a true-to-life likeness. After all, "the letter kills, but the Spirit gives life" (2 Cor. 3:6).[5]

Faithful to a distinguished historiographical tradition, Athanasius straddled the distance between history on the one hand and poetry and myth on the other.[6] History, according to Aristotle's *Poetics*, is concerned only with the particular, concrete, and transitory aspects of what Alcibiades, for example, did and what others did to him. Poetry, conversely, deals with things as they might have been or as they ought to be. That notion is already at work in the writings of Thucydides, father of "scientific" historiography, who in effect places words in the mouths of his characters that, according to him, they might have pronounced in the circumstances described.[7] Although he claims that the words reported are as close as possible to what was actually said, one need only read the elegant speech he puts into Pericles' mouth to realize that Thucydides chose words designed to "represent" the Athenian leader correctly rather than to reproduce those he actually spoke. Athanasius proceeds in exactly the same way.[8]

That narrative mode conceals a functionalist and didactic notion of the written word. The aim of "serious" writing has always been to change the reader, to improve him morally, to edify him. Any means can be used to that end. Athanasius, however, moves beyond the rhetoric of the faithful and reliable chronicler. He stresses to his reader the (moral and religious) contribution of figures such as Antony, so rich in significance that a simple account must inevitably be partial or it would end in failure. He challenges his reader to keep looking for more extensive information on the subject of Antony, immediately adding that even such additional information will never capture his personality.[9] True likeness being impossible, it would matter little if Athanasius' narrative were partial or even erroneous. Even if he had taken the trouble to gather testimony from the other hermits, his undertaking would have remained incomplete. Hence Athanasius offers a poetic "truth," not a historical truth.

The biography is composed of ninety-four chapters. The first ten relate Antony's early life up to age thirty-five, his decision to abandon the world, and his first ascetic experiences. After a battle against demons from which he emerges victorious, Antony receives a divine revelation (chapter 10) and decides to leave the inhabited world and go out into the desert. There he lives alone in the ruins of a fortress, where he reaches spiritual maturity and achieves a high level of asceticism. After twenty years of solitude, his admirers force him to come to them (chapter 14), and he begins a career as a spiritual guide. Chapters 16 to 43 are devoted to the long sermon in which Antony lectures his disciples on the ascetic's way of life. During the persecution of Maximinus Daia in 311, Antony arrives in Alexandria, aids Christians, and tries to die a martyr's death (chapter 46). Failing to attain this goal, Antony leaves the city. He intensifies his asceticism and decides to escape his horde of admirers by taking refuge on a mountain of the "inner desert," a place that tradition identifies as Deir el-Arab or Deir-Amba-Antonios, about thirty kilometers west of the Red Sea (chapter 50).[10] In the inner desert Antony performs a great number of miracles and is soon surrounded by admirers once again. Chapters 67 to 80 are devoted to Antony's orthodoxy: he respects the hierarchy and successfully opposes the Arians and pagans.[11] The last chapters relate Antony's power and influence, his death and burial, and the spread of his fame.

The biography includes several major elements that paved the way for saints' Lives in the following centuries: the path that leads the hero to God, his journey to his spiritual maturity, his departure from human society and his return to it, the ascetic's relation to the supernatural, and his connection to the hierarchy and to orthodoxy. Let us consider a few of these elements.[12]

Antony's Conversion

An ascetic is someone who has arrived at a turning point in his life. No one is born an ascetic; one must become one. Athanasius does not devote much time to the inner processes that led Antony to take such a dramatic turn in his style of life. The conversion and its psychological and social consequences are related economically—ascetically, we might say. At age eighteen, recounts Athanasius, less than six months after being orphaned, Antony goes to church, where he hears the following words read from the Gospel of Matthew: "If you want to be perfect, go, sell what you have and give to the poor, and you will have treasure in heaven; and come, follow Me" (Matt. 19:21–22). It seems to him that these words are addressed to him personally *(hos di' auton genomenou tou anagnosmatos)*. He immediately goes out of the church, divides up his lands and gives them to the people of the village, sells his chattels, and gives the money to the poor. He leaves only a modest sum for his younger sister.[13] On another occasion he enters the church and hears a different verse from the Gospel of Matthew: "Therefore do not worry about tomorrow" (Matt. 6:34). Antony hands out to the poor what little money he has kept for his sister, consigns her to the care of "respected and trusted virgins," and begins to live as an ascetic outside his home but within the confines of the village.

Only twenty lines or so are devoted to Antony's life before he turns away from the world, while thirty-two deal with the conversion itself. That brevity is not accidental. It serves to stress the vanity and insignificance of the hero's life before he chooses his career as an ascetic. The change comes about rapidly and unequivocally; the hero does not hesitate or look back. If he had doubts before the major turning point, they have all disappeared.

The determination and speed of the event attest to divine intervention: the words to which the hero responds as if they were addressed to him were in fact addressed to him. Such words have been pronounced an incalculable number of times, but only those who have ears to hear them will receive them. Only God's chosen respond to them so completely, as if to a command, as if they had been waiting their whole lives only for those words at that critical moment. Consider Athanasius' haste, how he reduces the interval between Antony's first decision to rid himself of his property and the decision to rid himself of his sister, that is, his last attachment to the everyday world. "On another occasion . . ." When was that? How much time elapsed between the time he heard the first fateful verse and the time he hears the second? Hours? Days? Months? Athanasius does not say exactly. Everything happened quickly. Give no thought to the past. How did the sister react? Did Antony maintain ties with this young girl whom he condemned to a life of poverty and self-denial? How did the people of the village react? None of that has any importance. The hero's profane life was an error. He was living a "normal" life, not realizing he belonged to a different world. What "normal" people would consider trivial opened his eyes, and from that moment on, he hastened to discover his true self, the self that was disguised and distorted by a life spent in a world of lies. As soon as he discovers his true nature, the Christian hero becomes truly involved in an exclusive relationship—with God. All other voices become a sort of drone to which the hero pays no attention. In the seventeenth century, John Bunyan's *Pilgrim's Progress* offered a symbolic narrative of man's journey from the "City of Destruction" to salvation. His wife and children run after him weeping, but the pilgrim covers his ears with both hands and, leaving his family behind, cries: "Life! Life! Eternal life!"[14] Anyone who hears the voice of God is deaf to the voices of human beings.

The event that brings Antony out of his psychic lethargy and launches him on the path of sainthood and asceticism cannot be attributed to chance. The words he hears are those of the Savior himself. Everything Christ says overflows the narrow confines of time and space, the concrete historical circumstances. His words are always pronounced in the eternal present where the word of God is realized. God speaks to Antony. Nevertheless, it is significant that Antony is set in motion by a text rather than by a direct revelation from God. In that way, Athanasius connects Antony to the world of books, of the church, and of the liturgy: the sacred and consecrated text stands in place of free-floating words pronounced by Jesus during a historical revelation made to a given person. The individual can relate to that text only through an implicit analogy, by saying, "I am like the apostles." Through the narrative of Antony's conversion, Athanasius stresses the centrality of the written word in ethical life and its role both in spurring and in restricting action. In addition, the text is transmitted through the church hierarchy, and the hero cannot become directly immersed in it, as he would be, for example, if he were reading to himself. The public reading of the public text connects the hero to human history, and he becomes a link in the chain, connected to the hierarchical community of the church, in which Athanasius and his peers occupy a central place, and where the charisma of the office is always more important than the charisma of the person.[15]

The Ascetic's Journey

Whereas the first removal from the world is rapidly sketched, the progress toward spiritual perfection is related with a great profusion of details, as a long, gradual process, both psychic and topographical. The more Antony represses his body, the more he strengthens his soul; the farther he moves from human beings, the closer he comes to God. At first, Antony stays in the village but outside his home. He seeks out instructors in asceticism whom he can imitate but apparently remains unsatisfied. Antony is on a quest, not for an orderly education in asceticism but for men he might imitate; he seeks not theory but practice. He borrows different elements from the ascetics he meets and strives to surpass them all in his zeal. Unlike Nietzsche's ascetics, Athanasius' Antony is not motivated by compunction or guilt.[16] He is not a repentant sinner, nor does he engage in self-punishment. He is a man in search of perfection, not absolution.

After living close to his home, Antony moves to the outer edge of the village, but he does not thereby become a marginal character. Although separated from his possessions and cut off from his family, he continues to be an integral part of the life of his community. He earns his living and gives alms to the poor. The community is sympathetic toward him but does not display any admiration. It becomes his extended family. The people consider him "son" and "brother," thus claiming a status higher or equal, not inferior, to his own. Nobody calls him "father." Antony has earned the right to be called *theophilos*, "one who loves God," but he has not yet become sufficiently removed from what is normal and conventional.[17] During a later crisis, more violent than that which led him to leave home, the devil assails Antony with doubts and mounting desires. Now he regrets the loss of his possessions, feels remorse for abandoning his sister, and begins to desire food, riches, and women. Antony responds to all these temptations by constantly making his asceticism even more severe: he reduces his hours of sleep and the quantity of food he absorbs, sleeps on a straw mat, and prays unceasingly. But that is still not enough. He decides to move farther away from the village. In a cemetery located at some distance, he sets himself up in a burial vault (chapter 8).

His confinement in a tomb illustrates the ascetic's attempt to die to the world in order to move to another, more elevated level of existence. In Palladius' *Lausiac History*, a collection of tales from the early fifth century, the author relates an encounter with an old hermit by the name of Dorotheus. The old man had persisted in working in the blazing noonday sun of the Egyptian desert to build cells for the hermits. "When I asked him: 'What are you doing, Father, killing your body in such heat?' [Dorotheus] answered: 'It kills me; I will kill it.'"[18] Here we see an attempt to push to the extreme the Pauline concept of the death of the old man and the resurrection of the new man in Jesus. For Paul, the symbol for that transition was baptism: death and resurrection were symbolic and spiritual. The ascetics attempted to destroy the body physically. In this respect they ascribed a new role to the body, making it the central location of the spiritual process rather than an insignificant annex to it.

But to live among the dead in the necropolis does not serve only as a symbol. The cemetery is the twilight zone of the community, the meeting place of demons, spirits, bandits, and the possessed. Antony's act represents both a symbolic declaration of his death and a test of his courage and determination. Antony overcomes temptation and doubt. Then the demons change their strategy. They attack his body. They beat him black and blue until he loses consciousness. A friend who has come to bring him food finds him in that state and believes he is dead. He takes him to the village church. But Antony refuses to be integrated just yet. He returns to his vault, where he becomes the victim of increasingly violent attacks by demons taking the form of wild beasts and serpents. Terror and pain threaten to overwhelm him, but in the end Antony prevails. The demons disappear, and Antony earns the right to a first divine revelation in the form of a heavenly beam of light that illuminates him from above. "Where were you?" asks Antony. "Why didn't you appear before, so that you could stop my suffering?" "I was here, Antony," replies the Lord, "but I wanted to watch your struggle. And now, since you persevered and were not defeated, I will be your helper forever, and I will make you famous."[19]

Asceticism, then, is not just a rigorous regime of spiritual and physical exercise; it is a challenge and a battle *(agon)* for life and death between the forces of good and evil. Like Perpetua's fatherly referee, God expects his champions to take the beating and win the fight. The spiritual empowerment of the ascetic and the mystic concentration of force around him attract both God and the forces of evil. Infernal and heavenly powers themselves cannot remain indifferent to the ascetic's powers. Antony has overcome the ordeal; he has earned the right to take the decisive step and separate himself completely from human society.[20]

The day after his divine revelation, Antony leaves the vault and goes out into the desert, far from any inhabited place.[21] The Egyptian desert is a region where life is almost impossible: the heat is oppressive, and there is a shortage of water. Peter Brown compares Antony to an astronaut in outer space. It is a striking image. The desert was the vast unknown. Caravans passed like spaceships transporting their cargo at their own risk and peril;

any mistake could lead to death. Antony cuts himself off from all lines of supply and goes to test the limits of humanity. In the desert, which myths of the time peopled with monsters and demons, the ascetic becomes a recluse (*monakhos*), a hermit (*eremita*), a man of the desert (*eremos* in Greek).[22] There are no longer any friends to carry him to a church in an emergency or other ascetics to offer advice or company. Antony installs himself in the ruins of an ancient fortress teeming with serpents (which, upset by his presence, abandon the place when he arrives). There is a source of water, and a friend is supposed to come twice a year to bring him a supply of bread. Antony allows no one into the fortress and lives there for twenty years without seeing a human face. Outside the city, says Aristotle, one is either a beast or a god.[23] In the eyes of Athanasius, the withdrawal to the desert is Antony's heroic innovation, the ultimate test. After twenty years, when the hermit's admirers force their way in, they do not find a creature who has lost all trace of humanity after so many years of physical distress and solitude. No, Antony appears before them as if he were a Stoic sage living "in accordance with nature," perfectly well balanced and perfectly serene:

> Neither fat from lack of exercise [*agymnaston*], nor emaciated from fasting and combat with demons, . . . [he] was just as they had known him prior to his withdrawal [*anakhōrēseos*].[24] The state of his soul was one of purity, for it was not constricted by grief, nor relaxed by pleasure, nor affected by either laughter or dejection. Moreover, when he saw the crowd, he was not annoyed any more than he was elated at being embraced by so many people. He maintained utter equilibrium [*olos ein isos*], like one guided by reason [*hypo tou logou kybernomenos*] and steadfast in that which accords with nature [*kata physin estos*].[25]

Antony has overcome the worst ordeal a human being can face, at least in the eyes of the close-knit community of the fourth century. It is not suffering or demons that make the ordeal so terrible but separation from the very thing that makes us human. Twenty years of solitude has not caused Antony to lose his perfect equilibrium. The strange description of his state—of his physical state at least—attests to the deep influence of Stoic ideas on Athanasius. Equilibrium and serenity are the signs of victory over pride and desire. The Stoic sage is indifferent to external circumstances. Whether in the arena or in the desert, he remains perfectly in harmony with his true nature. Athanasius dresses Antony in the philosophical attire required if he is to be invited to the intellectual high table. Philosophical respectability was not necessarily important among the ascetics themselves, however. Other writers often described the ascetics as men and women who had crossed the line between the human and the animal: they lived among beasts and resembled beasts or monsters.[26] But the transformation to an animal state was only a phase at the end of which the ascetic recovered his humanity and transcended it. Outside the polis, if you are not an animal, you are a god. As soon as Antony has departed, his body and soul in perfect equilibrium like a god, divine charismata pour from him and radiate outward to others. He heals the sick and drives out demons. God confers on the ignorant and solitary hermit the marvelous ability to persuade his listeners to choose the right path.[27] The example he offers and his inspirational words are wonderfully effective. The desert fills with hermits. Men appear everywhere, having sold their property and handed out their money to the poor. They now walk in the footsteps of Jesus—and of Antony—to claim their share of heavenly treasure. "The desert," writes Athanasius, "was made a city" (*eremos epolisthei*).[28] Antony began his journey by fleeing the earthly city; he ends it by founding a heavenly city.

At least, that is what appears to happen. For a time, Antony takes on the role of spiritual guide without complaint. He becomes the mystic center, the living model of the group of hermits that gathered around him. They maintain the form of monastic life called *laura*. For most of the week the other hermits live in isolation in their cells, approaching the guide only from time to time. On Sundays they convene for mass. Athanasius has Antony give a long sermon to his disciples, but it seems that its philosophical and didactic content reflects the concerns of an Alexandrian bishop more than those of an ascetic leader. As Violet MacDermot writes: "The instructions of the master to the disciple concerned, not doctrinal matters, but the personal qualities required for a life of solitude and the austerities to be practised in daily life. Learning consisted in obedience to commands to carry out certain ascetic procedures. The life of the holy man himself was the example and incentive to progress for the disciple."[29] Teaching consisted of observation, imitation, and guided action. What the apprentice ascetic learned was not a theory but a technique.

Antony becomes the object of veneration and imitation; he reigns over the hermits like a biblical patriarch. That harmonious desert city reminds Athanasius of the prophecy of Balaam (Num. 24:5–6):

> How lovely are your tents, O Jacob!
> Your dwellings, O Israel!
> Like valleys that stretch out,
> Like gardens by the riverside,
> Like aloes planted by the LORD,
> Like cedars beside the waters.

Images of plenty, fertility, and security abound. To quote Isaiah (35:1), "The wilderness and the wasteland shall be glad . . . , And the desert shall rejoice."

But the idyll does not last. About six years after Antony has returned to human society, news arrives in the desert that the Christians of Alexandria are being persecuted by Emperor Maximinus Daia. For the first time in twenty-five years, Antony leaves the desert. He hastens to the city in the hope of achieving martyrdom. He assists the prisoners, attends all the public interrogations, and does everything he can to get arrested, though he does not hand himself over to the persecutors (an act that Peter, the bishop of the city, has explicitly prohibited). When the authorities ban hermits from appearing in the city (probably to avoid having to condemn them to death), Antony remains in Alexandria. He even solemnly washes his tunic (unusual for him) and installs himself in a high place in the city. To no avail.

Disappointed and sad at his failure to die a martyr, Antony returns to the desert. (Athanasius explains that God wanted him to be a model for others, since the mere act of watching him led people to follow his example.)[30] Upon his return, Antony is overcome with anxiety. He increases his fasting, wears a hair shirt, and performs his ablutions even less often. He stops washing his feet. Antony becomes a "martyr of the soul" *(kath' emeran martyron suneidesei).*[31] He increasingly shuts himself away in his cell and finally decides he can no longer tolerate the company of his admirers and disciples. He joins a caravan of Saracens and moves to an oasis in the "inner desert," three days and three nights from the desert "city."

What led Antony to that crisis at the age of sixty, when he was apparently in full command of his faculties, sure of himself and his path, and surrounded by faithful disciples? The answer, it seems, lies in the belief, shared by Athanasius and Antony, that martyrdom is the pinnacle of Christian perfection. Antony went into the desert to find perfection. The encounter with the martyrs of Alexandria must have reminded him that asceticism, harsh as it is, is only a pale substitute for martyrdom. Whoever aspires to true perfection must shed his blood for the faith.[32] When the persecutions ended, Augustine recounts, certain fanatical Donatists engaged in an "artificial" martyrdom: they threw themselves from high rocks or asked their followers to push them over. The followers then collected the broken bodies of the "martyrs" and venerated them as if they were true martyrs.[33] That phenomenon, which Augustine condemns in the harshest terms, may have been the most extreme expression of the Christian community's difficulty in adapting to the new, less heroic life of the Christian empire. Those who are not ready to compromise choose to go to extremes. Antony's crisis results from his being unable to go far enough.

But the hermit's retreat into an ever more remote desert is ultimately pointless. However remote it might be, the desert can never equal the arena. Nor can asceticism be the same as martyrdom. Antony understands this. The second retreat, to the inner desert, ends quickly. Followers and admirers return and surround Antony, who resumes his social activities as instructor and miraculous healer, moving back and forth between his two cells, the one on the inner mountain and the one on the outer mountain.

Beginning in the third century, some Christian sources compared asceticism, and particularly sexual abstinence, to martyrdom. Robert Markus argues that admiration for the martyr's heroism among those he calls "more thoughtful Christians" yielded to a preference for more philosophical qualities: steadfast perseverance and fidelity to God.[34] These more thoughtful Christians, it seems, were none other than intellectuals. The qualities they attributed to the martyr were always the result of an analysis after the fact, of learned theorization. The dramatic power and rhetorical force of martyrdom resulted not from the fact that it "expressed" something but from the direct and immediate shock it caused. Only shock can explain the intense feelings expressed by witnesses to martyrdom or by readers of martyrdom narratives. That shock, caused by the spectacle of the torture and death of innocent victims, allows us to understand why magical virtues were attributed not only to martyrs' blood but also to the blood of anyone put to death. The blood of condemned criminals and of gladiators, for example, was a commodity with a high market value in late antiquity.[35]

The act of identifying the ascetic with the martyr was an attempt to confer the highest spiritual status on the new heroes of Christendom. Athanasius and some scholars at the beginning of the ascetic movement used martyrdom as a metaphor, even making asceticism a kind of death one inflicts on oneself (mortification, in the primary sense of that term). Martyrdom for them was a state of mind. Actual death seems to have become marginal and fortuitous: Antony simply did not have the opportunity to die. What matters in any case was his total readiness to die. "The confessors of Christ who did not find any persecutions impelling them toward martyrdom," wrote Gregory of Tours, "tortured themselves as if they were their own tormenters, using various ascetic mortifications, in order to be considered worthy of God."[36] That attempt was partially successful: it satisfied the theologians. In the most popular biographies of ascetics, we see a radicalization of asceticism. Originally a semiphilosophical training exercise whose aim was to achieve equilibrium and serenity, it became a disturbing series of heroic acts of aggression against oneself. (We shall see an extreme example in Saint Simeon Stylites.) The purpose was to make asceticism as traumatic in its effect as martyrdom.

As soon as his personal crisis has passed and he has given up his heroic aspirations, Antony dedicates himself to his social functions. He heals the sick, drives out demons, goes to Alexandria to debate with the Arians, argues the truths of Christianity with the pagans, preaches, receives letters from the emperor, and offers good advice to judges. In short, the athlete of Christ becomes a responsible Christian leader, not just for the hermits (his disciples and imitators) but for the Christian community as a whole. He becomes respectable even in pagan society. Athanasius recounts that the idolatrous Greeks thronged to him, calling him the "man of god" *(tou theou anthropon)*, and asking to touch him. Antony agrees to accept his status and the social duties it entails. He even reprimands those who attempt to keep the crowds away from him.[37] Everyone, says Athanasius, called him "father," even strangers.[38] The man who loved God *(theophilos)* had become the man of God; the son and brother of his village had become the father of the Christian world, and perhaps not only of the *Christian* world. Reconciled with himself and with his community, Antony is able to foretell his imminent death, prepare for his burial (he demands that the place of his sepulcher be kept secret), and depart in peace to meet the Lord.[39]

SIX

The Ascetic Pendulum

THE EMERGENCE OF ASCETICISM as a central category of Christian perfection implied a widening of the concept of sanctity. When the persecutions ended in the fourth century, martyrdom became an extremely rare phenomenon. Parallel to the veneration of those who had died for the faith (martyrs), Christian society began to venerate those who had lived for the faith. They were called "confessors" (from the Latin *confessor*, "witness"). In the second and third centuries, that name was sometimes given to those who had been arrested during the persecutions, had proclaimed their faith, and, for various reasons, had not been executed. By the fifth century, not only those who had shown they were ready to die but also those whose mode of life served as testimony were called by that name. Asceticism had become the main method of achieving the status of saint. Even those who were not career ascetics were credited with a certain degree of asceticism, just as previously the apostles had been credited with martyrdom. While martyrdom retained its status as the highest form of Christian witnessing, asceticism replaced it as the "standard" requirement.

The transformation was not simple. In the previous chapter we saw how even the ideal ascetic, the famous Antony, felt inferior to the anonymous

Alexandrian martyrs. By his death the martyr manifested his indifference to the Earthly City. The martyr was not of this world; he belonged to the Heavenly City. Death was his ticket home. To be venerated, the martyr had to be absent. His career really began once he had left the public arena. The martyr could not make a fool of himself or of his admirers; he could not make embarrassing mistakes or misuse his power. From the social point of view, he was an object that could be made to speak only through intermediaries. The ascetic's situation was more complicated. To gain public recognition, to be acknowledged as holy—something not all ascetics wanted—he had to adopt two contradictory modes of behavior. He was expected to detach himself from the community and its values, but at the same time he had to be close enough to edify and serve the community and its often rather worldly needs. He had to act publicly in accordance with rigid conventional rules of conduct, respond sensitively to the cues of his audience, while seemingly displaying a total indifference toward that audience and acting as if no one were watching him. These contradictory demands account for the saint's spiritual and sometimes physical shuttling between the inside and the outside of society.

Outside Society, inside Society

The Belgian folklorist Arnold Van Gennep has studied rites of passage in traditional societies. He distinguishes three phases: in the first, the rites of separation, or preliminary rites *(rites de séparation, rites préliminaires)*, symbolize the initiate's detachment from his previous status; in the second phase, the liminal rites *(rites liminaires)* place the initiate in a marginal state *(stade de marge)*, a sort of twilight zone that Van Gennep calls the *limen* ("threshold" in Latin). In that zone, none of the usual social rules hold sway, not those of the initiate's prior situation or those of his future status. These rites express disorder, symbolic death, the rejection of rules, and social rupture. In the third phase, the initiate goes through rites of inclusion, or "postliminal rites" *(rites d'agrégation, rites postliminaires)*, which mark a symbolic resurrection and accession to his new status.[1]

The path the ascetic takes is not a rite, of course: it is not defined by fixed rules or limited in time and space, as are rites of passage in traditional societies. All the same, it entails a clear pattern of breach, temporary marginality, and reintegration. The English anthropologist Victor Turner has applied Van Gennep's model to nonritual processes. Turner offers a paradigm for studying social crises, or "social dramas," as he calls them.[2] These processes tend to occur in four phases: breach, crisis, redressive action, and reintegration or schism.

In the first phase, individuals or groups call social norms into question. Whether direct (a riot) or indirect (a movement that does not explicitly criticize the existing order), this calling into question is perceived as a threat by the authorities. How serious a threat? That is in the eye of the beholder. Societies may react passionately to seemingly inconsequential questions (a change in the national anthem) and take no interest in a change likely to affect society's foundations (changes in the modes of production, for example). A crisis develops when the society ceases to see the calling into question as a minor contretemps that can be overcome effortlessly, and conceives it as a threat to its way of life. In reaction to the crisis, certain members of society propose solutions ranging from widespread violence against dissidents to radical reforms. That, according to Turner, is the "liminal" phase par excellence. Society becomes open to "emergency measures." It is ready to renounce, temporarily at least, the usual rules or to create new rules and new divisions of labor—at least temporarily. A typical example of this is the granting, during periods of armed uprisings, of important roles to women, children, and minority groups. If the means used succeed in eliminating (physically or socially) the dissidents or in changing society in a way that integrates them, the drama ends with a sense that unity and social health have been restored. If they fail, society must recognize that it has suffered an irreparable rift.[3]

Turner's model does not differ fundamentally from Van Gennep's; in fact, the addition of the "crisis" phase, when the society becomes aware of the rift, does not make any significant improvement to that model. What matters in Turner's approach is that the liminal situations he describes may be not only conscious and calculated manifestations (rites) that mark symbolic breaks in social life but also spontaneous reactions to unforeseen crisis situations. Turner does not confine himself to the rather banal observation that crises create or allow confusion and consequently a redefinition of social rules. He discerns two further phenomena. The first is that individuals are willing to instigate artificial states of crisis that allow them to live in liminal situations, during which they experience a sense of elation and after which they feel integrated. Turner gives pilgrimage as an example: the pilgrim voluntarily separates himself from the society in which he lives and goes to a remote place. On the way, he experiences physical difficulties, dangers, and a temporary ambiguity in his status: he comes into contact with people who do not know him, his language, or his social rank. In the holy place itself, the pilgrim experiences a sense of brotherhood with the other pilgrims (what Turner calls *communitas*) and a sort of elevation of the soul that would not have been possible in the everyday world.[4] The pilgrim returns to his starting point, having undergone a transformation.

Even more interesting than the voluntary search for limited liminality, followed by a return to the norms, is the way, according to Turner, observer-participants react to "wild" (that is, unritualized) liminal situations. In rites of passage, the liminal situation is "delimited"; the unruliness obeys rules, and everyone more or less knows in advance where the situation begins and ends and with what results. Order always returns, and when it does, it is perceived as redemption from anarchy and chaos. The anxiety that ritual liminality engenders is ritualized. But when thrust into a liminal situation outside the safe world of the ritual process, people react with great anxiety. Onlookers do not know what scenario or what timetable they are following. Is liminality a step toward total integration (as in rites of passage, where the participant emerges from the liminal stage to become "one of us")? Does it lead toward an alternative mode of existence altogether (is it *we* who are going to change)? Is it an attempt to destroy society (the liminal person does seek to change himself or us; he seeks to destroy us)? Now crisis situations can give birth to liminal characters. But the opposite is also true: the arrival on the social stage of liminal figures can be not the result of a crisis but its cause.

The Christian ascetic is a classic liminal figure. The ascetic's journey out of society is a unique sort of pilgrimage that transforms the pilgrim himself into a walking holy place. The hermit renounces his "normal" social power (which depends on social, familial, and economic norms); he purifies himself of the everyday (the familiar and conventional) and transports himself into a world diametrically opposed to the social world and the laws that define it.[5] André Droogens lists pairs of opposites that characterize the social versus the antisocial: nature versus culture, nomadism versus stability, nonviolence versus violence, solidarity versus hierarchy, isolation versus social life, bodily discomfort versus comfort, filth versus cleanliness, poverty versus wealth, and hunger (or fasting) versus satiety.[6] A Syriac sermon from the fifth century, "Recluses, Desert Dwellers, and Mourners," shows these dichotomies at work. The recluses live isolated in the desert, look like beasts, and dwell among the animals of the desert. They reside in caves; they eat herbs and drink water, depriving themselves of rich food and wine; they sleep on rocks and not on cushions, eat off their laps and not seated at a table. Their bodies are not cared for with rich ointments but are darkened by the sun; they wander from one place to another, unclothed and unshod; they speak with angels and beasts and not with people in their families and city; they despise possessions; they ignore hierarchy and disputes; their bodies are covered with wounds and filth; they weep and wail.[7] Recluses are no longer part of society, not only because they have separated themselves physically but also because they have broken away from it mentally and psychologically: "They are like spirits, though among mortals; and like angels in heaven, though among men of earth."[8]

From the ascetic's point of view, asceticism is a mode of behavior by which one purifies oneself of the world of sin: "When the world became enslaved by wealth, they emptied themselves of it; because it choked on money, they treated it with contempt and scoffed at it. . . . They greatly afflict their bodies, not because they do not love their bodies, rather, they want to bring their bodies to Eden in glory. . . . Neither are they troubled by death, for it is rest from their labors. Since they have died here in their lives, they are alive there in God."[9] The logic of Christian asceticism, like that of martyrdom, is a logic of exchange: this world in return for the world to come; earthly power for heavenly power. That heavenly power which the ascetics possess can be enormously useful for society. The very existence of the righteous allows others to continue to exist and to indulge in all the sins that make life bearable and that create what we call culture: comfort, leisure, pleasures. "Civilization," continues the Syriac sermon, "where lawlessness prevails, is sustained by their prayers. And the world, buried in sin, is preserved by their prayers."[10]

The ascetic thus removes himself from society, seeking purity and salvation. For a period of time his status is deliberately ambiguous and his relationship to the known and normal uncertain. If society wants to make use of the "recluse," it must transfer him from the sphere of cultural meaninglessness (to which demoniacs, madmen, and wild men of the woods belong) to the sphere of those who seek religious perfection. Either the liminal figure indicates that, despite his chaotic behavior, he is following a plan that connects him to the world of normative religion—in other words, that his "mad" behavior is a performance—or, less commonly, society decides for its own reasons to affix the label of religious virtuoso to some figure, even without his cooperation. In the former case, the ascetic adopts modes of conduct that society identifies with religious asceticism (the Christian ascetic fasts and flagellates himself, for example, but does not eat excrement or castrate himself). From time to time at least he prays in a way that people can recognize; he uses conventional religious gestures (genuflection, the sign of the cross, joined hands). These signs need not characterize the ascetic at all times (he may also spend part of his time acting like a madman or a fool). They leave the ascetic great freedom to maneuver. So long as he respects an "iconographical"—that is, symbolically identifiable—minimum standard, he is free to add his own variations and even innovations. But it is by virtue of that iconographical minimum standard that certain onlookers "uncover" the saint (they say they have seen the "madman" praying at night before the altar for many long hours, for example). As soon as an audience has formed around the liminal figure, even if it is an audience of one, as soon as that audience considers him an astronaut in cultural space and not a UFO, the way is open for the recluse to start moving from the margins to the symbolic center of society. As Van Gennep writes, the sacred world is to be found outside society, outside the profane world as members of society see it.[11] In order not to squander these powers, the ascetic returns to society, and he brings it the enlightenment he has found in the "desert" as well as the power he has acquired to heal, unify, and correct.[12]

But there may be cases in which someone whom society chooses to identify as a saint refuses to cooperate. Then a crisis of another sort arises. Palladius relates the story of a nun from the monastery of Tabennisi who, according to him, feigned madness and demonic possession (morian kai daimona).[13] She disgusts the other sisters, and they refuse to eat with her. Out of everyone's sight, she eats the crumbs she has gathered from the tables and the leftovers she has scraped from the pans.[14] She does not wear a cowl like the other nuns but covers her head with a rag. She works at various lowly kitchen tasks and silently endures the insults and blows her sisters heap on her. The madwoman is within the physical boundaries of the monastery but outside its social boundaries. She is marginal, filthy, silent. No one knows whether she is sane or insane, whether she belongs to God by virtue of being a nun or to Satan by virtue of being possessed. Her "liminality" is passive and antiheroic. In the absence of identifying signs, the community considers her an "empty" person. Palladius compares her to a sponge—amorphous and entirely passive. That harmonic disharmony of the community is shattered by the holy recluse Piterum. An angel appears to him and sends him to the convent of the Tabennisiotes, where, he is told, a woman more virtuous than he is living. The hermit, says the angel, lives in solitude, but in his thoughts wanders through the cities, whereas she lives among the crowd, but her thoughts are always with God. Piterum will be able to identify her by the rag she wears on her head. Piterum leaves his cell and is respectfully received at the convent, since he is a famous holy man. He asks to see the sisters, but the madwoman is not among them. "Someone is missing," says Piterum. "We have an idiot [sale] in the kitchen," respond the nuns (in other words, she is of no importance). "Bring her to me," he commands. She refuses to come, and the sis-

ters drag her in by force, telling her, "The holy Piterum wishes to see you."
(Who are you to refuse?) When she arrives before him, he sees the rag on
her head and falls at her feet, exclaiming, "Bless me!" The nun falls at his
feet in turn: "You bless me, lord," she says. The sisters still do not understand what is happening. They think that Piterum is showing Christian humility (which he is), that the nun is refusing to cooperate with him, and
that perhaps she is even mimicking him (which is indeed the case). They
console him, saying: "Father, take no offense. She is an idiot." "It is you
who are idiots!" says Piterum. "This woman is my mother and yours. I
pray that I may be deemed worthy of her on the Day of Judgment."[15]

Let us look more closely at Palladius' description. The nun's asceticism
is secret and antisocial. It is not without reason that Palladius compares her
to a sponge: she soaks up blessings and powers, virtues and merits, without
sharing them with the other nuns. Instead of serving as a catalyst for the
virtues of the community—which could then admire her for her Christian
charity—instead of bringing it enlightenment, guidance, and miracles, she
persists on the opposite path and constitutes a stumbling block for the
blind community. As she accumulates merits through her patience and asceticism, the others accumulate sins. Piterum comes to remedy that situation. He blows the saint's cover and immediately calls for her to fulfill a social role ("Bless me!"), to take on the duties her status implies. This is not
just a call for solidarity, however, but a spiritual contest. Piterum falls to his
knees before the "madwoman": in the realm of asceticism, the lower is
higher. The nun responds in kind: she lowers herself physically, and to the
formula of humility ("You bless me") she adds the honorary title "lord"
(*kyrie*), which in this instance is an act of symbolic aggression. Her "uncivilized" behavior allows her to continue the charade. The nun's conduct is
perceived as an effrontery attributable to her madness. In the community's
eyes, she is truly inferior, not just pretending to be so (like Piterum). But
Piterum holds the trump card, for despite his humility, he *is* a *kyrios.* He
turns away from the nun who refuses to cooperate with him and addresses
the other sisters, over whom he exerts his authority as a holy monk: Pay no
attention to her. Whatever *she* may say, *I* tell you that she is our mother.

The nuns immediately react to the signal given them by the monk.

Henceforth they all imitate his behavior. They kneel before their sister and confess their sins. Their behavior, heretofore judged normal in the presence of a madwoman who elicits disgust, becomes a sin committed against a saint. But have they really discovered their sister's sanctity? Unlikely. It is Piterum's words that have magical power. They are an example of what J. L. Austin calls *performatives,* that is, words that do not describe a situation but create it.[16] When a priest pronounces the words "I now declare you husband and wife," he is not describing an existing state of affairs but creating a new one. From that moment on, the couple become husband and wife. Piterum's words change the nun's status in her community. The eyes of the sisters are not "opened." What matters to them is Piterum's authority. It is that authority they venerate. They are now ready to accept the idiot, the lunatic, the repulsive woman as a saint, because that is what the holy father has decided. From the moment her status is redefined, everything is turned upside down in Tabennisi. Whether she wishes it or not, the nun becomes the object of veneration, piety, and remorse. The community begins to squeeze the sponge, extracting merit, favors, miracles, holy example.

We do not know the historical basis for Palladius' amazing story. What matters is the principle that emerges from it: there may be cases when a community arbitrarily chooses a commonplace object to venerate. Any act by the object of that veneration, who under normal circumstances would have been taken for a madwoman, an idiot, or a demoniac, is declared that of a holy dissembler. Her actions become charged with meaning, and all interactions with her become ritualized theater.

The object of veneration may be hollow, and in many respects it is preferable that she be so; but she must cooperate with the community or at least not disrupt it. The idiot in this case refuses to be at the center of social veneration. She is aware that she cannot fight the interpretive aggression of the community, which now heaps admiration on her and assails her with requests for forgiveness, pushing her against her will from marginality to centrality. Finally she adopts the only effective path of opposition: she leaves the convent and is never seen again.[17]

Cases of saints in spite of themselves are rare. Success was short-lived even in the case of "the idiot," in spite of the assistance of Piterum. The "normal" saint must collaborate with a community of devotees. As soon as his status is established among his followers, the ascetic may (though he does not always) tone down his ascetic practices. His social activity justifies a more "normal" life, at least temporarily. That social activity may be very intense. Thanks to his indifference to earthly things, the ascetic can serve as an honest broker; thanks to his spirituality, he can serve as a mediator between mere mortals and God. When he feels that his liminal powers are beginning to wane, after a period of fraternization with human beings and their affairs, he is likely to remove himself once more from society to recharge his spiritual batteries. There is nothing harmonious about that swing of the pendulum. It often generates anxiety or provokes doubt and uneasiness, both for the ascetic and for the community as a whole.

Visitors Who Come to Stay

The fourth century was a critical turning point in the history of the Mediterranean basin. Tensions, both social and cultural, gradually changed the shape of the world. The radical break with the past and the political upheavals that followed led to a state of prolonged social-identity crisis. Society chose to remedy this crisis by seeking new mediators, go-betweens that would enable it to unite ideas, classes, and communities (both real and imaginary) that were drifting apart in a world that had lost its symbolic equilibrium and its cultural center.

The church was a giant mediating agency. Omnipresent, bringing people together from the four corners of the earth, linking the present to the past and to the future, associating the living with the dead, heaven and earth, it claimed to be indispensable. *Extra ecclesiam nulla salus.* There is no salvation outside the church. In the new Christian world there were to be no neutral zones. The pre-Christian Roman Empire was indifferent to what lay outside its boundaries, but the church's ambition was to gather under its wing the human race as a whole. Ascetics served as symbolic bridges: they connected the lax present with the heroic past and the visible with the invisible worlds, for they were men and women who had a foothold on either side of the symbolic chasm. They were also the church's sales agents. They infiltrated local communities where the Christian ideals of the center were considered too "distant," too unappealing, and offered a version of Christianity that was made to fit local needs and tastes. The ascetic's prestige did not depend on his formal status, nor did he need supply lines. He made his own name and gathered his own supplies. He was the man on the scene making problematic, but highly effective, compromises for the greater glory of God.

There were disadvantages as well. In a world where "truth" was perceived in absolute terms, any version that was not the exact replica of the canonical version was necessarily a deviation from it. At times the useful compromises went too far. In addition, the ascetic-turned-saint accumulated power that threatened to turn him from a representative of the central authority to a local lord.

Consider the following story, recounted by Saint Boniface in a letter to Pope Zacharias in 745. It deals with the exploits of a popular saint named Aldebert who caused him serious difficulties. Aldebert began his career as a humble dealer in holy relics. A man from a distant land—or an angel who had taken human form, according to Aldebert—gave him certain relics. As Boniface hastens to explain, these were "of a wonderful, yet dubious, sanctity" *(mire et tamen incerte sanctitatis)*. With the help of the relics and the marvelous powers he attributed to them, Aldebert managed to gain access to the peasants' homes. His relics worked miracles and wonders, by which means, it appears, he earned renown as an "apostolic saint." It was then that he managed to persuade a few "ignorant" bishops to ordain him (we may assume that the comment about the bishops' ignorance was added after the fact). Aldebert built churches, which he dedicated to martyrs and apostles, and strove to find out what people expected from the saints.[18] Enlightened by what he had learned, he built places of prayer *(oratoria)* dedicated to himself. He erected crosses and chapels in the fields near springs and there held public services. The population abandoned the bishops and the old churches, preferring to gather at his shrine. "Saint Aldebert's merits will help us," the people said. Aldebert handed over his nail clippings and locks of hair for the faithful to venerate, and he invited them to keep these items alongside the relics of Peter, prince of the apostles. Finally, as Boniface wrote indignantly, he committed a terrible crime of sacrilege. When people came to his shrine to confess one day, he told them: "I know your sins, for all your secrets are revealed to me. It is not necessary for you to confess. The sins of the past have been forgiven you. Return to your homes in peace, reassured and forgiven." When Boniface tried to drive Aldebert from the region, people protested, proclaiming that he would be depriving them "of the holiest of apostles, of their protector, their intercessor [*oratorem*], and of a worker of miracles and marvels."[19]

Note Aldebert's trajectory. Initially, he appeals to an external holiness (that of relics), which says nothing about his person. After acquiring the first hint of status, he feels the need to win the support of the clergy and takes care to be ordained. From then on, the relics are forgotten. Aldebert combines institutional charisma (ordination) with personal charisma ("apostolic sanctity"). The churches he erects are dedicated to the apostles, but it is he who decides where they will be constructed. At this stage the churches are apparently built in towns and villages, and their construction encounters no opposition. Building churches is an act of Christian piety. It is only when Aldebert's status is sufficiently well established that he begins to build churches dedicated to himself and removes himself from the bishops' sphere of influence. It is there, outside the cities, out in nature—in the fields, near springs, under the open sky—that Aldebert becomes a real danger for Boniface, who has lost all control over this renegade "agent." He has no recourse but to turn to the supreme authority of the pope in Rome. Aldebert, however, does not think he is working against the church. He does not deny the apostles' holiness; he simply thinks he is their equal: the clippings from his body are preserved next to Peter's relics, not in place of them. The fact that he has renounced hearing confession, which has so shocked Boniface, attests to his autonomy and not to a total negation of the need for confession. Only those who come to Aldebert are exempted from the ceremony; those who have charisma do not need technical aids.

In other circumstances "the Apostle of Germany" might have made his peace with Aldebert. The veneration of nail clippings and hair, the construction of churches in nature, and even paraliturgical rites can be found in canonical saints' stories. With all his problems, Aldebert and people like him contributed to the Christianization of Germany. Where paganism was still a real option, Aldebert offered the peasants his own version of Catholic Christianity, complete with a special veneration of Peter and of holy relics. Granted, he was preparing for even greater compromises between "nature" and "culture" and seems to have been overconfident about his own charismatic gifts. But that is not the essential thing. For Boniface, Aldebert was a threat who had to be removed because (among other reasons) their respective forms of charisma were incompatible and because they were operating in the same territory.

An episode from the histories of Gregory of Tours provides another example of the ambiguous role that personalities such as Aldebert played in the Christianization of Europe. Gregory tells the story of a Lombard deacon called Wulfilaïcus. This Wulfilaïcus had decided to imitate Saint Simeon Stylites.[20] He built a high pillar near Trier and installed himself at the top, where he spent his time praying and fasting. When not fasting, he ate a little bread and pure water. Predictably, the choice of that form of asceticism was at odds with the harshness of the climate. Exposing oneself to the natural elements in the Syrian desert is different from doing so in northern Europe. At the mercy of wind, snow, and ice at the top of his pillar, Wulfilaïcus suffered horribly. In the winter, he said, his beard froze and his nails split. That asceticism drew a large crowd of admirers, who came to listen to his word. Wulfilaïcus preached against the cult of Diana, which was still being practiced in the region. He called on his listeners to renounce idols and to help him topple the large statue of the goddess standing not far away. The eloquent living saint prevailed over the silent goddess. The good people were persuaded to destroy the idol. What the authorized agent—that is, the bishop (the region was nominally Christian)—had not managed to do, an independent agent accomplished. Technical problems during the destruction were solved through the saint's prayers. Total victory.

The question, of course, is *who* won. Not the bishop. Wulfilaïcus' success brought the bishop to the place. Until then the prelate had not found it necessary to grant Wulfilaïcus much attention. Now the bishop spoke to him, trying to convince him that he was not on the right path and that a man of obscure birth (*ignobilis*) like him was not worthy to follow in the footsteps of Simeon Stylites (himself an obscure Syrian shepherd). Wulfilaïcus allowed himself to be convinced, came down from his pillar, and joined the monks at the local monastery. He submitted to the authority of the head office. But the bishop was not satisfied. Shortly thereafter he sent Wulfilaïcus away on some pretext and had workers knock down the pillar with hammers and iron rods. When the stylite came back and saw that his pillar had been destroyed, he wept bitterly but did not dare rebuild it.[21] His ascetic career was over, and with it his status as a saint. Henceforth he would be an ordinary monk, not too useful in fighting paganism but no longer a thorn in the bishop's side. From the description of Wulfilaïcus' reaction, it seems he did not think that his life as a stylite was over. Perhaps he had intended to return to his pillar after awhile; perhaps he hoped it would host someone of higher birth. It is certain, in any case, that the bishop did not rest until he had obliterated the pillar, an unpleasant vestige of the ascetic's power in the past and a permanent threat of its return in the future.[22]

Like the story of Aldebert, that of Wulfilaïcus begins with a personal initiative that is not necessarily negative, even from the hierarchy's point of view. Wulfilaïcus does not come to replace the local authorities or to rival official Christianity—at least not openly. On the contrary, he makes use of a canonical Christian model (Simeon Stylites) and participates in the struggle to displace paganism. He operates in a manner that the hierarchy cannot. Instead of confining himself to preaching in churches, he goes "out in the field." Instead of simply blaming, he proposes a substitute: his pillar in place of Diana's pedestal, himself as charismatic personality in place of the statue of the goddess. The danger posed by Aldebert, like that posed by Wulfilaïcus, is the centrality of the charismatic person. As long as the charismatic is far away, he can work wonders. It is proximity that makes him intolerable for those lacking charisma; that is why charismatics are tolerated only when they constantly acknowledge their readiness to respect and obey the hierarchy. Unfortunately some things can be done only by the likes of Aldebert and Wulfilaïcus. Wulfilaïcus seemed docile enough, but one never knows with charismatics. The bishop found it better to be brutally safe than sorry.

Aldebert may have abused his powers, but Christian communities everywhere, from the fourth century on, were ascribing extraordinary powers to their saints. God himself had become dependent on his charismatic representatives. He was "Saint Aldebert's God," "Saint Antony's God," "Saint Simeon's God." The confusion of powers often arises against the wishes of the saint. When pagans refer to Antony as the "man of God," who is that God? Have they implicitly added Jesus to their pantheon, or have they paired Antony with a Roman deity? The source of power becomes unclear. What matters is the power itself and he who manifests it, namely, the saint. Saints must constantly remind their admirers that their power comes from God. From time to time the saints forget to remind them, or the admirers forget to remind themselves.

As agents of the church, saints were a package deal. Often they were out of control; too often they took great liberties with orthodox notions—at least as orthodoxy was defined by the hierarchy. They allowed and made possible the survival of local traditions that a theologian might not have permitted. But it seems that this very legitimization of the illegitimate, which in many cases depended on the excessive powers attributed to the local holy man, made a huge contribution toward the gradual spread of Christianity. Christianization was achieved by turning a blind eye to abuses, and by using agents whose excesses could be ignored and who could, if necessary, be denounced when their job was done. Although the collective effect of all the holy men taken together was considerable, none was irreplaceable. Of course, saints are inspired, but they lack technical precision. They need to be interpreted by the elite. The mediation of saints allows buyers and sellers in the cultural market (who are constantly switching roles) to keep their hands clean, to preserve appearances. Members of the elite can learn from saints, but without acknowledging that they are thereby assembling popular materials; and the community can obtain messages they trust from someone whose moral authority and charismatic power they have experienced directly, someone they trust and fear.

The ascetic saint's power was not achieved without opposition. Whether he was already an outsider or became one through his asceticism, the potential saint made his way in the community by excluding rivals. Social systems are governed by an economy of scarcity: there is no free available power. The accumulation of power at a given point weakens power elsewhere. In the eyes of those who possess legitimate religious power (the hierarchy, Boniface, Wulfilaïcus' bishop), the saint is always a usurper. Even if he does not articulate any explicit criticism, the ascetic considers what for "normal people" is an important part of their daily life a blot he must eradicate. The ascetic maintains that the system is corrupt and that his community's religious life is lukewarm, if not sinful.

The ascetic who has acquired supernatural inspiration and power has authority that dwarfs every other kind. The aspiring saint often progresses by way of undermining others' authority, first that of his family: "If anyone comes to Me and does not hate his father and mother, wife and children, brothers and sisters, yes, and his own life also, he cannot be My disciple" (Luke 14:26). The transition from the ordinary world to the "liminal" world of the desert is almost always accompanied by acts of social irresponsibility. The ascetic abandons his fiancée, his brothers and sisters, his parents. He disperses his possessions and his patrimony insofar as he has control over them: "So likewise, whoever of you does not forsake all that he has cannot be My disciple" (Luke 14:33). He is often perceived—and not without reason—as someone who is experiencing a mental crisis; he acts irrationally and impulsively. These are the many specters that accompany the ascetic when he arrives from the desert, armed with the terrible powers he has acquired there, to lay claim to his place. He *lays claim* to his place, since the ascetic comes back to society not as someone who accepts its rules but rather as someone who expects respect even though *he* does not respect the rules. If society does not accede to his demands, the powers he offers as a symbolic lure may well turn against it. The ascetic's return is an act of symbolic violence.

The ascetic elicits what Freud has called the feeling of *das Unheimliche* (the uncanny), that is, the sense of uneasiness we feel when faced with something or someone mingling the familiar and the alien.[23] According to Freud, the uncanny feeling coincides with the surfacing of elements repressed in childhood, primarily castration anxiety. I do not find this explanation very convincing. I am not sure that the eerie feeling of "something wrong" familiar to most of us always has roots in childhood sexuality. What I find interesting, however, is Freud's elaboration of the immediate cause of that sensation. When we encounter something that is both familiar and yet somehow out of place or out of order, we experience a sudden disorientation of the ego. Freud mentions the reaction of repulsion and dread we feel when we run into our double, that is, someone who looks like us and yet is not, someone who is totally familiar and totally alien. The "wild" ascetic rouses similar fears precisely because he blurs the line between the human and the animal, life and death, culture and nature, reason and madness. In the liminal world, there are not only beasts and gods but also monsters and demons. The saint is in close contact with them. There are few ascetics who reappear, like Antony, in a state of equilibrium after many long years of solitude. When the ascetic emerges from the desert— dirty, hairy, and covered with wounds—he elicits the revulsion we all feel when confronted with something that seems beyond the limits of civilization. He causes terror not because he is a totally alien being but, as Freud argues, because he is a combination of the familiar and the alien, someone who simultaneously attracts and repels. One of Simeon Stylites' spectators asks him quite simply, "Are you a man or a disembodied creature [*anthrōpos ei ē asōmatos phusis*]?"[24] The ascetic causes terror because he raises the question of human limits in all its sharpness.

Accommodating the Ascetic

In one way or another, society must confront and domesticate the destructive force and the terrifying personality of the ascetic who emerges from the sacred world to enter the profane world. A tale from the Babylonian Talmud provides a succinct example of the process of domesticating the saint's destructive powers (*Shabbos* 33b).[25] During the Roman persecutions, Rabbi Shimon bar Yochai and his son hid in a cave. God provided a spring and a carob tree for them (the magic spring and the fruit tree are common motifs in the legends of Christian saints). The cave is an enchanted place that connects the world above (paradise) with the world below. The two spent twelve years in the cave, buried naked in the sand from Sunday to Friday, so that their clothes, carefully preserved for the Sabbath, would not wear out. Burial in sand is a dual symbol. In studying the Torah with their bodies buried in sand, Rabbi Shimon and his son are in a sense trans-formed into disembodied heads. But since it symbolizes spirituality, that burial also represents their half-dead status (in the outside world, they are considered dead). For twelve years they lived in that twilight state: pure of all sin, separated from the world, from women, and from all human inter-action, their spirits were expanding while their bodily functions were lim-ited to the bare minimum.

After twelve years a voice from heaven told them that the persecutions had ended and they could come out of the cave. The time they had spent in the sacred world, however, made the profane world unbearable for Rabbi Shimon and his son. An everyday activity such as plowing or sowing—morally neutral in appearance—made them indignant: "[These people] are forsaking the pursuit of the World to Come, and occupying themselves instead with everyday concerns." The inner resources they had accumulated had become destructive for the normal society of the living: "Everywhere [Shimon and his son] would cast their gaze, [the object] of their vision would immediately be incinerated." Then a voice from heaven said: "Have you emerged [from the cave] to destroy My world? Return to your cave!"[26] The two men were sent back to the cave for another twelve months, that is, the length of time that the wicked among the Jews spend in hell, as the tale explains.

The cave, which had been a kind of paradise, now became a kind of hell. This time the period of confinement was no longer intended to in-crease the father's and son's worth but rather to diminish it. During that year the gap that separated them from the rest of humanity narrowed. When Rabbi Shimon bar Yochai and his son left the cave, they remained certain of their moral superiority, but that superiority was no longer destructive to others. Now they found worth in those they encountered and virtue in the humble way others fulfilled their religious obligations day by day. The destructive forces that had driven them did not disappear. Rabbi Shimon still had the power to reduce people to piles of bones solely by looking at them, but he now used that power to serve society and to deliver it from its enemies.

In the Talmudic legend, the mission of humanizing and socializing the holy ascetics falls to God. When God does not intervene, society is obliged to take on the task itself. Society may respond to the saint's symbolic violence with its own. Hagiographers prefer to tell of successes; the Lives of failed saints are rarely written, but there is enough in the saints' Lives to suggest that the saint's victory was far from assured. Not everyone coming out of the desert dressed in rags, burned by the sun, and fulminating against sinful society received an enthusiastic welcome. The encounter could elicit admiration mingled with fear, but also reactions less desirable to the ascetic. A community could choose not to listen to him, or refuse to attribute miracles to him, as it did to Jesus in Capernaum, or make him the village idiot instead of promoting him to the status of a local saint. It could declare open war on him, ascribing his asceticism and miracles to the devil: "For John came neither eating nor drinking, and they say, He has a demon" (Matt. 11:18). A community could also point out that it already had its own experienced and effective patron saints and did not need any others. Sometimes members of a community tempted the ascetic with merciless generosity, offering him money, rich food, sex, or comforts, with the sole aim of stripping away his saintly mask. The legendary saints always passed the test. Ascetics of flesh and blood were more vulnerable. The saint's power depended entirely on a specific community's propensity to grant it to him.[27] If a saint failed to gain a community's respect and yet would not leave, it was always possible to use real rather than symbolic violence against him: blows, expulsion from the town or the monastery, even death. Thus an ascetic who wanted to serve as a confessor might end up a martyr. Sometimes the same community that did not want him in the former role was quite happy to accept him in the latter.[28]

Even when the community was open to accepting the saint, a gradual process of reciprocal accommodation was required. Only rarely did the saint enjoy unanimous support. Saints' Lives attest to endless conflicts between admirers and detractors of the saints. These were not simply conflicts between institutionalized saints and popular saints, as in the case of Aldebert and Boniface. Gregory of Tours tells the story of a holy recluse from the region of Bruges who ate only wild fruit. One day his dead body was found in a wood, at the foot of an apple tree. The "people" buried him in the church, writes Gregory, and attributed healing miracles to him. But the term "people" disguises conflicting positions regarding the recluse's sainthood. One member of the community criticized his neighbor, who decided to make beer on the saint's feast day rather than go to church. The neighbor replied: "Does it seem to you that a man who has fallen from a tree because of his gluttony can be numbered among the angels and venerated as a saint? It is better to take care of necessary household tasks than to venerate such a saint."[29] Gregory hastens to tell us that the man was punished by God for his skepticism, but that story, like so many others, attests to chronic suspicion and disagreement.

Much of that disagreement had to do with local power politics. All power is political, including supernatural power. As soon as the saint placed himself—or was placed by others—in a given political camp, he made enemies for himself in the other camp. Those who had decided to accept his sainthood wanted to make use of it immediately: saints reward the good and punish the wicked. Who are the good and who are the wicked? It all depends, of course, on whom you ask. Antony may have been a saint for Catholics and the "man of God" for (some) pagans, but there is no doubt that he was not a saint for the Arians he was fighting. When Bishop Franco used Saint Mitrias to threaten a certain Childeric who had stolen lands belonging to the church, Childeric heaped insults on both the bishop and his protector.[30] One reason for the constant demand for new saints was that honest brokers were needed who were not interested in worldly affairs and who were not yet tainted by the local power games.

By threats and enticements, by applause and ridicule, communities tried to "domesticate" their saints, to make the alien and disturbing familiar and reassuring. In that process, something got lost: the saint's uncanniness showed that he belonged to the world of higher powers. The erosion of the uncanny element in him resulted in a diminution of the saint's power. There was one way to preserve the saint's powers without being constantly threatened by his liminality. Society used stories about real or imaginary saints as a mechanism for diminishing the powers of flesh-and-blood saints while keeping intact saintly power and complete otherness in an imaginary realm that was nonetheless "real." It is not hard to see that these stories are not realistic. This is usually explained as a reflection of the authors' desire to glorify "their saint." But although propaganda obviously played an important role in the composition of saints' stories, it does not explain everything. The stories' most important task was to reshape the dangerous real-life saints and align them with conventional models of sainthood. That process gradually turned the saint into a cultural cliché.[31] The first stories did not generally deviate from what, according to the norms of the time, listeners considered plausible, acceptable, and "commonsensical." The saint's cultural "noise" was suppressed, his eccentricity moderated or conventionalized, his behavior adapted to the canons of sainthood (a "normal" singularity). Over time, the saint might become increasingly less "real," part of the world of legend, where strange and marvelous events occur. In that world, anything is possible: people live without eating, angels and demons appear before everyone's eyes, martyrs suffer inhuman torments. That world bears no resemblance to everyday life. In the world of legend, the saint completely loses his individuality, becomes a prototype, a saintly caricature. Paradoxically, when the process is complete, the saint can again assume his terrible aspect: whereas real-life horror elicits terror, a horror film can be cathartic.[32]

In the encounter between the concrete saint and the legendary saint, the legendary saint's authority always prevails. The legend speaks of saints whose sainthood needs no proof and whose miracles have been exaggerated. Almost by definition, "literary" saints are more nearly perfect and their miracles more impressive than those of any real saint. Unlike the real saint, the legendary saint does not experience failure or display flaws, which are all duly effaced as the legend is elaborated. It is therefore possible to use the synthetic saint, distilled through the author's cultural filter, to make the real saint conform, if not to profane and sinful society, then at least to the society of saints. Saints' stories were constantly being rewritten with the aim of adapting them to changing cultural ideals. The popularity of the genre made it possible to guarantee that every potential saint would be exposed in childhood or adolescence to "reworked" saints' stories. (The original versions only rarely reach the general public.) Ideally, young aspirants would conform to the given model by their own free choice. If they did not do so on their own initiative, then spiritual guides, friends, and even admirers would direct would-be saints toward these models. The living saint would be compared to the great saints of the stories so as to flatter (you are like X) and guide them (you should behave like X).

That process is somewhat like the manufacture of a vaccine; the harmful substance is injected in diluted form so that it can protect the body against more harmful substances. This procedure is not always crowned with success. The saint is likely to claim his right to originality in the name of a higher authority (direct inspiration, holy scripture) and, moreover, he may not take into account the "reworked" models but may seek "unsuitable" precedents for himself in the vast corpus of saints' stories. In that case a crisis, a social drama in the Turnerian sense, will necessarily ensue. The saint's supporters and opponents will debate the question of the limits of social legitimacy (can we accept the unprecedented, uncanny behavior of this man or this woman?). The process will end either with an expansion of the norm or with the saint's exclusion. Whatever its means of defense, no social system is immune from crisis or schism.

The presentation of "model saints" to the living saint in order to guide his conduct is not necessarily an act of hostility. Comparison to the great saints of the past may go hand in hand with admiration. In fact, in a large proportion of cases, veneration is the most effective means for influencing the saint. As a social phenomenon, veneration can be defined as a series of rewards, symbolic or material, that a person receives for having respected certain norms. The Christian saint, for example, is supposed to renounce lust and gluttony. As we saw, he is also expected to avoid vainglory and pride. But where does unseemly behavior begin for a saint? A nonsaint can eat well without being considered a glutton, for instance. It is less simple for a saint. But whenever the invisible limit (which is elastic and changing) is crossed, he may find that his admirers have become critics. The saint need not actually cross the line; all it takes is a rumor spreading through the community to compromise his status. Veneration is not something the saint can command. If he does not wish to lose his status, he is obliged to remain within the sociocultural boundaries imposed by the community's expectations.

Devotees establish a client-patron relationship with the saint. It is not enough that the saint respect certain moral norms; he must render services to the community. His admirers expect him to be powerful all the time and to use his powers to serve and protect them. To ensure the constant flow of spiritual goods, the saint's admirers try to enter into an unwritten contractual bond with him. They make a commitment to offer him services, both tangible and symbolic. They may provide him and his disciples with food, refuge, and protection, may spread his fame, or may protest slanderous and vicious criticism. This relationship sometimes begins unilaterally: a community attributes a series of miracles to an insubordinate saint to push him toward establishing a "commercial" relationship between them. The goods provided may be symbolic, but the game complies with the law of supply and demand. Veneration makes the saint a vendor and a commodity on the cultural market.

Veneration brings the saint into a world whose rules are well known to his clients, and it builds a wall of expectations and mutual commitments around him. The greater the saint's social capital, the greater the expectations. It is not simply a question of the saint's ego: even an altruistic saint understands that his loss of prestige may well put an end to the social and religious projects dependent on his authority and status. To avoid that loss of capital, the saint strives to conform to expectations, at least publicly. His behavior becomes ceremonial and theatrical, and access to the saint is limited by his intimate circle, to prevent the real person concealed behind the saint's mask from revealing himself. His reputation thus serves as a barrier between the saint and the community. Even if the saint attempts to rebel, his followers will keep telling conventional stories about him. The reputation tends to make of the saint what the community prefers: a predictable and inoffensive cultural icon. The icon is stronger than the flesh-and-blood saint. The storybook saint always has the last word.

The Institutionalization of Asceticism

The desert produced strong medicine. Society needed it but feared its side effects. Gradually the community moved from dealing with ascetics as individuals attempting to regulate "the desert." From the start, society made a distinction between "useful" and "useless" ascetic saints and between legitimate and illegitimate liminality. Hermits living like animals among the beasts, for example, appear in different legends. They elicit astonishment and sometimes admiration, but to become a social force they must once again take human form. Otherwise, they are useless specimens of transformed humanity. More significantly, the desert remained largely closed to women living alone. Of course, several popular legends depict women practicing asceticism in the desert (the most famous being Mary of Egypt, a legendary prostitute turned saint), but society permitted it for only a few flesh-and-blood women. It considered women too "liminal" already. Did one have to make matters worse by permitting them to go off by themselves into the desert, outside men's control? Hence the church and secular authorities tended to encourage women seeking an ascetic life to manufacture a symbolic "desert" at home, generally in the company of other women.[33] For the authorities, that symbolic and collective desert—the convent—quickly became the favored solution for all ascetics, both men and women.

Different forms of control over the ascetic life developed at the beginning of the eremitic movement. Antony did not have a precise model for the life he chose for himself. There was no one to guide and supervise him. But as officially sanctioned models and "authorized" guides emerged, recluses found it harder to evade control or social pressure. When "the desert was made a city," the rules of the polis came into play: hierarchy, laws, institutional supervision, sanctions against wrongdoers. From the early years of the movement, hermits were encouraged not to live a totally solitary life. As we saw in Saint Antony's Life, hermits often broke their solitude to meet for a weekly mass and for meetings with their spiritual guides. Although they were not obliged to come to these meetings, attendance had become the expected norm. In some of the communities, a sort of "commercial center" developed where hermits brought baskets they had woven (basket weaving was a widespread occupation among anchorites) and where they procured their food rations. Sometimes bakeries were built next to the small desert churches. The spiritual leader of the eremitic community set the norm, and his disciples imposed it by physical coercion if necessary. The following story, from the *Lausiac History*, gives us an idea of how this was done.

Palladius relates that a Palestinian hermit named Valens lived in Macarius' community of Kellia (the cells) in the Nitrian desert (a community where Palladius himself had spent nine years). Valens believed he had been visited by angels; according to Palladius, he had been deceived by demons.

> It so happened that some guests brought pastries to the church for the brethren.
>
> The holy Macarius, our superior, took them and sent about a handful apiece to each of us in our cells, and to Valens as well. Then Valens, seizing and striking the one who carried them, cursed him, saying: "Go, tell Macarius that I am no worse than you that he should send me a gift [*eulogian*, alms]."
>
> Now Macarius knew that he was deceived and he went the next day

to talk to him. He said to him: "Valens, you were deceived! Stop at once!"

As Valens did not listen to his exhortations, he went away.

The demon then was fully satisfied that Valens was completely won over by his treachery, and he went and disguised himself as the Saviour. He appeared at night in a vision of a thousand angels carrying lamps and a fiery disc in which, so it seemed to Valens, the Saviour had taken shape, and an angel approached Valens, saying: "Christ has loved you because of your way of life and your sincere speech [*parhesia*], and He has come to visit you. Leave your cell now, and when you see Him from a distance, prostrate yourself and adore Him; then return to your cell."

So he went out, and when he saw marshalled in line those who carried torches and the Antichrist himself about a stade or so away, he fell down and adored. The next day he became so demented again that he went into the church and told all the assembled brethren: "I have no use for Communion, for I saw Christ this very day."

Then the fathers bound him and put him in irons for a year. They healed him of his too-high opinion of himself by prayers, indifference [*adiaphoria*], and the calm life they imposed on him. As the saying goes: "Opposites are cured by their opposites."[34]

How did Macarius and the other fathers know that Valens had had a demonic vision and not a divine one? Nothing in that vision or in Valens' life justified such an interpretation. Angels bearing torches, Christ in a chariot of fire, the dialogue between the visionary and Christ are all elements that appear in numerous saints' visions. The community's violent treatment of Valens was a reaction to the Palestinian ascetic's insubordination. Valens failed to see why he was inferior to Macarius. For Macarius' disciples this was a clear sign of dementia. His vision of Christ corroborated his (too) high opinion of himself. Valens did not deny the sanctity of Communion; he felt that having met Christ in the spirit, he did not need it that day. The hermits had no doubt that Valens was deceived: Macarius had said so even before the vision. In the community of outsiders, outsiders are not tolerated. The limits of the community are the limits of the sacred world.

That logic, characteristic of holy communities of every kind, finds expression in the following chapter of the *Lausiac History*. This time the culprit is not plagued by delusions of grandeur. The hermit Heron denies the authority of the spiritual leader, not by any particular authority of his own but on the principle of equality: "Those who obey your teaching are deceived," he tells Father Evagrius. "One need not pay attention to any teacher but Christ." He irritates Evagrius by quoting Jesus' words to the apostles: "But you, do not be called 'Rabbi'; for One is your Teacher, the Christ" (Matt. 23:8).[35] Heron also avoids participating in the mass. Like Valens, it seems, he sees it as an expression of hierarchy. For him, the distribution of "eulogies" by the priest (*eulogia* can mean consecrated bread) disrupts the equality that should prevail in the desert. Despite his humility, his erudition, and his asceticism, Heron is accused by Palladius (and by Evagrius) of pride. "He, too, was put into irons," writes Palladius.[36] The presence of irons in the desert is itself significant: where there is a city, there are chains. The hermits, who had rebelled against the earthly city, demanded an iron discipline in the heavenly city they had built.

The anchorites' semi-institutionalized forms of organization rapidly evolved, culminating in a tighter organization, the cenobitic community (from the Greek *koinos bios*, "life in common"). In 321 an Egyptian hermit, a former Roman soldier by the name of Pachomius, founded a community of hermits in Tabennisi. That community resembled both an Egyptian township and a military camp. It constituted an autonomous economic unit. It had its own industries, practiced agriculture, developed crafts, set up refectories (where monks ate in shifts). It had a uniform, or habit, a fixed schedule, and above all a written rule, a constitution it lived by. It had an established and centralized leadership composed of the abbot and of the superiors he had named. Everything was controlled vertically by the superiors and horizontally by the monks themselves, who were supposed to keep an eye on one another.[37] The hermit's individuality was kept in check by the rules of abstinence, poverty, and obedience. Obedience was the most important of the monk's virtues: the cenobitic community no longer tolerated the frenzied individualistic rush toward the unknown, toward undisciplined solitude, toward the limits of the human. Everything in the monastery was known, predetermined; everything was supervised. Pachomius greatly reduced the degree of isolation allowed in his community and prohibited all individualism in the practice of asceticism: any deviation from the norm had to obtain his authorization. Offenders were punished for all acts of insubordination. For serious violations of the rule, Pachomius expelled the wrongdoer from the monastery. It was the community, not the individual, that was holy.

Palladius relates that in Pachomius' monastery the monks were divided into twenty-four groups. Each of these groups was designated by a letter of the alphabet, from alpha to omega. That division into groups allowed better control of the monastery, which could number as many as three thousand monks. But these letters also had a secret meaning known only to the father of the monastery and to his confidants: they corresponded to the monks' spiritual and disciplinary status. The letter a monk bore also allowed the supervisor who did not know him personally to place him in a specific moral category and treat him accordingly.[38] Pachomius introduced the notion of organized initiation (novitiate) into eremitic life. In the desert, the master declared his disciple a hermit whenever he chose.[39] In Pachomius' monastery, the novice was on probation for three years before being accepted as a full member of the community. The novitiate entailed hard physical labor. There was nothing heroic about it. Novices were the object of constant surveillance; no idiosyncrasies were tolerated. Those who did not fit in were expelled. Pachomius strove to remove any external temptation from "weak" hermits: visitors from the secular world and even hermits belonging to a different community were kept in sectors reserved for them and communicated only with monks authorized by the abbot.

Pachomius' rule did not remain unique. There were others with even greater influence: the rule of Saint Basil of Caesarea (329–379) has continued down to our own time in Orthodox monasteries; the rule of Saint Benedict of Nursia (480–550) was the most widespread in the Latin West until the thirteenth century. In all these rules, the same view prevailed: a fear of individualism, of exaggerated asceticism, and of solitude; emphasis was placed on moderation, obedience, and discipline. A wonderful story in the *Lausiac History* describes a meeting between the two archetypical representatives of the two schools of asceticism, the eremitic and the cenobitic—Macarius of Kellia and Pachomius of Tabennisi:

> [Macarius] heard that the monks of Tabennisi possessed a great way of life; he changed his clothes, assumed the appearance of a laborer, and traveled through the desert for fifteen days to the Thebaid [the area where Tabennisi was located]. Arriving at the monastery of Tabennisi, he sought out their abbot Pachomius, a most experienced man who had the gift of prophecy, but who did not recognize Macarius. Upon meeting him, Macarius said: "I beg you, receive me into your monastery that I may become a monk." Pachomius said to him: "You are an old man; you cannot practice the ascetic life.[40] The brethren are ascetics and you would not be able to bear their labors; you will not be equal to the task and you will leave cursing them." He did not receive him on the first day or on the second, or on the next, until the seventh day. All that time Macarius waited, fasting, he said: "Receive me, Father; if I do not fast and work along with them, order me to be expelled."
>
> He persuaded the brethren to admit him. The monastic community at that time consisted of fourteen hundred men.
>
> He entered the community, then. Shortly after he entered came Lent. He saw that each one of the monks was practicing asceticism in his own way. One ate only at evening, another only every other day, another only once every five days—this one remained standing all night but sat by day. Macarius moistened a great quantity of palm leaves and stood in a corner until the forty days were over and the feast of Easter had arrived. He ate no bread and drank no water, nor did he bend his knee or lie down. He partook of nothing but a few cabbage leaves, and that on Sunday, so that he might at least *give the appearance* [my emphasis] of eating.

And whenever he went out for his bodily functions, he came back quickly and stood there, speaking to no one, not opening his mouth, but standing there in silence. Except for the prayer in his heart and the palm leaves in his hands, he did nothing. Having seen this, the others came protesting to their superior saying: "From whence did you bring this fleshless [*asarkon*] man for our condemnation? Either expel him or know that we are all leaving."

Realizing what [Macarius'] way of life was, Pachomius prayed to God that it might be revealed to him who this might be. Then it was revealed to him. Taking Macarius by the hand, he led him into the oratory where the altar was and said to him: "Come, Revered old man, you are Macarius, and you have concealed this from me. I have desired for many years to meet you. I am grateful to you for having boxed my children's ears so that they might not become haughty about their own ascetic practices. Go away now to your own place, for you have edified us enough. And pray for us." Then he left them as requested.[41]

Macarius was a restless hermit. Palladius relates that he had many cells in various places in the desert. At the beginning of the chapter just cited, he tells us that Macarius wanted to go into a garden-tomb. "This garden-tomb had belonged to the magicians who shared power with Pharaoh back in the old days." When he arrived at the tomb, "seventy demons rushed from the garden-tomb to meet [him], shouting and fluttering like crows in front of [him], saying: 'What do you wish, Macarius? What do you want, monk? Why did you come to our place?'" Macarius did not fight the demons and did not deliver Christian sermons to them. He did not intend to stay in that place. He said: "Let me but go in and look about, and then leave."[42] Macarius did not want to stay in Tabennisi either: he wanted to visit the place, display his power to all, then return to his home (or homes). What attracted him to that place was curiosity and the challenge. Macarius concealed his identity from Pachomius to add weight to his victory. The community was supposed to think that it had been taught a lesson not by a professional ascetic—the great Macarius—but by a dilettante whose ability to perform the simplest ascetic tasks they had doubted. If Macarius had immediately revealed his identity and asked to join the community, he would have enjoyed a place of honor at the top of the local hierarchy. But Macarius did not want an institutionalized position offered him in accordance with the rules of precedence. He wanted to surprise, to subvert; he wanted to acquire his status from below, to topple the powers that be. That subversion entailed dissimulation, hidden irony, and presumption, all under cover of silence and humility. It attacked the status of all others in the community. The moderate asceticism of the monks did not make any one of them a truly exceptional being. Every monk practiced his asceticism in a slightly different manner, but without distinguishing himself too much from the others. The ascetic acrobatics of Macarius introduced an element of competition and tension that threatened the harmony of the community. If the brothers did not want to give up their status, they had to meet the standards set by Macarius.

The brothers refused. They demanded that the supervisor expel this inhuman creature from the monastery. Let us note that for the cenobites the hermit was a "liminal," threatening element who elicited fear (was this fleshless creature a human being?). His presence required that Pachomius take special precautions. First, he asked God to reveal the anonymous hermit's identity. Once that identity was revealed, he still felt it necessary to drag the intruder to hallowed ground: there, in front of the altar, in the world of institutionalized religion, his destructive powers could be controlled. Subversive elements, such as Valens and Heron, try to avoid the church and the altar. Despite his professed desire to meet the famous ascetic, Pachomius was not eager to have him stay. What he had seen was enough. Macarius had forcefully edified the novices, but what was the lesson he had conveyed? Clearly Pachomius did not wish his disciples to imitate Macarius' behavior. It is possible that Macarius' performance represents a more subtle lesson: an example of pride that should be avoided. Pachomius did not chastise his disciples for their insubordination or for their lack of ascetic enthusiasm; he accepted their demand to drive out Macarius. The fear Macarius inspired, the revelation of his hidden identity, along with Pachomius' act of leading him to the church, pronouncing his name, and uttering a formula of expulsion ("Go away!"), bring to mind an exorcism, the effort to expel a foreign element that has introduced itself into the community and that threatens to destroy it from within. Macarius' Dionysian irony meets with an appropriate response in Pachomius' Apollonian irony: "You have edified us enough. And pray for us." From afar.

After a period of coexistence in the fourth and fifth centuries, the distrust of eremitic asceticism began to grow. In the sixth century, Saint Sabas and Saint Theodosius organized monastic communities in Palestine. Sabas was responsible for organizing the hermits, Theodosius the cenobites. In his biography of Theodosius, Theodore of Petra relates how the saint brought together the anchorites who had been living outside the community in the mountains and caves, without any responsible supervision. Those hermits, writes Theodore, practiced an unreasonable asceticism and attributed powers to themselves that they had received from the Messiah. The hermits, he writes, had lost their minds. Theodosius gathered them together in a sort of mental institution near his monastery, where they were gently but firmly reeducated.[43] It was the same asceticism as before, the same powers; only the attitude had changed. Were the screams heard in the Palestinian nights different from those that Antony let out at the sight of the monstrous demons and wild beasts that threatened to devour him? Was the sister who wore a rag on her head in Tabennisi *pretending* to be mad and possessed? Were the anchorites in the mountains and caves "really" mad and possessed? The answer to these questions always lies with society. Ascetic techniques, as Violet MacDermot shows, can lead to an altered sense of reality: "From the standpoint of modern medicine, the techniques of asceticism resemble those used in experimental 'sensory deprivation.' The isolation of the individual, the removal of external sensory stimuli and the stereotyping of the environment are conditions which, in modern man, are hallucinogenic. When, to these, are added the factors of sleep and food deprivation, it becomes clear that what are here described are also the conditions conducive to the production of the dream visions of the pre-Christian religions."[44]

There is no need to expand on this. The psychological and even bio-chemical interpretation of "mystic" phenomena is now almost a matter of course. But "scientific" assertions about the premoderns' sense of reality are based on an all-too-absolute confidence in our own conception of reality. In the past no one doubted that visible reality was only the tip of the iceberg. In modern terms, saints and mystics "had hallucinations"; in the terms of their time, "they saw clearly through the screen of deception which we call reality." The fact that so many hermits were considered mad or possessed in the sixth century was in no way the expression of a sudden surge of ecclesiastical rationalism. It was only the delayed reaction of the social body to the troubling "invasion" of ascetics. People began to think that the eremitic phenomenon needed better control. Society increasingly called "madness" what it had once been willing to call "sainthood." The real desert had become something to be consumed in small doses and perhaps best left in the hands of experts.[45] In 692 the council in Trullo of Constantinople made hermits subject to bishops' authority. Isolation, the council decided, would be permitted only to those who had spent three years in a cenobitic community and an additional year in "supervised" isolation.[46]

And yet despite this and other control mechanisms that were unleashed against it, eremitic asceticism did not go away.[47] From time to time people felt dissatisfied with the city, dissatisfied even with the artificial deserts of the monasteries. They left for the "true" desert and came back from it to haunt society and reassure it. In moments of crisis, when the spiritual powers of the domesticated saints seemed insufficient, Christian society once more turned to the forests and deserts for stronger medicine. Consumed by anxiety and guilt, it looked for men of God terrible enough to overcome its most terrible fears.[48]

SEVEN

Paul, an Ascetic in Paradise

CHRISTIAN ASCETICISM WAS AN ENORMOUS SUCCESS, and like any success, it whetted the appetite both for life in the desert and for new descriptions of it, in the style of Athanasius' *Life of Antony*. One of the most ambitious of these undertakings was the *Life of Paul, the First Hermit*, a very early work by Saint Jerome (347–419/420). It was written in the late 370s, apparently in Antioch. Jerome went on to write two more hermits' biographies: a *Life of Hilarion* in about 390 and a *Life of Malchus* a year or so later.[1] Of these three biographies, the *Life of Paul* was the most influential. There are six Greek translations, one Coptic, one Syriac, and one Ethiopian. The work was a great success in the Middle Ages and appeared in many collections of saints' legends.[2] Although Paul is obviously the product of Jerome's imagination, his remains were "invented" in the twelfth century and transferred to Constantinople, then, during the Fourth Crusade, from Constantinople to Venice, and finally to Buda, Hungary, to the Order of Saint Paul the Hermit. His head, sent to Rome, disappeared without a trace.

The biography of Antony recounts the life of the first hermit; Jerome's *Life of Paul* relates the life of the hermit before the first. Unlike the *Life of*

Antony, which has given rise to a considerable number of studies, the little biography describing Paul's conversion and death has not attracted the interest of scholars, who for the most part have been concerned with Jerome's major works—his translation of the Bible, polemics, and exegetical and theological works. This early text, however, marks an important stage in the development of saints' Lives as a genre. At first sight, the *Life* looks like a strange marginal note to the *Life of Antony* by an arrogant young scholar. Jerome, it would seem, read Athanasius' popular composition and sought to attract public attention to himself by claiming that he had discovered a hermit who *preceded* the famous Antony. The first hermit was the model for all subsequent generations. Precedence in time meant precedence in dignity; some of that dignity would cling to the person who first discovered the founding father. The *Life of Paul* does not attempt to offer a systematic outline for the ascetic life, unlike the *Life of Antony.* Paul does not transmit important moral or theological messages; he performs almost no miracles; he has but one disciple, Antony. In fact much of the work concerns not Paul but Antony. But since Paul is Antony's master, one can assume that everything Antony imparts to posterity has its source in Paul. The most important aim of the *Life of Paul,* then, is to show that Paul was the first hermit. Jerome's Antony acknowledges that anteriority and that superiority. But Jerome's work is not just a scholarly account. It is important precisely because it moves away from Athanasius' model of the philosopher hermit's exemplary life. The *Life of Paul* was not intended to serve as a model. It was not a sermon camouflaged as a biography but, to cite J. N. D. Kelly, "a romantic idealisation of monastic withdrawal, as full of wonders and fabulous creatures as a fairy-tale."[3]

There are supernatural and mythical elements in the *Life of Antony* and in martyr narratives, but in general they appear as rhetorical "proof" of the hero's moral stature. That is not the case in Jerome's *Life of Paul.* The vague moral messages almost disappear under the weight of the mythical. This shift from a history in which the fabulous is present but secondary (as in the *Life of Antony* or in the other biographies written by Jerome, those of Hilarion and Malchus) to fable pure and simple marks a critical turning point in hagiographical writing. With his *Life of Paul*, Jerome abandons the historical-educational model provided by Athanasius for a kind of writing that gives free rein to the creative imagination. Jerome is not the only one responsible for this turning point, and it would have occurred sooner or later in any case, but the authority of the translator of scripture and venerated doctor of the Latin church gave it important support.[4] From that moment on we can distinguish two parallel hagiographical currents: one portrays historical heroes by combining historical and fantastic elements, while the other is entirely mythical and fantastic. The second type of work describes an enchanted world of Christian and universal archetypes, even when the main character is historical, provided that his remoteness in time and space makes him well suited to be mythified. Of the two types, it is the fantastic that was destined to be more popular. Legendary saints, it seems, are more memorable than historical saints.[5]

The first chapter of the *Life of Paul* is pseudo-historiographical. It begins with a discussion of the supposedly pressing question of the time: Who was the first hermit? Jerome presents several opinions and dismisses them all. Elijah and John were prophets, not hermits, and the view that Antony was the first hermit is fit only for the ignorant masses. Anyone interested in the essence of the hermit and not in the name alone should know that Paul was the first hermit. How does Jerome know? Even Antony's disciples confirm it. To whose ears? Jerome does not provide his sources. Moreover, how does Jerome know what the masses do not? He does not tell. From what he reveals subsequently, it would appear that the source can only be Antony himself or his disciples. Jerome does not say how the account of Paul's life has traveled from Egypt to Syria. He warns against those who invent shaggy hermits no one has ever heard of who supposedly lived in underground caves (just like Paul). Evidence to the contrary notwithstanding, Paul is not one of them.

After briefly apologizing for taking up the pen—a common rhetorical device, but not pointless for someone claiming to dispute Saint Athanasius himself—Jerome presents the reader with the "historical" backdrop for Paul's conversion. It was in the early days of the major persecutions, a hundred years before the biography was composed. Jerome seizes the opportunity to tell his readers two short martyrdom stories "worthy of memory." Again, he does not give references; as far as we can tell, both stories are his "inventions." The first story tells of a martyr condemned to a particularly horrible type of execution:

> During the reign of the persecutors Decius and Valerian, when Cornelius in Rome and Cyprian in Carthage shed their blessed blood for the Messiah,[6] a violent storm ravaged many churches in Egypt and in the region of Thebes. The desire of Christians at that time was to die by the sword in Christ's name, but the perfidious enemy inflicted slow torments unto death, seeking to murder their souls and not their bodies. According to Cyprian, who was [also] tortured by the devil: "They want death and are not allowed to die."
>
> To display his cruelty more clearly, I will present two examples worthy of memory. . . . The devil ordered a martyr, loyal to his faith, who had prevailed over instruments of torture and a white-hot iron, to be dipped in honey and placed out in the blazing sun, hands tied behind his back, so that bee stings would kill the man who had prevailed over the burning-hot instruments.

Curiously, that first account breaks off. What happened then? Jerome does not say. Although we can assume that the martyr kept his faith, this is not explicitly stated, nor do we know whether he survived the ordeal. There is something troubling about the story's incompleteness. Jerome then continues to the second story:

> He ordered that an adolescent in the first flower of youth be taken to a pleasant garden. There, among white and red roses, a faintly babbling brook meandered nearby and the leaves on the trees gently rustled in the wind. He ordered that the young man be stretched out on a feather bed and, so that he could not escape, had him bound by finely braided cords. When everyone had left the place, a pretty prostitute

arrived and began tenderly to kiss him on the neck, and, even more criminally, to touch his virile member, with the aim of throwing herself upon him—as a brazen woman devoid of modesty—after exciting his body's desire. The soldier of God did not know what to do or where to turn. He who had overcome torments was about to be defeated by lust. Then he was seized with divine inspiration: he bit off his tongue and spit it in the face of the woman kissing him. So it was that great pain vanquished his awakening passion.[7]

The usual descriptions of torture do not appear in that second account. They are merely implied. No one asks the young man to deny Jesus or Christianity. He is led to a sort of garden of pleasures reminiscent of the descriptions of Perpetua's and Saturus' paradise; the worst danger threatening him is the loss of his virginity. Granted, the preservation of sexual purity was desirable, but in the tradition of Christian martyrology it was not central, at least not for men. What truly matters is the choice between denying Christ and being tortured to death. That entire scene seems rather to have been borrowed from one of the Greek romances widespread in the Mediterranean basin in the early centuries of the Christian era, whose heroes had frightening adventures while defending their virginity.[8] As in pagan accounts, the struggle to defend sexual purity is described provocatively (in the nineteenth century, this scene was removed from the Latin editions). Biting off the tongue alludes to the world of pagan heroes who stand up to tyrants and heroically bear torture and death. When Tertullian praises the martyrs, he gives a list of these individuals. In among the men—Greek philosophers and noble Romans—is an Athenian courtesan who spits out her severed tongue in the face of a tyrant so that, even if she succumbs to torture ("if she is vanquished," writes Tertullian), she will not denounce her companions.[9] There is no doubt that this description made an impact on the young Jerome, but in his work the prostitute and the tongue appear separately.

One might have assumed that the function of these two rather odd martyrdom narratives was to create a sense of continuity between the age of martyrs and the age of ascetics. But surprisingly, Jerome departs from what had become the standard model (which we have seen in the *Life of Antony*). He does not present Paul as a man seeking physical or spiritual martyrdom. Unlike Antony, Paul does not experience a spiritual crisis that would lead to conversion. His conduct is the antithesis of the heroic self-sacrifice of the two martyrs and of the young Antony. Despite the resemblance between Paul and Antony—they are both Egyptians, both have a sister, both are orphaned by wealthy parents at an early age—there is a significant difference between them. Whereas Antony rejects secular studies, Paul is described as a bilingual scholar, like Jerome. Although the love of God dwells in his heart, he does not seek to perform feats of heroism, and when the persecutions come, he calmly withdraws to his estate, waiting for the storm to pass.[10] Were it not for the greed of his brother-in-law, who wants to denounce Paul to the authorities so he can seize the young man's property, Paul would not have gone out into the desert at all. Rather than being a conscious moral and religious choice, Paul's ascetic career is almost fortuitous.

Paul's desert experience unfolds entirely in a marvelous cave, "a beloved dwelling offered him by God," more fit for a serene life of contemplation than for an ascetic life, for the scholar's *otium* rather than the anchorite's *askēsis*: "When he moved away the stone [which concealed the entrance to the cave]—men wish to know what is hidden from them—he avidly surveyed it and found a vast open-air courtyard covered by the large palms of an old date tree." Life in the cave does not even include extraordinary devotional practices. Paul prays. Jerome says no more than that. There is no mention of the holy scriptures, no visions, no penance, no mortifications, no temptations.

A Sacred Summit in a Heavenly Cave

Paul's life is not a battle for spiritual life or death. The triumph is achieved without effort—without asceticism, in fact. The anchorite's cave is an enchanted place that is not of this world. It is a universal symbol for the passage between worlds. Paul leaves the world of the living behind him. The place where he finds himself, like the cave of Rabbi Shimon bar Yochai and his son, is a sort of underground paradise: a cave with its own enclosed piece of heaven, a source of clear water, a palm tree bearing fruit that protects him with its shade, and even a crow which, like the crows that sustained Elijah in the Judean desert (1 Kings 17:6), brings the hermit his loaf of bread every day. Nothing here recalls the terrible heat of the desert, the thirst and the hunger, the painful labor, the terror of wild beasts, or the machinations of demons.[11] One wonders whether the disappearance of asceticism in Paul's account does not express Jerome's own decision to abandon the ascetic life, leave the desert, and return to the city.

Paul lives in his cave like Adam in paradise before the Fall, in holy idleness. As proof of the authenticity of his account, Jerome reports the ascetic experience of two Syrian hermits he had known personally. But in doing so, he only underscores the differences between his hero and the "ordinary" ascetic. The two Syrians lived in poverty and hunger: one was confined to a cell and lived on dry bread and muddy water; the second lived in a well on a diet of dried figs. That is a far cry from Paul's spacious and pleasant oasis. With a touch of unintentional irony, Jerome situates Paul's paradise near a secret mint for counterfeit money.

Having placed Paul in his cave, Jerome skips the next seventy years and turns his attention to Antony, to whom Jerome devotes almost the entire remainder of the account. When we first meet Antony, he is a victim of vainglorious delusions: there is no hermit in the desert more perfect than he, he thinks. But that very night he hears a voice in a dream that tells him, "There is someone farther out in the desert who surpasses you by far." The divine voice is not content to articulate Antony's moral inferiority; it sends him off on a long journey through the desert to meet the *truly* perfect hermit. The journey highlights the differences between the two hermits: Paul is sedentary, Antony nomadic; Paul is at the heart of the desert and of the earth, Antony is at the periphery and the surface; Paul has achieved perfection, Antony aspires to it.

Unlike Paul's peaceful progress into the desert, Antony's path is strewn with difficulties. The feeble old man advances under the blazing desert sun, suffers from thirst, confronts his fear of demons by day, of darkness by night, always uncertain. Jerome's desert is an enchanted world inhabited by fantastic creatures: Antony meets a centaur and a satyr.[12] These creatures appear suddenly, and then disappear immediately after their brief encounters with Antony. The centaur answers Antony's question "Where does the servant of God dwell?" with a mix of barbarously pronounced, incomprehensible words and howls. Yet it shows Antony the way with a gesture of its right hand. Jerome presents the centaur, half man and half beast, as a creature of uncertain moral status. Although it helps Antony, Jerome is not certain whether it is the devil who has taken this form to scare Antony or whether the desert, which breeds monsters, gave birth to this creature also. As for the second monster, which identifies itself as a faun, a satyr, or an incubus, there is no longer any doubt. It is a Christian monster. The creature offers Antony food (dates) and declares that it has come as a delegate of its species to ask the abbot to pray to their common Lord, who came for the salvation of the whole world. In retrospect, then, it seems that the centaur too was not a diabolical creature. Jerome's desert is not diabolical; its monstrosity is only external. It is the antithesis of sinful Alexandria. The blazing heat of the desert is innocent, unlike the "burning-hot instruments" with which the city torments martyrs. In the desert, even monsters help the innocent traveler; in the city, even his family betrays him. Jerome's decision to show the mythical creatures he has Antony encounter in a favorable light goes against the more common Christian tendency to see the creatures of pagan mythology either as figments of the imagination or as devils pure and simple. In addition, centaurs, incubi, and satyrs are specifically identified with heathen sexual violence and seduction.[13] In Jerome's description these creatures are harmless, faithful beings—worshipers of Christ, not his enemies.[14] In the enchanted world of the desert, the love of God crosses species boundaries: it is not only men but also monsters and beasts who seek salvation. For example, pious lions bury Paul.

When Antony arrives at Paul's cave, the noise he makes causes the old hermit to lock his door. It is surprising to find a door and a lock on a desert cave. Jerome seems to be thinking more of a scholar's study than of a penitent's hideout. Only after lengthy supplications and threats ("I will die here on your doorstep") does Paul open his door to Antony. It is not very clear why Paul refuses to let him in. There is no surprise here, no real threat as in Pachomius' encounter with Macarius. Paul knows who his visitor is, yet he lets Antony knock on the door from dawn till noon. This seems to be a way of underscoring Paul's superiority. He will open his door only after his "younger" brother has declared his baseness: "I know I am unworthy of seeing your face," declares Antony. He compares Paul to Jesus: "I sought and I found. I knock so that it will be opened to me."[15] He complains that Paul, who welcomes beasts, should surely welcome a man. Paul makes him wait. In an ironic role reversal borrowed from Virgil ("Such was his [Antony's] constant cry; unmoved he stood. To whom the hero [Paul] thus brief answer made"),[16] Jerome identifies the younger and more active of the two hermits with Anchises, Aeneas' passive father, who wishes to die where he is, and Paul with the hero who directs Aeneas to his dead father. For Jerome, the one who stays is the heroic savior; the one who goes searching needs to be saved.

When Paul opens the door, he says: "Prayers like these do not represent threats; there is no trickery in tears. Are you surprised that I do not welcome you when you have come here to die?" But Antony has not come to die (as it turns out, and as his host has known all along, he has come to bury Paul), nor should we take Paul's reassurances seriously. Paul smiles and jokes; Antony weeps. Paul does not explain to Antony why he has not allowed him to enter. He continues to address him ironically, as if his visitor were a man with knowledge of worldly affairs. He asks not about spiritual matters but about things that are of no real interest to a hermit who has forgotten the world and been forgotten by it. (How is the human race faring? Have new roofs sprung up in the ancient cities? What empire rules the world? Are there people who are deceived by demons?) Paul is so detached from human inconsequentialities that he asks not about a specific community but about the human race generally. Antony, by contrast, is identified with the "world," where politics and economics and deception reign.

Paul's irony is manifest in his description of himself as an old man on the brink of death, "his limbs decayed with age, his gray hair unkempt." Why should Antony wish to see such a man, he wonders. Yet is he not speaking to a ninety-year-old ascetic, a man whom Jerome had earlier described as "supporting and guiding his weak limbs with a staff"? In repeatedly treating a fellow ascetic as a person who cares about insignificant, external things, Paul is being sarcastic and condescending. Antony, despite his many years in the desert, is a rookie. Paul treats him like one.

For a brief moment, the differences in status between Paul and Antony are blurred. The heavenly crow recognizes the presence of Antony and delivers a double ration of bread. In the dialogue that ensues, neither of the two ascetics is willing to admit his own superiority over the other (recall the dialogue between Piterum and the "madwoman" of Tabennisi). There is an amusing bread-breaking scene in chapter 12: "And after they had thanked God, they both sat down on the bank of the bright spring. There a discussion ensued on the question of who would break the bread, and it continued until almost evening. Paul insisted on his guest's priority rights; Antony rejected that opinion, referring to the age of the man who had received him. Finally, they decided that each would grab one end of the loaf and pull it toward him, and that the piece remaining in his hands would provide him with nourishment."

But the signs of equality do not last. At dawn, a hierarchy is reestablished. Paul reveals to Antony what he has heretofore concealed: whereas Antony has only recently discovered Paul's existence, Paul has known of Antony's existence "for a long time." They may argue about priority rights in breaking bread, but since God himself told Antony that Paul surpassed him "by far," there can be no doubt about who is spiritually superior. Paul has already reached the finish line, and the victory wreath awaits him. Antony has been sent to Paul as a disciple to a master, to render him various services.

Antony's reaction shows signs of jealousy. He weeps again and begs Paul to accept him as a companion on his last journey. Revealing his irresponsibility, he asks that the race he is required to run be cut short and beseeches Paul when he ought to be beseeching God. Paul reprimands Antony for his selfishness: "You ought not seek your own, but your neighbor's good!"

It is then that Paul asks Antony to fetch the mantle given to him by Athanasius to serve as his shroud. The request has a double meaning: it demonstrates to the stunned Antony that the anchorite, who seems not to know "how the human race is faring," not only has known of his existence "for a long time" but also knows a detail as small as the existence of a mantle. Jerome makes it clear that Paul's request is not sincere: it hardly matters to Paul "whether his cadaver rots covered up or bare" (chapter 13). Paul simply wishes to remove Antony from his death scene. Since Antony has a tendency to become overemotional, the old man "spares" him the spectacle Antony so wishes to share. As we shall see, he bitterly regrets Paul's "generosity."

Athanasius' mantle may be insignificant in Paul's eyes, but it is not in Jerome's. It is the only point on which Jerome explicitly contradicts the *Life of Antony*. Athanasius relates that on his deathbed the hermit handed out the clothes he had worn: he ordered that one of his mantles be given to Bishop Serapion, bequeathed his hair shirt to his disciples, and ordered that the mantle Athanasius had given him be returned to its owner.[17] Athanasius' mantle does not envelop Paul's body. It is in his possession. He confirms that the mantle he had personally given to Antony when it was new has been returned to him, threadbare and "permeated" with the hermit's sanctity. In passing it on to Paul, Jerome removes an important relic from Athanasius' hands. It is he, Jerome, who knows better than Athanasius, just as *his* hermit is greater than Athanasius'. For Jerome takes away the mantle even as he radically devalues it. Paul does not even really need it: it was merely an excuse for sending Antony away. Finally, Jerome denies Antony the privilege of giving and makes him the one who receives. It is not that Jerome has contempt for saints' garments. The tunic Paul had woven for himself out of palm leaves is a sacred relic that Antony wears with devotion on feast days.

In the *Life of Antony*, the protagonist's death scene is orderly and conventional: Antony dies surrounded by his disciples; he preaches a sermon which is his spiritual testimony, gives precise orders concerning his funeral arrangements, and bequeaths his few earthly possessions.[18] Paul dies alone; he has no last words and leaves nothing to anyone. Antony is obliged to "claim" Paul's tunic from the man who "died intestate" (chapter 17).

Antony hastens to carry out the mission that Paul has entrusted to him. He fears—and his fears are not unfounded—that Paul will die before he returns. He is afraid that Paul will elude him, just as he managed to elude the rest of "the human race" throughout most of his life. For Paul, Antony is only an instrument, not a fellow traveler. He travels alone. Antony arrives exhausted at his monastery. When he meets with his disciples, he declares that he is a sinner unworthy of bearing the name of hermit. Here Jerome closes the circle: in the first chapter he had said that Antony was the first to have borne the name "hermit"; but now Antony himself affirms that he is not even worthy of bearing the name. Paul's preeminence becomes even clearer. The prophet Elijah and John the Baptist, who were called "more than hermits" at the beginning of the text, are now combined with the figure of Paul. "I have seen Elijah," Antony declares. "I have seen John in the desert; I have seen Paul in Paradise" (chapter 14).[19] On the return trip, Antony, carrying the requested mantle, has a vision of Paul in heaven among the prophets and the apostles. When Antony arrives at the cave, he realizes that Paul has eluded him one last time. Antony sees Paul kneeling in prayer. Forgetting his heavenly vision, he thinks that his master is still alive and prays with him, only to discover that he has prayed with a corpse.

After carrying Paul's remains out of the cave (paradise has no place for the dead), Antony realizes that he has no implement for digging a grave. As Jerome repeatedly portrays him, Antony, feeling powerless, turns to futile laments and instead of taking action wishes to die. Then two of the providential creatures that populate Jerome's desert appear, *ex machina:* two lions lie down at the corpse's feet and mourn the saint's demise. Then they dig a grave with their paws and lick Antony's feet, waiting for his blessing. Clearly these are pious creatures, like the centaur that guides Antony, the satyr that offers him dates and asks for his prayers, the she-wolf that shows him the entrance to Paul's cave (and Paul himself, who shows him the way to heaven). Still, something is different here. The other beasts appeared suddenly to Antony and then immediately disappeared. The two lions are in no hurry to leave; he has to *order* them to go. With Paul dead, Antony now *is* the most perfect hermit in the desert.

Having carried out his mission in the sacred heart of the desert, Antony dares not stay there. He returns to his world. To the monks who asked where he was taking Athanasius' mantle, he replies, "There is . . . / A time to keep silence / And a time to speak" (Eccles. 3:7). When Paul was alive, Antony had to keep silent. Now he can speak. He gives them a detailed report: he went to the desert to find Paul and to join him; he failed. Paul got away from him.

The pride that motivated him has disappeared, giving way to humility, true self-knowledge. On particularly formal occasions, he wears Paul's tunic. The relic reminds him and others that *he* has replaced the first hermit, but also that he is only a *replacement.*

Paul is the perfect gentleman-ascetic—all understatement and smiling irony. He does not need to shock his spectators or advertise his powers. They are obvious to anyone whose discernment is keen enough. As we shall see in the next chapter, not all ascetics were so understated.

EIGHT

Suspended between Heaven and Earth

Simeon Stylites

P AUL, "THE FIRST HERMIT," NEVER EXISTED, but Simeon Stylites is a historical figure.[1] Even in his lifetime he was universally acclaimed as the ultimate star of Syrian eremitism. His reputation was worldwide, extending from Ethiopia to Gaul and from Persia to England. The eastern emperors Theodosius II and Marcian turned to him for advice and prayer. He was an object of veneration and a saintly model. His type of asceticism, living on top of a pillar, was added to an already rich ascetic panoply. Stylites could be found in the Orient until the nineteenth century. A great deal has been written about Simeon: his contemporary Theodoret of Cyrrhus, a bishop and historian who produced a collection of Lives of Syrian saints, claims to have known and to have spoken with him and with his associates. Theodoret wrote a biography of Simeon during the saint's lifetime.[2] Two additional biographies were produced shortly after Simeon's death: one gives the "official version" of Simeon's disciples and is written in Syriac; the other, attributed to "Antonios," his servant and disciple, was composed in Greek.[3] Each of these biographies contains elements that are problematic from the historian's perspective; they are filled with miracles and marvels, and all three portray Simeon as the ideal manifestation of the author's idea of sainthood. Scholars believe that Theodoret's biographical account is historical for the most part, at least concerning the details he says he witnessed with his own eyes or heard from the mouth of the abbot of Simeon's former monastery. Most agree that Antonios provided authentic testimony of the saint's death. All three biographies incorporate the oral traditions of Simeon's disciples and admirers.

Simeon was born in 380 in the small town of Šiša in Syria, to Christian parents, probably peasants. In his youth he is believed to have been a shepherd (unless this is a pious cliché intended to associate him with the saintly pastors of the Bible). The three sources relate that, after a conversion experience in a church (an experience whose precise nature they do not agree on), the young Simeon chose the eremitic life. Theodoret recounts that the saint first joined a group of anchorites for a period of two years, after which (in 403) he went to live in a cenobitic community in Teleda. It is not known what Simeon did among the anchorites or why he transferred to a monastery. The Syriac biography adds that he had a cousin in Teleda, but that element does not play any role in the story. Simeon lived some nine years in Teleda (the exact duration of that stay differs from one source to another). After that, he removed himself (or was removed) from the community and began to live as a recluse in Tell-Neschin (Telanissos). He stayed there for three years, isolated in a small cell on a hilltop, living undisturbed as an ascetic. It is said he refused all food during the forty days of Lent. By Easter he was on the brink of death. Then he moved to another hill, where he lived outdoors, attached to a rock by an iron chain. Since Simeon's hill, now called Qal'at Saman, was located near one of the country's main thoroughfares, the crowds on that road began to take a slight detour to see the famous ascetic.

About eight years later Simeon began to live on top of a pillar (*styllos*)—

according to Theodoret, to escape the pressures of the crowd; according to the Syriac biography, after a revelation from Moses and Elijah. Antonios does not provide an explanation. Why did Simeon choose to live on a pillar? The response to that question is not clear. It is difficult to believe that perching on an object 1.80 meters high (supposedly the height of his first pillar) could have gotten Simeon away from his admirers. On the contrary, there is every likelihood that it only made him more visible. If we are to believe the second-century rhetor and philosopher Lucian of Samosata, there was in the region of Hierapolis (about a hundred kilometers from Qal'at Saman) a cult associated with a high pillar dedicated to the goddess Atargatis, a Syrian Astarte/Aphrodite. Twice a year a man climbed the pillar (which Lucian, perhaps ironically, called a "phallus") using a rope and installed himself there for a week, praying and transmitting believers' requests to the goddess. That cult, it was believed, brought blessings to all of Syria.[4] Nothing attests to the existence of the cult between the second and fifth centuries, so Simeon's pillar cannot simply have been the continuation of a pagan cult. Even when Theodoret feels the need to make excuses for that type of asceticism, he defends it not against the accusation of paganism but rather against the reproach of ostentation and unseemly innovation. Important differences separate Simeon from the pagan stylites: they merely climbed a pillar for a short period of time and did not practice asceticism; Simeon *lived* on his pillar, never coming down, practicing a rigorous asceticism, and presenting himself not just as a messenger but as a spiritual guide and a model of religiosity.

Nevertheless, it seems that the two phenomena were not totally unrelated. The cults of Baal and of Astarte were widely practiced on hilltops. As David Frankfurter demonstrates in a captivating article, there was a long tradition in Syria of erecting various types of pillars and mounds on mountaintops.[5] In the fifth century, Syria was far from Christian in the orthodox sense of the term. Not only was paganism not dead, as attested by the cult of Aphrodite's effigies among the Bedouins, mentioned by the editor of Theodoret's work,[6] but also a mix of Christian and pagan elements existed even in nominally Christian areas. Pagan state religion had disappeared by the time the large temples were shut down, but local religion, combined with Christian elements, continued. It is likely that Simeon did not consciously seek to imitate any pagan model. That said, his choice of a mountaintop and a pillar as his perch was judicious, since he was perpetuating an ancient practice, perhaps without knowing it. It is exactly this type of innovation/reintegration that "unauthorized" agents such as Simeon were offering to local populations.

Toward the end of his life, when he was perched on a pillar eighteen meters high, the saint himself became a distant figure, exchanging a fragmented dialogue with his audience (or one mediated through his assistants). In many respects, the pillar at that point was more important than the individual atop it. The cult of the pillar also continued after Simeon's death, in the sumptuous church erected around it.[7] The saint's relics went to the city and civilization, the pillar remained in its place in nature, the two cults competing with and complementing each other. All the same, even with Simeon's return to the city, nature was no longer what it had been before him. Simeon contributed toward the personalization and Christianization of local nature cults. Christianity added—or at least attempted to add—a personal and moral dimension to the cults of place and to impersonal rites. Although the pillar had its own traditional sanctity, it had become, even in Simeon's absence, *his* pillar. The community where anyone could climb a pillar to intercede with the deities had been replaced by a community built around a religious virtuoso. Suspended between heaven and earth, Simeon did not confine himself to transmitting the requests of believers; he was also judge and adjudicator, deciding what to transmit. He lived neither on earth nor in heaven but in an intermediate world between men and gods: the world of demons. We shall return to Simeon's demonic nature.

The biography I use in this chapter was written by Antonios, or by someone claiming to be Antonios.[8] It is shorter than the Syriac one and enjoyed greater popularity, in both its Greek and Latin versions. It is of greater interest than the more historical biography by Theodoret. It can tell us something more important than what Simeon did or did not do in "reality," namely, what people could or wished to *say* about him.

Asceticism and Power

It may be the "realism" of Antonios' *Life of Simeon* that most differentiates it from Jerome's *Life of Paul.* By "realism" I do not mean historical accuracy. In the *Life of Paul* nothing has an odor: everything, including asceticism, is disinfected, as in a dream. In Antonios' biography, the stench and the sweat, the blood and vermin are omnipresent. In the *Life of Paul,* nothing can disturb our peace of mind: everything is enchanted, clean, remote. In the *Life of Simeon,* everything is alive, described with a hyperrealism that turns the stomach. But there is more here than realism. Feelings of horror and compassion are combined with terror and admiration. Is this a man "born of parents endowed with reason?" wonders Simeon's abbot. There is none of the stoic serenity of Saint Antony, none of the detachment of Paul. Simeon is *unheimlich;* he is, in Antonios' words, *xenos kai paradoxos*—strange and out of the ordinary. In what is probably the strongest and most powerful scene in the narrative, Antonios departs from the "facts" in order to shock. Theodoret reports the event as he heard it from the abbot of Teleda himself. Simeon spent ten years at the monastery. While everyone else there ate once every two days, he ate only once a week. His superiors at the monastery disapproved. They were constantly reproaching him for his disobedience. One day Simeon took a thick rope made of palm leaves and tied it fast to his waist under his clothing. Ten days later, after the rope had cut into his flesh, one of the monks saw blood dripping from Simeon's body. He asked him where the blood was coming from, and when Simeon feigned ignorance, the monk felt Simeon with his hand, discovered the rope, and reported it to the abbot. The abbot scolded Simeon, lectured him on the merits of restraint, and, with some difficulty, managed to untie the rope. Simeon took no account of the superior's warning and refused to have his wound tended. Seeing that he was continuing to engage in similar practices (whose nature the narrative does not make explicit), the monks drove him out of the monastery. In the mountains, Simeon found a dry, not-too-deep well and went down into it. Five days later the superiors of the monastery, having changed their minds, sent two men to bring Simeon back. With the help of a few shepherds, the monks discovered Simeon, went down into the well with ropes, and pulled him out. Simeon came back to the monastery, but shortly thereafter left.[9]

Here, now, is Antonios' account. It deserves to be quoted in its entirety:

> The saint stayed in the monastery, serving all and loved by all and observing the rule of the monastery. One day he went out from the monastery and came across a bucket in front of the well from which the water was drawn. It had a rope attached, and he untied the rope, went to a secluded place, and wrapped the rope around his whole body. Over the rope he put his hair shirt. Then he reentered the monastery and said to the brethren, "I went out to draw water and did not find the rope in the bucket." The brethren said to him, "Be quiet, lest someone tell this to the abbot." No one perceived that underneath he was bound with the rope. So he remained a year or more with the rope wrapped around his flesh, and it ate into his flesh so that the rope was covered by the rotted flesh of the righteous man. Because of the stench no one could stand near him, but no one knew his secret. His bed was covered with worms, but no one knew what had taken place.
>
> He would accept his food but give it to the poor without anyone knowing. One day, however, one of the monks went out and found him giving the poor the bread and peas he had received. Now, everyone would fast till sundown, but Saint Simeon ate only on Sunday. One of the monks went in and reported Simeon to the abbot, saying, "I beseech your holiness: this man wants to destroy the monastery and the rule which you have given us." The abbot said to him, "How does he want to destroy the rule?" The monk said: "We were taught to fast till sundown, but he eats only on Sundays, and the bread and peas he

receives he secretly gives to the poor every day. Not only this, but the stench from his body is so unbearable that no one can stand near him; his bed is full of worms, and we simply cannot bear it. You must choose: either keep him here and we will leave, or send him back where he came from."

When he heard this, the abbot was astounded. He inspected [Simeon's] bed and found it full of worms, and because of the stench he could not stay there. The abbot said, "Behold, a new Job!" Taking hold of [Simeon], he said: "Human being [*anthrope*], why do you do these things? Where does this stench come from? Why do you mislead the brethren? Why do you undo the rule of the monastery? Are you a specter [*ei phantasma hyparkheis*]? Go somewhere else and live away from us. Wretch that I am, I might be tempted by you. For if you were really a man born of real parents, surely you would have told us who your father and mother and kinsfolk are and from whence you came." When he heard these things, the saint bowed his head to the ground and said not a word, but the place where he was standing was filled with his tears. Quite beside himself, the abbot said to his monks, "Strip him so we can see where this stench comes from."

Then they wanted to strip him, but they could not do it, for his garment was stuck fast because of the putrefied flesh. So for three days they soaked him in warm water mixed with oil, and in this way, after a great deal of trouble, they were able to strip him: but with the garment they also took off his putrid flesh. They found the rope wrapped around his body so that nothing of it could be seen, only the ends. There was no number to the worms that infested his wound. When they saw that terrible wound, all the monks were astounded and they asked themselves how and by what means they could extricate the rope. But holy Simeon cried out, saying: "Let me be, masters, brothers. Let me die as a stinking dog, for so I ought to be judged because of what I have done. For all injustice and covetousness are in me, for I am an ocean of sins."

The monks and the abbot wept when they saw that terrible wound, and the abbot said to him, "You are not yet eighteen years old: what kind of sins do you have?" Saint Simeon said to him: "The prophet David said: 'Behold, I was brought forth in iniquities, and in sins did my mother conceive me.' I am covered with such sins." The abbot was astonished at the wisdom of this answer coming from one who, though a young uneducated rustic, had been spurred on to such penance and such fear of God. Then the abbot called two physicians, who with great effort finally removed the rope with flesh stuck to it, although causing him such pain in the process that at one point they all gave him up for dead. The brothers tended him for fifty days, taking shifts, until he recovered somewhat. Then the abbot said to him: "Son, you are now healthy. Go where you wish."

Then Saint Simeon left the monastery. Now there was a well near the monastery that contained no water, but many unclean, evil spirits lived in it: not only unclean spirits, but also unimaginable numbers of asps, vipers, serpents, and scorpions, so that everybody was afraid to pass by that place. Unknown to anyone, Saint Simeon went there and, making the sign of the cross, threw himself into that well and hid himself against the side of the well.

Seven days after Simeon had left the monastery, the abbot saw in a dream an unimaginable number of men clad in white encircling the monastery. They held torches and said: "We will burn you up this very moment, unless you hand over to us the servant of God, Simeon. Why did you persecute him? What did he do that you threw him out of the monastery? What was his fault? Tell us before we burn you. Do you not know what you had in your monastery? For he will be found greater than you on that fearful, terrible day." When the abbot awoke trembling from his sleep, he said to his monks, "Truly I see that that man is a true servant of God! For I have suffered much evil this night in a dream because of him. I beseech you, brethren, spread out and find him for me; otherwise none of you can come back here."

They went out and looked for him everywhere, and when they could not find him, they went back to the abbot and said, "Truly, master, there is no place left where we have not looked except that place where no one would dare to travel because of the hordes of wild beasts." The abbot said to them, "My sons, praying and bearing torches, go out and look for him there." After praying above the well for three hours, they, with ropes, let down into the well five monks holding torches. At the sight, the reptiles fled into the corners, but on seeing them, Saint Simeon called out, saying: "I beseech you, brothers and servants of God, grant me a little time to die, I do not want to live anymore for I could not fulfill what I set out to do." But the monks overpowered him with much force and pulled him out of the well, dragging him as if he were a criminal. They brought him to the abbot, who, when he saw him, fell at his feet, saying, "Grant my wish, servant of God: become my teacher, and teach me what patient endurance [*karteria*] is and what it offers."[10]

Antonios' account of Simeon's stay in the monastery begins with a scene in which Simeon throws himself at the feet of the abbot. "Have pity on me . . . and save a lost soul eager to serve God," he exclaims. It ends with the abbot at Simeon's feet. At first the abbot wonders whether the stranger is not a runaway slave; in the end, the angels reveal to him that Simeon is his spiritual master. But when he finally understands that Simeon is worthy of being his master, Simeon decides that the abbot is unworthy of being his disciple, and leaves.

As in the *Life of Paul* and other saints' Lives, we find in Antonios' biography an obsessive preoccupation with power: the saint prevails over anyone who threatens his authority. Simeon's power emanates from him, together with the stench that fills the monastery. When it first appears, Simeon's sanctity is subversive. He hides it; he denies it; if it could not find an outlet, it would indeed destroy him, the rule, the entire community. Theodoret relates that, throughout his stay, Simeon was a disruptive element in the monastery. He persisted in doing more than the rest of the community and was often accused of disobedience. Antonios presents Simeon as an innocent lamb. Obedient and beloved of all, he fasts *in secret.*

No one knows anything about him, either externally (he hides his origins; *who* is he?) or internally (*what* is he, deep down?). When Simeon returns from the well with the rope around him, he lies to the brothers: the rope did not vanish into thin air, it vanished into his flesh. The gap continues to widen between what he really is and does and what the monks think they know about him. Simeon is rotting before their eyes, becoming increasingly less human and more divine, getting rid of his flesh, disincarnating; and yet "no one knew what had taken place."

In Antonios' account, it is neither the holy stench emanating from him nor the worms crawling in his bed that reveal Simeon's "secret"; it is virtue that gives him away. The exaggerated asceticism, which in Theodoret's version is only a blameworthy exhibitionism, becomes for Antonios an act of discreet charity. What little food Simeon possesses he gives to the poor. He finds surplus where other see scarcity. Ultimately, the monks take notice. Only then do they become aware of the threat he poses and rush to the abbot to demand, "Send him back where he came from!" Recall the scene in the *Lausiac History* between Macarius and Pachomius. Annoyed by Macarius' heroic asceticism, the monks say to Pachomius: "Where did you get this fleshless man for our condemnation? Either throw him out or know that we are all leaving."[11] The resemblance between the two texts is too strong to be accidental. In both cases, once the hermit finds himself in a community that does not allow anyone to stand out, he is described as a subversive and destructive element. But the atmosphere is different in the two accounts: Palladius' Macarius is fundamentally a good-natured trickster. He acts openly and seeks only to "prevail" over the monks and to demonstrate his superiority. When Pachomius "unveils" him, the potential threat evaporates. He is not merely an old laborer endowed with extraordinary powers; he is Macarius, the well-known and experienced ascetic. The community has been defeated not by an amateur but by a professional. The disclosure does not call the monastery's hierarchy into question but, on the contrary, reestablishes it. Pachomius can gently dismiss Macarius because his moral stature is no lower than the hermit's.

By contrast, the "unveiling" of Simeon does not solve the riddle or reestablish order in the monastery, nor does it reconfirm the abbot's authority. Quite the opposite. The rot that Simeon has introduced into the monastery spreads everywhere. The abbot's spontaneous reaction at the sight of his bed—"Behold, a new Job!"—is ambivalent. He perceives a dual presence, of God and of the devil. His physical gestures bring to mind those of Pachomius. He too grasps the saint by the hand in an attempt to establish his *real* identity, intending to exorcise the intruder. He fails. When Pachomius addresses Macarius, he already knows by the grace of God who he is: "You are Macarius, and you have concealed it from me." Simeon's abbot does not know. His gestures and words express confusion. Having accused him of disobedience, he now accuses him of not being human: "Are you some kind of [diabolical] specter?" Simeon's refusal to answer questions about his identity on the day he arrived at the monastery now takes on a new and threatening meaning in the abbot's mind: Is this creature human? He expels Simeon using an empty formula, "Go somewhere else and live away from us," but instead of chasing him out, he immediately continues to question Simeon in the vain hope of calming his own anxiety. To no avail. Simeon does not answer any of the abbot's questions. He is not ready to give him any information that will neutralize Simeon's demonic power. He remains mute.

The abbot's recourse to violence is a desperate effort to salvage his authority. He orders the ascetic's garment ripped off. But before the ruins of Simeon's devastated body, the community's determination and its leader's authority collapse; hostility gives way to stupefaction and tears. Yet Simeon's sanctity shows no mercy. He widens the moral gulf separating him from the others with protestations of unworthiness. The brothers who attempt to help him are addressed with the title "masters," while he calls himself a "stinking dog." He asks them to let him die in that state, since he is in an "ocean of sins." And what are his sins? He quotes a verse from Psalms: "Behold, I was brought forth in iniquity, / And in sin my mother conceived me" (51:5). Simeon cannot think of a single specific sin. He has committed no sin other than original sin, the sin of being born human. Most people have more sins for which to reproach themselves. Not Simeon. That sin troubles and torments him body and soul. Moreover, Simeon identifies himself with David. The author has already suggested that identification at the beginning of the text, when he says that in his youth Simeon "cared for his father's sheep, just as the prophet David had done." Now Simeon slips in a hint of irony when he declares himself a "stinking dog." The reader may be reminded of the ironic words of David, the true king, spoken to Saul, the usurper: "Whom do you pursue? A dead dog?" (1 Sam. 24:14).

The abbot does not succeed in shaking Simeon's steadfastness. He drives him away out of weakness, not strength, and that is why the expulsion ends in failure. The abbot's dream confirms his deepest anxiety. Like the bramble in the parable of Jotham (Judges 9:14–15), anyone who does not take refuge under Simeon's shade will be burned by fire. The abbot finds himself obliged to take Simeon back into his monastery and to attempt to neutralize his terrible powers by submitting to his authority and proclaiming him a saint. He is not Macarius, but perhaps he can be made a Macarius after the fact. The community can try to live in Simeon's shadow. But Simeon, who has made his home among the vipers, the scorpions, and the impure spirits, refuses to heal the community of the devastation he has brought upon it. He declines the role offered him. He speaks neither to the abbot nor to the brothers. He weeps and prays to God. Three years later he leaves the monastery *in secret*. Like the "madwoman" of Tabennisi, Simeon is not inclined to share his life with the community. He is preparing to exert his great powers all alone, far from the other monks, who admire him but are also his potential rivals. Simeon perches alone on his pillar and looks at everything from on high.

According to Susan Ashbrook Harvey, the central theme of Antonios' *Life of Simeon* is sin and repentance: unlike the other biographies, in which Simeon is a transcendent ideal, in Antonios' account there is only contrition and ugliness.[12] I find this view hard to accept. Apart from Simeon's grandiloquent declaration to the abbot in chapter 8 of the *Life* ("I am an ocean of sin"), references to sin in the biography (in chapters 18 and 20, for example) are rare and purely formal. Simeon's asceticism is never considered an act of penance for his own sins, nor is it connected to a sense of guilt. Moreover, as soon as Simeon installs himself on his pillar, his character changes. The descriptions of asceticism that appear in other sources—prolonged fasts, endless prostrations, and continuous prayers—disappear from Antonios' text. Worms reappear in Simeon's sores (in chapter 17), but this time the wounds are not self-inflicted. They are not God's but the devil's work, and Simeon merely bears them patiently.

Antonios' biography of Simeon is not a story of sin, penance, and ugliness but one of power, compassion, and even beauty. In the first part (chapters 1 to 12), Simeon becomes a very powerful figure by concentrating all the energy he carries within him. In the second part, his powers spill out beyond his person. The "power [*dynamis*] of Simeon" gushes forth and inundates men and women, sinful and righteous, even animals (the words "by the power of Simeon" is used by his devotees as a magic formula). Simeon, who refused to share his power with his monastic community, shares it willingly with his petitioners. And he does not try to stop the spread of his fame. True, he tells the sick whom he cures to attribute their healing to God and not to him; otherwise, he warns, they will relapse. But later we learn that they take no heed of the warning, yet are unaffected all the same (in chapters 22 and 31, for example). On one occasion Antonios has Simeon himself advertise one of his miracles (chapter 24). Once, when he was in a state of ecstasy, everyone thought him dead. But Simeon was very much alive. A ship bearing three hundred people was caught in a storm at sea. The poor souls called to him, uttering many vows. Simeon asked God to calm the waters. Then he said, "I held out my hand to them and saved them all." In this case, as in other references to Simeon's miracles, the same concluding remark is made: "The crowd glorified God because of Saint Simeon." That expresses at the very least a division of gratitude between God and his servant. Simeon also gives his faithful a pious instruction: it is not good to speak the name of the Lord in vain, he tells them. He does not propose that they refrain from swearing altogether; rather they ought to swear "by Simeon." It is God whom they seek, of course, but it is the saint's name on their lips.

The Ascetic Star and His Fans

Let us now turn to the Simeon in the second part of Antonios' account, when his transfigured personality distributes his miraculous gifts with incomparable largesse to all his petitioners. More than an ascetic, this Simeon is a miracle worker.

The surprising thing here is the conciliatory—mild and generous—attitude that Simeon displays once he has installed himself on his pillar. There is very little anger in him, no fire and brimstone. The only time Antonios' Simeon scolds his audience for their sins is recounted in chapter 26. The saint accuses of lust, faithlessness, and wickedness the crowd who have come to ask for his protection against an earthquake; but even this episode ends on a harmonious note. Simeon finds one righteous man in the crowd, and with the aid of his prayers, the many sinners escape divine punishment.

Simeon learns to be reconciled with the world. Having become a healer, he makes peace with his mother. According to Antonios, it takes the poor woman twenty years to find the most famous saint in the country, installed on his pillar one or two days' walk from his native village. Simeon's parents have already been mentioned in the text. In chapter 4 Simeon refuses to reveal their identity to the abbot at the monastery. He is willing to divulge only that they are freeborn and that he is not a runaway slave. In chapter 5 a single but eloquent phrase expresses the rift between them: while he was completely devoted to the service of God "his parents, with tears, ceaselessly looked for him."[13] Like a true servant of God, the saint denies his father and mother; he severs all ties with them and with the rest of his past.

But the past has ways of becoming present—very present. Simeon's mother finally finds her wayward son. She cannot approach him. On his pillar, he is beyond human reach. As a woman, she is not even allowed inside the enclosing wall around the pillar. To get closer to him, she tries to climb a ladder set against the wall of the women's enclosure, but the ladder collapses. The first words the son says to his mother express repentance: "Forgive me, Mother." It is human, not divine, forgiveness that Simeon seeks. The request for forgiveness is followed by the promise of reunion in the afterlife. But the mother is not ready to wait until then. On the contrary: "Having heard these words, she only longed more to see him."[14] Simeon, told of his mother's agitation, asks her to calm down, to rest a little. He will see her soon. The mother, impatient, gives up the ghost. Moved to tears, Simeon asks that the body of his mother be brought in and placed before his pillar. He prays to God to receive her soul in heaven. Then the mother's corpse seems to move and a smile appears on her lips. After that, it is no longer possible to separate the mother from her son. She is buried near the pillar and is frequently recalled in his prayers.

Simeon's conciliatory spirit is clearly manifested in the miracles he works in the animal world. In chapter 15 pilgrims are punished for slitting the throat of a doe after using Simeon's name to trap her. Their punishment is to see the difference between man and animal blurred. They lose the ability to speak and begin to bleat. In chapter 16 a serpent slithers into a woman's belly (a folk motif widespread in premodern medical literature and in saints' Lives)[15] and feeds on her flesh. The expulsion of the reptile is not accompanied by a horror of serpents or other crawling things. In the following chapter Simeon does not remove the worms that infest an abscess in his thigh; he orders that the worms which have fallen from his wound onto the ground be collected and put back on it, so they can "eat from what the Lord has given them."[16] The serpent, then, is punished for eating what was *not* given him to eat. The three chapters turn on ambiguities: the pilgrims are both human and animal; the woman consumes a serpent and is consumed by it from the inside. In addition, Simeon is eaten by worms, but they turn out to be pearls. In chapter 18 the king of the Saracens, who has come to obtain a prayer from the saint, having gathered up a worm that had fallen off the saint's thigh, opens his hand and exclaims: "Look! What you said is a worm is a priceless pearl by means of which the Lord has enlightened me."[17] In chapter 19 a large poisonous serpent that lives not far from the saint's compound is suffering because a piece of wood has lodged in its eye. It comes to the saint for a cure and behaves "like an innocent lamb." In chapter 25 a couple of serpents who come to ask that the female be healed of a tumor are careful to respect the decorum of the place.

The female remains in the external enclosure set aside for women (the *gynaeceum*), while the male joins the men to speak with Simeon. Hence in Simeon's proximity the oppositions between culture and nature, sublime and abject, man and beast become blurred. Simeon's generosity crosses all boundaries. Poisonous snakes, pagans, brigands, sinners, worms: all benefit from the saint's powers and from his goodwill.

From the start, Antonios' Simeon despises conventional rules. The miracles are only one more manifestation of that constant disregard for norms and boundaries. In chapter 23 the saint grants his blessing to a "sinful woman" who has disguised herself as a soldier. Whatever her earlier sins (usually when a woman's sins are unspecified, they are of a sexual nature), the woman violates the rules against dressing in men's clothing and intends to violate the rules of the saint's court by entering the men's enclosure. The saint knows who the "soldier" is, but he neither exposes the woman nor rebukes her. Before she has the chance to approach him, he sends her a blessing through her fellow soldiers. In response to their question "What good have you done in God's sight? [to deserve such a blessing],"[18] she can only reply that she very much wanted to see Simeon. The saint's generosity, like God's, is gratuitous and arbitrary.

In chapter 31 we find an even more astonishing miracle, the healing of a necrophiliac. Antonios relates that a spurned lover satisfied the passion that the living woman had refused him on the body of the dead woman. He was immediately struck deaf and dumb and became paralyzed. He found himself trapped in the tomb. A grave violation of the limits between the permitted and the forbidden, and between life and death, had occurred. When Simeon's body was taken to be buried in the city of Antioch, however, the mules carrying it suddenly stopped before the woman's tomb. The necrophiliac touched the carriage bearing the saint's remains and was completely healed. Why did Simeon grant his first post mortem miracle to a necrophiliac? This is not clear. We are not even told that the man repented of his sin or did willing penance for it, or even that he was particularly devoted to Simeon. Why, then? Because Simeon willed it.

Simeon is the liminal ascetic par excellence. Like other liminal persons, he makes subversive use of his power. He cannot be restrained by threats; only veneration softens his heart. Veneration and the responsibility that comes with authority domesticate Simeon, turn him from *unheimlich* to *heimlich*; they make it possible for him to moderate his asceticism and to control the negative powers that drive him. When he makes his peace with his inner demons, he can be reconciled with the world. He becomes charitable and forgiving. The most serious punishment he inflicts, on a man who attempted to kill him (chapter 27), is a case of painful gout in the man's hands and feet.

Suspended between heaven and earth, neither man nor god, neither dead nor alive but demonic, Simeon is close enough to human beings to help them and far enough away for them to tolerate his presence.

NINE

Saints' Stories and the Rise of a Popular Literature

THE FIRST SAINTS' LIVES were written in the East. In late antiquity, it was there that the empire's cultural center of gravity was located. The superiority of the East was not only religious (most of the important theologians came from there) but also political. These two realms were not unrelated, of course. Ever since Constantine, the first Christian emperor, had founded the new Rome in Constantinople and had begun to grant imperial favors to the Christians, the cultural center of gravity had coincided with the political center of gravity. The inferiority of the western part of the empire only increased with the beginning of the "Great Migrations" in the late fourth century. Between 376, when Emperor Valens allowed the Visigoths to cross the border into the empire, and 476, when Romulus Augustulus, known as "the last western Roman emperor" (he was not in fact the legitimate emperor but a usurper), was dethroned by Odoacer, imperial power in the West was in decline. In the fifth century the western empire was divided into several independent Barbarian kingdoms. A century later the Byzantine emperor Justinian the Great (r. 527–565) attempted to restore imperial sovereignty in the West. His success was limited and ultimately did more harm than good. In Italy the Byzantines put an end to the Gothic endeavor to reestablish order and to the relative economic recovery that the area had enjoyed under the Ostrogoth kings. The peninsula endured two centuries of war, political instability, and economic and cultural devastation, made worse by the plague brought by the invading armies from the East and by new waves of invaders from the south, east, and north. Between the seventh and eighth centuries, northern Africa, the islands of the Mediterranean, and Spain were occupied by the Muslims. The Lombards wrested away parts of the Byzantines' conquests in Italy. The dream of imperial unity had evaporated.[1]

Parallel to the political divisions, the West went through a series of cultural transformations. "Classical" Roman culture was dying out. Its two pillars were collapsing: an educated elite and the state's massive investment in the public sphere (spectacles, architecture, art, civic religion). The new political elites (Barbarian and barbarized Roman) based their power not on a bureaucracy and on written law but increasingly on personal loyalty and unwritten custom. The intense commercial activity that had characterized the empire was gone. When the Mediterranean basin ceased to constitute a common economic sphere, the standard of living dropped sharply. Thoroughfares were abandoned, and the circulation of people and commodities between the two halves of the empire slowed. These events gravely affected the West, a longtime consumer of products and ideas from the East. The crisis lasted from the sixth to the mid-tenth century, with some vicissitudes. The overarching preoccupation of the early Middle Ages was to survive the constant threats of invasion from the outside, the collapse of the central power, and the threat of famine that came with the disappearance of surplus in almost all spheres of life. Most elements of society not engaged in producing food had disappeared: merchants, bureaucrats, urban craftsmen, intellectuals. Slavery had disappeared as well, and freedom was radically curtailed. The overwhelming majority of the western population lived as serfs, producing basic foodstuffs. According to estimates, the rest—warriors and churchmen—represented only about 5 percent of the population.

The collapse of imperial power in the West also had critical repercussions for the church. Once Christianity had become the state religion, in the era of Constantine and his successors, the church established powerful contacts with the Roman political elite, and bishops became part of that elite. The Barbarians were also Christians, but Christians of a different sort. They embraced Arian Christianity, whereas most of the population in the West was Catholic. The disappearance of its former protectors obliged the Catholic Church to adapt. It did so by combining innovation and conservatism. Church leaders understood immediately that times had changed. They promptly elaborated a theology justifying the fall of the Christian empire after centuries of pagan victories. They reshaped old-time religion to suit new tastes, new needs, and new masters. They adopted many Barbarian customs without hesitation. They presented Jesus more as a powerful warrior-God than as a meek Galilean social revolutionary. While many Romans regarded their new masters with consternation and even contempt, churchmen were quick to offer their services and support. Times had indeed changed, and only the church would remain steadfast, provided, of course, it knew how to change with the times.

Simultaneously, however, the church preserved important elements of the ancient world out of institutional nostalgia: ritual aesthetics (a large part of church ceremonial imitated Roman state ceremonial); garb (originally, priests wore the ceremonial robes of Roman officials); the structure of the basilica (the "house of the king," the Roman public building); and most important in a world where power was becoming increasingly a personal affair, the strict separation between person and office. Unlike the Barbarian warrior, who owed personal fidelity to his leader, the churchman was like the Roman official: he obeyed his superior, whoever he might be. The church's nostalgia was especially manifest in its conservation of the Roman administrative divisions of provinces and dioceses, which no longer had any political meaning in the new world. A bishop stood at the head of each diocese. Although cities in the strict sense had disappeared from the West, the locality of the bishop's headquarters, or "throne" (*cathedra*), and of his church, the "cathedral," continued to be called "city" by churchmen, whatever its dimensions and importance. The church's notion of culture also remained unchanged. "Culture" was written culture—Latin, erudite—in a world in which language, reading, and writing were quickly being forgotten outside the church, and where being "cultivated" was no longer a measure of status.

Cassiodorus and Benedict: The Monastic Program

As the secular clergy gradually joined the new political elite (with Barbarians and Romans exchanging goods and values and sharing power), monasteries remained intentionally anachronistic islets. The reorganization of the monastic movement has generally been attributed to two Italians, Cassiodorus and Benedict. Cassiodorus developed a course of study in which learning became an essential part of a monk's life; Benedict compiled a very influential monastic rule that established a community where asceticism was played down and there was limited contact with the world, even as the community deliberately preserved its autonomy and cultural anachronism. It was the combination of these two monastic models that would allow that un-heroic Western monasticism to assume such an important role in preserving the Western culture of antiquity.

It is difficult to say with certainty the degree to which we are justified in attributing the cultural phenomenon of monasticism to these two founding fathers. Their paternity is increasingly disputed. We may assume that the monastic enterprise had many fathers. Its character during the early Middle Ages depended not on one or two men but on a large mass of anonymous cultural agents making "small" choices, not always perceptible from a distance of centuries. One might argue that neither Cassiodorus nor Benedict was a great innovator, and that both had only limited influence in their time. The importance granted them is in great measure the result of hindsight. It is therefore better to consider them mythic founders, ideal types whose historical choices were not necessarily foremost at the time but were recognized in retrospect as critical for later generations. What were these choices? Primarily they had to do with ways of adapting to the new world: What part of the old could be given up, and what had to be preserved?

In the 530s the Roman aristocrat Magnus Flavius Cassiodorus left the service of Theodoric the Great, Ostrogoth ruler of Italy. After years of public activity in Rome and Ravenna, and an exile of some fifteen years in Constantinople, he retired to the monastery of Vivarium, which he had founded on his family estate of Squillace. For him that withdrawal did not represent an act of asceticism. He did not seek to suffer bodily pain or to forget the world in his monastery. He wanted rather to pursue studious calm *(schola)*, without which there can be no culture. At issue was Roman— Christian but also pagan—culture. Cassiodorus was not the defender of pagan culture per se. He rejoiced in the triumph of Christianity, but the old bureaucrat believed that foundations were indispensable to any culture. These foundations happened to be pagan. Unfortunately Cassiodorus' monks were not the refined and cultivated aristocrats who could still be found in old Roman families a generation or two earlier. They were only pale and ignorant shadows of the past. Knowledge of Greek, an essential condition for participating in Mediterranean culture, had almost disappeared in the West. More and more even the educated were now monolingual. One had to accept the facts. Boethius, one of Cassiodorus' predecessors in the service of Theodoric, had undertaken to translate a selection of Greek philosophical texts into Latin. Executed in 524, he left that work uncompleted. For centuries to come, the West's knowledge of Aristotle was limited to what Boethius had had time to translate. The fact that the death of one man could have such a huge influence on an entire civilization demonstrates the fragility of the culture of the time. A handful of intellectuals fought not to create something new but to preserve as much as possible of the glorious past, which was dying out before their eyes.[2]

Cassiodorus' monks were unable to conduct very sophisticated philosophical or theological debates. Many of the theological controversies of the East could hardly be understood by a West lacking the necessary theological vocabulary, even in Latin. Cassiodorus' monks had to be taught the basics: grammar and logic, arithmetic, rhetoric, geometry, astronomy, and music—the liberal arts. Cassiodorus required his monks to devote a few hours every day to copying both pagan and Christian manuscripts patiently and meticulously. But even in his own monastery the monks had trouble accomplishing the relatively simple tasks they were assigned. At the age of ninety-three, Cassiodorus found himself forced to yield to their demands to compile a simple manual that would teach them Latin spelling. "What import can the ancients' thinking have, or even your own for that matter," his monks asked, "if we are unable to transcribe or spell an illegible hand?"[3] Even in the protected Vivarium in southern Italy, far from the political and social tribulations of the time, and despite the monastery's rich library (Cassiodorus' private collection), and the presence of one of the greatest scholars of the West, written culture was disappearing.

Vivarium was not a success. After its founder's death, it rapidly declined. But Cassiodorus' didactic writings, the translations done under his supervision, and above all the conservative principles he promoted and legitimated and that others, whose names have been forgotten, defended after him, were adopted by a monastic movement that would have much greater success: the Benedictine movement. By making the copying of manuscripts rather than manual labor the occupation befitting a monk, Benedictine monasteries became the curators of classical culture in the West. The copyists did not always understand the works they were copying. Copying was an act of piety toward a vanished culture and included semimagical elements: transcription, the very act of drawing letters on parchment, became a sacred act. That enterprise guaranteed continuity. Thanks to the copyists, these manuscripts became accessible to all those—few at first, but increasingly numerous later on—who *were* interested in the content.[4]

Initially, Benedictine monasteries were not centers of knowledge. According to tradition, Saint Benedict of Nursia compiled the rule in the 540s for the monks of the monastery of Monte Cassino, based on an ancient model known as the "Rule of the Master," *regula magistri*. Its purpose was to serve as a guide to living for the monks, who sought to "forget the world and to be forgotten by it." Unlike Cassiodorus, Saint Benedict did not write books to guide monks in the intricacies of Roman culture. His community's intellectual occupations were minimal. Monks were expected to know how to read and write, and to understand holy scripture and saints' Lives as they were read to them at mealtimes. They had to read a book from the monastery's library during the Lenten fast, not to satisfy their intellectual thirst but to avoid sloth. Reading was work.[5]

That was not much. But in a world where books and erudition had disappeared, it was more than could be found elsewhere. Benedict preferred that his monks spend their time in manual labor and prayer rather than study, but the sons of the upper classes who increasingly found refuge in the monasteries considered work in the fields demeaning. They were workers in God's fields, not serfs. Writing was work that the masses did not do. Over time, the study and copying of texts, along with prayer and ritual, came to constitute the prototypical "work" of Benedictine monasteries, at least those of the old school.[6]

The choice of an intellectual occupation was not the only imaginable substitute for manual labor. The monasteries could have been turned into centers of mystical activity, like some of the Buddhist monasteries in the East, for example. The centrality of texts and of books, of "bookish" culture, served the Benedictine community's desire to maintain the distance separating it from the surrounding world not only in religious or moral terms but in cultural terms as well.[7]

The monasteries that adopted the Benedictine rule were not just pockets of cultural anachronism where Roman culture was preserved. They were also the vestiges of a Christianity that was disappearing outside their walls, "Latin" Christianity. The monks led a "regular" pious life, trying to cultivate the ancient Christian norms, in a world where the religion of most of the population was a mixture of watered-down paganism and highly diluted Christianity. It is not easy to analyze the components of that mixture.[8] This was not, as some have claimed, idolatry thinly covered by a veneer of Christian symbols, but it was no longer the urban Christianity of the Mediterranean past either. Western "rustics" (who were now in the majority) adopted Christian structures and symbols: linear time alongside cyclical time, the personalization of the forces of nature, a god who became man, a savior who suffered like a man, a moral cosmos ruled by the hope of future reward and the fear of eternal punishment. But they absurdly and tenaciously continued to believe in the old sacred topography (of mountains, caves, and springs) and in morally neutral forces dominating nature, fertility, and daily life. The ancient deities lost their status as masters of the cosmos, which was now dominated by the divine trinity of the new masters; but certain forces, whose religious nature was vague, continued to play an important role for most people and undermined the sharp Christian dichotomies between good and evil and between Christian and non-Christian. The ecclesiastical elite manifested disdain toward the ignorant hardworking peasants: the term "pagan" (from the Latin *paganus,* inhabitant of the *pagus,* or "countryside") was synonymous with "idolater." That did not mean that the peasants were actually idolaters, however. They were Christians, at least in that they considered themselves part of a community in quest of salvation by the grace of Christ. Yet a widening rift opened between the elite and the majority of the population. In Western medieval society, several types of Christianity coexisted. They had things in common, but major differences separated them.

The Flock and the Shepherds

The monastic elite of the early Middle Ages, although it regarded popular Christianity as superstitious and semipagan, did not make any great effort to bridge the gap separating that Christianity from "true" Christianity. In the society of the time there was a sharp division of labor: the common people, and especially the peasants, were satisfied with a minimal religious faith, while members of the secular clergy concerned themselves with the affairs of the church in the world. Monks were the only ones to realize the pure Christian ideal—or at least, they were supposed to do so. So long as enough true faith existed in society, there was little reason to insist on its equal distribution among the different sectors. Ascetics, holier than their own salvation demanded, allowed society as a whole to feed on the surplus they produced. No one saw the point of imposing on the masses a complex theology that was difficult to understand. On the contrary, such an attempt could be harmful. Individuals are always part of a community, enjoying its privileges and paying its social debts. Even a Benedictine community was not perceived as a group of individuals in search of salvation; it was not a collection of personal careers but a joint effort. In the holy community the whole was always greater than the sum of its parts. For Benedict, salvation was too heavy a yoke to be assumed by a single man; it could be achieved only through collective effort. Anyone who stepped out of line (whether by doing less than his share or more) endangered the community's salvation and his own. The supreme virtue required of the monk was obedience: "Without an order from the abbot . . . monks may not have the free disposal even of their own bodies and wills."[9]

In 595 Pope Gregory the Great, who has been called the last man of antiquity and the first man of the Middle Ages, described the division of spiritual labor that was to characterize medieval Christianity. In his *Moralia in Job,* he commented on the passage from scripture "The oxen were ploughing, and the asses feeding beside them" (Job 1:14):

> What else do we take the oxen to mean in figure, but well-doers; what the asses, but certain men of simple ways? These are properly described to be feeding beside the oxen, because simple souls, even when they are incapable of comprehending deep mysteries, are near to the great, inasmuch as they account the excellencies of their brethren to be their own also by force of charity; and while envy of the knowledges of others is a thing unknown, they are never divided at pasture. The asses then take their food in company with the oxen, in that duller minds, when joined with the wise, are fed by their understanding.[10]

The relative indifference of the elite toward the "simple" people allowed uneducated Christendom to remain fairly free. It is no accident that, between the fourth and eleventh centuries, no one in the West was executed for heresy. According to the elite's criteria, the masses were ignorant, but that ignorance did not represent a threat to the "professional" clergy and did not prompt them to provide the masses with systematic education. As long as the asses were prepared to graze in relative calm on the spiritual grass set aside for them, and as long as there were enough oxen in society to procure virtues for all, the situation was tolerable; indeed, harmony could reign.

The gap between popular practice and learned religion in the period between the seventh and eleventh centuries meant that one of the principal forms of expression of popular Christianity—namely, the cult of saints—functioned with only a minimal reliance on texts. In the ancient world, hagiographical texts had great importance as didactic tools and propaganda. Granted, not all the saints who had a cult possessed a biography, and not every literary saint had a cult, but the veneration of saints took place within a textual environment. In the West at the end of antiquity, there had been an attempt to write the Lives of western saints, either to imitate or to rival the saints of the East. Sulpicius Severus' *Life of Saint Martin*, written in about 410, describes the life and ordeals of Martin, a former Roman soldier, monk, and the bishop of Tours; and Gregory the Great's *Dialogues*, compiled in 593, relates, among other things, the life of Saint Benedict of Nursia.[11] Sulpicius Severus' biography tries to adjust the eastern model of Athanasius' *Life of Antony* to the western audience. The saint of Tours is not described as an ascetic philosopher engaged in an internal battle in the desert and leading a monastic community away from the secular world. Martin is a bishop active in public affairs who leads both his ascetics and his lay flock. The biographical part of Gregory's *Dialogues* attempts to present a model of sainthood to the monks in the West. In both works the emphasis is placed on external matters at the expense of internal ones. The saints' actions, and especially their miracles, take center stage. This may attest to a certain pessimism about readers' capacity to assimilate an overly spiritual text.

These two works, which were the most influential hagiographical writings in Latin until the twelfth century, were composed on the premise that written texts have a major impact on shaping consciousness, and that Christian texts can contribute greatly to the shaping of Christian consciousness. In his *Confessions*, written in the late fourth century, Saint Augustine relates how, after hearing that two young men had been led to convert after reading Athanasius' *Life of Antony*, he too experienced an internal transformation.[12] Texts are instruments of spiritual transformation. The *Confessions* itself ultimately seeks to bring about readers' conversion through a biographical account, Augustine's own in this case.[13] That phenomenon was destined to disappear almost completely in the West. Gregory the Great's writings were among the last to have in mind a relatively broad readership. People continued to write saints' Lives in the West; these writings, however, were no longer intended for a mixed audience of ecclesiastics and secular readers, but primarily for monastic communities. The ordinary Christian (layman and cleric) had all but stopped consuming texts.[14] Between the seventh and eleventh centuries, the saint's biography was written not to convince a skeptical or semipagan audience, but to glorify a venerated protector whose sanctity was not doubted by the community, to serve as part of the liturgy, and to place a particular ecclesiastical community within the sacred history of divine grace.[15]

The fact that religious texts were primarily intended for monastic communities does not mean they were without effect outside the monastery. The saints venerated by the laity in the early Middle Ages were for the most part martyrs from the first years of Christianity.[16] The common people obtained basic information from specialists on the saints in question. Granted, sometimes these people developed a cult of "popular" saints whose sainthood the elite did not recognize; but in general they had no reason to attach themselves to unauthorized saints, since saints "authorized" and endorsed by the religious and political elite fit the bill perfectly. Monks, guardians of the holy relics—and themselves semimagical figures—gave the local relic or location of the cult an identity that inscribed them within ecclesiastical time and space. But that identity remained fairly vague for most consumers. For the monks, the authors and readers of saints' narratives, their content was more or less standard: a detailed history and edification—moral Christian messages. The peasants were less clear about the saint's character and curriculum vitae. In addition to the fact that peasants could not read the full narratives in Latin, the saint's life had no importance for the practice of his cult. Even when artistic representations of the saint happened to be placed at the cult site, it is very doubtful that the complex symbolism and the allusions to written texts had much significance for ordinary consumers. Often they would create an alternative saint for themselves from the fragments that had come down to them, rearranged by creative misunderstanding and wishful thinking. This alternative saint was different from the monks' saint. The popular saint was not the complete, more or less well-balanced saint of the scholarly texts. He did not always have a beginning, middle, or end, and his different parts were not necessarily well proportioned. Above all, he was not an educator or aspirant for perfection but a healer and fixer. All the other elements of his personality were secondary.[17]

The cult of relics and of holy places does not require an elaborate corpus of narratives, or in any case not a corpus of "historical" narratives that relate with precision how the holiness of the place or person developed. The consumers of holy powers do not need detailed knowledge about the *source* of power, just as in general we do not seek to learn the biography of our physician before seeking his advice, or even worry very much about his formal professional credentials. The plate affixed to his door, the certificate on the wall of his office, and his reputation are all we need. Some of the information transmitted between various kinds of consumers and impresarios of the saint was of that order. The saint had a label ("martyr," "confessor," "ascetic," "apostle"), a general description ("expert in fertility miracles," "spiteful and vindictive," "compassionate to sinful women"), and some exemplary miracles to his credit. In place of a certificate on the wall, there were conventional signs (a "typical" architecture designated a holy place even if the source of its holiness remained unknown; the many candles and ex-votos proved that the saint was active and successful). Other consumers constituted an important part of the decor. They confirmed that the place or saint had established a consensus. Everyone wants to eat at a crowded restaurant. Having often visited modern cult sites, both Christian and Jewish, I have noted that most of their consumers have an extremely imprecise, and sometimes even erroneous, knowledge of the saint whose favors they are soliciting. Even when they can easily obtain more extensive information (from books or from experts), they rarely do so. When there are conversations about the saint at the site, they almost always have to do with his powers and not his biography.[18]

But though a cult does not require complex narratives to thrive, such narratives do sometimes surface. They grow in size and significance when there is a community to make use of them. Contrary to the widespread view that saints' Lives are a propagandistic genre created by the elite but destined for the people (its "opiate"), it appears that biographies written before the twelfth century were destined primarily for the psychological—not just liturgical—benefit of the elite. The saints' stories allowed the educated people to digest more easily the wilder aspects of the cult of saints. The cult may strike the learned spectator as uncivilized and pagan, but in the written texts the "true" saint emerges. There the educated monk could find a more palatable saint and an explanation for the cult that he could live with. The written text often arrived *post factum.* A cult could exist for many long years without the faithful knowing anything more about the saint than his name. In an active cult, the dialogue between the saint and his clientele always takes place in the present: the past matters little. A saint who does not act now is not really a saint. The learned could not accept such an empirical and ahistorical attitude. The saints' stories "saved" the saint for the learned while redefining the popular cult as a corruption of an imaginary purity that existed only on parchment.[19]

The widespread phenomenon of attributing one saint's biography to another saint obviously expressed the intellectual's profound need to legitimate the popular cult by applying it to a "saint," even if that saint was totally synthetic. When the scholar encountered a cult without a biography, in which the saint was no more than a name or a collection of miraculous accounts, she attempted to find biographical details about the object of the cult. If she did not succeed, he could assimilate the anonymous saint with a saint whose biography was known—Q.E.D.![20] The fact that the biography had no empirically demonstrable relation to the cult was unimportant. The purpose of the biography was to make the saint follow canonical rules, not to establish historical truth.

Although the didactic potential of saints' Lives did not escape the attention of the elite when the cult of saints emerged in the fourth century, only gradually was it exploited in the West in a systematic way. Before it could use the saint's story to shape public opinion, the ecclesiastical elite had to persuade itself that the public was worth convincing. The church shifted from the passive mode (it is futile to try to change the world; it is enough that the world does not change us) to active (it is our duty to re-create the world in our shape and image). That evolution came about between the tenth and thirteenth centuries. The first signs of it can be seen in the reform movement of Benedictine monasticism identified with Cluny. The movement did not initially seek to call into question the social division of labor; on the contrary, it aimed to make sure that monastic communities were truly pure, as those whose virtues are in the service of society as a whole must be. The reformers also wanted to make the secular clergy more "regular" in order to make the whole church a true spiritual elite. Monks had to return to the strict observance of the Benedictine rule (note the redefinition of the present as the corruption of an ideal fabricated after the fact), and the clergy had to practice celibacy and reject simony.

The monastic reform rapidly spilled out into the world, that is, into secular society. In the late tenth century, monks, and the churchmen who supported them, organized the movement known as "Peace of God," whose aim was to reduce violence in society by declaring some of its elements—churchmen, merchants, peasants—protected by God and his saints. In the eleventh century, the reform faction took over the papacy and became involved in the struggle against the emperor for the right to name the bishops (the so-called Investiture Contest). The papacy emerged victorious: from a modest institution with essentially symbolic preeminence, it became the true ruler of a unified hierarchy throughout Europe and a major player in international politics. By the twelfth century, the division of labor holding sway in the early Middle Ages had disappeared. The new ecclesiastical elite, with the pope at its head, was up to its neck in the affairs of this world, from calls for a crusade to matters relating to marriage, which the church now annexed to the spiritual sphere. Monks did not lock themselves in their monasteries; they were advisers, polemicists, and leaders.

Eleventh-century reformers criticized their predecessors for having become too involved in the affairs of this world. That reproach appears paradoxical, since they themselves were much more involved in the politics and
economics of their time than their predecessors. But it was not paradoxical
in their own eyes: unlike their predecessors, who were involved in a world
whose rules they accepted, the new men were setting the rules—or so they
claimed. With this new conception of itself, the ecclesiastical elite had
come to grant increasing importance to the church's pastoral role. Education was its chief weapon. Since the church had chosen not to arm itself, it
could influence only those who believed in the force of its spiritual sanctions. Whenever it wanted to extend its power, it had to educate new
publics and reeducate old ones. In the early stage of the ecclesiastical revolution, between the eleventh and twelfth centuries, the elite sought primarily to reeducate the warrior class, from the local lord to the emperor. Warriors were a physical and social threat to the clergy. With the aim of
reeducating these warriors, the church took on the task of creating a new
ideal type, the Christian knight, defender of widows and orphans. Armed
with narratives, images, and sermons, the church strove to move warriors
from a culture of shame to a culture of guilt. In other words, it tried to
persuade members of the ruling class to fear God and his secret agent in
the soul (the conscience) more than the mockery and contempt of their
peers. That pedagogical project was only a partial success. It took many
years to break the old habits of the warrior class.

While trying to reeducate the ruling class, the church collided with an
unanticipated factor, the "common people." The "common people"—
those good asses grazing peacefully beside the oxen—came on the scene in
the eleventh century, brayed, kicked, and made mischief. The world had
changed. The huge demographic boom of the eleventh century came with
a revolution in agricultural techniques that allowed medieval society to
produce enough food to feed more mouths and still produce a surplus.
The resumption of trade favored the circulation of merchants, products,
and ideas on the roads of Europe. Everywhere, old structures were being
undermined. New urban centers and new needs produced unprecedented
modes of life and thought. The asses awakened from their torpor. It was

not so much hunger that gnawed away at them as a thirst for new pleasures and new freedoms.

When in 1095 Pope Urban II summoned Christian knights to go and free Jerusalem and the Holy Sepulcher from the infidels, the "common" people arrived en masse, uninvited, to participate in the First Crusade. They left their manor without permission and filled the roads to old and new pilgrimage sites. They formed confraternities to engage in religious activity outside the church. More seriously, they were increasingly drawn to charismatic preachers, who often criticized the church for the fruits it had reaped—power and wealth—in its battle against the secular elite. These attacks did great damage, especially since they based their criticism on the Sermon on the Mount and the Acts of the Apostles, sacred texts conceived in a different world for a different society. It had taken centuries of exegesis to take the edge off the Sermon on the Mount and to legitimate power not only in the world to come but also in the world here below. It turned out that the old raw texts had not lost their power. Since it was not possible to disregard the sacred texts, the only solution open to the church was to wage an all-out war on anyone who seemed to be calling into question the *magisterium*. The church had a monopoly on the interpretation of scripture. Anyone who said differently was a heretic. Heretics were not just political opponents and theological rivals. They were antisocial elements who sought to destroy everything that was good and decent.[21] The evil intentions and horrors attributed to the heretics (they ate excrement, engaged in sexual debauchery, practiced homosexuality, cannibalism, and infanticide, and secretly fomented the destruction of society in the service of the devil) combined a cynical strategy aimed at wiping out a dangerous rival and real anxiety about a threat that was at least partly imaginary.[22]

Between the eleventh and thirteenth centuries, the papacy was the most audacious innovator in religious matters. More than once it was the church and not those it accused of heresy that abandoned the earlier ways and redefined the notions of "faith" and orthodoxy, supposedly in the name of tradition. The actions of the church took the form of revolution disguised as conservatism, both in the Investiture Contest and in the war against heresy. In both cases its sociopolitical interests were camouflaged behind a doctrinaire religious rhetoric. These two conflicts were not of the same nature, however. The Investiture Contest was essentially an internal quarrel about the division of powers within the elite, though with repercussions for other parts of the population, especially the new bourgeoisie. The war against heresy was, at least initially, a battle of the elite against the new masses, especially in the towns. It should not be surprising to discover that the secular authorities generally collaborated with the church to suppress heresy, even at the height of their own struggle against church authorities. Fear of the common enemy was greater than mutual hostility.

The effort to prevent the new masses from forming anti-ecclesiastical associations was not necessarily antagonistic in nature. Along with the stick—persecutory legislation, Inquisitorial courts, massacres—the church also used a carrot: a growing awareness of the spiritual needs of religious consumers. The asses demanded more and better spiritual hay, and the church procured it for them by the same means it had previously used for the political elite: education and propaganda. How was one to educate the masses, primarily city dwellers, whose political and economic importance was increasing? The church conducted a threefold policy: it created new monastic orders, encouraged preaching tailor-made for the different strata of the population, and increasingly intervened in the most popular religious practice of believers, the cult of saints. These three orientations were not unrelated.

Religious orders—a network of communities obeying not only a single rule but also a single central authority—were a relatively new phenomenon in the West. A Benedictine "order" appeared in the tenth century, with the creation of a chain of "reformed" abbeys that accepted the authority of the abbot of Cluny. Centralization was one of the means used by followers of the monastic reform to augment their power. Because of its conservatism and its tendency to separate monks from the world, the Benedictine rule—the only one that had enjoyed official recognition in the West since the ninth century—did not satisfy the new needs. The more monks strove to follow the rule scrupulously, the less they could be involved in pastoral activity.[23] In the eleventh century, communities of canons regular who followed the Augustinian rule (a new rule attributed to Saint Augustine) began to form in the West. For the most part, these priest-monks operated in the cities and offered religious services to the new urban communities.[24] Simultaneously, a new eremitic movement was emerging in Europe.

Initially these anchorites, whose numbers had swelled, lived on the margins of society without submitting to any rule. They preached and practiced a "wild" asceticism like the desert fathers in the East. Unlike Benedictine monks, the hermits were not confined to a fixed place, nor were they committed to serve a given community, as were Augustinian canons. Moreover, the hermits were not obliged to pass through the filter of the Benedictine novitiate, which tended to rein in or even punish any behavior outside the norm. They were idiosyncratic charismatics who disregarded propriety and good manners. The new masses, hungry for immediate religious experiences and charismatic leadership, were drawn to these men, whether they were "orthodox" or "heterodox." Although they remained a relatively small group, these medieval hermits, with an ambiguous status and an elastic code of behavior, played a prominent role in the social transformations of the time. They were, like "wild" ascetics everywhere, the experimental laboratory of the church: they experimented with new types of behavior and congregations, and with new types of dialogue with the community. If they turned out to be a nuisance, they were fairly easy to disband or to force to toe the line. An eremitic phase often served as a springboard for more regulated forms of religious organization. The "wild" hermits were often hard to distinguish on the outside from heretics. There was one clear sign of their orthodoxy, however: they remained loyal to the pope.[25]

Benedictine monks were the avant-garde of the religious and social movements of the eleventh century. The twelfth century was a time of socio-religious experimentation in which canons and hermits played a crucial role—canons by working within the community, hermits by placing asceticism and charisma once more at the forefront.[26] But neither was equipped to serve as the avant-garde in a medieval society that had reached its maturity. It took a combination of the two. These were the Mendicant orders.[27]

Like all members of religious orders, the Mendicants, chiefly Franciscans, Dominicans, Carmelites, and Augustinian friars, took a vow of individual poverty, but in addition they made the commitment not to accumulate property as a community. They made their living through manual labor and begging. They moved from place to place, preached, and offered their example and spiritual services, especially in the cities. Unlike the "wild" hermits, however, the Mendicants did not constitute an undisciplined, decentralized element. Mendicant friars were characterized by scrupulous obedience to their superiors and to the pope and by strict observance of the rule. The Mendicants resembled the heretical movements in that they provided a literal interpretation of the apostolic ideal, especially with regard to "apostolic poverty," but unlike heretics, the friars refrained from criticizing the church for not sharing their ascetic practices. The papacy saw the huge potential of a centralized, obedient group that retained many of the attractive traits of charismatic asceticism which had served heretics so well in their struggle against the church. The Mendicants were effective anti-heresy fighters. The papacy hastened to grant them its support and protection. Between the beginning of the thirteenth century and the Reformation, they fulfilled essential functions in all areas of religious life and in all ranks of Christian society, from the papal court and the universities to the streets of cities and towns.

The Mendicants became the authorized agents of the papacy. Their mode of life disputed the validity of the heretics' propaganda: moral purity and asceticism did not necessarily imply rejection of the papacy. On the contrary, it was possible to be an ascetic and a saint while remaining a faithful son of the Church of Rome. But in the war against heresy it was not enough to preach by example. One had to preach by the word, to convince the undecided. The Mendicants preached well, and they preached a great deal. Their preaching attained a scope that had no precedent in the history of the West.

Preaching is one of the duties of the bishop, the spiritual pastor of his flock. Every bishop was obliged to preach a sermon on Sundays and major feast days. Since the bishop sometimes had trouble getting to all the churches of his diocese and was sometimes away, he was allowed to authorize priests to preach in his place. Most of the bishops were very busy people who did little preaching and did not concern themselves with training replacements. This was not simply a logistical problem. The bishops preached little because they did not think that an ordinary believer truly needed systematic instruction in religious matters. During the early Middle Ages only a small minority of believers had the privilege of hearing a real sermon. This state of affairs began to change in the eleventh century, when itinerant preachers—heretics and hermits for the most part—addressed communities directly, bypassing the bishops.[28] The secular clergy proved incapable of keeping up with them.

That would be the job of the Mendicant orders. The friars preached in an orderly manner in the churches associated with them and also wherever they happened to be. Preaching occupied a central place in the life of the Dominican order, as its official name, the Order of Preaching Brothers (*Ordo fratrum praedicatorum*), attests. But preaching also played an important role in the lives of the other Mendicant orders. The preachers inculcated the elements of the true faith in their listeners, promised reward and punishment after death, and warned against heresy.

Rewriting Saints' Lives

The orders that saw preaching as their essential mission began to take an interest in preaching techniques and preaching aids, from model sermons to concordances designed to facilitate the search for pertinent verses.[29] The Mendicant friars understood the important role that narrative can play in popular preaching. Abstract didactic messages were not easy to assimilate. They were boring and repetitive; they called for obedience; they spoke to the intellect and not the heart. The new preachers sought to sugarcoat the bitter pill of obedience and doctrinal purity with amusing narratives. The use of brief moral narratives (exempla) had a long tradition in the Christian world. On several occasions Gregory the Great mentioned the tremendous rhetorical power of the exemplum, and other authors followed his lead, at least in their declarations of principle. Exempla could be found here and there in the ninth and tenth centuries. But it was only when the awareness of the audience's needs and sensibilities developed—that is, in the tenth and eleventh centuries—that the exemplum became a central element of medieval literature. In the twelfth century, the Latin *exemplum* entered the French vernacular as *essample*, evidence of the growing importance of that literary genre in medieval culture.[30] What constitutes the effective exemplum? Which narratives are likely to serve both playful and didactic ends at once? Some of the narratives came from popular culture, folktales, and the oral tradition. They had only to be adapted to the preachers' educational needs. The new preachers proved to be surprisingly receptive to materials "from below."[31] But folk materials were not always easy to adapt. There was, however, a ready-made corpus of narratives that was just begging to be put to use in the church's educational program: saints' stories.[32]

The cult of saints was perhaps the most important form of religious activity for the laity; certainly it was the most popular. Anyone seeking to influence the religious practice of medieval laymen had to have control, or at least a certain influence, over the cult of saints. In the twelfth century, and even more clearly in the thirteenth, the church intervened in the cult in three different ways: first, it created the control mechanism known as "canonization," whose objective was to submit candidates for sainthood to strict quality tests;[33] second, it promoted the veneration of certain saints, both canonized and uncanonized, over others, in an effort to encourage models of sainthood that it approved of; and third, it encouraged the rewriting of the hagiographical corpus for popular use. Since most laymen could not read, the way to reach them was by creating collections of saints' Lives that could be used as materials for preaching. This was done particularly by members of the Mendicant orders.[34]

The project of restructuring the West's hagiographical narrative corpus for educational use obliged churchmen to take two opposing approaches. Ancient saints constituted excellent raw material. Since it was the church that brought them to the community's attention, it could ascribe to them words and feats that fitted its purpose. The trouble with ancient saints was that they were passé. They had lived in the remote past; their acts, wondrous as the clerical imagination made them, belonged to a fabulous world totally different from the present one. They were admirable but hard to imitate. The modern saint—the one who still lived in the community or who had only recently died—was more useful in the war against the heretics: the modern saint knew heretics personally and, in plain view of everyone, defied them through his mode of life or his words. He resembled the people around him but was different enough to prove that the Holy Spirit was still active in the church. He might be less awe inspiring than the ancient saint, but he was probably more likely to be emulated.

The ecclesiastical elite fished in both ponds, the ancient and the new. It neglected a good number of Merovingian, Carolingian, and Ottonian saints, the memory of whom was preserved in Benedictine monasteries. Either it did not find material about them especially inspiring, or these saints too vividly represented the ideals of the premonastic reform era, an era which was still threatening to the new elite. But the compilation of ancient saints' legends and the composition of modern saints' Lives were encouraged. This entailed, first, translating and adapting the stories of martyrs and monks that arrived primarily from Byzantium, and second, developing a genre of "realistic" hagiography of modern saints.[35]

For a modern saint's biography to be effective, readers—that is, educated people—had to be convinced that its subject was truly a saint. This could not be done by parading hagiographical clichés. After all, educated readers had often used those very clichés themselves. For readers, then, a more elaborate image had to be constructed, with a sufficient dose of shadow and nuance apt to lend credence to the narrative.[36] Conversely, to gain influence over an *uneducated* audience, the complex nuanced structure of the scholarly biography had to be broken down and simplified, made more striking and more didactic. In their complete and "pure" form, hagiographical Latin texts were designed for the elite that had written them. But the common man needed a *Reader's Digest,* or rather a *Listener's Di-*

gest, version. The modern saint of the original version was simplified, stripped of the doubts and human defects that made him "real" in the eyes of the learned. The narratives were reduced to the essential: a set of edifying clichés, exempla.[37]

In the thirteenth century a new "canon"—a *commune sanctorum*—was created. By the end of the century, when this process was complete, the ecclesiastical "impresarios" were seeking to impose the new corpus on the cult of saints. The principal objective of the saints' stories had always been to calm the doubts that the elite harbored about the cult of saints. But beginning in the twelfth century, the elite ceased to produce them solely to ease its own theological anxiety. The elite now turned outward, toward the masses, intending to persuade them that the narrative preceded the cult rather than the reverse. Didactic narratives placed the emphasis on the saint's morality and integrity, and presented her magical power as an external, relatively negligible manifestation of her virtues.[38] What made someone a saint in God's eyes were her virtues. A person could be a friend of God and still not perform miracles. Conversely, many miracle workers were not saints, and their power came from an impure source. The church never tired of telling believers that miracles were not the most reliable expression of sainthood but rather one of its least reliable manifestations. The cult itself was presented primarily as an act of recognition of a person's virtues, not as a contract with a patron for the exchange of material and spiritual goods.

It is difficult to judge the success of the church's effort to control the cult of saints. On the one hand, the cult did not become disciplined or centralized, as church authorities wished. People venerated dubious saints and refused to venerate very good ones—from the hierarchy's point of view, that is. Often they persisted in drawing the wrong conclusions from perfectly good exempla. Even today the cult of saints remains a phenomenon that is difficult to control. It was even more so in the Middle Ages. On the other hand, the cult did become subject to the elite's way of thinking as never before, for now the authorities were shaping the cult not just by controlling access to relics or sites but by making saints' stories so popular and omnipresent. The story did not totally take over the cult of the saints, but it became an inseparable part of it.

From the thirteenth century on, hagiography enjoyed a popular success similar to what the cult of saints had enjoyed since the fourth century. After holy scripture, the most popular work in the Middle Ages and the early modern period was a collection of saints' Lives known as *The Golden Legend*, written by Jacobus de Voragine. Stories of new saints, as well as new versions of ancient saints' histories, became part of the cultural heritage of the West. Saints took on very distinct features. One could say that the western Christian pantheon took shape in the thirteenth century. Saints' Lives became a unifying element, at least at the cultural level: throughout Europe, people knew the same legends, and the same artistic illustrations of the same popular saints could be found everywhere.[39] Even the Reformation, which to a large degree managed to eliminate the cult of saints, did not succeed in obliterating saints' stories. They have remained popular in the modern secular world, which has renounced almost all other aspects of medieval religion.

But let us not be deceived by the great success of the church's educational project. Granted, the narratives enjoyed enormous popularity, but in what measure did they transmit the messages they were supposed to transmit? It seems that success in that regard was only partial. Sometimes the medium prevailed over the message. How many times did listeners swallow the juicy narrative fruit and spit out the dry, but all-important, moral stone? Too often listeners enjoyed all the wrong things: they were more delighted with the horrifying descriptions of the tortures endured by the saint, for example, than with his faith in Jesus. More significant was the profound ambivalence that could be detected not simply among consumers of the narratives but in the narratives themselves. Several of the most popular stories in the new corpus conveyed very ambiguous messages from the church's standpoint and even from a social perspective. But it may be precisely the ability to express ambiguous messages that was and still is the secret behind the power of the cult of saints and of saints' stories. In the religious sphere, drugs without side effects are ineffective.

We shall next examine a few of the most popular saints' stories, almost all of them set in the mythical golden age of the great persecutions, though they became popular in the late Middle Ages. But first let us pause to consider two biographies of "modern" saints—Saint Francis of Assisi and his disciple, Fra Ginepro. The biography of Saint Francis of Assisi, founder of the Order of Friars Minor, better known as the Franciscan order, is one of the most famous saints' Lives of the Middle Ages. Francis, an astonishing mix of naïveté and shrewdness, conservatism and innovation, lived his life as if he were preparing a series of exempla for believers. He had a very clear awareness of the considerable importance of saints' Lives, and he shaped his own to constitute the ideal *Vita*. And in fact his Life—or rather his Lives, since there were several—were an enormous success, so much so that they shattered his order and caused the church itself to tremble on its foundations.

TEN

Francis of Assisi,
a Joyful Ascetic

S AINT FRANCIS OF ASSISI (1181–1226) was one of the most influential
leaders of the cultural revolution of the twelfth and thirteenth centuries. He founded the first and most popular of the Mendicant orders,
helped make popular preaching a central element of the church's program
of action, and served as a catalyst in the great resurgence of hagiography in
the late Middle Ages. To a significant degree, the saint's enormous popularity can be attributed to his willingness to take risks and to place some of
the most radical ideas of his age in the service of the church. Francis proposed a religious model that suited the most dynamic element of society,
members of the new urban classes (he was a cloth merchant before his conversion). Franciscan spirituality was founded on individual experience, not
ritual, on heroic action and personal expression, not on collective discipline
and inactive contemplation—*theoria*. Like other reformers of the time, he
legitimated religious innovation by presenting it as a reconstruction of the
mythical past (the apostolic life), but he also called for a bold return to the
very source of all authority, to Christ, thus bypassing, at least implicitly,
everything that stood in the way. It was now time to *imitate* Christ. Imitation for Francis meant direct, almost instinctive contact, not careful, re-

sponsible interpretation. This was dangerous stuff. That is why it was so powerful.

Francis blurred the boundaries between the religious and the profane worlds by creating a loose-knit community, like an eremitic band: in Francis's day, Franciscans traveled in pairs, without supervision; they had no buildings, and friars who felt that their superiors were not strictly observing the rule were expressly told to disobey them. Francis recruited laypeople without serious examination and without a novitiate. He bestowed the right to preach on uneducated laymen. Francis himself deliberately refused to be ordained and remained a deacon. His men often dressed in rags that bore little resemblance to habits and wore deliberately small tonsures.

The combination of radical ideas and institutional vagueness came dangerously close to the profile of heretical movements. In 1184, barely twenty-five years before the founding of the Franciscan order, Pope Lucius III had denounced the Waldensian movement as heretical. Its notions were relatively orthodox, and its founder, Waldo, was willing to proclaim his total fidelity to Catholic doctrine.[1] What had changed between 1184 and 1209 was not lay attitudes but papal *Realpolitik*. The urban classes were still seeking outlets for their religious aspirations, but if in the twelfth century the curia had believed that these new aspirations could be dismissed out of hand, by the thirteenth it realized they could not. The Waldensians were told to choose a recognized monastic rule and give up popular preaching. They could not be both inside and outside the church. The Waldensians refused. Unfortunately, papal denunciations and excommunications failed to stop them. In the two generations that followed their denunciation by the pope, they became a real presence in the new urban centers, increasingly critical of the hierarchy.

In the early thirteenth century, under Pope Innocent III, the church, having reached the pinnacle of its political power, realized its weaknesses—the many Waldensians were not going to disappear just because they were ordered to do so—and its strengths: it was powerful enough to try radical solutions. The church needed to fight fire with fire. It needed its own

"Waldensians," like Barbarian garrisons stationed on the *limes* to stop waves of new, more dangerous Barbarians. The church was now strong enough—in the pope's opinion at least—to absorb the subversive force of its new recruits. Francis and his small band of brothers were received into the church more or less on their own conditions, with a very different rule from the other monastic rules in force up to that time, a rule much more problematic from the perspective of church discipline.

Most historians consider Innocent III's welcoming of the Franciscans into the ranks of the church a stroke of genius. In many respects, that is an apt judgment. The Franciscans and the other Mendicant orders that soon followed played a prominent role in the battle for the hearts of the new masses. But the service they rendered may have come at a high price. At first the threat to the authorities was only indirect: Francis of Assisi's companions seemed to respect the church's doctrine and institutions. But without explicitly refuting its teaching—that mere mortals were incapable of imitating the life of Christ and his apostles—the Franciscans showed by example that the apostolic life was possible here and now. The Franciscans embodied the greatest hope of the thirteenth century. If it was possible to live the Sermon on the Mount, to live the life of the apostles, then surely the Second Coming was imminent. The sense that they had of abolishing the intermediary and reestablishing contact with the source had strong eschatological implications. Saint Francis was perceived as a second Jesus. Like Christ, he had managed to overcome man's sinful nature and to recover the primal innocence of Adam before the Fall. He was no longer just another monk imitating Jesus, on an onerous and ultimately absurd mission, but an extraordinary messianic figure who had actually achieved that imitation. He was a second Christ, of the same form as Christ (*conformis Christi*).[2]

Francis's status as "alter Christus" was reinforced about two years before his death. In September 1224, after a long period of isolation and contemplation on Mount La Verna, Francis had a vision of a seraph bearing the semblance of the crucified Jesus. The seraph hovered above the saint, filling him with anguish and joy. When the seraph disappeared, Francis discovered bleeding wounds on his hands, feet, and side. In the center of the wounds on his hands and feet were also excrescences, black and rounded like nail heads. On the other side they looked like bent nails flattened by hammer blows. Francis now bore the stigmata of the living God on his flesh—the first human being found worthy of such an honor.

According to contemporary sources, the saint, in his modesty, attempted to conceal the miracle. He covered his hands and his feet with bandages. But the blood constantly staining his shirt and his bandages awakened the suspicions of some of his close friends. Finally, the saint revealed the truth to them, provided they not divulge it during his lifetime.[3] Despite the prohibition, rumors of the miracle spread among the members of the order. On the day Francis died, the whispers became an uproar. In a letter sent to every member of the order, Francis's successor, Brother Elia, described the stigmata in the most solemn terms and with the deepest emotion: "I bring you joyous tidings, a new thing among miracles, a sign never seen before except on the son of God, Christ the Lord. Shortly before his death, our brother and father was seen crucified, bearing on his flesh five wounds, the stigmata of Christ. On both hands and feet, signs resembling nail holes appeared, with the scars and imprint of the nails still on them. His side seemed to have been pierced by a lance and frequently bled."[4]

Not only had the Franciscans managed to live like the apostles, but they also had a leader who was like Christ.[5] This was not imitation but conformity (*conformitas* had a much stronger sense than it does today, signifying participation in the essence). Since someone had appeared on earth whom Christ himself had accepted as a faithful reproduction of the original, why did his disciples have to accept the superiority of a "vicar"? At most, the pope enjoyed a technical superiority. There was no need for a frontal attack on the Church of Rome and on the pope. Like the Roman Empire at the time of Christ, the Roman Church in Francis's time was an instrument in God's hands. Although rebellion was forbidden, it was important to keep in mind the distinction between what was Caesar's and what was God's. Francis expressed that conviction in his most radical text, the spiritual testament he wrote shortly before his death in 1226:

And then God gave me—and still gives me—such a great faith in the priests who observe the way of life of the Holy Roman Church by virtue of their ordination that I will turn to them if they persecute me. And had I the wisdom of Solomon and found priests wicked sons of this world in the parishes where they dwell, I would not preach against their will. These priests, and all the other [priests], I will fear, love, and respect as my masters. And I will not seek out their sins, for I see the son of God in them, and they are my masters. And I do it not because I see the eminent Son in their flesh in this world, but because I see in it the image of the most sacred body and the most sacred blood, which they receive and which they alone transmit to others [the Eucharist].

And after God gave me brothers, no one guided me, no one told me what had to be done. It is the supreme God himself who revealed to me that I was to live the life of the Holy Gospel, and that is what I dictated, simply and in few words, and the lord pope confirmed it for me.

I urgently order all my brothers, by virtue of the vow of obedience, that wherever they are, they dare not request any letter from the Roman curia, either personally or through an intermediary, either for a church or for some other edifice, either in the guise of a sermon or because their body is being persecuted, but that they flee any place where they are not welcome and go into another country, and do penance with God's blessing.

And if there are any among them who would not perform their duties according to the rule, or would wish to deviate from them in any other manner, or would not be Catholic, all brothers, wherever they may be, are required, by virtue of the vow of obedience, should they find one of these sinful brothers, to bring him before the custodian of the place where they are, and the custodian is urgently required, by virtue of the vow of obedience, to watch him conscientiously, as if he were bound day and night, so that he cannot escape until he has been handed over to the minister general [*minister*]. And the minister general is urgently required, by virtue of the vow of obedience, to place him in the hands of the brothers, who will watch him night and day, as if he were bound, until he is placed in the hands of Monsignor Cardinal of Ostia, who is the master, the protector, and the corrector of that brotherhood.

And to all my brothers, priests and laymen, I urgently order, by virtue of the vow of obedience, that you not add interpretations to the rule or to these words saying, "This is how they must be understood." But since God had me say and write the rule and these words simply and purely, it is thus that they must be understood, simply and without interpretation. And follow them with a sacred zeal to the end. And all who observe them will be rewarded in heaven by the blessing of the supreme Father, and on earth by the blessing of his beloved Son and of the mediating Holy Spirit, and by the blessing of all the heavenly powers and all the saints. And I, Brother Francis, your humble servant, confirm that sacred blessing to those of you inside and to those of you outside, as much as it is in my power. Amen.[6]

In the first paragraph Francis explains that, unlike heretics, he fully accepts the authority of Catholic priests. But he adds in the same breath that the only reason for his respect is, in a sense, technical: ordination confers on priests alone the power to bring Christ back to this world through the Eucharistic miracle. There is nothing positive about the priests, therefore. The ones he mentions are wretched persecutors devoid of all charisma. Francis *does not want* to preach against them. He wants to love and respect them. Why? Because that is his will.

In the second paragraph Francis explains that he sees the church as an instrument. It is God alone who revealed to Francis how he ought to live; the pope only confirmed for Francis what was at every level a fait accompli. (Could the pope have failed to obey God?) The prohibition—which has no legal foundation—on asking the pope for privileges, even to prevent an injustice or to obtain what is needed to serve the church's interests, also attests that Francis considered the church a source of impurity from which he sought to protect his order. That attitude is further accentuated in the paragraph concerning the deviant elements within the order. Francis describes a mechanism designed to drive rebels into outer darkness, the world of reality and compromise represented by the cardinal protector and the curia. It seems that the cardinal protector is less the overseer of the order than its agent and liaison officer. Finally, in the last paragraph Francis expresses great distrust toward textual interpretation, the cornerstone of the church's power. He seeks to prevent the interpreters from giving new meanings to his texts (the rule and the testament). By commanding that the two documents always be read together, Francis tries to impose his noninterpretive interpretation on posterity. But something much more radical can be glimpsed behind that invitation to interpretive restraint. After all, the New Testament was also written with simplicity and purity, and it too was dictated by God. Might the ecclesiastical interpreters be distorting its messages with their glosses, as they threatened to do to Francis's rule and testament?

That was all very troubling. No one thought that Francis was a heretical wolf in saintly sheep's clothing. As far as we know, he himself sincerely thought that it was possible to reconcile formal obedience to and respect for the church with the radical implications of his words (and acts). The church was much less certain, especially since Francis of Assisi had a considerable number of followers ready to draw the most unpleasant conclusions from his words. The church refrained from attacking Francis directly. It preferred to cover him with authoritative interpretations. About four years after the saint's death, a bull (*Quo elongati*) declared his testament legally void. After that, Pope Nicholas III offered the "correct" interpretation of the Franciscan rule in the bull *Exiit qui seminat* (1279). The papacy demanded that the order fall into line in terms of its organization: that it regulate the admission of aspirants, reduce the number of laymen within the order, live in convents, and own property. Since this was an abomination in Francis's eyes, the order's property was defined as belonging to the church so that the appearance of collective poverty would be preserved. In addition to the technical problems raised by the order, there was its enormous prestige, especially the fact that it constituted an "apostolic" alternative to the Church of Rome. The church had to make the Franciscans less holy by imposing compromises and materialism on them and by stressing the gap between their lofty ideals and their less than lofty behavior. That process, already begun during Francis's lifetime, accelerated after his death. The popes granted many privileges to the order and, contrary to its founder's explicit wishes, made its members participate in the church's governance: political (as bishops, advisers, and cardinals), legal (as inquisitors and papal judges), and intellectual (as university professors). Those who did not want to compromise were forced to do so.[7]

A series of crises ensued, both within the order and between it and the papacy. In the end it was the church that prevailed. In becoming institutionalized, Franciscan charisma lost a great deal of its power; the "carrots" of power and wealth had had an impact even before the papal "stick" was brandished. Nevertheless, to deliver the deathblow to the Franciscans' claim to a distinct moral status within the church, the papacy ultimately did resort to the stick. During the first half of the fourteenth century, John XXII systematically attacked the Franciscan notions of poverty through a series of papal bulls. Those who refused to compromise were condemned as heretics and persecuted by their more accommodating brethren, among others. The more moderate brothers diluted their idealist wine with a great deal of pragmatic water. The Franciscans' radicalism cooled. The ideological threat of the movement waned until it no longer constituted a threat at all. The papacy demonstrated that, taken literally, the apostolic life was impossible, even harmful. The Franciscans ceased to be serious candidates for the role of the spiritual angelic order prophesied by Joachim, the great seer of Fiore in the twelfth century,[8] and became one order among others. Several women in rival orders received stigmata, which put an end to Francis of Assisi's singularity. Meanwhile, scandals linked to the order's name stripped away what little prestige it still enjoyed.

The definitive decline of the Franciscan order in the fourteenth century put an end to the course of events Innocent III had initiated in the early thirteenth. To a certain extent that process can be considered a victory for the church: the essential threat represented by popular heresy had been warded off. Heretics had not completely disappeared, of course, but by the beginning of the fourteenth century, it seemed that the church no longer needed to reach compromises with radical elements in order to deal adequately with them. But bringing the Franciscans into line came with a price tag. What the church gained in discipline, it lost in enthusiasm. The posthumous defeat of the *Poverello* of Assisi was accompanied by widespread disillusionment, cynicism, and a loss of confidence in the church and its leaders. The domestication of the Franciscans with everything they represented played a major role in the radical devaluation of the church's status during the late Middle Ages.

In the battle waged over the definition of the Franciscan ideal, the founder's biography likewise played a key role. It illustrated the growing value of narrative in the cult of saints while also contributing greatly to that value. For Francis's admirers, his acts, even the most mundane and seemingly trivial ones, were no less significant than his miracles were—perhaps more significant, in fact. The cult of Francis was manifestly that of a living saint and was not linked to miraculous relics. Great supernatural powers were attributed to Francis, as they were to other important saints, but his greatest work, in his own eyes and in those of his admirers, was his life itself.

The precedence given to the quality of one's life over one's miracles was part of the church's educational effort, designed to change the cult of saints by establishing a necessary connection between power (given to both saints and nonsaints) and the moral right to power (granted exclusively to saints). But the centrality of action also reflected a change in the perception of the saint's spirituality. That spirituality came to be closely linked to the idea of conversion not simply as a turning away from "the world" but as an inner transubstantiation that allowed the saint to move in the world with a sense of real freedom: the freedom to act without precedents or reflection. An expression of this change can be found in the first sentences of the testament: "God allowed me, Brother Francis, to begin my repentance in this way: when I lived in sin, seeing lepers was a very bitter experience for me. God himself guided me into their midst and among them I performed acts of charity. What appeared bitter to me became sweetness of soul and body. After that, I stayed with them briefly and then I left the world."[9]

Francis does not begin his testament by describing his worldview or by giving a chronological account of his path to God. He does not invoke the famous scene in which he undressed before the bishop of Assisi and denied his father, nor his encounter with his first disciple, nor even his meeting with Pope Innocent III. All these dramatic events, of course, had great importance: they were milestones on the road to Francis's religious maturity. Yet the saint chose to mention a completely personal event impossible to situate at a precise moment. What happened to Francis among the lepers was a substantial change. He did not learn to overcome his disgust or to tolerate the lepers' presence for the sake of Christ; he did not grasp the symbolic meaning of the lepers and of the care he offered them; he did not follow the rules of charity and of Christian compassion. Francis recounts what happened in emotional and sensual terms: what was bitterness became sweetness of soul and body. After the transformation came about, he no longer needed to overcome his revulsion through charity or self-sacrifice because the revulsion was gone, having given way to spiritual and corporeal sweetness. Someone who moves through the world feeling that what is bitter for others is for him sweetness of soul and body can act with absolute certainty that he is on the right path. Francis made spontaneity a value: someone who becomes a transformed man acts as if he has an internal compass guiding his steps.

The last phase of Francis's transformation was the stigmatization. It was not necessarily the culminating point, since the truly important things are not visible, but it attested to his success. The stigmatization was a miracle of a particular kind, an "aesthetic" miracle. It was not a healing or a resurrection or the deliverance from danger, nor was it an act of control over the forces of nature. In itself it was only an external change of the flesh, but that change was a witness for others of the internal change that had come about in Francis's soul. It allowed everyone to see what only God had seen until then: Francis's transformation into a Christ-like figure, from an imitator to a model of imitation. Francis was not simply a supplier of miracles. He himself was the greatest miracle of all.

Francis could ignore existing models because he felt directly connected to the source, to Christ, but interestingly, he did not expect his disciples, like him, to imitate Christ and only Christ. Francis served as their mediator and model. Their need for him to be a mediator stemmed, on the one hand, from his historical role—he was the first to have retraced the path toward salvation—and, on the other, from the extraordinary charismatic power he possessed. Anyone who, like him, has experienced an internal change no longer needs models; anyone still struggling needs Francis as an intercessor. That role imposed a heavy responsibility on him. He lived his life as if it were an ethics lesson. He spoke to the audience that had come to listen to him; but also and above all, he spoke through it to the crowd without number in Christendom as a whole and to future generations.[10] Stories about Francis of Assisi do not merely aim to demonstrate that their hero is worthy of the miracles attributed to him; they are a "user's manual" for those in quest of salvation. They are designed not just to enlighten but to instigate action. They offer a series of direct and specific injunctions (act exactly like me) that should not be interpreted and adapted but imitated to the letter. If the path to salvation entails imitating Saint Francis, then the best way to instruct the brothers once he is no longer there is through a careful narration of his acts and words. Francis's biography is a key tool of reform.

Saint Francis and His Friends

What kinds of things were deemed worthy of memory by the saint's comrades, by those "who were with him"? We are fortunate to be able to answer this question. A collection of stories compiled by the saint's close friends—Leo, Rufino, and Angelo—has survived. It was sent to the authorities of the order in 1246, about twenty years after Francis's death.[11] An official and exhaustive biography (the *Vita prima*) had been written in 1229, barely five years after the saint's death, by a learned friar, Thomas of

Celano. But it soon emerged that the text did not satisfy the brothers. They wanted to know "everything" about Francis. Hence in 1244 the authorities of the order called on the brothers to provide additional information, with the aim of compiling a second biography (*Vita secunda*), which would also be by Thomas of Celano.

The letter from the three friends is one of the most interesting hagiographical texts to have come down to us from the medieval period. Its authors had not intended to write a biography. For them, the stories they sent were merely raw material for the biography that would be written by the order's official biographer. They did not take the trouble, therefore, to arrange the information systematically by date or theme. This is relatively unpolished material (written in Latin, it is of course a translation of words originally spoken in Italian), expressing the views of the saint's immediate entourage before these views were smoothed out by a representative of the order's leadership. The letter is problematic material. It is all the more astonishing, then, that it had a profound influence on Thomas of Celano and that much of it was incorporated into the *Second Life* without radical change. When the friends sent their letter to the authorities of the order, Francis's spiritual legacy was already being called into question. The proponents of compromise were arguing with the purists over what Francis's true legacy was: Was the order to keep its charismatic rigor alive and risk confrontation with the papacy, or was it time to build institutions and look at the (political) big picture?

The three friends, it must be noted, were not Franciscan fundamentalists (as they are sometimes portrayed). Although they obviously side with the purists, that is not because they wish to preserve the past or to reinstate it, but because they are calling for a permanent revolution. That revolution is founded on the opposition Francis established between "interpretation" and "sweetness of soul and body." For him, "interpretation" means the examination of texts and of actions with the aim of creating a rational system free of contradiction, of fostering order. It is an act of human pride to try to impose false order on the world. To find a single explanatory principle is not merely impossible; it is the surest way to distort the deep meaning, whose internal power proceeds precisely from its external contra-dictions. Only a strictly literal reading of Francis's texts and a humble imitation of his acts can produce a meaning that is not intellectual but truly spiritual. What the friends' stories of Francis attempt to achieve is a transformation of the reader/listener. Imitation, no longer a theatrical and empty reiteration, will become an instrument of inner transformation.

To a great extent, Thomas adopted the friends' approach and identified with their presentation of the saint as a man in conflict with his nominal collaborators, especially with the order's hierarchy. The *Second Life* is full of descriptions in which the founder opposes the compromises the officials of the order seek to impose on him. No less important is the fact that, al-though Thomas abridged the text of the friends' stories and polished the style, a considerable portion of the second biography he wrote (197 of the 224 chapters) is a collection of episodes from the saint's life that are not ar-ranged in chronological order. The *Vita* begins by retelling the story of Francis's conversion (that is, the internal change that makes him worthy of being imitated). Then the orderly narrative disappears, broken down into a series of examples out of context. These are not events that follow the in-ner logic of the saint's life but lessons, sermons in action that transcend the saint's biography.

The *Vita secunda* was received by the order's authorities with some reserva-tions. At first they felt that the emphasis was placed on the actions at the expense of the miracles, that Francis was too much an object of imitation and not enough an object of admiration. In 1252–1253, Thomas of Celano published an appendix, "On Miracles."[12] It was an awkward solution: the narrative later had to be reworked so as to tone down the radical elements, a task so important that the minister general of the order took it upon himself. Thus, in 1263 the new minister general, Bonaventura, published yet another official biography of Saint Francis of Assisi (the *Legenda maior*), and in 1266 the general chapter of the order ruled that all previous biogra-phies should be destroyed. Most copies of these biographies did in fact perish. But the effort to silence the Francis of the friends' letter failed. Too many people were already familiar with the old versions. The leadership of the order may have offered a more moderate Francis, a saint less literal in his demands, more accommodating to spiritual interpretations, a saint in formal dress, but the old, tattered, uncompromising beggar refused to go away.

Who, then, is the Francis we discover in his friends' accounts? He is a very human saint, sure enough of himself to demand strict observance from his brothers and to disregard his own principles when necessary. He orders his followers to rise to a very high degree of asceticism: he forbids them from preparing their food in advance or from asking for more alms than they need for one day (chapter 4); but he also departs from his usual asceticism by eating with brothers who are hungry in order not to shame them (chapters 1 and 5). Chapter 19 recounts how a young peasant from a small township close to Assisi joined the order. Francis explains to him that he must sell his possessions and distribute the money to the poor, as the Gospel commands. The young man is prepared to obey without question and to sell his ox immediately. But when Francis realizes how poor the candidate and his family are and what a blow it would be for them to lose the ox, he allows the young man to give it to his relatives as alms. The compromises that Francis allows seem to contradict his demands for intransigent and inflexible action, but the essential thing for him is not legalistic consistency but the right state of mind; that is more important than strict observance of the rules. This attitude finds expression in chapter 19 in the account of the conflict between Francis and the young man, now Brother John:

> He indeed was of such simplicity that he believed himself bound by anything that the blessed Francis did. So when the blessed Francis stood in church or in some distant place for prayer, he too wanted to see him and observe him attentively so that his every gesture would conform to those of the saint. If the blessed Francis knelt or joined his hands to heaven, or if he spat or coughed, John did the same. The blessed Francis began to reproach him with great joy for these marks of simplicity. Brother John replied: "Brother, I promised to do every-

thing you do, so I want to do everything you do." That amazed the blessed Francis and filled him with joy at the sight of such purity and such simplicity in his companion. John began to be so perfect in his virtues and his merits that the blessed Francis and the other brothers were greatly astonished by his perfection. Shortly thereafter, John died in that holy perfection. With inner and outer joy, the blessed Francis took to relating John's way of life to the brothers, and he called him not "Brother John" but "Saint John."[13]

Francis reproaches his young companion for imitating him without discriminating between what is worthy of imitation and what is not. Surely coughing and spitting are not integral parts of the friar minor's way of life. Is John's imitation, then, not a mechanical, external repetition? John denies the accusation. His imitation is not mechanical; it is the result of a conscious decision to refrain from choosing, that is, from interpreting. Francis accepts this explanation with great joy. John has truly followed his precepts "simply and without interpretation," just as his testament would have it. Moreover, by combining internal conversion with action, John too has become worthy of imitation, and it is Francis himself who takes to "relating his way of life to the brothers."

Two other chapters show the great importance Francis grants to internal change and its connection to acts. In chapter 3 Francis at first refrains from requiring his brothers to go out and beg, realizing that they would be ashamed to do so. Francis then understands that he is wrong on two counts: in the first place, if he does not share the burden, he will ultimately succumb to it; and second, begging is important for the *brothers'* spiritual well-being. Francis does not ask them to overcome their shame; he enjoins them to stop feeling it and to ask for alms joyfully, telling them:

> "My dear sons and brothers, do not be ashamed to go begging, for behold, the Lord became poor for us, and that is why we have chosen, on the basis of the example he set for us, the path of true poverty. . . . That is our heritage, the heritage that Jesus Christ our Lord acquired

for us and left for us and for all who follow his way and want to live a life of holy poverty." And he also said: "I tell you truthfully: many of the nobles of this world and its wise men will come to this community and will be honored to beg. Go then confidently and with a joyful spirit, beg with the Lord's blessing. You must go out with a desire and a joy greater than that of someone who out of one denier gained one hundred."

Because there were so few of them at the time, he could not send them out in pairs, and so he sent them one by one into the villages and small towns. And when they came back, each showed the blessed Francis the alms he had collected, and they said to one another: "I have collected more than you." And the blessed Francis was greatly delighted in seeing them joyful and affectionate.

Note that it is only after the brothers have actually gone begging that the change desired by Francis comes about: joy in what others consider "bitter" and shameful. Inner change requires more than consent; it requires action.

Chapter 88 offers an even more striking example of that lesson: Francis expresses the agony of his humiliation by briefly relating a situation in which he was publicly scorned by the brothers and shamefully driven out: "It does not seem to me that I am a [true] friar minor if I do not delight as much when they despise and reject me shamefully, when they do not want me as their superior, as when they respect and admire me." Internal joy, indifferent to scorn and convention, is thus the most profound characteristic of the Franciscan friar. Although in this case it is not an act proper but a mental exercise, action is still privileged as the ultimate test. Francis is not content to express the abstract idea that the Franciscan is obliged to accept the good and the bad with the same cheerfulness. He places his words in a dramatic context, and the principle takes concrete form. A good story, whether it has actually taken place or not, can have the necessary impact on its listeners.

In chapter 39 Francis reenacts, for himself and his spectators, the imaginary humiliation evoked in chapter 38:

Once, when he had recovered a little from a serious illness, he reflected and it seemed to him that he was guilty of indulgence, though he ate very little (because of his various long illnesses, he could not eat [much]). He rose one day before he was completely cured of a quartan fever and convoked the people of Assisi to gather for a sermon in the public square. When he finished the sermon, he commanded that no one should leave the place until he had come back to stand before them. He entered the church of San Rufino in the company of Brother Peter Catani, whom he had elected to be the first minister general of the order, and several other brothers. He ordered Brother Peter to obey without protest everything he ordered him to do or say about him. To which the brother replied, "Brother, I cannot and must not want anything for myself or for you except what pleases you." The blessed Francis took off his garment and ordered Brother Peter to lead him naked before the people with a rope around his neck. He ordered another brother to take a plateful of ashes, to go up to the place above where he [Francis] had given his sermon, and to pour the ashes over his head. (That brother refused to comply because of the pity and mercy he felt for Francis.)

Brother Peter rose and led the blessed Francis as he had been ordered, weeping bitterly, as the other brothers wept along with him. When [the saint] thus returned naked to the people [who were waiting for him] at the place where he had given his sermon, he said: "You take me for a holy man. And others think like you, and have abandoned the world to join the order and the brothers' way of life. But I confess before God and before you that during my illness I ate meat and gravy." Almost all those present began to weep from pity and mercy, for it was winter and bitterly cold, and he was not yet cured of his fever. They beat their chests and confessed, saying: "If this saint, whose way of life we know, and who, because of his excessive abstinence and austerity against his body since his conversion to Christ, we see living in flesh that seems already dead, accuses himself so shamefully for the just and manifest needs of his body, what shall we poor souls do, we who live and wish to live by our passions and the desire of the flesh?"

The narrators do everything they can to show that the consumption of food did not really exceed the limits of the plausible and permitted, since it did not deviate from what Francis allowed others. Nevertheless, beyond the "objective" justification of Francis's confession, two themes surface: first, that of subjective justification; and second, that of pedagogical duty. Francis feels that his act was not performed in the proper mental state. He did not eat meat with mindfulness (otherwise his act would have been totally justifiable) but did so without awareness, or worse, while feeling guilty. Since there was no joy in the act (as there was in eating with the hungry brother), it was wrong. In chapter 85 Francis grants a similar concession to his sick body (he patched his tunic with some pieces of cloth to keep himself warm). And even though he judges after the fact that he was wrong, he does not feel the need to punish himself. He feels that his motives were pure, and so he can feel great joy *(magna letitia)* even as he recounts his mistake. It is not because his state of mind was wrong but because of his duty to set an example to the brothers that he removes the patching.

As a spiritual leader Francis must constantly turn his life into an exemplum. This theme is repeatedly invoked in the letter. Thus, for example, in chapter 85: "We who have been with him cannot count the necessities he denied his body in food and clothing to set a good example for the brothers, and so that they would bear their necessities more patiently. The blessed Francis's chief and supreme wish was always—especially once the brothers began to grow in number and he gave up his role as leader—to teach the brothers what they should do and what they should refrain from doing, by acts rather than words."

Francis was forced to relinquish the leadership of the order in 1220, under pressure from the order's hierarchy. In the eyes of the provincial ministers, Francis was an irrational element that threatened to slow the order's development. As a result of being "deposed," his distrust of calculated rationality increased. The calculation of profit and loss is completely at odds with the holy simplicity that characterizes the true Franciscan. Hence the great importance Francis granted to teaching by acts rather than words. If one is to make one's life an exemplum, the memorable aspects of the message must be emphasized. When one speaks to the last rows in the theater of life, it is necessary to raise one's voice above its "natural" level. Acts must have a dramatic effect; they must shock to bypass the spectators' "rational" defense mechanisms.[14]

The theatricality of the saint's acts was obvious to others as well. They understood it as pedagogy and cooperated with the saint. Sometimes they encouraged him to act. In chapter 100 a brother urges the dying Francis to die well so that his death will remain forever engraved in people's memories.

> One day a brother told the blessed Francis . . . "Father, your life and behavior [*vita et conversatio tua*] have been and are a light and a mirror not only to your brothers but to the entire Church of God, and so will be your death. . . . You know in truth that unless God sends a heavenly cure to your body, your sickness is incurable and you have little [time] left to live, as the doctors have also said. I tell you this to comfort your spirit, so that you will always be joyful in the Lord, internally and externally, and even more, so that your brothers and the others who come to visit you will find you joyful in the Lord (since they know and believe that you will die soon), so that your death will become a memorial [*memoriale*] for those who see it and for others who will hear about it after your death.

Francis's death scene shows that he has internalized the lesson. He has made his death a lesson, a memorial. He directs his death as a series of edifying scenes, culminating in a Last Supper in which he performs the role of the Savior. For once he does not expect his followers to imitate him. He has played his part well. He deserves applause.[15]

ELEVEN

Fra Ginepro, the Holy Fool

THE OLDEST SOURCE TO MENTION Fra Ginepro (or Brother Juniper) is the biography of Saint Clare of Assisi, attributed to Thomas of Celano. When the saint was dying, "priests and brothers reputed for their spirituality," including Leo and Angelo, came to visit her "to support her with pious words and with the story of Christ's Passion. Fra Ginepro, the eminent fisherman [or lancer] for God, who used to enunciate God's Word fervently, also appeared among them, and she was once more filled with joy, and asked him if he had anything new to tell her about God. He opened his mouth and brought forth word-sparks from the blazing furnace of his heart and with his proverbs brought consolation to the virgin of God."[1] In the early fourteenth century, Ginepro appears in the *Speculum perfectionis* (The Mirror of Perfection), a work linked to purist circles. In it Saint Francis offers Ginepro as a model for the brothers: "[They must imitate] the patience of Fra Ginepro, who has achieved perfect patience by always acknowledging his baseness [*vilitas*], and whose greatest aspiration has been to imitate Jesus on the Way of the Cross."[2] According to both sources, then, Ginepro incarnates Franciscan virtues: he is humble and patient, a fervent and inspiring preacher, and he is determined to imitate the crucified Jesus.

Idealized descriptions of early brothers, such as Ginepro, who were faithful to the founder's teaching circulated widely among critics of the order's leadership, especially after the destruction of the first biographies of Saint Francis. Such stories did not usually amount to full hagiographical narratives. The saintly brothers appeared in isolated episodes where the central theme was their loyalty to the pure Franciscan ideal.

In the first half of the fourteenth century, a Franciscan friar, Ugolino di Monte Santa Maria, produced a collection of narratives about Saint Francis and the first generation of Franciscan friars. It was titled *Acta beati Francisci et sociorum ejus* (Acts of the Blessed Francis and of His Companions). Between 1370 and 1380 an unknown Italian Franciscan translated Brother Ugolino's collection into Italian and reworked about two thirds of it, adding an essay on Saint Francis's stigmatization and several accounts borrowed from other sources. This work is known as *The Little Flowers of Saint Francis (I fioretti di San Francesco)*. The *Little Flowers*, which enjoyed great popularity, reflected the worldview and the narrative model of the friends' letter. The demand for these pious narratives was so great that it could not be controlled by issuing orders or repressed by burning manuscripts. During the same period Fra Ginepro resurfaces in another Franciscan text, the *Chronica XXIV generalium* (Chronicle of the Twenty-four Ministers General). That text, which deals with Francis's successors up to the 1370s, includes a brief collection of narratives about this companion of Saint Francis.[3] The Latin in which Ginepro's exploits are related clearly reflects the influence of spoken Italian, and the Italian version that appeared shortly thereafter must be considered a more faithful expression of the original oral narrative.[4] The story of Fra Ginepro seemed so close in spirit to the *Little Flowers* that in many manuscripts, and later in printed editions, it appeared with a number of other short texts as an appendix.[5]

Where did Fra Ginepro suddenly appear from after so many years of obscurity and why? Does his Life reflect oral traditions about the historical Ginepro, or is it an entirely new work, created in purist circles? It is hard to know.[6] In any case, nothing of what we find in the early accounts about the pious friar prepares us for the new biography. The fervent and austere preacher who brings forth "word-sparks from the blazing furnace of his heart" has vanished, making way for a clown—not a *jaculator* (fisherman or lancer) but a *joculator* (joker, player) for God. Of the fourteen stories included in the *Life of Fra Ginepro*, eight describe a character who at times behaves in a manner that is not just silly and illogical but truly scandalous. Ginepro cuts off the leg of a live pig, refuses to proclaim his innocence when accused of crimes he did not commit and is almost executed, gives to the poor indiscriminately and irresponsibly, falls into disrepute for his strange behavior, and in his folly allows large quantities of food to spoil which were needed to sustain the brothers. At times it is hard to decide whether Ginepro is a fool for Christ or simply a fool.

But it would be a mistake to think of the Fra Ginepro stories as comic relief in the drama of spiritual perfection. They are much more than that. They take to extremes a central, altogether serious aspect of the Franciscan worldview. In all the stories of the saintly *joculator*, the same motif returns: Ginepro refuses to act in accordance with conventional logic and received social norms. A true "spiritual" (for that is how the purists, or *zelanti*, came to be known) Franciscan is closer to the Cynic notion of asceticism than to the Stoic. He despises social norms and seeks to subvert them by his scandalous behavior. When a true Franciscan acts with complete, confident spontaneity, everything he does is good. Franciscan simplicity and poverty are not merely outward modes of behavior; they correspond to an existential position that renounces the defense mechanisms provided by the Earthly City (wealth, power, practical logic) in order to be worthy of the Heavenly City. Francis himself could not completely ignore practical logic. He may have forbidden his disciples to prepare food for the next day and may have refused ecclesiastical prelacies, but he did agree to be leader of *his* order. Again and again Francis refers to the Order of Friars Minor as *his*. It is the one property he is not willing to renounce. But with property comes attachment, worries, responsibilities, "economic" considerations. Francis was a propertied man. He was constantly obliged to think of the future of the order and to hold positions of power, to compile rules and letters of instruction, to organize general chapters, and to conduct political negotiations.

Even more problematic than his need to run the order was the tension that existed between the demand for full spontaneity and the institutional requirement to set an example for his followers. Ideally the saint sets an example without realizing it, simply because he is a saint; in reality, Francis was obsessed with the pedagogical and political implications of every act and gesture. "The blessed Francis's chief and supreme wish—especially once the brothers began to grow in number and he gave up his role as leader—was always to teach the brothers what they should do and what they should refrain from doing, by acts rather than words."[7] Spontaneity is difficult under such conditions.

Francis was caught in a dilemma: as head of the order, he acted with too much "spontaneity"—that is, with institutional irresponsibility. That conduct ultimately got him removed from office. But as a private Franciscan, he was not spontaneous enough, since he was constantly directing himself to achieve the most edifying dramatic effect. In the end, no political leader, not even Francis, can be a true Franciscan. But a simple brother can. Ginepro fully realized the ideal that Francis, occupied with his duties as educator and political leader, could implement only to a limited degree. Precisely because he appeared irresponsible and was constantly taken for a fool or a madman, Ginepro, even more than Francis, was the ideal Franciscan: "But God has chosen the foolish things of the world to put to shame the wise, and God has chosen the weak things of the world to put to shame the things which are mighty" (1 Cor. 1:27).[8] It is no accident that in the first two stories of the *Life of Fra Ginepro*, Ginepro is portrayed as surpassing Francis. In the first, Ginepro acts with a spontaneity that threatens to bring trouble to the order. Here, then, is the story:

> One of the most elect first disciples and companions of St. Francis was Brother Juniper, a man of such unshakable humility, patience, and self-contempt that the rushing waves of temptation and tribulation could not move him. His patience is said to have been so remarkable that no one ever saw him disturbed, even when under great pressure. He reached such a degree of self-contempt that he was considered

stupid and foolish by those who did not know how perfect he was. Therefore St. Francis, once when he was speaking about the outstanding virtues of his companions, said: "He would be a good Friar Minor who had attained to Brother Juniper's contempt of self and of the world."

Now one day Brother Juniper was visiting a certain sick friar at St. Mary of the Portiuncula. And when he saw him suffering very much from his illness, Brother Juniper's heart melted with compassion and burned with fervent charity. So he asked the friar: "Can I help you in any way? Do you want something to eat?"

The sick friar answered: "I would love to eat a pig's foot if I had one. . . ."

Brother Juniper quickly said: "Leave that to me—I'll soon have one and prepare it the way you want!"

He went and took a knife from the kitchen and ran into the fields, where he found a group of pigs feeding. He ran after one of them, caught it, and cut off one of its feet with the knife. Leaving the pig with its leg maimed, he came back and washed and dressed and cooked the pig's foot. And after he had prepared it well, he brought and served it with great kindness to the sick friar. The latter ate it very eagerly, to Brother Juniper's intense joy and consolation. And to entertain him, Juniper gleefully described how he had caught the pig.

Meanwhile, however, the man who was guarding the swine and who had seen him cut off the foot, told his master the whole story with great indignation. When the master heard about it, he went to the friars' Place and shouted at them, calling them hypocrites, thieves, forgers, bandits, and evil men for having with deliberate malice cut off one of his pig's feet. At all the noise he was making, St. Francis came out with the others and very humbly made excuses for his friars, saying that he had not known about what had happened. Yet to appease him, he promised that he would make good the damage. But the man would not calm down. Raging with anger, he uttered many curses and threats, repeating over and over that the pig's foot had been cut off with deliberate malice. He refused to accept any excuses or promises, and he left in unappeased anger and indignation, shouting curses and insults.

While the other friars stood around in amazement, St. Francis prudently thought the matter over and said to himself: "Could Brother Juniper have done this out of indiscreet zeal?" He immediately summoned Brother Juniper privately and asked him: "Did you cut off the foot of a pig in the fields?"

Then Brother Juniper, acting not like someone who has done something wrong but like one who believes he has performed a great act of charity, answered joyfully: "Dear Father, it is true I cut that pig's foot off. And now listen compassionately to the reason. I went to visit that sick friar . . ." And he told him the whole story.

On hearing it, St. Francis was very sad. And with zeal for justice, his face flushed, he said: "Oh, Brother Juniper, why did you bring this great disgrace on us? That man is quite right in being angry at us. And now maybe he is complaining about us and spoiling our reputation throughout the town—and he has good reason to do so! Therefore I now order you under holy obedience to run right after that man until you overtake him, and to throw yourself on the ground before him and admit your guilt to him. And promise to make good the damage—and do it—in such a way that he will have no more reason to complain against us. For this certainly has been a most serious wrong!"

Brother Juniper was very much surprised at these words, as he marveled that anyone should be angry over such an act of charity. For to him all these material things seemed like nothing, except if they were put to use in practicing charity. And he replied: "Father, you can be sure I will quickly give him full satisfaction. But why should he be so angry when something that belonged to God rather than to him was used to perform such a real act of charity?"

Then he ran off and overtook the man, who was still so angry that he had not an ounce of patience left. With intense joy and fervor Brother Juniper told him all about the amputation of the pig's foot, as though he had done him a great favor for which he deserved a reward. The man's anger only increased, and he became so enraged that he shouted insults at him, calling him a fool, a lunatic, and the worst kind of criminal—and he almost struck him.

Brother Juniper was amazed at these ugly words, although he rejoiced at receiving the insults. And because he thought that the man had not understood what he had said (which seemed to him a matter for joy rather than anger), he told the same story over again. And he embraced the man, explaining how it had been done only out of love, and urging the man to congratulate him for doing such a good deed, and even inviting the man to give the rest of the pig for the same purpose.

Then that man was overcome by so much simplicity and humility. And recovering his senses when he heard that the cause of the deed had been an act of charity, he knelt down and wept and admitted that he had been wrong in insulting Brother Juniper and the other holy friars. And he acknowledged that perhaps he was greedy and ungrateful to God for the good things which he possessed. So he went and caught and killed the pig and had it cooked and well dressed. And with great devotion and weeping he brought it to St. Mary of the Angels and gave it to those holy friars to eat as compensation for the wrong which he had done them.

Now St. Francis, considering the simplicity and self-contempt and patience under adversity of that holy Brother Juniper, said to his companions and the other friars who were standing around: "My Brothers, if only I had a great forest of such junipers!"

To the glory of Christ. Amen.[9]

Ginepro behaves outrageously. Not only does he cut a leg off a live pig but he is not even worried about who the animal's owner might be. For him the pig "belonged to God rather than to him" and was used to perform an act of charity. "For to him all these material things seemed like nothing, except if they were put to use in practicing charity." In other words, Ginepro applies the Franciscan rejection of ownership to the secular world. Everything belongs to God, and we have no right of ownership *(dominium)* over things, but only right of use *(usus)*. If someone has a greater need for a thing in another's possession, nothing prevents a third person from handing it over to him. Hence in another episode Ginepro removes silver "ringlets" from the frontal of an altar and gives them to a poor woman (chapter 5). "Don't be upset about those ringlets," he tells the sacristan, "because I gave them to a poor little woman who was in great need. They were good for nothing here except to make a display of worldly vanity."[10] Moreover, Ginepro acts with total spontaneity and great joy. He has fully *internalized* the Franciscan spirit. It is now not a strategy but second nature.

Francis does not explicitly reject the principle of universal (or divine) ownership. But knowing that it is not accepted by "worldly" people, he is upset by the repercussions that the theft—at least in worldly terms—of the pig's leg may have on the brothers' reputation. The problem is not the act but its consequences. There is the possibility of scandal, anger, malicious gossip. Fra Ginepro's reaction to Francis's anxiety is that of a true Franciscan: he is astounded because "all these material things seemed like nothing, except if they were put to use in practicing charity." When he meets the pig's owner, it does not occur to him to apologize. He considers the entire affair a misunderstanding, explains that he acted not out of a sense of ownership (in which case taking an object from its owner would have been unwarranted), but solely out of love (which renders void the rules of this world). He is confident that love, true love, will triumph. Francis, who naturally despises earthly things, is more realistic. He has less faith than Ginepro in the power of love among those who live in the secular world. Such people, he knows, do not share the Franciscan contempt for property. Ginepro's sin, then, consists of not respecting other people's conception of the world and in not realizing that his fervor may come with a price tag. But the story proves Francis wrong. The saint did not have enough faith. The peasant himself acknowledges the soundness of Ginepro's attitude and apologizes to *him*. In most Franciscan stories it is Francis who teaches others a lesson. His example puts them to shame. Here the roles are reversed. Francis has learned something. He expresses the wish to have many more brothers like Ginepro. In the second episode of the Life, Francis once again acknowledges Ginepro's superiority. When he drives out demons, Francis does it in the name of Ginepro, whose wild "folly" (demons are afraid "of that fool Ginepro") reinforces the more restrained, political folly of Saint Francis.

Alongside stories in which Ginepro acts like a fool there are others in which he is consciously seeking to be *considered* a fool as an act of radical humility. In some episodes (1, 3, and 5) Ginepro deliberately refrains from defending himself against false accusations. In others he arranges for his humiliation by walking naked through town (episodes 8 and 11). In episode 9 we find him in Rome. A crowd gathers, and the usual displays of admiration and favor seeking ensue. Ginepro then ejects a child from a seesaw and doggedly plays on it until the crowd tires of the spectacle and some start calling him an imbecile.

In the only episode that appears exclusively in the Latin version of Ginepro's Life, the friar explicitly speaks of humiliation as the road to spiritual perfection. Suddenly the description in the *Speculum perfectionis* comes to mind: Ginepro is the brother who achieves "perfect patience by always acknowledging his baseness." The Latin text relates a conversation between Ginepro and a friend.[11] The question arises of how they would like to die. The friend replies that he would like to die surrounded by Franciscan friars praying for the salvation of his soul. These were indeed the circumstances of Saint Francis's death (chapter 117 of the friends' letter) and of the death of Saint Clare. Ginepro's response is completely different: "And *I* should like to stink so badly that no brother could come near me; finally they would throw me away in some valley where I would die alone and despised, without burial, and dogs would eat my corpse."[12]

Ginepro does not wish to experience Francis's historical death but seeks instead to imitate his imaginary humiliation, which leads to perfection: "It does not seem to me that I am a [true] friar minor," says Francis, "if I do not delight as much when they despise and reject me shamefully, when they do not want me as their superior, as when they respect and admire me" (chapter 83 in the friends' letter). The ultimate test is the capacity to bear constant humiliation to the very end.[13] But again Ginepro takes the Franciscan ideal a step further. For even when Francis publicly humiliates himself (when he confesses to the people of Assisi that he ate meat during Lent), he is not a laughingstock for the spectators. On the contrary, he is a tragic-heroic figure who shocks his audience into tears and even greater admiration. Ginepro gives up his last possessions by making himself ridiculous and contemptible. And indeed, immediately after that imaginary dialogue with the friend, the narrator comes back to the real world. Ginepro is received admiringly by a layman. He constantly acts like an idiot (as he did on the seesaw in Rome), but to no avail. His host offers him a bed and clean sheets. Ginepro soils the sheets and the room with his excrement, finally gaining the contempt and disgust he was hoping for.

Unlike spontaneity, which is good in itself, humiliation is formulated by Ginepro in terms of profit and loss (in this world and in the world to come). Thus in episode 12 Ginepro says: "O my Brothers, who in this life is so noble that he would not willingly carry a basket of manure from St. Mary's all through town, if he were given a house full of gold? . . . Ah, why do we not want to endure a little shame in order to gain eternal life?"[14] For Ginepro too, then, as for Saint Francis, self-humiliation is at least partly a pious masquerade. But there is a difference: unlike Francis, Ginepro does not teach. His acts do not end in catharsis for his spectators. In fact, quite often they put people at great spiritual risk.

What are we to make of Ginepro? Does Francis mean it when he says he wants "a great forest" of Ginepros? Unlikely. Sometimes one can have too much of a good thing. Ginepro must not be imitated to the letter. If the Franciscan order were to adopt his attitude, it would be for extraordinary beings only. Ginepro elicits admiration; he awakens astonishment and stupefaction, which make the religious experience come alive. But his lessons are hard to follow, and in this respect he represents the opposite of the Franciscan spirit. Consider episode 5 in the Life:

Once when Brother Juniper was at the friary in Assisi for the Feast of the Lord's Nativity, he was in the church near the main altar, which was very beautifully draped and decorated. At the request of the sacristan, he stayed to guard the altar while the sacristan went to get a bite to eat.

While he was devoutly meditating, a poor little woman begged him to give her something for the love of God. And he answered: "Wait a minute. I'll see if I can find anything to give you from this richly decorated altar."

Now there was on the altar a very costly frontal from which were hanging some silver ringlets. And when Brother Juniper looked at the ornate altar, he saw the silver ringlets and said: "These ringlets are superfluous." And taking a knife, he cut all of them off the frontal and gave them to the poor little woman, out of compassion.

Meanwhile the sacristan, after eating three or four mouthfuls, began to remember the ways of Brother Juniper and to fear that in his zeal for charity he might do some damage to the richly decorated altar which he had left in his guard. So he quickly rose from the table and went to the church. And when, on looking over the ornaments of the altar, he saw that the ringlets had been cut away and stripped from the frontal, he became exceedingly angry and indignant.

Brother Juniper saw how excited he was and said: "Don't be upset about those ringlets, because I gave them to a poor little woman who was in great need. They were good for nothing here except to make a display of worldly vanity."

On hearing this, the sacristan became furious and immediately ran through the church and the whole city anxiously trying to find the woman. But not only did he not find her—he found no one who had seen her. So he returned to the friary and angrily took the frontal to the Minister General, who was then in Assisi, and said: "Father General, I demand justice from you against Brother Juniper, who has destroyed this frontal for me—and it was the finest one in the sacristy! Now look how he has ruined it and stripped away all the silver ringlets! And he says he has given them to a poor woman."

The General answered: Brother Juniper did not do this—but your foolishness, because you assigned him to guard the altar! Don't you know his ways? I tell you I am surprised he did not give away the rest. However, I am going to correct him severely for this fault."

And after vespers were chanted, he summoned all the friars in chapter. And calling Brother Juniper before him, in the presence of the whole community he rebuked him very strongly about the ringlets. And as his anger increased, he raised his voice until he became rather hoarse.

Now Brother Juniper did not particularly mind those words, as he rejoiced in being blamed and humiliated, but he began to worry more about the General's hoarseness and to think of some remedy for it. So after receiving the scolding, he went into the city and had a bowl of porridge prepared with butter.

He returned late that night. And lighting a candle he took the bowl of porridge to the General's cell and knocked. On opening the door and seeing him holding the lighted candle and the dish, the General asked quietly: "What do you want at this hour? What is it?"

Brother Juniper answered: "Father, when you were scolding me in chapter for my faults, I noticed that your voice became hoarse from overstrain, I believe. So I thought of a remedy and had this porridge made for you with butter. Please eat it—I am sure it will relieve your throat and chest."

The General said: "What an hour for you to bother people!"

Brother Juniper replied: "Come—it was made for you. Please eat it. It will do you good."

But the General was angered by the lateness of the hour and his insisting, and said: "Go away, you brute! Do you think I am going to eat at this hour?"

As Brother Juniper realized that neither begging nor persuading would help, he said to him: "Father, since you do not want to eat—and this porridge was made for you—at least do this for me: hold the candle, and I will eat."

Then the General, who was a very pious and devout man, was won over by Brother Juniper's great compassion and simplicity and charity—for he had done it out of devotion—and he answered: "Well now, Brother, since you want to, let's both eat it together!"

And because of Brother Juniper's insistent charity, they both ate the bowl of porridge. And they were refreshed far more by their devotion than by the food.

From the beginning there is a moral and cognitive dissonance between the one representing a moral ideal (contempt for all "earthly things") and the many who are supposed to act like him but care about vanities. Like Francis, Ginepro is giving to the poor what the poor in spirit have but do not own. The minister general tries to get Ginepro to behave like everyone else. Ginepro pays him no mind. He does not argue. He simply treats his superior's words as meaningless sounds. Their only significance is that they make the general hoarse. By bringing him a bowl of porridge and insisting that he eat it in the middle of the night, he makes a mockery of the general's authority. That symbolic act of aggression is seemingly made by a complete fool, a man who cannot tell the sublime from the ridiculous. Unlike Simeon's abbot, the general does not feel that his authority has really been threatened. Remember the words of the sisters in Tabennisi to Saint Piterum: "Father, take no offense. She is an idiot." Because Ginepro does not have to be taken seriously, the general can react with charity. He does not conclude that all should act like Fra Ginepro, any more than that the owner of the pig should now share his property with the needy. Ginepro is an exception whose simplicity and "importunate" charity can be admired.

In episode 10 Ginepro lets a great quantity of food spoil. On the pretext of leaving the brothers free to devote themselves to prayer, he prepares gruel "for the next fortnight" which is so nasty that "not a single hog in the city of Rome would have eaten [it]."[16] The custodian does not think that the saint should be imitated, though he considers his act exemplary. An example, yes, but not one to be imitated. The custodian urges the brothers to reflect on the *motivation* behind Ginepro's act and the spiritual lessons to be drawn from it. In other words, Ginepro is not to be read "literally." He needs "interpretation."

To behave like Ginepro, one must be Ginepro. Normal people do not behave that way, and in reality it is better that they do not. Therein lies the major difference between this text and the older texts devoted to Saint Francis. In appearance, it is very difficult to imitate Francis. Unlike the humble brother, Francis is an important religious leader, a miracle worker who was marked with the stigmata by God himself. But in fact Francis models his actions in such a way that they will remain within reach of the brothers. It is precisely because he has given up spontaneity, which in his eyes is at the very heart of the Franciscan ideal, and because he sets a "serious" and practical example taking into account social conventions and politics, that the Francis of Assisi of the friends' stories remains a radical, dangerous power. It is precisely because the stories about Ginepro propose an idealization of uncompromising spontaneity, a total disregard for human sensitivities and needs, that he is ultimately a conservative figure devoid of moral power. Ginepro elicits our admiration; Saint Francis demands that we imitate him.

TWELVE

The Golden Legend

THE GROUP OF STORIES TO WHICH we now turn is drawn entirely from a single work, Jacobus de Voragine's *Golden Legend*. Originally the title of the work was simply *The Legend of the Saints (Legenda sanctorum)*, but because of its enormous popularity, it acquired over the years the epithet *aurea*, "golden." Jacobus (1230–1296), a native of Varazze, near Genoa, joined the Dominican order at fourteen and held various administrative positions. He was the provincial prior of Lombardy from 1267 to 1277 and from 1281 to 1286. In 1292 he became archbishop of Genoa. Jacobus wrote several books of sermons, an interpretation of Saint Augustine, and a history of the city of Genoa.[1] None of his works had a success even remotely comparable to that of *The Golden Legend*, which he composed in the 1260s. Apart from holy scripture, *The Golden Legend* was the most widely copied work in medieval Europe. It was translated from Latin into all the languages of western Europe and has been preserved in some thousand manuscripts, many more than even standard university textbooks. With the advent of printing, hundreds of editions of the book were published, and to this day it is one of the rare works from the Middle Ages to be brought out in new editions.

The Golden Legend is divided into the liturgical periods of the year, and the saints appear on their feast days. Of the *Legend's* 182 chapters, 149 are dedicated to saints. The 33 others deal with Jesus, Mary, church feasts, and the liturgical seasons. Most of the chapters dealing with saints tell the life of a single saint, but some relate the lives of several (some two hundred saints in all). For the most part, the saints—evangelists, apostles, Latin and Greek church fathers, martyrs, desert fathers, popes, bishops, and missionaries—lived in the early centuries of the Christian era, about 120 of them between the first and fourth centuries and 40 others up to the seventh century. Jacobus included only six "new" saints in his collection: Bernard of Clairvaux and Thomas Becket (from the twelfth century), Francis of Assisi, Dominic, Peter Martyr, and Elizabeth of Thuringia (from the thirteenth).

Jacobus was not an original author. He generally reworked existing versions of saints' Lives. At times he abbreviated and revised one version; at others he borrowed from several sources, creating his own mélange. That method led to his being widely criticized (even by members of his order). The criticism did not adversely affect the book's success. It is estimated that Jacobus used more than 130 diverse sources from the twelfth and thirteenth centuries.[2] Although most of these sources were considered reliable in his time, he did not hesitate to take from sources whose reliability was doubtful even in his own eyes. He made generous use of the Apocrypha, the church fathers, contemporary chronicles, liturgical texts, and encyclopedic works. Three of his main sources were collections of saints' Lives written by Dominicans of his time—Vincent of Beauvais's *Speculum historiale* (Mirror of History), Jean de Mailly's *Abbreviatio in gestis et miraculis sanctorum* (Short Guide to the Acts and Miracles of the Saints), and Bartholomew of Trente's *Liber epilogorum in gesta sanctorum* (Book of Abstracts of the Acts of the Saints).[3] These works, like Jacobus', were part of the Dominican effort to reorganize the church calendar by filling it with new saints' stories. All three were almost forgotten after the appearance of *The Golden Legend*.[4]

Most chapters of the *Legend* begin with an etymological analysis of the saint's name, aimed at showing how that name, and sometimes the vowels and consonants composing it, both symbolize and foreshadow the saint's particular character and destiny. In most cases these etymologies are not "scientifically" valid. Jacobus had a limited knowledge of Greek and Hebrew, and even in the analysis of Latin names he gave free rein to his imagination. After the etymological introduction, he proceeds to the central part of the chapter, the account of the saint's adventures and of his or her miracles. Most of the chapters end with the saint's post mortem miracles. Jacobus does not always adhere to that model: sometimes the chapter does not begin with an etymological commentary or does not end in posthumous miracles.

For whom was this collection intended? The fact that it was written in Latin indicates it was directly addressed to the clergy. The organization of the chapters according to the church calendar and the simplified theological discussions indicate that these were probably materials for the preparation of sermons.[5] The preacher could consult the *Legend*, find the saint whose name was commemorated on a specific day, and use his or her story in his sermon. *The Golden Legend* was thus a text for which the principal addressees were not its readers. The learned preacher did not need Jacobus' collection for *his* spiritual needs. For his own edification, he could read more sophisticated materials—either theological tracts or unabridged saints' legends. But the preacher stood between the text and the less educated listeners. He did not simply read the text out loud. Rather the text was supposed to serve as a starting point on which he expanded, and which he glossed and modified to fit his own and his audience's tastes and needs.

At first sight this might seem a surprising statement. In a text intended for the laity, one might have expected the author to strive to bring the heroes closer to the audience by choosing lay, married, and contemporary or near-contemporary saints. That is not the case. *The Golden Legend* is very remote from the everyday experience of thirteenth-century listeners. The collection includes only four thirteenth-century saints. There are very few lay saints (apart from the martyrs). Women are underrepresented (forty-one out of about two hundred saints—predominantly martyrs). Moreover, the *Legend*'s saints are not ordinary human beings. For the most part they are described as superior creatures endowed from birth with superhuman powers. They are characterized by unwavering piety; most are virgins, and almost all the confessors are clerics. The saints of *The Golden Legend* despise this world and practice extreme forms of asceticism. They live in an enchanted realm that does not obey the laws of the historical world. And as if to increase the distance between the texts and concrete reality, Jacobus provides few psychological or historical descriptions. The saints lack psychological depth, and even when dates are provided, this has no effect on the text: fourth-century saints are in no way different from sixth- or twelfth-century saints.

In one sense, the *Legend* seems to be strangely "out of touch" with the spirit of the time. In the twelfth and thirteenth centuries, more and more new Lives were devoted to contemporary saints. Historical context and psychological insight had become very important as part of the individualism and realism that were emerging in the new urban centers. If we compare *The Golden Legend* to the Franciscan narratives we have examined, the difference is glaring: the latter deal with "little" everyday situations, human drives such as vainglory, gluttony, and envy; the former depicts saints who resemble angels, undisturbed by such trivialities and more divine than human. Jacobus' collection looks like a relic from the monastic centuries when liturgical texts were written for the convinced.

But Jacobus was working against the spirit of the time only in appearance. Once we understand that *The Golden Legend* was not supposed to be the end result, that it was not intended to satisfy either readers or listeners "as is," the picture changes. The "shallowness" of Jacobus' text, the one-dimensionality of the characters, the stress on action and miracle rather than inner conflict—these were not flaws but advantages. What Jacobus provided were prototypes, extremely powerful "clichés." It was the preacher's job to draw conclusions, elaborate analogies, and add to the heroes the type of inner depth that was most suitable for his listeners. *The Golden Legend* thus offers no Franciscan-style examples to be imitated, no materials for deep contemplation. It gives the preacher a captivating story of the remote world shared by all Christendom, along with theological reflections adaptable to any public. Jacobus leaves it to the preacher to make the adjustments that will edify his flock.

The Golden Legend was successful not only as a preacher's aid, however. Its huge success made it a dominant factor in the newly "narrativized" cult of saints. Iconography often followed the themes and narrative patterns of Jacobus' collection. Saints became identified with the *Legend's* now "canonical" version. Although some intellectuals harbored doubts about *The Golden Legend*, ordinary preachers adopted it with enthusiasm. They used it in their sermons and as a guide for artists painting and sculpting images of the saints; they composed vernacular versions of the legends for the masses. Within a short period of time, *The Golden Legend* was ubiquitous. Reading it was like walking through familiar territory. Almost as much as holy scripture, it had become part of the cultural core of late medieval Europe.

The success of *The Golden Legend* offers historians an extraordinary key to medieval culture. Historians need not wonder—as they often do—whether this text had an impact on its culture. *The Golden Legend* reached an enormous audience. Hundreds of thousands, if not millions, of medieval listeners heard one version or another of the text and saw it painted on the walls of their churches. The success of Jacobus de Voragine's *Golden Legend* is one of the most astounding expressions of the narrative revolution of the late Middle Ages. By examining a few of the most popular of the *Legend's* stories, I attempt to draw attention to the problematics of this new narrative repertoire. Anyone studying these stories closely will be struck by the highly problematic nature of some of these supposedly stereotypical saints. The heroes break rules and cross boundaries—between life and death, between natural and supernatural, between Christian and pagan, between moral and immoral, masculine and feminine. We assume that edifying stories will carry one-dimensional, easily understandable messages, but that is not the case.[6]

Mary Magdalene

The Mary Magdalene of the Christian tradition is a fusion of different women who appear in the Gospels: the woman from whose body Jesus drove seven demons, the sinful woman who anointed Jesus' feet with fragrant oil, the sister of Martha and Lazarus, and the woman who stood at the foot of the cross and to whom Jesus revealed himself after his resurrection. When these different characters were united into a single person, Mary became one of the most fascinating female characters in the New Testament. Mary represents human experience in its entirety: before reaching the heights of sainthood, she drinks deeply from the waters of sin. The brazen bodily contact she forces on the Messiah when she bathes his feet with her tears, anoints them with precious oil, and wipes them with her hair—an erotic attribute that a decent woman must cover—even before she has been forgiven of her sins, elicits not blame as one would expect but praise. This is the only occasion in the New Testament when someone has such intimate contact with Jesus.[7]

Jacobus chooses not to focus on the biblical Mary. The sacred text allows him too little room to maneuver. After a brief prologue, he proceeds to the post-biblical career of the Magdalene in Provence. Under European skies, Mary acquires a new character and a new history.[8] Once Mary and her companions arrive in Provence, Jesus no longer plays a role in their lives, nor is any importance attached to her repentance. We move from the moral world of the New Testament, with its poor day laborers and argumentative Pharisees, to the world of legend. Mary and her companions set off in a boat without sails and oars and arrive unharmed in Marseilles. The marvelous journey is a common folk motif. It transfers the hero or the heroine into an enchanted world, often in a strange craft (a cradle, a box made of rushes, a wooden chest, a big fish, a boat without sails). Jacobus links that motif to the more religious one of martyrdom: it is idolaters who put the Christians in the boat so that they will drown. God's grace saves the Christians, but they do not find safe haven in Marseilles, for this too is an idolatrous town. And yet these enemies of the faith do not threaten the new arrivals with horrible torture and gruesome death. In fact, the threat of violence comes from an unexpected quarter: Mary is not threatened; she threatens.

The miraculous journey of Mary, Martha, and Lazarus to Provence is associated with the vast exodus of saints' relics from the Holy Land (an important site from a religious, but not a political, point of view) to the new Christian centers. Between the tenth and fourteenth centuries there were quite a number of more or less miraculous arrivals from the Holy Land. Saint James the Great was placed in a boat after his martyrdom, and seven days later his body landed in Spain, where various miracles led it to its final resting place in Compostela. Saint Mark's body, stolen by Italian mariners from Muslim Alexandria, led them to Venice. Saint Nicholas's body, stolen from Myra, was brought to Bari. In the fifteenth century the house belonging to the Virgin Mary traveled from Nazareth to Fiume, then to Recanati, finally ending up in Loreto. As for Mary Magdalene, her remains were first claimed by Ephesus (probably in the fifth century); in the ninth or tenth century her relics were transferred to Constantinople, and during the great plunder of relics in the Fourth Crusade (1204), some of her relics were transferred to Europe. Paying no mind to that tradition, Geoffroy, abbot of the monastery of Vézelay, declared in the eleventh century that Mary's grave was to be found in his monastery. The monks of Vézelay did not offer an explanation as to how the saint had gotten to France, and did not display any of her relics. Their reply to the skeptics was that nothing is impossible for God. In the thirteenth century, doubts grew, fewer and fewer pilgrims came, and the monks had to give more elaborate explanations. They claimed that Mary had arrived in Marseilles from the Holy Land, and that she died there after living in seclusion in Aix for many years. In the ninth century, they said, the city of Marseilles was laid waste by the Saracens and a devout monk transported the saint's remains to Vézelay. Giving credence to that story was the rediscovery of Mary's remains in Vézelay in 1265, with a (forged) document beside them from "King Charles" attesting to the authenticity of the relics. A papal delegation confirmed that discovery.[9]

The matter did not end there. The monks of Vézelay had not foreseen that their story would spur rival claims about Mary Magdalene's bones in Provence, where, according to them, she had debarked from the Holy Land. In 1279 the remains of Mary Magdalene were discovered in the church of Saint-Maximin, between Marseilles and Aix. These remains were also accompanied by a document which explained that they had been transported in a special coffin during the Arab invasions, some thirty-five years *before* the "transfer" to Vézelay. To mislead relic hunters, other remains had been placed in the original tomb, and it is *they* that were transported to Vézelay. Thus the good people of Vézelay found themselves defeated by their own weapons. In that battle of forged documents, Saint-Maximin prevailed, and it is there that the saint's remains can be found to this day.[10]

Let us return to *The Golden Legend*. In the pagan city of Marseilles, Christians were received without enthusiasm but also without hostility, like any other group of anonymous immigrants. The residents did not offer them refuge, but they did not prevent them from installing themselves under the roof of the local temple and from preaching against idolatry. Although the locals did not become Christians, they were amazed by Mary's beautiful words. At this point it is already obvious that Mary is the undisputed leader of the group and that, despite the presence of men—Mary's brother Lazarus and the blessed Maximinus, both priests destined to become bishops—she is the only one to preach to the crowd. That element of the story is far from a matter of course, since Saint Paul had explicitly forbidden women from preaching, especially if a man capable of doing so was present: "And I do not permit a woman to teach or to have authority over a man, but to be in silence. For Adam was formed first, then Eve. And Adam was not deceived, but the woman being deceived, fell into transgression" (1 Tim. 2:12–14). Commentators often added that the sight of a woman preaching necessarily elicited lustful thoughts in her audience. Jacobus does not mention any heated debates raised by Mary Magdalene's preaching, nor did the beautiful Mary elicit lust among the Marseillais.[11] It is obvious that the woman beloved by Christ does not need to obey the rules to which mere mortals are subject.

But surprisingly, "the mouth which had pressed such pious and beautiful kisses on the Savior's feet"—to quote Jacobus—does not produce the mass conversion one might expect.[12] Mary has her greatest success with the governor, and even that success is modest. Under her influence the governor, while not accepting Christianity, gives up making sacrifices to the gods. He steps into a religious no-man's-land—betwixt and between. Mary now focuses her efforts on him. She moves from the everyday world, where she and her companions are powerless immigrants, into the spiritual sphere, where she surpasses the governor in power and authority. First, Mary appears in a dream to the governor's wife. We are naturally reminded of Pilate's wife warning her husband not to harm Jesus for she has "suffered many things . . . in a dream because of Him" (Matt. 27:19). But Mary does not speak of Jesus, whose crucifixion and resurrection she has witnessed, nor about Christian salvation. She threatens the wife and then the governor himself with divine retribution for more earthly things: How can they live comfortably, filling their bellies and sleeping between silk sheets, when God's servants are hungry and cold? The governor and his wife comply out of fear. Whoever the god may be in whose name she threatens them, he is powerful enough to intervene in their dreams and to menace them in their sleep. It is better not to contend with him and to bow to his demands.

The governor sees to it that the Christians are provided with food and lodging. This seems to satisfy Mary. She continues to preach, seemingly without result. It is the governor himself who takes the initiative in moving closer to Christianity. He does not suddenly see the light. Rather, he and his wife desire a son. Mary's preaching and threats have prevented them from praying to their gods to have their wish granted. Hence the governor proposes barter: he and his wife will give themselves to Mary's god in exchange for a son. The deal is accepted, and the wife becomes pregnant. But the governor remains undecided. He has already realized the power Mary possesses. In proposing that bargain, he promised to do as she told him, but he did not promise to believe in her god. Now he needs a man, Peter, to "find out whether what Magdalene preached about Christ was the truth."[13]

Three journeys divide the story into distinct narrative units. The first journey occasions the meeting between the governor and Mary and creates the dramatic situation; the second separates them and precipitates the crisis; the third brings them together a second time to close the circle with a catharsis. The crisis is not long in coming. The pilgrims have only just left for Rome, openly displaying the sign of the cross as if that posed no danger, when the sea—the merciful element that led Mary and her company to Marseilles—begins to take everything away from the governor. First, his wife dies onboard ship while giving birth to the promised son. Unexpectedly, the sailors demand that the governor throw the body into the water; otherwise, they explain, the storm will not cease. That scene echoes the story of Jonah fleeing for Tarshish. A mighty tempest sent by God threatens to break up the ship carrying the prophet. When all prayers are in vain, Jonah himself tells the mariners to pick him up and throw him into the sea. When they do so, the sea stops raging. It is clear why Jonah, fleeing God, endangers the ship's crew, but why is the poor mother's corpse so threatening to the sailors? Is it because she symbolizes bad luck? Is it as punishment to her husband for wavering, like Jonah? The reason is not clear. It might be no more than a narrative device to separate the governor from his family (for the father is certain that his son will not survive without his mother). What follows is even stranger. The sailors, who have been unable to control the ship because of the woman's presence onboard, are persuaded by the governor to bring mother and child to the nearest shore. They then manage to guide the ship without difficulty to terra firma. But the ground is too hard for digging a grave, so the tearful husband abandons his wife's body on a hillside, the child clinging to her breast. The governor wails and blames Mary for all his misfortunes. *Her* landing on his shore has brought ruin upon him.

The father loses everything at once. There seems to be no reason for him now to embrace Christianity, which he was willing to do only in return for a son. Mary played the role of midwife badly, and her God has failed. All the same, the governor continues to Rome. There the meeting with the holy *man*, Saint Peter, makes him forget his misfortunes. Peter consoles him with ambiguous words: "Do not take it amiss that your wife sleeps and the infant rests with her. It is in the Lord's power to give gifts to whom he will, to take away what was given, to restore what was taken away, and to turn your grief into joy."[14] Does he mean that she sleeps in the Lord, or is she simply asleep? The saint does not say. Then Peter takes the husband along to Jerusalem, shows him the holy sites of the city, and gives him what he did not receive from Mary: "thorough instruction in the faith." Interestingly, the man does not ask Peter to save his son. That type of contractual relationship is something he has with Mary. With her it is not faith but tangible proof that matters.

We get evidence of that on the return trip to Marseilles. The governor stops at the shore where he has left his wife and his son. We learn for the first time that the child is alive. The governor is overjoyed: "He lifted the boy and said: 'O Mary Magdalene, how happy I would be, how well everything would have turned out for me, if my wife were alive and able to return home with me. Indeed I know, I know and believe beyond a doubt that having given us this child and kept him alive for two years on this rock, you could now, by your prayers, restore his mother to life and health.'"[15] Now, with the miraculous proof in his arms, the governor believes beyond a doubt. And indeed Mary does not fail him: the wife too turns out to be alive. For two years she has remained immobile and silent, has taken neither food nor drink, but her full breasts have continued to nurse her child, who has grown healthy and beautiful.

The governor now realizes how deceiving appearances can be. The misfortunes he endured were not truly misfortunes. Mary did not fail him. Quite the contrary: "O blessed Mary Magdalene," exclaims the wife, "you did me a midwife's service and waited upon my every need like a faithful handmaid."[16] Moreover, while Peter was instructing the husband, Mary served as the wife's tour guide, and the two listened reverently to Saint Peter's words. Upon their return to Marseilles, the couple receive baptism from Saint Maximinus. They easily get the residents of the city to do what years of apostolic preaching failed to achieve—convert to Christianity, destroy the temples of the idols, and build churches instead. The second cycle then ends with a complete conversion: the dead are alive, the idle are industrious, the idolatrous are Christianized, and losses turn out to be gains. Things are not what they seem to be.

With the end of the second miraculous cycle, the third cycle opens. The governor and his wife disappear. Mary, who once so forcefully demanded food and shelter, now becomes an ascetic; she who has worked for others "like a faithful handmaid" now abandons human society. She retires to the wilderness, where there are no streams of water, no grass or trees. There she spends thirty years as a recluse, without food or drink. But this is neither asceticism nor the purifying torments of penance.[17] Suffering is completely absent, and earthly food is replaced by heavenly food. Every day at the seven canonical hours she is carried by angels to heaven and hears the singing of the celestial choirs. For thirty years, then, Mary enjoys in life what others enjoy only after their death. She lives the greater part of her life in heaven; the time she spends on earth is dull and meaningless. Like the governor's wife, Mary is one of the living dead. She is dead to this world but alive in Christ; she seems immobile, but she is constantly on the move; she does not eat, yet she is perfectly well nourished. Appearances are deceiving. The ascetic experiences not suffering but ineffable pleasures; the desert is a paradise, and the dead woman is alive.

The paradox is complete with the description of Mary's death. An anonymous priest sees her rising to heaven borne by angels. Mary then sends the priest with a message to Saint Maximinus: he should wait for her at his church on the day of the Lord's resurrection. On the given day she appears at the church, receives communion from the bishop's hands, and dies before the altar. As long as she was away from the world and ate no earthly food, everyone considered Mary dead, but she was alive; when she returns to the company of human beings, to the church and its rituals, when she eats the physical host, she dies—that is, she lives.

Mary must return to the world in order to leave it, must proclaim that she is alive in order to die, must die in order to live. The third cycle thus closes with yet another return—Mary's. The message of the second cycle is reaffirmed: death and life are only an appearance. The dead may be alive, and the living may well turn out to be dead, like the knight whom Mary brings back to life only so that he can confess his sins and be dead again.[18] But the saint does not merely cross the line separating life from death. Mary erases all boundaries. She is a sinner and a saint, lazy and hardworking, neglectful and conscientious. She expresses, or rather the narrative expresses, the fragility of appearances, the fact that opposing forces (sin and reward, life and death, truth and lie) cannot hold back God and his saints. The lines are crossable, and they are crossed. Nothing coming from God can be surprising: like a magician pulling white doves out of his hat, he draws out of our suffering the white doves of hope.

Saint George

Like Mary Magdalene, George crosses boundaries. Mary the holy sinner does so in a roundabout way, whereas George does so openly, audaciously, with a lance. Who is not familiar with that Christian knight and his dragon? George's dragon, as it happens, appeared relatively late, and initially in artistic representations. In the eleventh century, the dragon suddenly cropped up in illustrations of the story of George's torments. (The saint is designated in Greek sources as the great martyr—"megalo-martyr.")[19] Perhaps it represents an attempt to provide a symbolic image of the saint's persecutor, the devil, who is sometimes designated as *drakōn* in Greek—a fabulous serpent or dragon.[20] At first, then, the dragon was only a symbol for the martyr's demonic enemy. Gradually it acquired a life of its own and a distinct character, inseparable from the saint himself. The shift from image to text did not come about all at once. There is no allusion to Saint George's dragon in the collection of saints' legends compiled by the Dominican Jean de Mailly in 1243.[21] Two years later it is mentioned for the first time by Bartholomew of Trent, not as a symbol but as a true monster, and a few years later it appears with all its attributes in Jacobus de Voragine's *Golden Legend*. From then on, in countless stories, images, statues, medallions, and key rings, the saint and the beast appear side by side, or rather, the saint appears on his horse with the dragon at his feet. George is far from behaving like a victim: he attacks the dragon forcefully and courageously. As for the dragon, it gazes at the saint, half admiring, half resigned to its fate, as if knowing it is destined to die not in a battle with the lance-bearing hero but defeated and domesticated, its throat slit.

Before the dragon's first appearance, two elements had determined George's character: his profession as a soldier and his marvelous capacity to withstand torture. The tradition that made him a Roman soldier contributed to his popularity among the upper classes. There was something refreshing for them about a saint who knew his way around a lance. Military saints were particularly effective defenders against the forces of evil—spiritual and physical (they were, after all, security experts). And they were, naturally, the patron saints of Christian warriors. Between the living and dead warriors a professional and class solidarity was established, a brotherhood in arms. The church encouraged knights to choose models and patrons from among its saints. In the tenth century, Saint Odo of Cluny tried to fashion a new model of the Christian knight with the figure of Saint Gerald of Aurillac,[22] but that patron saint of knights had only limited success. There was nothing heroic about Gerald. Was it conceivable that a warrior, even a Christian one, would attack his enemies with his lance facing backward so as not to do them any harm? Knights were more inclined to admire warriors such as Charlemagne and Roland, who were less timid in the use of force (both enjoyed semiofficial cults). The Crusades—the church's attempt to channel European violence outward—also contributed to the popularity of military saints. In Sicily and the Orient, Christian warriors became aware of the Byzantine traditions of saints such as Theodore, Mercurius, and George, soldier-saints and the protectors of armies.[23] Of all these soldier-saints, it was George who enjoyed the greatest popularity.

Eastern legends attributed to George a series of tortures so extraordinary that even the church fathers, though inured to such things, could not keep from harboring a few doubts.[24] These doubts did not trouble the saint's admirers, however.[25] On the contrary, the soldier provided a good dose of healthy violence to a public hungry for distractions. But what captivated the Crusaders' imagination was not the saint's battle against his persecutors, however heroic that may have been. Chroniclers of the First Crusade describe him leading an army of angels, who had come to support the Crusaders at the siege of Antioch in 1098.[26] A similar role was attributed to Saint James of Compostela in the battle against the Moors in Spain.[27]

But whereas Saint James remained a very Spanish military saint (for the rest of the world he was more one of the apostles than the "Slayer of Moors"), George became a saint of fighting Christian knighthood everywhere in Europe.[28] His only rival was Saint Michael. The cult of the archangel (an unusual case of an angel enjoying a cult), established in the West in the fifth century, experienced a resurgence in the eleventh and twelfth centuries. Michael was venerated not because he was part of the angelic choir but because he was the leader of the heavenly host who had overcome the dragon (that is, the devil who rebelled against God). George's dragon thus grew on fertile symbolic ground. The monster contributed toward transforming the martyr into a warrior, the passive victim of violence into the active perpetrator of it.

Although both Saint Michael and Saint George were dragon slayers, there was nothing particularly Christian about George's dragon. A creature of the cultural borderline, it belonged both to the fantastic Christian cosmos, where men are constantly tortured without dying and wield unheard-of magical powers in the name of the crucified Savior, and to the universal world of archetypes, where good and evil, conscious and unconscious, the earth with its monsters and heaven with its denizens, fight it out.

In *The Golden Legend* the saint's story begins with the dragon. We know nothing of George's past. Even his religion is revealed to us only after the fact, when he informs the young girl threatened by the beast that he will save her in Christ's name. The first part of the narrative does not mention persecutions or the quest for perfection. It begins with the story of a city in the grip of an ecological danger: a dragon threatens to pollute the air of Silena (in Libya) with its venomous breath. That threat, it appears, is a reaction to an act of aggression by the Silenians themselves. At first the monster seems rather peaceful, minding its own business. It is the humans who initiate the hostilities. Yet even when attacked, the monster is content to make its aggressors flee without harming any of them. But after many such assaults, it loses patience. The dragon demands that the residents hand over two sheep a day. This is a reasonable price to pay for keeping the city's air clean. But "running out of sheep,"[29] the residents decide to give the dragon young children, and every day they send it a sheep along with a boy or girl. There is something strange about this. The dragon seems to be more or less endowed with intelligence, able to enter into agreements and respect them. He is also quite modest in his demands. More important, this monster does not thirst for human blood. It seems to prefer sheep, in fact. It is only for want of sheep that the dragon devours humans. Everything suggests that the townspeople, too, are very fond of their sheep, since they begin to send their children to the dragon's pond well before they run out of livestock.

When the king's daughter is selected by lot and her father attempts to ransom her, his subjects are not happy. They threaten to burn both him and his palace if he does not abide by his own decrees. That description recalls the biblical story of Jephthah's daughter. In both cases cruel fate forces the leader to obey his laws by sacrificing his own daughter. All the same, the comparison is not flattering to the king. Jephthah does not seek to go back on his word, even when he learns that it is his daughter who has been selected. The daughter of Jephthah has been singled out, and it is she who must die if her father's oath to God is to be kept, whereas in George's legend a replacement can be found: the king says he prefers to die before she does. There seems to be nothing to prevent him. Immediately thereafter, however, he sends her to the dragon.

It is at this moment that George appears in the story, astride his horse, armed with his lance. It is not known how or why he has come; in any case, these are not pertinent questions in legends. He is there to save the princess. For her part, she does not seem to have a great deal of confidence in the knight. She enjoins him to save himself before he too dies, for the townspeople have not sent the day's sheep with her, and the dragon may assume that George has come to replace one of Silena's much-loved animals. But as soon as she explains the danger to which he is exposing himself, George displays a fatherly attitude: he consistently calls her "child," as if he were inclined to replace the somewhat less than loving father who, along with the whole town, watches her without lifting a finger. As they converse, a change comes over her. At first she calls him "good youth," but later "brave knight," and finally "my good lord." It is then that George attacks the dragon. He does not kill the monster, as might be expected, however, but only captures it. After delivering the blow that knocks it senseless, George asks the young woman to throw her girdle onto the beast, a gesture that immediately tames it. The saint does not vanquish the dragon by Christian methods, then. Granted, he makes the sign of the cross before the attack, but the battle is physical, not spiritual. The miraculous domestication of the monster is also achieved not in the name of Christ (as promised) but with the young woman's girdle, a symbol of virginity exercising a magical influence over fabulous beasts such as dragons, unicorns, and unmarried men. Why does George not kill the dragon? Because he needs it to force the townspeople to accept Christian baptism. It seems that the dragon, in becoming tame, will no longer pollute the city unless the saint orders it to do so. It also appears that George does not have a great deal of confidence in his powers of persuasion. As for the townspeople, they are already accustomed to blackmail. Given the choice between salvation and air pollution, they choose salvation. It is only then that George kills the dragon.

Dragons frequently incarnate evil. They symbolize the powers of the unconscious that rise up out of the earth. They are half serpent, half fabulous lizard. They threaten to poison earth dwellers. One of the gods of heaven, or one of their representatives on earth, must fight and slay them. These myths are common to many beliefs: Baal fights against Yam, Marduk against Tiamat and her monsters, Yahweh against Rahab and its sea monster attendants, and even Michael fights against the terrible dragon of the Apocalypse. Perseus saves Andromeda from the sea monster. But George's battle with the dragon does not assume these cosmic proportions. Precisely because Jacobus places the dragon in the nonreligious world of fantasy and folklore, it remains a relatively innocuous monster. George can use it, then get rid of it, more because he does not know what to do with it than because of any great danger it poses after its subjugation. Thus, on the one hand, the dragon does not represent altogether terrible and negative forces, as in the mythic epics; on the other, it does not represent any threat to the young woman's sexual purity, as it often does in legends. Jacobus de Voragine uses the princess almost incidentally: with the dragon's defeat, he forgets her entirely. Not only does she not marry the hero (who is supposed to symbolize a restrained sexuality, unlike the unbridled and threatening sexuality represented by the monster), but Jacobus does not even make her the hero's asexual companion in martyrdom. She simply disappears.

After the Christianization of the city, the king builds a church dedicated to Saint Mary and to George. All that remains for the young man, who is dead while still alive (since he already has a church to commemorate him), is to die—properly, that is, like a martyr. Similar to the dragon and George himself, martyrdom appears out of nowhere. We are suddenly told of a horrible persecution under the governor Dacian which has already taken the lives of seventeen thousand men and women. Is this a different kingdom? A different region? How did the rumor reach George's ears in Christian Silena? We do not know. George arrives at the place of persecution, rids himself of his soldier's uniform, and puts on "the garb of Christians" (we are not really sure what this consists of). It is clear that, even before changing his clothes, the saint was already Christian, but his act symbolizes the transition from the legendary and folkloric sphere to the Christian mythical sphere. Only there, in the world of religion, do truly great evil and truly great good reside. The dragon that appears in the first part of the narrative pales in comparison to the true dragon in the second part, which is none other than the murderous pagan tyrant.

The account of George's martyrdom is in three parts. First, the saint endures the most horrible tortures, but the vision of the Lord makes them seem insignificant. As usual in this sort of narrative, the narrator does not take the trouble to explain how the saint's body survived the torments inflicted on it. Nothing is impossible for God's favorites. In the second part, a sort of competition of magical forces, passive and active, takes place between the Christian saint and pagan magician. George drinks a great quantity of poison, a motif also found in the Lives of John the Apostle and Saint Benedict, and he overcomes the torments of the wheel and the cauldron of molten lead. Then he calls down fire from heaven, which consumes the temple and its priests, and the earth opens to swallow up their remains. The triumph is not just physical; it is also moral. The saint's spirit has not faltered. George then manages to convert the magician who attempted to kill him, as well as the wife of the tyrant who is attempting to break down his resistance. The heroic death of these two characters, executed by the tyrant, provides further proof of George's power and of his tormentors' wickedness. The third part, which concludes the story, is as usual commonplace and predictable. Something must put an end to the saint's series of successes: otherwise he would lose his right to be a martyr. After prevailing over the dragon and the magician, after emerging unscathed from the wheel and shackles, torches and hooks, molten lead and poison, after calling on heaven and earth to aid him, he is executed by decapitation without further ado.[30] His first post mortem miracle is to finish off his torturer. Once he has accomplished his mission, that dragon too can disappear.

Saint Christopher

The patron saint of travelers appears on an incalculable number of good luck charms. For a long time he has assumed the aspect of a kind old man bearing the baby Jesus on his shoulders. That was not the case at the start of his career.[31] Christopher appears for the first time in the fourth-century Gnostic text *The Acts of Saint Bartholomew*, where he is described as belonging to the tribe of cynocephali, cannibalistic monsters with human bodies and dogs' heads who had been tamed by Christian baptism. That version had been known in the West since the eighth century. Jacobus rejects it, and turns the giant cynocephalus into an enormous Canaanite, "fearsome of visage" but completely human.[32] As in numerous other narratives in *The Golden Legend*, there is a clear separation between the "universal"-mythical part of the story and the properly Christian part. The hero first completes his journey in the world of universal symbols and motifs, and only then enters the Christian sphere, where he suffers martyrdom. The "universal" part is not devoid of Christian connotations. The hero is Christian, but his

hope (vain, of course) of escaping his fate, Julian flees to a distant country and marries a widow as a reward for his great service to the community—a somewhat toned-down reminiscence of the Oedipus story. It is then that the parents, who have been seeking him all over the world, arrive and are received by the wife. The sexual motif is not totally absent from the story of the Christian saint: "Finding the two, his wife and her lover, sleeping together in his bed he silently drew his sword and killed them both." His wife and her lover—his mother and his father. The immediate decision to punish himself with sexual abstinence (the husband and wife now address each other as "my brother" and "my sister") proves that this is not merely a sin of violence; this is a crime of passion.

Julian and his sister-wife take people across the river. That role has a dual meaning: if the river marks the boundary between life and death, the ferryman is a *psychopompos*, a conductor of souls—like Charon, boatman of Hades, who ferries souls across the Styx. But even though saints are indeed symbolic ferrymen, intermediaries between men and God, it is difficult to maintain that our two saints are really fulfilling that role. At the time they are ferrying others, the two have not yet ferried themselves across the mystic river. They are clearly ferrying bodies, not souls. It seems that in both legends the role of ferryman signifies marginality. The river, like the hospice, is located on the outskirts of the city, and is a place open to everyone—good and bad, saints and sinners. By taking people across the river without asking questions, the saint renounces his moral and religious status, which would have allowed him to choose and to impose conditions. It is clear why Julian is pushed to the margins: he is a sinner seeking repentance because he has killed innocent guests who came to find shelter under his roof. He has murdered his parents. But why was Christopher sent to the river? Probably to learn a lesson in humility. Christopher, who seeks only the company of the most powerful prince in the world, is not worthy of that aim until he is ready to serve without distinction anyone who turns to him.

Having met Christ, Christopher goes to the city to seek martyrdom. The period and the place remain unclear. How does one find persecution as a Christian in a world where the saint's first master, the ruler he thought to be the most powerful king in the world, is Christian? It is pointless to ask such nagging questions. It is enough to realize that all the standard elements are present: all of a sudden the saint becomes utterly Christian. Jacobus has forgotten that the giant Canaanite is not in the habit of praying: now he attributes great power to his prayers. He performs a miracle and leads thousands of idolaters to convert to Christianity and to die for the glory of Christ. Since no one can impose anything on him, Christopher goes to his martyrdom on his own initiative. When he meets the tyrant, they exchange the usual invectives. As always, we are dealing with a tragedy of errors. The tyrant believes that his worldly power makes him superior; the saint knows that only spiritual power matters. It is the persecutor, not the persecuted, who is really on the path to a horrible end. We encounter another classic motif here, which we encountered in Jerome's *Life of Paul*: the attempt to break the saint's spirit by seducing his body. It fails. The two seductresses convert and are martyred after jeering at the pagan gods and throwing a large number of idols onto the ground using their girdles (a symbol of sexual abstinence we also saw in the story of Saint George). The women's sexuality had no power against the saint; their chastity is all-powerful against the idols.

What more is there? Christopher is left unharmed by iron rods, a red-hot iron helmet, a fiery iron chair. A volley of arrows launched at him freezes in the air and never reaches its target. Only the sword prevails over him. He dies decapitated. If he was a cynocephalus, his dog's head is now gone for good.

Saint Alexis

The story of Saint Alexis is unusual: the hero is neither a martyr nor a miracle-working hermit.[36] He is a saint who has chosen to live in poverty and humility within the city, and he does not perform a single miracle during his lifetime. The oldest version of the Alexis legend is a fifth-century Syriac text, the *Life of Mar Risha* (*Mar Risha* means "the holy pauper").[37] According to this version, the saint was the son of rich Christian parents living in Rome. The day before his wedding he suddenly decides to set out in a boat for the East, to leave everything behind, and to live as a beggar. He distributes the few valuables he is carrying with him and lives as an ascetic in Edessa. Emissaries who come from Rome to find him do not recognize him. After a while, the doorkeeper of a church learns in a vision that the unknown beggar is a saint in disguise. He watches him pray and perform his ascetic practices, and forces him to admit his saintliness. The saint implores the doorkeeper not to reveal to anyone what he has seen and heard. Later, the poor man falls ill. The doorkeeper persuades him with great effort to go to the hospital for the indigent, where he visits him every day, but God answers the saint's wish to remain anonymous. On the eve of the saint's death, the doorkeeper is held up by urgent affairs and does not pay his daily visit. The next day he learns that the man has died and has been buried among the other poor beggars who died the same day. He hastens to the bishop, tells him the story, and together they open the tomb. But the saint's body has disappeared; only his rags are left. He remains without a body, without a name, and without a cult. The ancient versions of the legend in Greek greatly resemble the Syriac version. But they give the anonymous saint a name: Alexius.[38]

Alexis was unknown in the West before the tenth century, when he was "imported" by Archbishop Sergius of Damascus, who was exiled to Rome in 977. The archbishop was amazed to discover that the locals were unfamiliar with that Roman saint, and was even more amazed to find his relics in the very church where he was residing, the church of Saint Boniface on the Aventine Hill. The Latin text is based on the Syriac and Greek versions but adds new elements to them (perhaps under the influence of the Greek legend of John Calibite, a Roman anchorite who returned to Rome and lived in a shack near his parents' house). In the eleventh and twelfth centuries the legend was translated, generally in verse, into several European languages. A French version of the story, according to the Chronicle of Laon, played a role in the conversion of Waldo, founder of the Waldensian heresy. The chronicler relates that Waldo heard the story of Alexis sung by a jongleur and decided to portion out his possessions and devote his life to Christ.[39]

The Latin legend begins with a description of Alexis' parents, Euphemianus and Algaes, a rich and charitable couple, apparently irreproachable. The description of the belated birth of their son after years of barrenness only reinforces our impression of their piety. The parents do not complain about their sterility. They simply increase their prayers and give away enormous sums to charity. Ultimately God grants them a male child. Children born under such circumstances are God's favorites: Isaac, Samuel, Samson, and John the Baptist are destined from birth for great feats. These children belong more to God than to their parents, and the parents in fact dedicate them to God, who has allowed them to raise the children for him. Isaac, whose parents tried to exempt him from consecration, is suddenly claimed by God, and it is only the father's willingness to sacrifice him that saves him from death. Samson, Samuel, and John the Baptist are in the service of God from youth. Alexis' parents try to back out of dedicating the child to God by offering themselves in his place. When he is born, they give up all sexual relations and thereby devote themselves to God. Their sacrifice is not accepted. Alexis belongs to God, not to his parents. He is going to demonstrate it unequivocally.

When Alexis reaches adulthood, his parents wish to marry him to a girl of the imperial household. On the wedding night, after the celebration, Alexis urges his wife to remain in the pure state of virginity. He gives her his golden ring and his girdle, and leaves without consummating the marriage. He then seizes a portion of his father's possessions and secretly flees the city for Edessa in Asia Minor. Young people (and especially young women) who refuse to marry are not rare in saints' legends. We often encounter young Christian girls who do not want to marry the pagans who desire them (for example, Cecilia, Catherine of Alexandria, and Margaret of Antioch). Sometimes a young woman wishes to live chastely and her parents try to force her to marry. In both cases there is a conflict, sometimes violent, and the saint must cope with the hostility of those around her. In the story of Alexis there is no indication of the slightest hostility

toward him. Everything takes place in a Christian empire. All the protagonists, from the parents to the bride, are good, pious Christians. This is also
not a story about a saint and his parents having conflicting wishes: the
marriage was not imposed on Alexis; the bride was worthy; he went
through the wedding rites without protest. If he wanted to remain celibate,
why did he not say that to his devout parents? If he wanted to live chastely
beside his spouse (as his parents had done), why did he abandon her on the
wedding night? Why did he flee like a thief in the night?

These questions caused uneasiness even among medieval readers. One
French version, *La vie de saint Alexis*, attempts to describe Alexis' flight as a
response to a sudden moral anxiety. The saint senses his desire for his wife
awakening and understands that he will be unable to live in chastity beside
her. Hence he flees so as not to succumb to the flesh.[40] A different French
version, *Li roumans de saint Alessin*, tries to smooth out another difficulty by
relating that the saint obtained the consent of his wife to live chastely.[41] But
the saint's decision raises not only moral problems but legal ones as well.
The Christian norm is that a decision to live chastely cannot be made
without the spouse's consent.[42] Alexis' wife says nothing, and even if she
did agree to live chastely, it seems quite clear from her reactions later on
that she did not expect to live apart. It is also perplexing why Alexis would
leave without his father's consent. A father's authority over his son (*patria
potestas*) did not end with the son's marriage—particularly if the son did
not consider himself married. Only baptism received against the wishes of
a non-Christian father constituted an exception to the rule. That is obviously not the case here. Yet Alexis does not ask for his father's consent to
depart; worse, Alexis takes possession of a portion of his father's goods
without permission, which, at least in legal terms, has to be considered
theft.

The Latin version does not answer these questions. It does not mention
any attraction on Alexis' part to the young bride, who throughout the narrative remains a drab and marginal figure. It is not she whom Alexis flees
but his parents. The gold ring and the girdle he gives her just before he
leaves are symbols with a sexual connotation, the ring symbolizing mar-

riage and the belt the capacity to accomplish or renounce the sexual act. They also attest to the bond with the father: all of his servants wear golden girdles. Alexis renounces his. It is not primarily sexual desire that threatens Alexis but the wealth and status associated with his father. In Edessa, and then in Rome, Alexis makes a career of poverty and anonymity.[43] That career, which is in itself a fairly common choice in Christianity, takes a disturbing turn. There is something detached and merciless about the saint's path toward salvation. Alexis walks alone. He does not attach himself to fellow travelers; he uses them as instruments and ultimately abandons them to their fate. What makes his journey even more problematic is that the narrator chooses to place innocent people in his path: his wife, his mother, his father. In the course of the narrative, these three characters experience great suffering, but there is not the slightest trace of hesitation in the saint. He is not moved by compassion for a single instant. It is not easy to love Alexis. It is possible to accept a saint who, on his path toward heaven, passes over the heads of his enemies and persecutors. It is more difficult to bear with someone who makes his loved ones his stepping-stones.

What exactly does Alexis seek in Edessa? Anonymity, detachment, alienation. He settles in among the beggars, in front of the church of Mary the Mother of God, content to go unrecognized by his father's servants, who give alms to him as to the other beggars. But Alexis is not a beggar like any other. Not only did he begin his stay in Edessa by distributing a portion of his father's enormous wealth, not only did he *choose* the life of poverty, but also, unlike ordinary beggars, he continues to play the philanthropist in rags. Like Simeon, of the alms he collects he keeps only what he needs to survive and distributes the rest to the poor.

The gap that separates Alexis from others becomes even more marked when the narrator begins to describe the situation in the house he left behind. His father sends servants throughout the world to find him, and his mother and wife mourn him continually. On one side, then, the saint disperses possessions and accumulates good works; on the other, his father futilely squanders his capital in search of his son. The saint displays total indifference toward his wife, while her life is entirely centered on him, and she languishes desperately for him. The saint lives beside the Mother of God, but his own mother suffers terribly from his absence.

Things might have continued like this, but a turning point suddenly occurs in the story. Alexis is exposed—not by someone who wishes him ill, but by God himself. After seventeen years, "the image of the Blessed Virgin that was in the church spoke to the watchman saying: 'Bring in the man of God, because he is worthy of the kingdom of heaven. The Spirit of God rests upon him, and his prayer rises like incense in the sight of God.'"[44] The heavenly parents who have replaced the earthly parents want the son to unveil himself, to be fruitful, to grow up, to give others more than scraps and leftovers. It is time for him to offer *spiritual* charity.

Alexis refuses. He disobeys God and the Mother of God. Outwardly he is fleeing the crowds of admirers that gather around him, but in fact, like Jonah, he is fleeing God, who wants to force him to serve. Alexis tries to seek refuge in Tarsus, in a house dedicated to Saint Paul; but God, who has dominion over the seas, has other plans. He causes a storm that brings Alexis back to Rome. The return is a key moment in the story. Alexis, finding himself in Rome, does not leave. In a stupefying decision he makes up his mind to go home and spend his last years there. "I will go and stay unknown in my father's house," he proclaims, "and so will not be a burden to anyone else."[45] Up till now, Alexis has tried to separate himself as much as possible from his home and to take refuge in faraway churchyards, among anonymous beggars. Now he changes his mind, and instead of moving away, he moves closer. In a Christian version of Edgar Allan Poe's "Purloined Letter," the place where he is most visible is the last place people look. Alexis is confident that he will not be recognized in his father's house among his family and servants. He intends to be a prophet without honor, in his own country and among his own relatives, and in his own house (Mark 6:4). In his father's house he will also be able to escape God, who is pursuing him. He will no longer beg alms or distribute them. He will withdraw entirely into himself, seeing but unseen.

At first glance the reunion between Alexis and his father is reminiscent of the scene of the Prodigal Son's return (Luke 15:11–32). In both cases the son leaves the paternal home with a portion of his father's wealth. The Prodigal Son squanders his money out of vice, while Alexis does so out of virtue. The Prodigal Son, who is left penniless, decides to return home, to be a servant in the father's house; Alexis returns to his native city and decides to live by begging in his father's house. At this point the two stories diverge. In the parable, the father recognizes his son from afar, falls on his neck, and kisses him. The son recognizes his moral inferiority: "I have sinned against heaven and in your sight, and am no longer worthy to be called your son." The father forgives him, "for this my son was dead and is alive again; he was lost and is found." He makes everything return to order: he dresses his son, orders the fatted calf killed, and places a ring on his finger. In the story of Alexis, the father does not recognize his son in Rome, just as his servants failed to recognize him in Edessa. Alexis' words to his father are laden with irony: "Servant of God, give orders that I, a stranger, be taken into your house, and that the crumbs from your table be given to me as food. And may the Lord deign to be merciful on the one you have in a strange land."[46] Alexis appeals to his father's pity by virtue of his love—the love for the son lost in a foreign land—and the father remembers his son and is overcome with sympathy. Except the son is no longer in a foreign land; he has been found. But now, perhaps even more than before, Alexis is "in a strange land." Like Mary Magdalene, Alexis is one of the living dead. Since he does not reveal his identity, nothing returns to order. He does not ask forgiveness, nor does he offer embraces. The father's ring, which was given to the wife, does not return to the son's finger. He remains unattached, uncontrolled, uncontrollable. The father offers him food and drink as well as refuge, but Alexis is not ready to accept his father's fatted calf. He eats almost nothing, does not speak, does not leave the house. He is there day and night, nourished by his fasting, by the mockery of his servants, by his terrible, terrible silence.

Alexis returns to life when he dies. "For this my son was dead and is alive again; he was lost and is found." On his deathbed, after seventeen years of lies and dissimulation, Alexis writes out his story. It is then that God exposes him for the second time. In the church a voice is heard once

more from heaven, and it proclaims the presence of the man of God: he is
at the home of Euphemianus. The pious old man rushes back to his house.
He does not realize that God was referring to his son. His son is lost. He
finds the beggar dead, holding a parchment. He tries but fails to remove the
parchment from Alexis' hand. Even dead, Alexis is not ready to extend his
hand to his father. It is only when the pope and the two emperors arrive
that the dead man's grip is loosened. They read the parchment and learn
the truth at last. Euphemianus falls in a faint onto the ground, then rends
his clothes and pulls out his hair and beard. Throwing himself on his son's
body, he cries out: "Why have you saddened me this way? Why have you
stricken me all these years with grief and lamentation?" The mother's accusations are equally bitter: "Why did you do this? Why have you treated
us so cruelly? You saw your father and miserable me shedding tears, and
did not make yourself known to us."[47] The wife's reaction is much less
emotional than the parents'; she does not touch Alexis' body or reproach
him. It seems that she rightly understands that Alexis' hostility was directed
not against her but against his parents. She was only an accidental victim of
the situation, collateral damage. After finally being reunited with his parents—or definitively escaping them—Alexis comes out of the cubbyhole
where he lived. He performs miracles and even makes his saintliness public
through the fragrance given off by his grave. The circle is closed.

It is difficult to understand the motivations of a fictive character such as
Alexis. Why does he act as he does? What is the message that the story
conveys about this saint? Since we do not find the usual villains, such as pagans who despise Christ, or simply sinners, there is also no clear division
here between good and bad. The people around Alexis are God-fearing
Christians who are not accused of any specific sin. Why does he choose to
hurt them so? There is no catharsis here. "Now," says the father, "my mirror is broken and my hope gone. Now begins the grieving that has no
end."[48] Has Alexis chosen to demonstrate his resolve to overcome the most
difficult ordeals that proximity to the beloved represents, like the hermit
who spends the night beside a naked woman? I do not think so. Nothing
indicates that love or compassion tempts Alexis. What is the reason, then?

It seems to me that the story of Alexis deals with the conflict between a son and his parents and, more particularly, between a son and his father. More than the mother, it is the father who suffers from his son's ironic distance. The father's righteousness proves that there is nothing at stake morally in this conflict; rather it expresses the hostility that paternal authority itself provokes in the son. This prodigal son is not ready to forgive his father for being his father.

Cecilia and Margaret

To conclude this discussion of *The Golden Legend* we consider two martyrdom narratives, those of Margaret of Antioch and Cecilia of Rome. The two, like many of the most popular saints in the late Middle Ages, never existed. Their stories are very different from Perpetua's touching prison journal with which we began, and more than the stories we have examined so far, they call attention to issues of gender and sexuality.

Margaret first appeared in the East (where she is known as "Marina") in the fourth or fifth century. In the sixth century her story was declared apocryphal by a "decree" (wrongly) attributed to Pope Gelasius I. The legend arrived in the West in the eighth century. In the ninth we find the saint mentioned in several liturgical collections, and her legend also appears in manuscripts as a separate text. By the twelfth century, Margaret was becoming increasingly popular—a popularity that *The Golden Legend* helped consolidate.[49] The saint of Antioch was one of the "Fourteen Holy Helpers," a group of saints whose aid in case of misfortune was considered particularly effective.[50] It was her voice, along with those of Saint Michael and Saint Catherine of Alexandria, whom Joan of Arc heard commanding her to save France.

The story of Cecilia was apparently written between the late fifth and mid-sixth centuries. The legend was probably composed to provide an explanation for the name of a Roman church, taken from the matron who had it built.[51] The cult of the saint was active in Rome from antiquity, but like that of Margaret, it experienced a revival in the twelfth and thirteenth centuries. Cecilia is the patron saint of music and musicians. In the twentieth century, when a papal commission of historians revised the calendar, her name was removed, together with the names of other saints declared spurious or doubtful. But Cecilia's popularity prevailed over the experts' skepticism because of "the veneration of the masses."[52] It is good to be popular.

The story of Cecilia was linked more than once to that of Saint Alexis. Both narratives are about saints who defend their virginity *after* being properly wed. Both inform their spouses of their vow of chastity on their wedding night, and both succeed in preserving their virginity. But there are differences. Alexis flees the house and severs all ties with his wife. Cecilia remains at her husband's side until his death. In the story of Alexis there are no pagans. Alexis lives in a Christian empire and dies in his own bed, while the tale of Cecilia and her husband begins as a story about preserving moral purity but ends as a story of martyrdom. More important, for Alexis sexuality represents just one of the ties that bind him to a world from which he wants to cut himself off. For Cecilia virginity is the essential thing. He is an ascetic; she is a virgin.

Cecilia goes through the marriage rites in a state of high anxiety. She fears defilement. If her body is defiled, she will be "ruined." Unlike Alexis, she does not feel she has the capacity to preach and to persuade, let alone decide unilaterally. In the silence of the bridal chamber she confesses to her husband, Valerian, that she has a lover—a confession that would have meant her physical "ruin" under normal circumstances—but she immediately adds that it is a supernatural lover, a jealous angel who watches over her body with exceeding zeal. If Valerian dares touch his wife with lust, the angel will strike him. That declaration has very weighty implications. Not only does the saint designate an angel—who often appears in religious and profane narratives to announce an imminent birth—with the problematic term "lover," but she also runs the risk that her husband will refuse to believe the lover's angelic nature and kill her straightaway. The dialogue between husband and wife, then, begins not with an effort to persuade the husband that virginity is important but with a challenge. The angel is not a chaste guardian of her virginity but a jealous lover. Valerian has to accept this not out of respect for virginity but out of respect for power. The angel's invisible power is greater than his. But the threat is followed by a promise of reward, a bargain: if the husband agrees to Cecilia's request, he will enter a world where he too will have access to that invisible power.

Valerian bows to the threat but sets conditions all the same. He declares that he will let his wife remain a virgin if it turns out that her lover is more powerful than he; but if the latter is a mere man, he will kill both his wife and her lover. It is only then that Christianity enters the picture. Cecilia responds with a condition of her own: if he wants to see the angel, her husband must become a Christian. Valerian then allows himself to be baptized, not out of deep Christian faith but as part of his marriage arrangements.

Valerian goes to see Urban, bishop of Rome, to be baptized. He then has a vision of an old man dressed in white holding a book written in gold letters (Paul? God himself?). This frightens him so much that he faints. Cecilia's Christian supporters are real and dangerous, it seems. As soon as Valerian has been baptized, he is permitted to see the angel in his bride's room. Somewhat surprisingly, however, the angel is not Cecilia's spiritual husband, as we might have deduced from Cecilia's words. In fact, he serves as best man in a new, spiritual wedding, in which the spouses present each other with wreaths of flowers: lilies, a symbol of virginity, and roses, a symbol of martyrdom. Two elements deserve our attention. First, because Cecilia is not designated as Christ's bride, she can remain the (virgin) wife of Valerian. (In other words, she does not tamper with the familial system.) Second, the body plays an important role in establishing the spiritual system of relationships. The purity of the body is an indispensable condition for the purity of the soul and the vision of divine grace. Only "those whom chastity pleases" will be able to see God.[53] But while seeing the invisible requires chastity and baptism, chastity is not without sensual manifestations. When Valerian's brother Tiburtius enters the couple's room, he senses a powerful odor of roses and lilies.

As soon as the relationship between Cecilia and Valerian has been ar-ranged, they become equals. Whereas at first they exchanged threats, now they operate on a footing of complete, nonhierarchical understanding, since what makes the woman subservient to the man is sexual desire ("Your desire *shall be* for your husband, / And he shall rule over you" [Gen. 3:16]). Without desire there is no longer servitude. Without lust there is real, unfettered sensuality. Valerian wants his brother Tiburtius to join them in a chaste ménage à trois. "There is nothing sweeter[54] to me in this life than the love of my only brother," he declares. The image is sensual; like the fragrance emanating from Cecilia's and Valerian's blossoming wreaths, spiritual love is sweet. As we learn from Cecilia's words to Valerian, the invisible world does not have a totally different set of parameters and values. But it is something more. It is better.

Once this chaste circle is closed, we are transferred from the world of competing forms of sensuality and virginal liberation, where Christianity plays a secondary and instrumental role, to the world of martyrdom, entirely centered on the struggle between a spiritually aggressive Christianity and a physically aggressive paganism. In that world sexuality no longer plays any role. The evil prefect Almachius does not try to seduce Cecilia and does not threaten her virginity. In the dialogue between the martyrs and their torturers, the same motif returns again and again: the opposition between the deceptive force of the visible world and the true force of the invisible world. "Am I hearing this in a dream, Valerian, or are the things you are saying true?" asks Tiburtius. "We've been living in dream, but now we dwell in the truth," replies his brother.[55] When the brothers refuse to sacrifice to Jupiter, they are beheaded. Their executioner testifies that he saw "the martyrs' souls going forth like virgins from the bridal chamber."[56] Then Cecilia too is beheaded in a boiling bath where she lay without feeling as much as a drop of perspiration.

Lust plays no role in Cecilia's story. This is not a typical story of ascetic struggle against dangerous passions. Cecilia and Valerian do not have to suppress their lust. The entire account is about the absence of lust. The story of Margaret, by contrast, begins with a mix of strong feelings, sexual and religious. Margaret's father *hates* her because she has converted to

Christianity, and the prefect Olibrius burns with desire for her. The body in Margaret's account is not marginalized. It is present as a subversive, destructive force. Margaret's beautiful flesh ignites Olibrius' passion and is indirectly the cause of his hostility toward her religion, since the legend does not mention any persecution of Christians before the encounter between the saint and the prefect. Olibrius' reaction to Margaret's beauty combines the sexual and the political, the physical body and the body politic. "No beautiful and noble girl like you should have a crucified god," he exclaims.[57] We might have expected Margaret to inform her suitor that, her religious preferences notwithstanding, she has a heavenly lover, but she does nothing of the sort. She simply ignores the prefect's passion and engages him in a theological debate. If he believes in Christ's crucifixion, he should also believe in his resurrection. But Olibrius does not ignore the body; it is now transmuted from a source of pleasure to a battleground of wills: "Vain girl, pity your beauty and adore the gods. . . . Unless you yield to me, I'll have your body torn to shreds."[58] Lust seems to have disappeared; Olibrius is more interested in Margaret's willful pride than in her sexual favors. This is not a matter of course. For example, in the life of Saint Catherine of Alexandria—like Margaret, a beautiful Christian virgin—for example, the evil emperor's threats are accompanied by propositions that she become his lover or wife. Catherine declares that she is the bride of Christ, who is her sweetness and delight. It is him she loves.[59] The English versions of the legend of Saint Margaret make desire the principal motive and the desire for Christ a replacement for earthly passion.[60] But in Jacobus' version the lust for power—the desire to break down the adversary's spiritual resistance—matters more than carnal lust. Hence he rejects the very popular version of her tale that has Margaret swallowed by the devil, who appears in her prison cell as a dragon. Inside the belly of the beast, the saint makes the sign of the cross, the dragon explodes, and the virgin emerges unharmed. Jacobus dismisses the story as "apocryphal and not to be taken seriously."[61] It is surprising to find such scruples in an author who generally tends to reproduce the most fantastical descriptions without too many questions, and who added Saint George's dragon to the mythical Christian repertoire.

Jacobus has nothing against dragons. The difficulty with *Margaret's* dragon is that this monstrous symbol of the devil devouring her expresses an intimacy—albeit momentary—with the earthly, phallic forces of passion and the body. The saint swallowed by the dragon penetrates its body and becomes assimilated with it. She escapes intact and immaculate, of course, but she has experienced something physical, carnal even. Popular tradition was less scrupulous than Jacobus might have wished. The virgin of Antioch was venerated as the patron saint of midwives and women in childbirth—that is, of the consequences of desire. In *The Golden Legend* the devil appears in the form of a man. He does not swallow the saint but tries to stop her from praying. He fails. Margaret grabs him by the head, throws him to the ground, and plants her right foot on his muscular neck. This is an allusion to the serpentine nature of the devil, trampled underfoot by the Blessed Virgin Mary. The devil does not really threaten Margaret—any more than he would threaten the Holy Virgin. Margaret does not touch the devil. She allows the sole of her right shoe to touch his neck. That is all. And like Olibrius, Jacobus' devil is more preoccupied with status than with desire. He regrets that it is a woman who crushes him. He has no desire to devour or to be devoured, to penetrate or to be penetrated. He converses with Margaret about this and that, religion and ethics, topics wholly unrelated to the passion with which the circle opened and which will close with the heroine's death. After a while she tires of him, and the Father of Lies is shown the door like a mere nuisance. She endures the usual tortures and is finally decapitated.

We are approaching the end of this book, and we have our own circle to close. Margaret's encounter with the devil brings to mind our first heroine, Perpetua. On the eve of her execution she has a vision of a contest with the devil. There too the Old Serpent ends up eating dust, trampled underfoot by a woman. But there seems to be a world of difference between the tender African mother and the virgin of Antioch. The fictive heroine is supremely confident of the narrator's ability to let her overcome any obstacle. The true heroine, beset by fears and doubts, struggles to make sense of her life. In the end, she writes, she feels confident in her victory. But can one really know? Who can tell what was going on in the mind of this sensitive young woman when she was murdered in the arena? "This is what I have done until the eve of the games. Let whoever wishes to do so tell what happened during the games." These are the last words Perpetua wrote.

Concluding Reflections

I can imagine another Abraham, who, to be sure, would not make it all the way to patriarch, not even to old-clothes dealer—who would be ready to carry out the order for the sacrifice as a waiter would be ready to carry out his orders but who would still never manage to perform the sacrifice, because he cannot get away from home, he is indispensable, the farm needs him, there is always something that must be attended to, the house isn't finished.

Franz Kafka to Robert Klopstock, Matliary, June 1921

THE CULT OF SAINTS GAVE RISE to a new genre of religious narratives. With the collapse of classical culture in the West, saints' stories became separated for centuries from the cult of saints and were confined to churches and monasteries. Between the eleventh and the late thirteenth centuries the genre made a forceful comeback, becoming a central element in the religious life of Western society. Everyone participated in that process:

the suppliers of religious materials offered narratives to spur action—and, more often, to serve as substitutes for action—and the religious consumers learned to absorb these narratives as an integral part of their religious diet, whether around the saints' shrines or in the church's celebrations. By the late thirteenth century, the triumph of that narrative revolution in the West was decisive. Latin culture and its offshoots created a new narrative canon whose popularity crossed national and class boundaries. The foundations of the new hagiographical cosmos lay in a certain expanded and revised version of *The Golden Legend*, a work that was as important for the cult of saints as the *Malleus maleficarum* was for the witch hunt. The attacks of humanists and reformers broke the spell of Christian consensus. After the fourteenth century, very few ancient saints were added to the number of popular saints, and by the sixteenth century, modern saints were by definition controversial.

The complex social process that resulted in the narrative revolution raises two questions: *Quomodo?* (how did Christian society in the West create its narrative repertoire?) and *Cui bono?* (what purpose did it serve?). I have addressed the first question throughout these pages. The second I have discussed in various chapters, in concrete situations and in terms of specific audiences. I would now like to focus on some more general aspects.

What was the purpose of saints' stories in the Middle Ages? The simple answer is that they served the political interests of the church. Power and domination are keys that open every door. They provide a simple response to a very complicated question. In this view religious stories of all kinds, produced by the ecclesiastical elite or under its authority, constituted a control mechanism. Through them, the elite transmitted messages—supposedly religious, but in fact political—of social obedience, the *virtus heroica* of any authoritarian regime. In other words, saints' stories, like religion itself, are "the opiate of the people." They are the pie in the sky that distracts people from focusing their sights on the hard facts of reality. Such a view of religion was attractive to critics of the ecclesiastical establishment from both ends of the political spectrum (on the left the church was accused of being too keen on brainwashing, on the right of not being keen enough). The church-as-opium-dealer approach represents the ideal mix of conspiracy theory and self-proclaimed enlightenment. Other people's religions are to be tolerated in the name of multiculturalism; our own established religion is an obstacle to true open-mindedness. True open-mindedness is anticlerical, anti-organized (Christian) religion. Of course, now that the church has lost much of its power, the need to blame it for being the source of all impurities is less pressing. Religion has become just one narcotic among many others in the political elite's conspiracy to numb the masses by controlling the media. Propaganda is no longer an ecclesiastical term. As in Marx's time, the strategy of those who envision cultural production as indoctrination is not merely description or analysis: it is an ethical-political act of the intelligentsia in a world where elites hungry for power strive to perpetuate their domination, and where hordes of subject-victims swallow the drug dispensed to them and derive only the "right" hallucinations from them. Enlightened intellectuals (and nowadays enlightenment often involves denouncing the historical Enlightenment as itself part of the great conspiracy) expose the dirty games of the political and economic elites. In so doing they keep oppression in check: they dispel their readers' illusions and make them see things as they are. In the best of cases they speak to the oppressed; most often they speak to other members of the intellectual elite. But then initiates do not need "demystification"; on the contrary, they hold it for an article of faith that power, any power, spends its time deceiving the good common people. Offer them new evidence and they will merely nod their heads knowingly.

More than anything else, this interpretation reflects the poverty of certain historiographical and philosophical schools linked to the contempt intellectuals feel for the lower classes. It is not that the elite or elites do not seek to perpetuate their own domination, or that they do not advocate the virtue of obedience. Of course they do. The question is not what the intentions of the elites are but what means are at their disposal and how gullible consumers are. The analysis of symbolic oppression often falls short in two important respects. First, it tends to disregard the inner contradictions and the ineffectiveness of many of the religious messages the elites produce or help to diffuse. Second, it does not take into account the use their consumers make of them: in the symbolic realm, consumers are never passive; they engage in creative consumption.[1] They stubbornly insist on "not getting it," or at least on not getting it right. That "misunderstanding" is not necessarily conscious. The worst subversives act with the self-assurance of good citizens. If religion is an opiate, it is a drug to which the dealers are probably more addicted than the average consumer. Members of the ecclesiastical elite have internalized their own messages much more than the masses they were supposed to dupe.

How were the messages brought home? By way of morality tales. Morality tales, a category to which all saints' stories belong in theory, can be divided into three subcategories: stories whose message is unambiguous and coherent (common but ineffective), stories whose messages are openly revolutionary (extremely rare, since their dangerous potential is obvious and the authorities do their best to suppress them), and stories whose message is neither clear nor coherent (the overwhelming majority, appearances notwithstanding).

Let us begin with a morality tale of the first category. A child plays with matches, even though his parents have expressly forbidden it. One day he sets his bedroom on fire, all his toys burn up, and he suffers painful burns. Lessons: Do not play with matches; daddy and mommy know best. The tale seeks to make a causal relationship concrete for the child; in the morality tale, parents' warnings always come true, unlike in daily experience, where a child may perfectly well play with matches without any harm coming to him. The religious narrative often describes an ideal moral reality that rectifies the amoral reality of the real world. In the world here below, martyrs are tortured and die with no harm to their tormentors; the righteous suffer and the evil prosper. By contrast, the stereotypical martyr's story punishes the wicked, and no villain benefits from his villainy. In the real world, goodness may go unrewarded, but in the world of religious narratives, descriptions of paradise show the church's promises fulfilled and the moral order reestablished. In everyday reality the good are often weak and hesitant, whereas in the world of the religious story they are forceful and decisive. Since the stereotypical religious narrative deals with the social order—that is, with much higher stakes than burned toys and scorched fingers—it tends to be more dramatic than our little morality tale: the sins are gruesome, the virtues heroic, the reward marvelous, the punishment horrible.

If all religious narratives were so simple, and if all children were willing to draw the right conclusions from their parents' warnings, politics would be a much easier game. The problem with the stereotypical morality tale is that it quickly loses its shock value. The revolver that makes an appearance in the first act will go off in the third; the hero will be saved and the villain punished, just as in a Hollywood film. The saint's list of virtues is always the same, and it is a short list. The dramatic effect is limited. Worse, the strict rules of saints' narratives prevent the hero from being heterodox, from deciding, for example, to embrace a career as a seducer, from losing his faith, or from ending his life as a pirate. Morality tales are predictable, and audiences accustomed to hearing them develop an immunity to their lessons. If the political message (obedience is good for you) is too direct, the peasants may believe that an obedient and servile saint is a fool or an invention of the masters. Thus, either they make up an alternative story reflecting their own, probably more problematic tastes, or they adopt the old strategy of children obliged to listen to their parents' morality tales: they pretend to listen and immediately put it out of their minds. At least part of the narrative must sugarcoat the politico-moral message enough so that it elicits no opposition, boredom, or indifference. The message must be camouflaged.

Camouflaging the message is a difficult task, and it is not always crowned with success. One possible solution is to make the hero less one-dimensional. Thus listeners swallow the juicy story without noticing the moral hook it conceals. Take the story of the boy who played with matches: if the storyteller adds a name, a concrete environment, personal traits, and a more intricate story (he is, for example, the best soccer player in his school), the hero becomes more alive, more interesting, though the message does not change. He is still the child who, in playing with matches, sets fire to his toys and burns his fingers. From our perspective, what is added to the tale is only an agreeable and incidental noise that camouflages the disagreeable but important lesson (those who disobey are punished). Nevertheless, these embellishments, which the storyteller tends to consider neutral and morally colorless, convey messages of their own that may well deviate from the intended message or even contradict it. The boy in question may be punished for playing with matches, but he is a good soccer player whose talents as a scorer earn him the admiration of girls and the jealousy of the other boys. In these relationships the preconditions of success are not moral fiber but beauty, physical strength, and social skill. The listeners may choose to ignore the main point and internalize the accidental "embellishments."

The heroes of Christian narratives too are more than their virtues. Apart from the fairly simple core of the martyr's story (the hero gives up his life for the Christian faith) or of the confessor's (the hero overcomes the temptation to increase her pleasure in this world to enjoy eternal pleasure in the kingdom of heaven), religious narratives contain elements that are at the very least ambiguous. The emphasis sometimes placed on the heroine's beauty or on the hero's social status attests to a value system that is problematic from the Christian perspective. Sometimes the discrepancy is glaring. Think, for example, of the very popular Saint Alexis. The hero disobeys his parents, remains outside any churches, ignores the demands of God and the Mother of God, and behaves in shockingly antisocial ways. Yet the saint is not criticized for his behavior but, on the contrary, is praised and glorified by the storyteller. Why? Because of his contempt for the world. Now contempt for the world can be a very dangerous attitude, especially when it is not ritualized. Mary Magdalene preaches publicly, and in her relationship with her devotees serves more as a provider of miracles than as a spiritual guide; Simeon Stylites protects runaway brigands and offers grace to pagans and necrophiliacs; Francis embraces a mode of life that implies a disastrously dangerous criticism of the established church; Ginepro acts like a perfect idiot; and Saint Nicholas is willing to serve as a watchdog in a Jew's house and suffer a beating when the house is robbed by thieves.[2]

These examples are but a random sample of the vast set of ambiguous messages to be found in saints' Lives. It goes without saying that a narrative which contains *only* such messages would be unacceptable: to convey unconventional messages, the narrative needs a passport, a religious laissez-passer. Alexis could not have been considered a Christian saint if, alongside the subversive aspects of his behavior, he was not also a devout Christian ascetic, and if there were not acceptable, albeit strained, explanations for the problems the narrative raises. Alexis prays and gives up his possessions *for God*; if he flees God, it is out of an excess of Christian humility. In acting cruelly toward his parents, he overcomes his feelings in order to enjoy heavenly reward. Mary Magdalene behaves as she does in obedience to Saint Peter and to Christ; Ginepro is not simply a fool but a holy fool; Christopher and George willingly give up their fabulous powers to become martyrs. Nevertheless, just because the narratives can be reconciled with an orthodox interpretation does not obliterate their subversive potential. We shall return to this question.

It is not just by presenting protagonists with seemingly negative or socially unacceptable traits that stories can be ambiguous and confusing. Sometimes the didactic message, which is supposedly the essential thing, becomes marginalized in the story. In many of the most popular saints' stories, the canonical Christian portions give way to supposedly less important elements. Saint Eustace is remembered for his talking stag and picaresque adventures and not for his martyrdom. In fact the Christian ending seems to have been appended almost as an afterthought to the folktale. George's dragon, like Margaret's, has totally devoured the saint's martyrdom in the collective mind. And when the Franciscan context of his actions was forgotten, Ginepro became an amusing clown whose decontextualized stories entertain children. The medium may not be the message, but it can sometimes precede it in the race for the listener's attention.

But does not this observation contradict what I have argued concerning Jacobus de Voragine's *Golden Legend*—namely, that the *Legend*'s stories were designed not to be read by laypeople but to be used in sermons, where the subversive message would be neutralized by the preacher's cautious commentary and expansion? I do not think so. *The Golden Legend* is in fact a classic example of a medium acquiring a life of its own. For it seems that the elite that produced it and similar collections like it soon lost control of its creations. Instead of being just one ingredient in the preacher's mixture, it was imbibed straight by laypeople who read it *without* appropriate interpretation. It was hard for thirteenth-century intellectuals to foresee the growth in the number of readers or the hunger of new audiences for hagiographical texts. But it is precisely the inability to foresee consequences that makes social dynamics so unstable. Moreover, texts can convey the wrong messages, even when performed "properly," by the "right" preacher, one who provided his listeners with a cautious commentary that put the "message" back on the pedestal from which it was removed in the heat of narration. The reason is twofold. First, consumers understand messages in terms of their own aptitudes and preferences; they choose, consciously or not, to memorize and to retain (that is, to internalize) certain elements of the message to the exclusion of others.[3] Sometimes the misunderstanding is so widespread that the church is forced to canonize the "noise"; hence George's dragon, and Saint Nicholas's bag full of gifts (a misinterpretation of images of the saint freeing three soldiers from a tower), and of course Cecilia's and Christopher's cults, which thrive despite the church's doubts as to the saints' existence. Nonexistent saints, it turns out, can be quite resistant.

But the distorting use (conscious or not) of the stories was not reserved for consumers alone. The suppliers were also far from the consistent and conformist group that modern commentators often make them out to be. Indeed, saints' stories were not simply read aloud; every "performance" meant a rewriting of the text, and potentially its inventive misappropriation for ad hoc purposes. Slight or not so slight variations meant to drive the message home in a particular set of circumstances were inevitable. Such variations could gradually upset the inner balance of the text: minor characters suddenly took center stage; unintended characteristics became attached to the protagonist. Even when such performances were intended to promote the cause of the hierarchy, it is obvious that they did so in a dangerous way, using too many agents whose degree of identification with the symbolic center varied and whose comprehension of and conformity to the center's interests were limited.

Every society contains within it the forces of change. Political and cultural elites attempt to avoid changes in the power structure that might undermine their hegemony, but that attempt is doomed to failure. Change cannot be avoided because no strategy for retaining power is foolproof, and no system as complex and dynamic as human society can ever be predictable. Worse, the more authoritarian the regime, the greater the energy required to conserve the power structure, and the less likely it is to succeed. True conservatism demands an enormous effort exerted by too many unreliable agents; it wastes energy on relatively trivial things, and because the social image of continuity is all-important, substance is often sacrificed for appearances. That does not mean that all elites lose their social hegemony at the same pace. Obviously some elites are more successful than others in clinging to their power. But it does mean that in seeking to hold on to their power, elites are more than once forced to make tacit concessions and to rely on unreliable allies. Furthermore, they must invent an imaginary status quo that is to be preserved. In reality there is always more than one status quo. This is often not acknowledged, which makes a realistic appreciation of circumstances difficult. Thus different members of the elite attempt to reconstitute different status quos—all in the name of the imaginary common cause. Since it is impossible to reproduce the cultural order in its entirety, some of them attempt to reproduce at least what seems important to them. These different schemes are bound to contradict one another.

What is the nature of the golden past? What is that old-time religion? It all depends on whom you ask. Different members of the ecclesiastical elite (priests, bishops, theologians, even popes) had very different ideals, and very different ideas, even about the one area where they were forced to reach a consensus—the nature of orthodoxy. They rarely had a clear, shared concept of the past (let alone the present). And in most cases they did not possess the conceptual and political means to realize fully and precisely their projects, however limited. It is the cultural elite's inevitable lack of effectiveness that makes moral, political, and cultural systems dynamic.

Agents never fully achieve their moral ideals or their concrete objectives. Thus it is in the nature of conservative societies to think in terms of failure. That failure can be explained in various ways: heterodoxy and insubordination (of subjects), corruption and laziness (of the elite). To fight against fluctuations in the status quo, it is necessary to resort to emergency measures that can succeed only at the price of the most radical change, by taking scandalous liberties with "normal" rules. In the twelfth and thirteenth centuries, the Catholic Church, in the name of restoring a largely imaginary past, became the principal agent of change in society.[4] In its struggle against heterodoxy it used cultural and political means that themselves constituted a serious distortion of orthodoxy and orthopraxis. The failure of an elite to replicate itself, however, is not necessarily a political failure. Emergency measures and reforms can succeed in keeping power in the hands of a specific political class. It may well be, in fact, that cultures which fail in their attempts to reconstitute the past "faithfully"—or which have totally given up on the idea of faithful replication—"succeed" better from a pragmatic standpoint than societies which invest huge efforts in saving appearances.

Medieval society exemplifies the tension between smooth surfaces and raging undercurrents. While the elite invested an enormous amount of effort in formulating its official doctrine, both by bringing its most gifted elements to bear on it and by disciplining and punishing, it allowed the less exalted field of hagiography to develop almost unsupervised. The intellectual abilities of Jacobus de Voragine hardly measured up to those of Saint Thomas Aquinas or Henry of Ghent. Jacobus' collection of saints' legends was much less studied and criticized than the theologians' works. It was "less important." And yet—and this would be shocking for students of theology—it had a much greater influence. Saints' stories, as we have seen, could contain with impunity subversive elements inconceivable in the works of theologians. The level of supervision and political attention was much lower when it came to hagiography. Saints' Lives were not important for the elite; ergo, they were not important. The popular literature of the Middle Ages was a relatively unsupervised market where suppliers with limited abilities (from the standpoint of the system's declared interests) met uneducated, often uncommitted consumers.

What was the effect of these ambiguous, subversive materials, slipped— for the most part inadvertently—into the hagiographical narratives? Let me first note that the subversive *potential* of many saints' stories does not necessarily make them radical texts. The critical issue from the politico-cultural perspective is not whether there is a subversive potential and a psychological apparatus able to give it concrete form, but whether and how that potential can be realized. It is often politically inconsequential whether a text, read in a certain way, contains elements contesting the dominant notions of the social order. Readers or listeners may *choose* to understand it as a conformist text, or they may be incapable of understanding it any other way. They ignore the irony, the internal contradictions, the revolutionary allusions, and the hidden criticisms. The text's subversive potential remains unexploited and awaits a society or a reader capable of making use of it.

It is clear that whatever subversive content we may see in them, saints' Lives did not spur the Christian public to man the barricades. Even the most audacious reading of the messages hidden in the texts cannot lead us to expect that. It is true that Waldo began his career as a religious reformer and consequently a heresiarch after hearing a jongleur singing the story of Saint Alexis; but such radical reactions were rare. Besides, did the example of the saint drive Waldo to stand up to the authorities, or did it only make him decide to leave the world behind? Who knows? It is likely that, in most cases, the messages that have the greatest impact in the long run are not those that lead to direct political action. What the saints' stories created was a system of thought that existed alongside the official system created and dominated by the elite and that subverted it with no conscious plan of action behind it. That unheralded system spread confusion, not by protesting openly, but by producing "noise" in the official system, sand in the social machinery. The effectiveness of these stories was inversely proportionate to the clarity of their messages. If they were too direct, they would risk bringing the censors' wrath down upon their authors' heads. That was the case, let us recall, for the first Lives of Saint Francis.[5] Their subversive messages were too obvious and struck where it hurt. The whole point of hidden forces is that they must continue to be considered unimportant.

It would be impossible to describe the countless ways the alternative messages of saints' stories have influenced the *populus Christianus,* just as it would be difficult to identify the thousand ways inertia, silent hostility, and subterfuge obstruct the actions of tyrannical regimes. Think, for example, of the combined effect of all these elements on the Soviet empire. Every day millions of people found small ways to thwart the system— shirking work, performing badly, telling anticommunist jokes, buying and selling on the black market, embezzling small sums. It all adds up. The changes in attitude and behavior brought about by dangerous cultural materials are often too small to be visible. Change comes through the accumulation of incalculable little glitches in the system, none of which on its own is critical or worth pointing out, especially since the area in which it occurs is by definition "unimportant."[6] What the historian can detect are the moments of crisis, moments when a new understanding of a sacred text or a hallowed institution becomes thinkable and socially meaningful, as when Martin Luther realized the revolutionary potential of the Epistle to the Romans.

The Lutheran crisis was not unrelated to the cult of saints. Luther saw his rereading of Paul as an antidote to the ecclesiastical degeneration he associated with the "idolatrous" popish cult of saints. But whereas the Epistle to the Romans is an example of a text whose revolutionary potential was well known (it was an "important" text), saints' Lives exemplify material whose revolutionary potential was not acknowledged. Theologians were aware of the problematic nature of Paul's writings, but since they had been canonized by the church, they had no other choice but to attempt to coat them with forceful exegesis, a coating they knew was brittle and ready to crack. In contrast, the impresarios of the cult of saints did not foresee that this phenomenon could cause much harm—especially after the disappearance of paganism. No one could seriously accuse the saints' devotees of idolatry. Idolatry was dead. At worst there were superstitious elements

in the cult that were quite harmless, given the good intentions of its followers. For reasons we shall examine shortly, however, the cult's impresarios were impelled by the mounting expectations of their audience to produce increasingly extreme, irrational, and in many respects unorthodox
hagiographical texts. In their minds, these were harmless concessions of
the learned oxen to the unlearned asses. The Protestant criticism of the
cult of saints (preceded by the humanist criticism) was the moment when a
social commonplace was reread with new eyes. For Luther the cult of
saints did not have a revolutionary potential; it was the (disastrous) expression of an already completed revolution, the victory of magical, idolatrous,
and ritualistic elements over the original, purely scriptural Christianity Luther wanted to revive. Protestantism in that sense was a *counter*-revolution.[7]

The polemic between Protestants and Catholics regarding the cult of
saints, however, took place within the usual channels of theological debate,
focusing on the question of the cult's dogmatic validity and its religious
purity. In a way this involved extracting a social phenomenon from its natural habitat and discussing it in terms that made realistic assessment of its
causes and effects impossible. Even now, this attitude is very much alive
among religious authorities and academics. In Israel, for example, the sudden blossoming of cults of Jewish saints in the early 1980s is still considered from the perspective of religious purity: Are these cults idolatrous, or
are they a legitimate expression of Jewish religious feeling? Are they an un-
objectionable concession to the "primitive" masses or a respectable phenomenon with roots in the canonical Jewish past? Framed in these terms,
the debate on Jewish saints and their veneration conceals the heterogeneous, "impure" nature of *any* religious system in the name of a certain
imaginary religious purity. Instead of adopting the binary vision of the
theologian (pure or impure, orthodox or heterodox, Christian or pagan),
we can use the Christian cult of saints as a privileged "field" to understand
how alternative, unspoken theologies come into being. To do so, we must
refrain from mentally filling in the blanks in the narratives and from instinctively "saving" them by reading them in a way that will smooth out
their contradictions and make them conform to the "correct" (that is,

official) theology. Religious systems suffer from multiple personality disorder. Orthodoxy is one of the personalities. Underneath the orthodox surface lurk other, unconfessed possibilities that can be deduced from seemingly "innocent" cultural expressions. It is those other personalities, those hidden theologies, those implicit worldviews that we must try to reconstruct.

The medieval church was aware of the existence within it of parallel systems of belief, and to a great extent was ready to tolerate them, so long as they were not formulated systematically. Take, for example, the statement of Pope Innocent IV (r. 1243–1254) on the question of how much faith is needed for salvation:

> There is a certain measure of faith to which all are obliged, and which is sufficient for the simple people [*simplicibus*] and perhaps for all laymen—that is: every adult who comes to the faith must believe that God exists and that he rewards all good people. He must also believe the other articles of the Creed implicitly [*implicite*], that is, he must believe whatever the Catholic Church believes is true. . . . [Bishops must be familiar with all the articles of the Creed and capable of explaining them with the help of experts.] As for lower clerics, it seems clear that if they are poor and cannot attend school because they lack money for tuition fees or teachers and have to earn their living with their own hands, it is enough that they know as much as simple laymen, and a little bit more [*aliquantulum plus*], about the Eucharist. For they must know that in the Eucharist the true body of Christ is being made [*conficitur*], and that is because they deal with it daily and on a regular basis, more than laymen.
>
> Such is the power of implicit faith that there are those who say that if someone has it—that is, if he believes in everything the church believes—but his natural reason [*ratione naturali*] makes him hold the erroneous opinion that the Father is greater than the Son or precedes him in time, or that the three persons are separate beings, he is neither

a heretic nor a sinner, so long as he does not defend his error and so long as he believes that it is the faith of the church. In that case, the faith of the church replaces his opinion, since, though his opinion is false, it is not his faith, rather his faith is the faith of the Church.[8]

It is not surprising that the pope should acknowledge that the depth of faith and of theological understanding varies from person to person and from class to class. As we saw in previous chapters, the church perceived faith as a heavy burden to be borne in common. Some are oxen; others asses. The important thing is that there is always enough true knowledge for all. What *is* surprising about Innocent IV's text is that it explicitly recognizes and even accepts the existence of other belief systems under the church's broad umbrella of explicit faith. A man can have an erroneous belief, even concerning the very core of Christian faith—the doctrine of the Holy Trinity. That person may even express his erroneous opinion with impunity, provided he is not aware of his error. So long as he believes that there is no conflict between his belief and that of the church, and so long as others have not forced him to realize his error, he can hold a belief not just at variance with dogma but even contrary to it.

The pope's discussion of "implicit faith" shows how misleading it is to perceive religious praxis in binary terms. The pope himself points out that there are vast areas (after all, the laity and the lower clergy constitute the majority of the faithful) where heterogeneity is possible and permitted. Pope Innocent is not really concerned that most of the faithful do not believe what they ought to believe. What troubles him is disobedience—believing consciously and willfully against the church's teaching. That is the legal definition of heresy. A heretic is not someone who does not believe rightly. (The beliefs of most people are approximations of the true faith. Only a small group of experts represents an exception.) A heretic is someone who *knows* he does not believe rightly and persists in his error. It is possible to believe, and to state, that "the Father is superior to the Son and precedes him in time," that is, to be explicitly Arian, and still be perfectly Catholic, thanks to "implicit faith." That is why the vast majority of the faithful are not heretics, even though they harbor manifestly heretical beliefs. That arrangement exempts the asses from the uncomfortable dichotomy in which the oxen live. So long as the ass is content to believe without confronting the authorities head-on, he enjoys considerable freedom: he can tell sacred stories in his own way, invent practices that will largely escape the control of the authorities, invent saints, venerate saints in accordance with his tastes and needs, and tell unorthodox stories, or at least understand orthodox stories in radically unorthodox ways.

Of course, the asses' freedom is conditional, implicit, and founded on a tacit contract. The church does not recognize freedom of conscience. It is simply tolerant, while reserving for itself the right to intervene as it will, when it will. This it does when it sends in its inquisitors, for example. But the spectacular actions of these frightening figures have made us lose our sense of historical proportion. Most communities never met an inquisitor. Moreover, there was only a tiny risk that a medieval inquisitor would meddle in the life of a community, unless there were suspicions of "explicit" heresy. Inadvertent heresy rarely interested the authorities. The villagers of Montaillou were unlucky: they ran into Jacques Fournier, an atypical and extraordinarily ambitious inquisitor (how many inquisitors became pope?). But even Fournier sought only "true" Cathar and Waldensian heretics and left the merely "confused" alone.[9] When Stephen of Bourbon discovered by chance that the peasants near Dombes venerated Guinefort, a saint he had never heard of, and that the saint was in fact a martyred greyhound, he forbade the cult but did not punish anyone. (In fact, as Jean-Claude Schmitt shows, the cult continued until the twentieth century.)[10] We do not know how many Guineforts there were in the Middle Ages. The church did not know either.

What theological and ethical notions can we draw from the acts of the saints as described in the Lives, texts that were the closest thing the common man had to a theological worldview? An understanding of that implicit theology, which is very different from the explicit theology of the professionals, is associated not just with the saints, of course.[11] It can be found wherever professional theologians were absent.[12] Here are a few preliminary observations.

One of the most obvious differences between the theologians' and the

concrete religion, see Edith Wyschogrod, *Saints and Postmodernism: Revisioning Moral Philosophy* (Chicago: University of Chicago Press, 1990).

3. *Babylonian Talmud, Baba Bathra* 12, in *Hebrew-English Edition of the Babylonian Talmud,* ed. I. Epstein, trans. Maurice Simon and Israel W. Slotki (London: Soncino Press, 1976).

2. The Beginnings

1. All biblical citations are to the New King James Version.

2. The traditional Jewish exegesis, which sees the "servant of God" as the people of Israel, is just as arbitrary as the Christian exegesis that views him as Jesus Christ.

3. See Origen, *Contra Celsum* 5.25.

4. See Mark S. Burrows, "Christianity in the Roman Forum: Tertullian and the Apologetic Use of History," *Vigiliae Christianae* 42 (1988): 209–235.

5. Tertullian, *Apologeticum* 40 1, in *Apology; De spectaculis,* trans. T. R. Glover (Cambridge, Mass.: Harvard University Press, 1931), p. 183.

6. Minucius Felix, *Octavius* 9.6; Eusebius of Caesarea, *Historia ecclesiastica* 5.1.14. On the pagans' attitude toward the Christians, see R. L. Wilken, *The Christians as the Romans Saw Them* (New Haven: Yale University Press, 1984).

7. A clear description of the first waves of persecutions can be found in Robin Lane Fox, *Pagans and Christians* (New York: Random House, 1989), pp. 419–492.

8. Tacitus, *Annales* 15.44.

9. G. W. Bowersock, *Martyrdom and Rome* (New York: Cambridge University Press, 1995), pp. 1–21.

10. There is a well-known exception to that rule in the figure of Eleazar in 2 Maccabees 19–31. As in the story of the woman and her seven sons (7:1–39), we see here an act of defiance resulting in execution, and the notion that the martyr's death brings salvation to others. It is no accident that the story of Eleazar, like the Book of Maccabees as a whole—written under a strong Hellenistic influence—has remained marginal in the Jewish tradition, whereas Eleazar and the woman had a glorious career among the Christians. See Theofried Baumeister, *Die Anfänge der Theologie des Martyriums* (Münster: Aschendorff, 1980), pp. 45–51.

11. Quotations from *Hebrew-English Edition of the Babylonian Talmud,* ed. I. Epstein, trans. Maurice Simon and Israel W. Slotki (London: Soncino Press, 1976). [Translation modified by the author.] Here and subsequently, the citation is given in the text. On the Jewish precedents and parallels concerning martyrdom, see H. A. Fischel, "Martyr and Prophet: A Study of Jewish Literature," *Jewish Quarterly Review* 37 (1946–47): 265–280 and 363–386. Fischel does not pursue far enough the distinction between *kiddush hashem* (literally, sanctification of God's name), which, among Jews, especially during the first three centuries A.D., means a readiness to die, not a glorification of death, and Christian martyrdom, which sees death as a major path to salvation. See Moshe David Herr's important essay on how the conception of Jewish martyr-

dom evolved, "Religious Persecution and *Kiddush Hashem* in the Time of Hadrian" (in Hebrew), in *Holy War and Martyrology in the History of Israel and the Nations* (Jerusalem, 1967), pp. 73–92. Herr maintains that the Jewish concept of martyrdom came closer to the Christian concept at the time of the Roman persecutions of Christians, that is, between the second half of the third century and the fourth century. See also S. Safrai, "Martyrdom in the Teaching of the Tannaim," in T. C. de Kruijf and H. van der Sandt, eds., *Sjaloom* (Arnheim, 1983), pp. 145–164; J. W. van Henten, ed., *Die Entstehung der jüdischen Martyrologie* (Leiden: Brill, 1989). Even though a new form of martyrology appeared in Judaism at that time, the attitude toward martyrdom remained very ambivalent until the twelfth century. On the medieval change in attitude, see Israel Y. Yuval, "Vengeance and Damnation, Blood and False Accusation" (in Hebrew), *Zion* 58, no. 1 (1993): 63–75; Haym Sloveitchik, "Religious Law and Change: The Medieval Ashkenazic Example," *AJS Review* 12, no. 2 (1987): 205–221.

12. See Judith Perkins, "The Apocryphal Acts of the Apostles and Early Christian Martyrdom," *Arethusa* 15 (1985): 211–230; and Perkins, *The Suffering Self: Pain and Narrative Representation in the Early Christian Era* (London: Routledge, 1995), pp. 25–31.

13. Arthur J. Droge and James D. Tabor, *A Noble Death: Suicide and Martyrdom among Christians and Jews in Antiquity* (San Francisco: Harper, 1992), pp. 129–165.

14. Ignatius of Antioch, *Epistula ad Romanos* 2–7, in *The Epistles of St. Clement of Rome and St. Ignatius of Antioch*, trans. James A. Kleist (Westminster, Md.: Newman Bookshop, 1946), pp. 81–83.

15. This motif is emphasized in *Ad Martyras*, written by Tertullian in about 197 for a group of Christian prisoners awaiting execution.

16. Barbara G. Melamed et al., "Psychological Consequences of Torture: A Need to Formulate New Strategies for Research," in *Psychology and Torture*, ed. Peter Suedfeld (New York: Hemisphere, 1990), pp. 13–16, esp. pp. 15–16; Peter Suedfeld, "Torture: A Brief Overview," ibid., pp. 1–11.

17. On the public's reaction to Roman executions, see K. M. Coleman, "Fatal Charades: Roman Executions Staged as Mythological Enactments," *Journal of Roman Studies* 80 (1990): 44–73.

18. Tertullian, *Apologeticum* 50.14, in *Apology*, p. 227.

19. See Maureen A. Tilley, "The Ascetic Body and the (Un)Making of the World of the Martyr," *Journal of the American Academy of Religion* 59, no. 3 (1991): 467–479.

20. My analysis is influenced by Richard Trexler's brilliant study of the execution and martyrdom of Brother Michele da Calci in fourteenth-century Florence, *Public Life in Renaissance Florence* (Ithaca: Cornell University Press, 1980), pp. 205–211.

21. The saint's "birthday" (*dies natalis*) is actually the day of his death—the day when he dies in this world to be reborn in the world to come.

22. *Martyrium Polycarpi* 18.

23. On the role of the community in the formation of martyrdom and the role of

memory in the formation of the community, see Eugene Weiner and Anita Weiner, *The Martyr's Conviction: A Sociological Analysis* (Atlanta: Scholar's Press, 1990).

24. See James Fentress and Chris Wickham, *Social Memory* (Oxford: Blackwell, 1988), pp. 144–172.

25. Hippolyte Delehaye, *Les légendes hagiographiques*, 3rd rev. ed. (Brussels: Société des Bollandistes, 1927), pp. 57–100.

26. On the pagan precedents for the stories of martyrdom and their influence on the genre, see Herbert A. Musurillo, *The Acts of the Pagan Martyrs: Acta Alexandrinorum* (Oxford: Clarendon, 1954), pp. 236–246.

27. Manichaeism was a dualist sect that appeared in the 240s and was popular in Asia and North Africa.

28. See Cyprian of Carthage, *De lapsis* 8, in *Corpus Scriptorum Ecclesiasticorum Latinorum* (hereafter *CSEL*) 3.1.

29. Tertullian, *Apologeticum* 50.12, in *Apology*, p. 227.

30. Ibid.

31. On the influence of that notion on medieval culture, see Gerhart B. Ladner, "*Homo Viator*: Medieval Ideas of Alienation and Order," *Speculum* 42 (1967): 233–259.

32. Tertullian, *De spectaculis* 30, in *Corpus Christianorum, series Latina* (hereafter *CCSL*), 1:252–253.

33. Charles Pietri, "Le succès: La liquidation du paganisme et le triomphe du catholicisme d'État," in *Histoire du christianisme: Des origines à nos jours*, ed. Jean-Marie Mayeur et al., vol. 2 (Paris: Desclée de Brouwer, 1995), pp. 399–434.

34. There is one biblical description of miracle-working bones. We are told that people threw a body into the tomb of the prophet Elisha; barely had the dead man touched the bones of the prophet when he immediately came back to life (2 Kings 13:21). Nevertheless, a cult of relics did not develop in Judaism.

35. Ambrose himself relates the events in a letter to his sister: Ambrose of Milan, *Epistula* 22.2, in *Patrologiae Cursus, series Latina* (hereafter *PL*) 16, cols. 1019–20.

36. Ibid., 22.12, in *PL* 16, col. 1023.

37. Paulinus, *Vita Ambrosii* 29 and 33, in *PL* 14, cols. 37 and 38.

38. Ibid., 15, in *PL* 14, col. 32. They also claimed that it was demons who recognized Vitalis and Agricola as saints. On the political role of the discovery, see E. Dassmann, "Ambrosius und die Märtyrer," *Jahrbuch für Antike und Christentum* 18 (1975): 49–67; Neil B. McLynn, *Ambrose of Milan: Church and Court in a Christian Capital* (Berkeley: University of California Press, 1994), pp. 209–219.

39. See Gregory of Tours, *Liber in gloria confessorum* 18.21, in *Monumenta Germaniae Historica, Scriptores rerum Merovingicarum* (hereafter *MGH, SRM*), 1.2:307–308, 310–311.

40. Lucian, *Epistola ad omnem ecclesiam*, in *PL* 41, cols. 807–815.

41. On the discoveries, see Hippolyte Delehaye, *Les origines du culte des martyrs* (Brussels: Subsidia Hagiographica 20, 1933), pp. 73–91. A historical description of the cult of saints in the third, fourth, and fifth centuries, including a study of the ar-

chaeological discoveries, can be found in Victor Saxer, *Morts, martyrs, reliques en Afrique chrétienne aux premiers siècles* (Paris: Théologie historique 55, 1980).

42. On similar customs in Judaism, see Rivka Gonen, "Prayer and Charity, Fire and Water: Customs around the Tomb of the Righteous Man" (in Hebrew), in *In the Tombs of the Righteous: Pilgrimages to the Tombs and Rejoicing in Israel,* ed. Rivka Gonen (Jerusalem, 1998), pp. 87–103.

43. Gregory I, *Register* 4.30, in *CCSL* 140:248–250.

44. In the account of the execution of Cyprian, bishop of Carthage, in the third century, it is said that the crowd threw sheets and handkerchiefs at the bishop's feet. That is probably the first account of something akin to the veneration of saints' relics (*Acta procunsularia Cypriani* 5, in *CSEL* 3.3:113).

45. Victricius of Rouen, *Praising the Saints,* trans. Gillian Clark, *Journal of Early Christian Studies* 7, no. 3 (1999): 365–399.

46. For a study of the cult of relics as an expression of conceptions of the body in late antiquity and as a cause of change, see Caroline Walker Bynum, *The Resurrection of the Body in Western Christianity, 200–1336* (New York: Columbia University Press, 1995), pp. 43–114.

47. Annabel Wharton, "The Baptistery of the Holy Sepulchre in Jerusalem and the Politics of Sacred Landscape," *Dumbarton Oaks Papers* 46 (1992): 313–325.

48. Peter Brown, *The Cult of the Saints: Its Rise and Function in Latin Christianity* (Chicago: University of Chicago Press, 1981), pp. 8–9, 31–33, 125.

49. Chap. 83, in *CCSL* 149:204–205.

50. On the water cult of Saint Julian in Brioude and Vienne, see Paul-Albert Février, "Loca Sanctorum," in *Histoire de la France religieuse,* ed. Jacques Le Goff, vol. 1, *Des dieux de la Gaule à la papauté d'Avignon* (Paris: Éditions du Seuil, 1988), p. 161. On water cults in general, see Brigitte Caulier, *L'eau et le sacré: Les cultes thérapeutiques autour des fontaines en France du Moyen Âge à nos jours* (Paris: Presses de l'Université Laval, 1990).

51. Gregory of Tours, *In gloria confessorum* 2, in *MGH, SRM,* 1.2:299–300.

52. See Robert Markus, *The End of Ancient Christianity* (New York: Cambridge University Press, 1990), pp. 125–135; Arnold Angenendt, *Heilige und Reliquien: Die Geschichte ihren Kultes von frühen Christentum bis zum Gegenwart* (Munich: C. H. Beck, 1994), pp. 123–137.

53. See John M. Howe, "The Conversion of the Physical World: The Creation of a Christian Landscape," in *Varieties of Religious Conversion in the Middle Ages,* ed. James Muldoon (Gainesville: University Press of Florida, 1997), pp. 63–78.

54. William A. Christian Jr., *Apparitions in Late Medieval and Renaissance Spain* (Princeton: Princeton University Press, 1981), p. 20. See also Christian's excellent study on the relationship between nature-community and leaders in holy places in the twentieth century, *Visionaries: The Spanish Republic and the Reign of Christ* (Berkeley: University of California Press, 1996), pp. 302–315.

55. Augustine, *Sermo* 273.3.

56. Jerome, *Contra Vigilantium* 7, in *PL* 23, col. 345.

57. Augustine, *Contra Faustum* 20.2.

58. See Aron Gourevitch, "Santi iracondi e demoni buoni negli 'exempla,'" in *Santi e demoni nell'alto medioevo occidental (secoli v–xi)* (Spoleto: Settimane di studio del Centro italiano di studi sull'alto medioevo 36, 1988), pp. 1045–63.

59. As I shall later show, even then there was no uniformity in religious practice, but in the eleventh and twelfth centuries we find an aspiration to uniformity backed by rhetorical and authoritarian means.

60. Gregory I, *Register* 11.56, in *CCSL* 140A:961.

61. See Peter Brown's description—brilliant as usual—of the "popular" reaction to the church's attempt to monopolize the saints, in *Cult of the Saints*, pp. 125–126.

62. See David T. M. Frankfurter, "Stylites and Philobates: Pillar Religions in Late Antique Syria," *Vigiliae Christianae* 44 (1990): 177–179.

63. A similar process of paganization (the continuation of pagan cults under cover of Christianity) was at work in the Americas during the colonial period. Hence the cult of Saint Mary of Guadalupe in Mexico developed at the site of the cult of Tonantzin Cihuacoatl, our holy mother the snake woman, an Aztec deity. Today the cult is entirely Christian. See Jacques Lafaye, *Quetzalcoatl et Guadalupe* (Paris: Gallimard, 1974).

3. On the Way to Heaven

1. The historical backdrop is described in the introduction to the excellent critical edition of the text, *Passion de Perpétue et de Félicité suivi des Actes*, ed. and trans. Jacqueline Amat (Paris: Éditions du Cerf, Sources chrétiennes 417, 1996), pp. 19–83, hereafter cited by chapter and line in the text. In my analysis I will not consider the relationship between the Latin and Greek texts or the philological and archaeological questions. Readers are invited to consult the critical edition. See also Joyce E. Salisbury, *Perpetua's Passion: The Death and Memory of a Young Roman Woman* (New York: Routledge, 1997), pp. 59–148; Victor Saxer, "Afrique latine," in *Hagiographies: Histoire internationale de la littérature hagiographique latine et vernaculaire en Occident des origines à 1550*, vol. 1 (Turnhout: Brepols, 1994), pp. 25–95.

2. See Brent Shaw, "The Passion of Perpetua," *Past and Present* 139 (1993): 2–45, esp. pp. 12–20.

3. On the influence of the work, see Amat, *Passion de Perpétue et de Félicité*, pp. 79–83.

4. On the instruction of the common people, see my "*De agone christiano*: The Preacher and His Audience," *Journal of Theological Studies* 38 (1989): 16–33.

5. The procurator was responsible for managing the finances of the province. Hilarianus concerned himself with criminal law only temporarily, because of the death of the proconsul.

6. Louis Robert, "Une vision de Perpétue martyre à Carthage en 203," *Comptes rendus de l'Académie des inscriptions et belles-lettres* (April 1982): 229–230. Robert methodically analyzes martyrdom in the arena and the Pythian Games as the source for Perpetua's arena images in the fourth vision.

7. See Shaw, "The Passion of Perpetua," p. 5.

8. For an excellent discussion of execution by beasts in general, and of condemned men and women disguised as pagan deities, see K. M. Coleman, "Fatal Charades: Roman Executions Staged as Mythological Enactments," *Journal of Roman Studies* 80 (1990): 44–73.

9. See, for example, Romans 9:21; 1 Thessalonians 4:4.

10. See J. Armitage Robinson, ed., *The Passion of S. Perpetua* (New York: Cambridge University Press, 1891).

11. See Peter Dronke, *Women Writers of the Middle Ages: A Critical Study of Texts from Perpetua (†203) to Marguerite Porete (†1310)* (New York: Cambridge University Press, 1984), pp. 1–7.

12. In Egyptian myths and in Mithraism, the soul must climb a ladder surrounded by demons and monsters. In the Upanishads and in the medieval tales of Lancelot, the hero must cross a narrow bridge sharp as a blade, which cuts his hands and feet. See Franz Cumont, *After-Life in Roman Paganism* (New York: Dover, 1959), p. 88; Origen, *Contra Celsum* 6.22.1; Joseph Campbell, *The Hero with a Thousand Faces* (Princeton: Princeton University Press, 1968).

13. Cées Mertens notes the absence of nightmares in martyrs' narratives. I am more inclined to believe that martyrs passed over their nightmares in silence than that they all fully accepted what awaited them. Cées Mertens, "Les premiers martyrs et leurs rêves: Cohésion de l'histoire et de rêves dans quelques 'passions' latines de l'Afrique du Nord," *Revue d'histoire ecclésiastique* 81, no. 1 (1986): 5–46.

14. Marie-Louise von Franz proposes a captivating Jungian interpretation of the dream. She sees the serpent as a symbol of earthly materiality and femininity, a role it often plays in pagan myths. In placing her foot on the serpent's head, Perpetua renounces materiality in favor of spirituality and femininity in favor of virility, whose representative is Saturus. See Marie-Louise von Franz, *The Passion of Perpetua: A Psychological Interpretation of Her Visions* (Toronto: Inner City Books, 2004), pp. 39–40. See also Pierre Hadot's critique, "Patristique latine," *Annuaire EPHE* 75 (1968–69): 184–189.

15. Jacqueline Amat, *Songes et visions: L'au-delà dans la littérature latine tardive* (Paris: Études augustiniennes, 1985), pp. 117–119.

16. "Pasteur (bon)," *Dictionnaire d'archéologie chrétienne et de liturgie*, ed. Fernand Cabrol (Paris: Letouzey et Ané, 1907–1953), 13.2, cols. 2272–2390; "Orphée," ibid., 12.2, cols. 2735–2755. On the good shepherd (in its "Orphic" variant) as a motif in Christian baptisteries and mortuary art (Perpetua may have combined the two spheres in her imagination), see Lucien de Bruyne, "La décoration des baptistères paléochrétiens," *Miscellanea Mohlberg*, vol. 1 (Rome, 1948), pp. 191–200.

17. In chapters 5 and 6. Already in the fifth century, the North African bishop Quodvultdeus identified the shepherd with Perpetua's father. Quodvultdeus, *Sermo de tempore barbarico* 6, in *PL* 40, col. 703: *acciperat ab illo pastore simul et patre bucellam lactis.*

18. The complete history of Orpheus is related in *Georgics* 4.453–527.

19. Among the characters in the underworld, Virgil also mentions young men burned at the stake before their parents' eyes *(impositique rogis iuvenes ante ora parentum)*; *Georgics* 4.475–477.

20. Virgil, *Aeneid* 6.645–647 and 660–665.

21. See Pierre Prigent, *L'art des premiers chrétiens: L'héritage et la foi nouvelle* (Paris: Desclée de Brouwer, 1995), pp. 127–143.

22. Martial, *Liber spectaculorum* 21. That is the interpretation of the event given by Coleman ("Fatal Charades," p. 62). Note that according to other commentators, this was an accident and not a ceremonial execution. I find Coleman's interpretation more convincing.

23. "Abandon all hope, ye who enter here" *(lasciate ogni speranza voi chi entrate)* are the words inscribed over the gates of hell in Dante's *Divine Comedy*.

24. Dronke, *Women Writers of the Middle Ages,* p. 11; Amat, *Songes et visions,* pp. 128–131.

25. See note 17.

26. Saturus' dream bears the stamp of Perpetua's first dream, for example, in the description of the garden, the ascension to paradise by climbing, not floating, and the man with the white hair *(canum)*.

27. Egypt stands as the antithesis of Israel. Since Christians identify with Israel, it is logical that Egyptians represent the devil. In addition, the Egyptians were reputed to have a knowledge of magic and the occult, activities that the Christians considered diabolical. See Peter Habermehl, *Perpetua und der Ägypter, oder Bilder des Bösen in frühen Afrikanischen Christentum* (Berlin: Akademie Verlag, 1992), pp. 130–144.

28. Eusebius of Caesarea, *Historica ecclesiastica,* bks. 5–7.

29. See Victor Turner, "Religious Paradigms and Political Action: Thomas Becket at the Council of Northampton," in *Dramas, Fields, and Metaphors: Symbolic Action in Human Society* (Ithaca: Cornell University Press, 1974), pp. 60–97.

30. A scholarly edition of the *Acta* appears in the Amat edition of *Passion de Perpétue et de Félicité,* pp. 278–303.

31. *Acta* 1.7.2; *Acta* 2.7.2.

32. *Acta* 1.3.6–7; *Acta* 2.3.6–7.

33. *Acta* 1.3.6; *Acta* 2.3.6.

34. *Acta* 1.6.1–6.

35. Jacobus de Voragine, *The Golden Legend: Readings on the Saints,* trans. William Granger Ryan, 2 vols. (Princeton: Princeton University Press, 1993), 2:342.

4. The Ascetics

1. Plato, *Phaedrus,* in *Phaedrus and The Seventh and Eighth Letters,* trans. Walter Hamilton (New York: Penguin, 1973), p. 63.

2. Friedrich Nietzsche, *Genealogy of Morals,* trans. Walter Kaufmann and R. J. Hollingdale (New York: Vintage, 1967), p. 141.

3. See Tertullian, *De ieiunio* 9.4, in *CCSL* 1:1266.

4. For a good glimpse at the beginnings of the eremitic movement, see Derwas J. Chitty, *The Desert a City: An Introduction to the Study of Ethiopian and Palestinian Monasticism under the Christian Empire* (Oxford: Basil Blackwell, 1966); Henry Chadwick, "The Ascetic Ideal in the History of the Church," in *Monks, Hermits, and the Ascetic Tradition,* ed. W. J. Sheils (Oxford: Basil Blackwell, Studies in Church History 22, 1985), pp. 1–23. On the hermits of Syria, see Susan Ashbrook Harvey, *Asceticism and Society in Crisis: John of Ephesus and the Lives of the Eastern Saints* (Berkeley: University of California Press, 1990), pp. 1–21.

5. See, for example, *Babylonian Talmud, Taanith* (Fasting) 11, in *Hebrew-English Edition of the Babylonian Talmud,* ed. I. Epstein, trans. Maurice Simon and Israel W. Slotki (London: Soncino Press, 1976). Essene asceticism was Jewish in character: the purpose of the restrictions and prohibitions that members of the community imposed on themselves was ritual purification. The prohibitions came to distinguish members of the community from the world of sinners and had no positive value.

6. For a brief comparison between the ascetic notions of Judaism and Christianity, see Veronika Grimm, "Fasting Women in Judaism and Christianity in Late Antiquity," in *Food in Antiquity,* ed. John Wilkens, David Harvey, and Mike Dobson (Exeter: University of Exeter Press, 1995), pp. 225–241.

7. Plato, *Phaedrus,* p. 57.

8. Porphyrus, *Vita Plotini* 1–2.

9. Epictetus, Discourse 1.1.21–24, in *The Moral Discourses,* trans. Elizabeth Carter (New York: E. P. Dutton, 1910), p. 5.

10. Ibid., 3.13.11–16, p. 157.

11. Ibid., 4.12.1–3, pp. 249–250.

12. Musonius Rufus' text (discourse 6) can be found in Cora E. Lutz, "Musonius Rufus, 'The Roman Socrates,'" *Yale Classical Studies* 10 (1947): 52–56.

13. Patricia Cox, *Biography in Late Antiquity: A Quest for the Holy Man* (Berkeley: University of California Press, 1983), p. 25.

14. Derek Krueger, *Symeon the Holy Fool: Leontius's Life and the Late Antique City* (Berkeley: University of California Press, 1996), pp. 72–89.

15. On the resemblances and differences between the Stoic and Christian conceptions of the world, see M. J. Lagrange, "La philosophie religieuse d'Épictète et le christianisme," *Revue biblique,* no. 9 (1912): 5–21, 192–212.

16. Tertullian, *Apologeticum* 42.1–3, in *Apology; De spectaculis,* trans. T. R. Glover (Cambridge, Mass.: Harvard University Press, 1931), p. 191.

17. See Robert Kirshner, "The Vocation of Holiness in Late Antiquity," *Vigiliae Christianae* 38 (1984): 105–124.

18. Epictetus, *Discourses* 3.12.

19. Ibid.

20. On religious practice and its reciprocal relationship to theory, see my "Why Is God Not Silent?" (in Hebrew), *Zemanim* 53 (1995): 4–17.

21. Augustine, *De civitate dei* 22.8, in *CCSL* 48:815–816.

22. Lellia Cracco Ruggini, "Miracolo nelle cultura del tardo impero," in *Hagiographie, cultures et sociétés, IVe–XIIe siècle* (Paris: Études augustiniennes, 1981), pp. 161–202.

23. See Athanasius, *The Life of Antony* 20, in *The Life of Antony and the Letter to Marcellinus*, trans. Robert C. Gregg (New York: Paulist Press, 1980), pp. 46–47. I have consulted the French scholarly edition, *La vie d'Antoine*, ed. and trans. G. J. M. Bartelink (Paris: Éditions du Cerf, Sources chrétiennes 400, 1994).

24. These are Jovinian's assertions. Jerome distinguishes between what is permitted to the ordinary Christian and what is demanded of someone seeking perfection. Asceticism is a condition sine qua non for the latter. See Jerome, *Adversus Jovinianum* 1.3 in *PL*, vol. 23, col. 214; and Jerome, *De perpetua virginitate Mariae Adversus Helvidium*, in *PL* 23:183–2206.

25. Athanasius, *Life of Antony* 67.1–2, p. 81.

26. Vigilantius, one of asceticism's first critics, accused the careerists of the desert of being selfish and of evading their obligations to the community. In his response to that criticism, Jerome accepts these accusations in great part. See Jerome, *Contra Vigilantium* 15–16, in *PL* 23:351–352.

5. Antony, the First Hermit

1. Gregory of Nazianzus, *Oratio* 21.5.

2. Athanasius, *Vita S. Antonii* 3.1 [not in English translation—Trans.].

3. On the tendency in antiquity to explain a social phenomenon by referring to its founder, see James Francis, *Subversive Virtue: Asceticism and Authority in the Pagan World of the Second Century, c.e.* (University Park: Pennsylvania State University Press, 1995), p. 139.

4. Athanasius does not explicitly designate the recipients, but they were probably ascetics living in Italy or Gaul. See G. J. M. Bartelink's scholarly edition of *La vie d'Antoine* (Paris: Éditions du Cerf, Sources chrétiennes 400, 1994), p. 46.

5. See Patricia Cox, *Biography in Late Antiquity: A Quest for the Holy Man* (Berkeley: University of California Press, 1983), p. 45: "Biographies of holy philosophers were creative historical works, promoting models of philosophical divinity and imposing them on historical figures thought to be worthy of such idealization."

6. On the connection between pagan models and ancient Christian hagiography, see Martin Heinzelmann, "Neue Aspekte der biographischen und hagiographischen Literatur in der lateinischen Welt (1–6 Jahrhundert)," *Francia* 1 (1973): 27–44.

7. Thucydides, *History of the Peloponnesian War* 1.22.

8. See Nancy Partner's interesting essay on modern parallels to the mix of "fiction" and "reality," "Historicity in an Age of Reality-Fictions," in *A New Philosophy of History*, ed. Frank Ankersmit and Hans Kellner (Chicago: University of Chicago Press, 1995), pp. 21–39.

9. Athanasius, *Life of Antony*, in *The Life of Antony and the Letter to Marcellinus*, trans. Robert C. Gregg (New York: Paulist Press, 1980), prologue 3, pp. 29–30.

10. Otto F. A. Meinardus, *Monks and Monasteries of the Egyptian Deserts*, rev. ed. (Cairo: American University in Cairo Press, 1989).

11. Arianism was a fourth-century movement whose name comes from its leader, the priest Arius. In the Holy Trinity according to the Arians, only the Father is eternal in the full sense of the term, whereas there was a time when the Son was not.

12. On hagiographical conventions, elaborated in great part on the model of the *Life of Antony*, see Alison Goddard Elliot, *Roads to Paradise: Reading the Lives of Early Saints* (Hanover, N.H.: University Press of New England, 1987), pp. 77–130; Derek Krueger, *Symeon the Holy Fool: Leontius's Life and the Late Antique City* (Berkeley: University of California Press, 1996), pp. 36–47.

13. Athanasius, *Life of Antony* 2.4–5, p. 31.

14. John Bunyan (1628–1688), *The Pilgrim's Progress*, beginning of pt. 1.

15. Athanasius, *Life of Antony* 3, pp. 31–32. Antony's uninterrupted prayer is presented as a commandment from holy scripture. On the use of holy scripture in the biography, see pp. 48–53 of Bartelink's critical edition of *La vie d'Antoine*; and Brian Brennan, "Athanasius' *Vita Antonii*: A Sociological Interpretation," *Vigiliae Christianae* 39 (1985): 209–227.

16. Patricia Cox considers the *Life of Antony* "a sinner to saint tale" (*Biography in Late Antiquity*, pp. 53–54). I think that she is mistaken on this point. The work is closer than she imagines to the classic model she describes.

17. Athanasius, *Life of Antony*, 4.4, pp. 32–33.

18. Palladius of Hellenopolis, *The Lausiac History*, trans. Robert T. Meyer (New York: Newman Press, 1964), p. 33.

19. Athanasius, *Life of Antony* 10.2–3, p. 39.

20. Brennan believes that the beam of light that appears to Antony in the vault echoes the initiation rites of the mystery sects of antiquity ("Athanasius' *Vita Antonii*," p. 213).

21. According to Athanasius, Antony was thirty-five years old when he went into the desert. It is clear that the process related by Athanasius is a very abridged account of the seventeen years that have passed since Antony's conversion.

22. In the ascetic-eremitic tradition, "desert" designates any place that is physically difficult to live in and isolated from human society. In Europe, for example, the term "desert" is generally associated with forested mountains.

23. Aristotle, *Politics* 1.1253a.2–7.

24. The word *anakhōrēseis* means "the act of setting oneself apart, of retiring (from the world)"; hence the word *anachorete* (anchorite), "a hermit who isolates himself."

25. Athanasius, *Life of Antony* 14.3–4, p. 42. For a further "Stoic" description of the equilibrium between Antony's body and spirit, see *Life of Antony* 67.5–8, p. 81.

26. Violet MacDermot, *The Cult of the Seer in the Ancient Middle East: A Contribution*

to the Current Research on Hallucinations, Drawn from Coptic and Other Texts (London: Wellcome Institute of the History of Medicine, 1971), pp. 229–294. We will later examine the reasons for these differences.

27. Samuel Rubenson uses the letters attributed to Antony to present him as a sort of learned and sophisticated Origenist theologian. That attempt does not seem convincing to me. The presence of the letters (if they were indeed written by Antony) does not prove that the hermit could read and write (most letters in Antony's time were dictated). Rubenson finds many complex philosophical meanings in the simple words of the correspondence. What emerges clearly is a greater emphasis than in the biography on enlightenment and knowledge. There is not necessarily a connection between knowledge and erudition. See Samuel Rubenson, *The Letters of St. Antony: Origenist Theology, Monastic Tradition, and the Making of a Saint* (Minneapolis: Fortress Press, 1995).

28. Athanasius, *Life of Antony* 14.7, pp. 42–43.

29. MacDermot, *Cult of the Seer*, p. 31.

30. Athanasius, *Life of Antony* 46, pp. 65–66.

31. See Robert A. Markus, *Gregory the Great and His World* (New York: Cambridge University Press, 1997), pp. 59–62.

32. According to Susan Ashbrook Harvey, in the Syrian region the rarity of persecutions and their late appearance (not until the fourth century) created a unique situation in which asceticism took precedence over martyrdom both chronologically and conceptually: "Syriac martyr passions draw on the ascetic imagery of Syriac spirituality rather than the reverse." Susan Ashbrook Harvey, *Asceticism and Society in Crisis: John of Ephesus and the Lives of the Eastern Saints* (Berkeley: University of California Press, 1990), p. 9. I am not entirely convinced that Harvey is right. If she is, this was an unusual phenomenon. Both in Latin and in Greek Christianity the martyr serves as the ultimate model of Christian perfection.

33. Augustine 28.5, in *Miscellenea Agostiniana* (Rome, 1930), p. 539.

34. Robert A. Markus, *The End of Ancient Christianity* (New York: Cambridge University Press, 1990), p. 72; see E. A. Malone, *The Monk and the Martyr: The Monk as the Successor of the Martyr* (Washington, D.C.: Catholic University of America Press, 1950); A. de Vogüé, "'Martyrium in occulto': Le martyre de temps de paix chez Grégoire le Grand, Isidore de Séville et Valerius de Bierzo," in *Mélanges J. M. Bartelink* (Steenbrugge: Instrumenta Patristica 19, 1989), pp. 125–140.

35. Franz Joseph Dölger, "Gladiatorenblut und Märtyrerblut: Eine Szene der Passio Perpetuae in kultur-und-religions-geschichtlichen Beleuchtung," *Vortäge der Bibliothek Warburg, 1923–1924* (1926): 196–214.

36. Gregory of Tours, *Vitae patrum* 2, Praefatio, in *MGH, SRM* 1.2:218.

37. Athanasius, *Life of Antony* 70.2–3, p. 83.

38. Ibid., 88.3, pp. 94–95.

39. On the social functions of the saint as a "professional outsider" who can serve

as broker, conciliator, and protector, see Peter Brown's classic essay "The Rise and Function of the Holy Man in Late Antiquity," in *Society and the Holy in Late Antiquity* (Berkeley: University of California Press, 1982), pp. 103–152.

6. The Ascetic Pendulum

1. Arnold Van Gennep, *Les rites de passage* (Paris: É. Nourry, 1909), pp. 26–27, 93–163.

2. Victor Turner, "Social Dramas and Ritual Metaphors," in *Dramas, Fields, and Metaphors: Symbolic Action in Human Society* (Ithaca: Cornell University Press, 1974), p. 37: "Social dramas, then, are units of aharmonic or disharmonic process arising in conflict situations."

3. Ibid., pp. 38–41.

4. Victor Turner and Edith Turner, *Image and Pilgrimage in Christian Culture: Anthropological Perspectives* (New York: Columbia University Press, 1978).

5. See Antoine Guillaumont, "Le dépaysement comme forme d'ascèse dans le monachisme ancien," *Annuaire EPHE* 75 (1968–69): 31–58.

6. André Droogens, "Symbols of Marginality in the Biographies of Religious and Secular Innovators," *Numen* 27 (1980): 105–106. See Victor Turner, "Betwixt and Between: The Liminal Period in *Rites de Passage*," in *The Forest of Symbols: Aspects of Ndembu Ritual* (Ithaca: Cornell University Press, 1967), pp. 93–111. Apart from the useful list of antonyms, Droogens's article is a good example of how *not* to use a theoretical model.

7. Joseph P. Amar, trans., "On Hermits, and Desert-Dwellers, and Mourners," in *Ascetic Behavior in Greco-Roman Antiquity*, ed. Vincent L. Wimbush (Minneapolis: Fortress Press, 1990), pp. 68–80.

8. Ibid., line 129, p. 71.

9. Ibid., line 369, p. 76; line 189, p. 72; line 245, p. 73.

10. Ibid., line 501, p. 79.

11. Van Gennep, *Les rites de passage*, p. 36.

12. Max Weber enumerates similar phases in the career of the charismatic figure: breaking off from friends and family; joining an exclusive initiatory community (the recluse may join a community assembled around a guru, but he does not always do so); training physically and mentally to generate ecstasy; going through ordeals, which include bodily torture and shock; and achieving the status of those whose charisma is recognized. The ascetic achieves the status of saint and is henceforth able to guide others on the path he has taken. Weber's divisions between phases may be too sharp, but he also points out the importance of the antisocial and ascetic phase for forming the charismatic personality. Max Weber, *Economy and Society: An Outline of Interpretive Sociology*, ed. Guenther Roth and Claus Wittich, trans. Ephraim Fischoff et al., 2 vols. (New York: Bedminster Press, 1968), 2:1111–57.

13. Palladius of Hellenopolis, *Lausiac History* 34, in *The Lausiac History*, trans. Robert T. Meyer (New York: Newman Press, 1964), pp. 96–98.

14. The motif of eating in secret as an act to be ashamed of also appears in Athanasius, *The Life of Antony*, 45.3, in *The Life of Antony and the Letter to Marcellinus*, trans. Robert C. Gregg (New York: Paulist Press, 1980), p. 65. See also Palladius, *Lausiac History* 1.3, p. 31.

15. [Translation modified by the author.] Piterum uses the honorific title *amma*, the feminine equivalent of *abba*, given to the father of the monastery. In both cases it is the title for someone who has acquired the status of spiritual authority.

16. J. L. Austin, *How to Do Things with Words* (Oxford: Oxford University Press, 1962); John Searle, *Speech Acts: An Essay in the Philosophy of Language* (New York: Cambridge University Press, 1969).

17. My interpretation is deeply influenced by Michel de Certeau's brilliant analysis in *La fable mystique* (Paris: Gallimard, 1982), pp. 49–58.

18. The sentence *et interrogavit quid voluissent homines visitando limina sanctorum apostolorum* has been interpreted to mean that Aldebert was placing in doubt the usefulness of the pilgrimage to the apostles' tombs in Rome. It is very unlikely that such an expedition could have been more than an extremely rare occurrence in eighth-century Germany. It is more plausible that Aldebert, who himself built churches in tribute to the apostles, wanted to find out why people would wish to visit the apostles. He then built churches dedicated to himself, where, we may suppose, he applied what he had learned from the faithful.

19. *MGH, Concilia* 2:39–40.

20. On the popularity of Simeon among the Gauls, see Joseph Nasrallah, "Survie de S. Siméon l'Alepin dans les Gaules," *Syria* 51 (1974): 171–197.

21. Gregory of Tours, *Libri historiarum* 8.15, in *MGH, SRM* 1.1.380–383.

22. A similar battle took place near Tours. Saint Martin "recognized" that a bandit was buried at the location of a popular cult and destroyed his grave (Sulpicius Severus, *Vita S. Martini* 11).

23. Sigmund Freud, "Das Unheimliche," in *Gesammelte Werke*, vol. 12 (London: Hogarth Press, 1947), pp. 229–268.

24. Theodoret of Cyrrhus, *Historia monachorum* 26.23.

25. *Hebrew-English Edition of the Babylonian Talmud*, ed. I. Epstein, trans. Maurice Simon and Israel W. Slotki (London: Soncino Press, 1976).

26. On the saint's dependence on his onlookers, see my *Prophets in Their Own Country: Living Saints and the Making of Sainthood in the Later Middle Ages* (Chicago: University of Chicago Press, 1992), pp. 1–20, 99–125.

27. Ibid. [Translation modified by the author.]

28. The classic case is Thomas Becket, who became the patron saint of the kings of England, a surprising example of a murder that benefited the murderer (physically and spiritually). On the variety of means available to sixteenth-century Christian so-

ciety to get rid of a troublesome saint, see Jean-Michel Sallmann, *Naples et ses saints à l'âge baroque (1540–1750)* (Paris: Presses universitaires de France, 1994), pp. 177–210.

29. Gregory of Tours, *In gloria confessorum* 80, in *MGH, SRM* 1.2:349.

30. Ibid., 70,1.2:339. See Kleinberg, *Prophets in Their Own Country*, pp. 149–162.

31. See Michael A. Williams, "*The Life of Antony* and the Domestication of Charismatic Wisdom," *Journal of the American Academy of Religion, Thematic Studies* 48, nos. 3 and 4 (1982): 23–45, esp. 36–41.

32. See Kleinberg, *Prophets in Their Own Country*, pp. 52–54; Alain Boureau, *L'événement sans fin: Récit et christianisme au Moyen Âge* (Paris: Les Belles Lettres, 1993), pp. 33–37.

33. Gillian Clark, *Women in Late Antiquity: Pagan and Christian Life-Styles* (Oxford: Clarendon Press, 1994), pp. 102–104; Susana Elm, "*Virgins of God*": *The Making of Asceticism in Late Antiquity* (Oxford: Oxford University Press, 1994), pp. 311–312; Jo Ann McNamara, *Sisters in Arms: Catholic Nuns through Two Millennia* (Cambridge, Mass.: Harvard University Press, 1996), pp. 61–88.

34. Palladius, *Lausiac History* 25.2–5, pp. 84–85. [Translation modified by the author.]

35. Ibid., 26.1, p. 86.

36. Ibid., 26.2, p. 86.

37. Ibid., 32, pp. 92–95. A. Boon, ed., *Pachomiana Latina: Règle et épîtres de S. Pachome, épître de S. Théodore, et "Liber" de S. Orsiesius* (Louvain: L. Durbecq, 1932).

38. On a similar method of control of workers in Robert Owen's textile business in New Lanark, Scotland, see James C. Scott, *Domination and the Arts of Resistance: Hidden Transcripts* (New Haven: Yale University Press, 1990), pp. 46–54.

39. See Palladius, *Lausiac History*, 22.9, p. 79.

40. One might rather expect that advanced age would be an advantage, since the passions of youth cool over the years, but desert people perceived asceticism as physical and mental hard work that should be undertaken when one is relatively young and strong. Palladius, *Lausiac History* 22.2–3, p. 77.

41. Ibid., 18.12–15, pp. 61–63. [Translation modified by the author.]

42. Ibid., 18.5–9, p. 60. [Translation modified by the author.]

43. Pierre Canivet, "Erreurs de spiritualité et troubles psychiques: À propos d'un passage de la *Vie de S. Théodose* par Théodore de Pétra (530)," *Recherches de science religieuse* 50 (1962): 161–205; Susan Ashbrook Harvey, *Asceticism and Society in Crisis: John of Ephesus and the Lives of the Eastern Saints* (Berkeley: University of California Press, 1990), pp. 19–20.

44. Violet MacDermot, *The Cult of the Seer in the Ancient Middle East: A Contribution to the Current Research on Hallucinations, Drawn from Coptic and Other Texts* (London: Wellcome Institute of the History of Medicine, 1971), p. 48; George W. Fenton, "Hysterical Alterations of Consciousness," in *Hysteria*, ed. A. Roy (Chichester: John Wiley, 1982), pp. 229–246.

45. Elm, *Virgins of God*, pp. 331–372.

46. Chapter 41, in Mansi, *Sacrorum consiliorum nova et amplissima collectio* 11.964. The same notion also appears in Saint Benedict's monastic rule *(Regula S. Benedicti* 1). On the later institutionalization of solitary eremitism and the details of its systems of control, see the tenth-century text by Grimlaicus, *Regula solitarium* 15, in *PL,* vol. 103, cols. 593–594. See also s.v. "Érémitisme" in the *Dictionnaire de spiritualité ascétique et mystique, doctrine et histoire,* ed. Marcel Viller (Paris: G. Beauschesne et ses fils, 1932–1995), 4.1:944–945.

47. On the resurgence of eremitism in eleventh-century Europe, see Henrietta Leyser, *Hermits and the New Monasticism in Western Europe: A Study of Religious Communities in Western Europe, 1000–1150* (New York: St. Martin's Press, 1984); Gregorio Penco, "L'eremitismo irregolare in Italia nei secoli XI e XII," *Benedictina* 32 (1985): 201–221; Phyllis G. Jestice, *Wayward Monks and the Religious Revolution of the Eleventh Century* (Leiden: Brill Academic Publishing, 1997), pp. 141–151.

48. John Howe, "The Awesome Hermit: The Symbolic Significance of the Hermit as a Possible Research Perspective," *Numen* 30, no. 1 (1983): 106–119.

7. Paul, an Ascetic in Paradise

1. The three *Vitae* appear in *PL,* vol. 23; *Vita S. Pauli eremitae,* cols. 18–28.

2. See J. N. D. Kelly, *Jerome: His Life, Writings, and Controversies* (London: Duckworth, 1973), p. 60; Philip Rousseau, *Ascetics, Authority, and the Church in the Age of Jerome and Cassian* (Oxford: Oxford University Press, 1978), pp. 133–139; Manfred Fuhrmann, "Die Mönchsgeschichten des Hieronimus: Formenexperimente in erzählenden Literatur," in *Christianisme et formes littéraires de l'Antiquité tardive en Occident,* ed. M. Fuhrmann (Geneva: Fondation Hardt, 1977), pp. 69–82; Walter Berschin, *Biographie und Epochenstil im lateinischen Mittelalter,* vol. 1 (Stuttgart: A. Hiersemann, 1986), pp. 134–138; E. Coleiro, "St. Jerome's Lives of the Hermits," *Vigiliae Christianae* 11 (1957): 161–178; I. S. Kozik, *The First Desert Hero: St. Jerome's "Vita Pauli"* (Mount Vernon, N.Y.: King Lithographers, 1968).

3. Kelly, *Jerome,* p. 60.

4. On the tradition of the manuscripts of the *Life of Paul,* see W. A. Oldfather, ed., *Studies in the Text Tradition of St. Jerome's "Vitae Patrum"* (Urbana: University of Illinois Press, 1943).

5. Several saints' Lives very closely imitate the *Life of Paul,* for example, *Vita Onuphrii, Vita Macarii, Vita Marci,* and *Vita Mariae Aegiptiacae.* See Alison Goddard Elliot, *Roads to Paradise: Reading the Lives of Early Saints* (Hanover, N.H.: University Press of New England, 1987), which proposes a structuralist analysis of the *Life of Paul* (pp. 42–76).

6. What Jerome writes is not accurate. The emperor Decius (r. 249–251) ordered the persecution in 250. The pope executed under his reign was Fabian. His successor, Cornelius, was exiled from Rome under Gallus (r. 251–253) and died a natural death in Civitavecchia in 253. Valerian (r. 253–260) ordered the persecution of Christians in 257. A year later, Cyprian, bishop of Carthage, was martyred.

7. On the classical sources for Jerome's martyr narratives and on their avatars, see Hippolyte Delehaye, *Les légendes hagiographiques*, 3rd rev. ed. (Brussels: Société des Bollandistes, 1927), pp. 33–34.

8. On the analysis of that aspect in three of the romances—*Chirias and Callirrhoe, The Ephesian Tale*, and *Leucippus and Cliotophon*—see Judith Perkins, *The Suffering Self: Pain and Narrative Representation in the Early Christian Era* (London: Routledge, 1995), pp. 41–76, esp. 68–73; Elliot, *Roads to Paradise*, pp. 46–51. Jerome repeats the motif of the man as sexual victim and the identification of sexual abstinence with martyrdom in the *Life of Malchus: Vita Malchi* 6, in *PL* 23:56–57.

9. Tertullian, *Apologeticum* 50.8, in *CCSL* 1:170.

10. See Athanasius, *Life of Antony* 1–11, in *The Life of Antony and the Letter to Marcellinus*, trans. Robert C. Gregg (New York: Paulist Press, 1980), pp. 30–40.

11. In his two later biographies, Jerome adopts more "classical" models and devotes a considerable portion to asceticism (see, for example, *Vita Hilarionis* 4–11, in *PL* 23:30–32).

12. The creature identifies itself as one of those called "fauns, satyrs, or incubi." Faunus was the Roman god of agriculture, the grandson of Saturn and the father of Latinus. With the expansion of the cult of the Greek god Pan in Italy, the two gods became conflated, and both are represented with goat's horns and hooves, like the satyrs, lustful deities of the woods. The incubi are sometimes identified as monstrous creatures that appear in nightmares. They lie on a person while he or she is sleeping and rape or strangle him or her. Because of the strong sexual connotation of the three groups, the wood deities (fauns, pans, sylvans) were also called *incubi* in Late Latin. See also Jerome, *Commentarii in Isaiam* 12.

13. Jerome's younger contemporary Augustine also identifies the sylvans and pans (or fauns) with those popularly called incubi and with creatures that, "according to credible sources," seduced and raped women. See Augustine, *De civitate dei* 15.23.

14. In the ancient world, many testimonies of "true" satyrs circulated, like the one seen in Constantinople in Constans' time. Jerome probably knew the passage from Plutarch's *Life of Sylla* in which a living satyr is brought to Sylla and dies shortly thereafter. The satyr tries to produce sounds, which resemble a combination of a horse's whinny and a goat's bleating. The description is similar to that of the talking centaur in Jerome. See Plutarch, *Vita Syllae* 27.3–4.

15. See Matthew 7:7: "Ask, and it will be given to you; seek, and you will find; knock, and it will be opened to you."

16. Jerome combines two different verses from Virgil's *Aenead*. The first (in book 2) describes Anchises, father of Aeneas, refusing to leave Troy in ruins; the second (in book 6) anticipates Musaeus' instructions to Aeneas and to the Sibyl in the Elysian Fields, after they asked where they could find the hero's father, who had died in the meantime.

17. Athanasius, *Life of Antony* 91.8–9, pp. 96–97.

18. Ibid., 91–92, pp. 96–98.

19. There is an oblique reference here to Paul the apostle's presence in heaven (2 Cor. 12:1–6).

8. Suspended between Heaven and Earth

1. On Simeon, see Hippolyte Delehaye, *Les saints stylites* (Brussels: Subsidia Hagiographica, 1923), pp. i–xxxiv; André-Jean Festugière, *Antioche païenne et chrétienne: Libanius, Chrysostome et les moines de Syrie* (Paris: De Boccard, 1959), pp. 347–406; P. Peeters, "Un saint hellénisé par annexion: Syméon Stylite," *Analecta Bollandiana* 61 (1943): 29–71, 123–132; Arthur Vööbus, *History of Asceticism in the Syrian Orient*, 3 vols. (Louvain: Corpus Scriptorum Christianorum Orientalium Subsidia, 1958–1988), 2:208–223; Susan Ashbrook Harvey, *Asceticism and Society in Crisis: John of Ephesus and the Lives of the Eastern Saints* (Berkeley: University of California Press, 1990), pp. 15–21; Harvey, "The Sense of a Stylite: Perspectives on Simeon the Elder," *Vigiliae Christianae* 42 (1988): 376–394.

2. Theodoret of Cyrrhus, *Historia monachorum* (hereafter *HM*) 26. The text exists in French translation in the "Sources chrétiennes" collection of Éditions du Cerf. There is also an English translation: *A History of the Monks of Syria*, trans. R. M. Price (Kalamazoo, Mich.: Cistercian Publications, 1985), pp. 160–176.

3. For a discussion of the sources, see Festugière, *Antioche païenne et chrétienne*.

4. The description appears in Lucian of Samosata's short work *De Dea Syria*. See J. Toutain, "La légende chrétienne de S. Siméon Stylite et ses origines païennes," *Revue d'histoire des religions* 65 (1912): 171–177; David T. M. Frankfurter, "Stylites and Philobates: Pillar Religions in Late Antique Syria," *Vigiliae Christianae* 44 (1990): 168–198.

5. Frankfurter, "Stylites and Philobates," pp. 184–198.

6. *HM* 26.13.

7. Georges Tchalenko, *Villages antiques de la Syrie du Nord*, 3 vols. (Paris: P. Geuthner, 1953), 1:227–276.

8. I have used the edition of the Greek text edited by Hans Lietzmann, "Das Leben des heiligen Symeon Stylites," *Texte und Untersuchungen* 32, no. 4 (1908): 20–78; and Festugière's French translation, *Antioche païenne et chrétienne*, appendix 3, pp. 493–506. Some believe that the Latin versions of the biography are closer to the source: see Guillaume de Jerphanion, "Les inscriptions cappadociennes et le texte de la *Vita Simeonis auctore Antonio*," *Recherches de science religieuse* 21, no. 3 (1931): 340–360; 22, no. 1 (1932): 71–72.

9. See HM 26.5–6.

10. *The Lives of Simeon Stylites*, trans. Robert Doran (Kalamazoo, Mich.: Cistercian Publications, 1992), pp. 88–91. [Translation modified by the author.]

11. Palladius of Hellenopolis, *Lausiac History* 18.15, in *The Lausiac History*, trans. Robert T. Meyer (New York: Newman Press, 1964), p. 63.

12. Harvey, "The Sense of a Stylite," pp. 386–387: "[The Life] presents the ugliness of the saint's practice as exactly that. It is not the angelic life, nor is it transcendent" (p. 387).

13. *Lives of Simeon Stylites*, p. 88.

14. Ibid., p. 93.

15. See Yaara Bar-On, "Woman and the Serpent: Another History—Historical Reality and Legends," in an instruction manual for midwives, *Literature and History* (in Hebrew), ed. R. Cohen and Y. Mali (Jerusalem: Merkaz Zalman Shazar, 1999), pp. 125–144.

16. *Lives of Simeon Stylites*, p. 93.

17. Ibid., p. 95.

18. Ibid., p. 226.

9. Saints' Stories and the Rise of a Popular Literature

1. Robert A. Markus, *Gregory the Great and His World* (New York: Cambridge University Press, 1997), pp. 3–8; James J. O'Donnell, *Cassiodorus* (Berkeley: University of California Press, 1977), pp. 1–12; M. Rouche, "Grégoire le Grand face à la situation économique de son temps," in *Grégoire le Grand*, ed. Jacques Fontane et al. (Paris: Éditions du CNRS, 1986), pp. 43–44.

2. O'Donnell, *Cassiodorus*, pp. 198–255.

3. Cassiodorus, *De orthographia* 143.1–6.

4. Pierre Courcelle, *Les lettres grecques en Occident de Macrobe à Cassidore* (Paris: De Boccard, 1943), pp. 313–388; Henri-Jean Martin, with the collaboration of Bruno Belmes, *Histoire et pouvoirs de l'écrit* (Paris: Librarie académique Perrin, 1988), pp. 121–177; Ludo J. R. Milis, *Angelic Monks and Earthly Men: Monasticism and Its Meaning to Medieval Society* (Woodbridge, U.K.: Boydell Press, 1992), pp. 92–114.

5. *Regula S. Benedicti* 48.

6. Lutz Kaelber, *Schools of Asceticism: Ideology and Organization in Medieval Religious Communities* (University Park: Pennsylvania State University Press, 1998), pp. 68–74; Friedrich Prinz, "Mönchtum und Arbeitsethos," in *Askese und Kultur: Vor- und Frühbenediktinisches Mönchtum an der Wiege Europas* (Munich: Beck, 1980), pp. 68–74.

7. Jean Leclercq, *L'amour des lettres et le désir de Dieu* (Paris: Éditions du Cerf, 1957); Harvey J. Graff, *The Legacies of Literacy* (Bloomington: Indiana University Press, 1991), pp. 34–74.

8. John van Engen, "The Christian Middle Ages as an Historiographical Problem," *American Historical Review* 91, no. 3 (1986): 519–552.

9. *The Rule of Saint Benedict*, trans. Abbot Gasquet (London: Chatto & Windus, 1909), 33, p. 56.

10. *Moralia in Job* 2.30.49, in *CCSL* 143:88–89; Gregory the Great, *Morals on the Book of Job*, vol. 1 (London: Oxford, 1844), p. 100.

11. See Clare Stancliffe, *St. Martin and His Hagiographer: History and Miracle in Sulpicius Severus* (Oxford: Clarendon Press, 1983); Jeffrey Richards, *Consul of God: The Life and Times of Gregory the Great* (London: Routledge and Kegan Paul, 1980); William D. McCready, *Signs of Sanctity: Miracles in the Thought of Gregory the Great* (Toronto: Pontifical Institute of Mediaeval Studies, 1989).

12. Augustine, *Confessions* 8.4.15.

13. Aviad Kleinberg, "We Did Not Know It Was So: Three Autobiographies from the Middle Ages" (in Hebrew), *Alpayim* 13 (1996): 44–64.

14. John Howe calls this period, which extends from the compilation of Gregory's *Dialogues* to that of the "Dialogues" of Desiderius of Monte Cassino (1058–1087), the "hagiographical dark ages." John Howe, *Church Reform and Social Change in Eleventh-Century Italy: Dominic of Sora and His Patrons* (Philadelphia: University of Pennsylvania Press, 1997), p. 22. Others maintain that saints' Lives continued to be read to laypeople until the ninth century. In any case, these were short texts designed to be heard during religious ceremonies. See Marc van Uytfanghe, "L'hagiographie et son public à l'époque mérovingienne," *Studi Patristica* 16 (1985): 54–62; Lynda L. Coon, *Sacred Fictions: Holy Women and Hagiography in Late Antiquity* (Philadelphia: University of Pennsylvania Press, 1997), pp. 6–7.

15. See the interesting article by Jean-Yves Tilliette, who deals with saints' Lives written in verse between the tenth and twelfth centuries: "Les modèles de sainteté du Xe au XIIe siècle d'après le témoignage des récits hagiographiques en vers métriques," in *Santi e demoni nell'alto medioevo occidentale (secoli V–XI)*, 2 vols. (Spoleto: Centro italiano di studi sull'alto Medioevo, 1989), pp. 381–406.

16. Thomas Head, *Hagiography and the Cult of the Saints: The Diocese of Orleans, 800–1200* (New York: Cambridge University Press, 1990), pp. 1–5.

17. In 878 Hincmar of Rheims wrote a biography of Saint Remigius in which passages for the clergy and passages for the laity appear side by side. This is a rare example of a text designed for a mixed public. See Aron Gourevitch, "Paysans et saints," in *Culture populaire au Moyen Âge*, translated from the Russian by Elena Balzamo (Paris: Aubier, 1996), pp. 51–52.

18. Patrick Geary shows how the peasants of Calais-sur-Anille "banalized" Saint Calais (Carilef) and established quid pro quo relations with him. See Patrick J. Geary, "Humiliation of Saints," in *Living with the Dead in the Middle Ages* (Ithaca: Cornell University Press, 1994), pp. 112–114.

19. On the different techniques for elaborating the saint's biography, see the interesting article by Charles Altman, "Two Types of Opposition and the Structure of Latin Saints' Lives," *Mediaevali et Humanistica*, n.s., 6 (1975): 1–11. See also Thomas J. Heffernan, *Sacred Biography: Saints and Their Biographers in the Middle Ages* (Oxford: Oxford University Press, 1992).

20. Aviad Kleinberg, *Prophets in Their Own Country: Living Saints and the Making of Sainthood in the Later Middle Ages* (Chicago: University of Chicago Press, 1992), pp. 23–24.

21. On the emergence of popular heresy, see R. I. Moore, *The Formation of a Perse-cuting Society: Power and Deviance in Western Europe, 950–1250* (Oxford: Blackwell, 1987), pp. 11–27 and 66–69.

22. André Vauchez, "Diables et hérétiques: Les réactions de l'Église et de la société en Occident face aux mouvements religieux dissidents, de la fin du Xe au début du XIIe siècle," in *Santi e demoni nell'alto medioevo occidentale*, pp. 573–601; R. I. Moore, "New Sects and Secret Meetings: Association and Authority in the Eleventh and Twelfth Centuries," *Studies in Church History* 23 (1986): 47–68.

23. Georges Duby, *Le temps des cathédrales: L'art et la société, 980–1420* (Paris: Gallimard, 1976), pp. 71ff.

24. Richard W. Southern, *Western Society and the Church in the Middle Ages* (Harmondsworth: Penguin, 1990), pp. 240–250.

25. J. Becquet, "Érémitisme et hérésie au Moyen Âge," in *Hérésies et sociétés dans l'époque préindustrielle, XIe–XVIIIe siècle* (Paris: Mouton, 1968), pp. 139–145; Paolo Golinelli, *"Indiscreta sanctitas": Studi sui rapporti tra culti, poteri, e società nel pieno medioevo* (Rome: Istituto storico italiano per il Medio Evo, 1988), pp. 169–184.

26. Henrietta Leyser, *Hermits and the New Monasticism: A Study of Religious Communities in Western Europe, 1000–1150* (London: Palgrave Macmillan, 1984), pp. 87–96.

27. Phyllis G. Jestice, *Wayward Monks and the Religious Revolution of the Eleventh Century* (Leiden: Brill Academic Publishers, 1997), pp. 141–160.

28. In the twelfth century the church tended to regard any preaching by laypeople with suspicion. The Waldensian movement became a heresy because its members re-fused to stop preaching.

29. Richard H. Rouse and Mary A. Rouse, *Preachers, Florilegia, and Sermons: Studies on the Manipulus Florum of Thomas of Ireland* (Toronto: Pontifical Institute of Mediaeval Studies, 1979), pp. 1–64.

30. Claude Bremond, Jacques Le Goff, and Jean-Claude Schmitt, *L' "Exemplum"* (Turnhout: Typologie des sources du Moyen Âge occidental, 1982), pp. 43–63; C. Delcorno, *Exemplum e letteratura* (Bologna: Mulino, 1989); Hans Jörg Gilomen, "Volkskultur und Exemple-Forschung," in *Modernes Mittelalter: Neuer Bilder einer populärer Epoche*, ed. J. Heinzle (Frankfurt-am-Main: Insel, 1994), pp. 165–208. See the impor-tant article by Baudouin de Gaiffier, "L'hagiographie et son public au XIe siècle," in *Miscellanea historica in honorem Leonis van der Essen* (Brussels: Éditions universitaires, 1947), pp. 135–166; Michel Zink, "Les destinataires des recueils de sermons en langue vulgaire au XIIe et au XIIIe siècle: Prédication effective et prédication dans un fauteuil," in Actes du 99e Congrès National des Sociétés savantes, Besançon, 1974, Section de philologie et d'histoire jusqu'à 1610, 1: *La piété populaire au Moyen Âge* (Paris, 1977), pp. 59–74; Beverly Mayne Kienzle, "The Typology of the Medieval Sermon and Its Development in the Middle Ages," in *De l'homélie au sermon: Histoire de la prédication médiévale* (Louvain-la-Neuve, 1993), pp. 83–101.

31. Jean-Claude Schmitt, "La parole apprivoisée" (1979), reprinted in *Le corps, les*

rites, les rêves, le temps (Paris: Gallimard, 2001), pp. 183–210. Alain Boureau shows how the process began with the expansion of the corpus of holy scripture through Christian exegesis, which granted new legitimacy to apocryphal accounts, ancient and modern. That inclusive approach allowed the introduction of narratives from different sources. See Alain Boureau, *L'événement sans fin: Récit et christianisme au Moyen Âge* (Paris: Les Belles Lettres, 1993), pp. 22–27.

32. See Felice Lifshitz, "Beyond Positivism and Genre: 'Hagiographical' Texts as Historical Narrative," *Viator* 25 (1994): 106.

33. Canonization had limited influence on the cult of saints. The church never managed to make "authorized" saints the only objects of worship and had to be content with recognizing saints who had earned official authorization as an elite group, at least among the authorities. See Kleinberg, *Prophets in Their Own Country*, pp. 21–39.

34. On the shift from collections of saints' Lives for the contemplation of monks to collections for popular sermons by preachers (not just Mendicants), see A. Dondaine, "Le dominicain français Jean de Mailly et la *Légende dorée*," *Archives d'histoire dominicaine* 1 (1946): 115–116. Dondaine attributes the shift to Jean de Mailly, dating de Mailly's collection of saints' Lives from between 1225 and 1230.

35. Boureau, *L'événement sans fin*, pp. 32, 58–74.

36. Kleinberg, *Prophets in Their Own Country*, pp. 40–70.

37. On the mnemonic aspects of secular narrative in French epics, see Eugene Vance's excellent article "Roland and Charlemagne: The Remembering Voices and the Crypt," in *Mervelous Signals: Poetics and Sign Theory in the Middle Ages* (Lincoln: University of Nebraska Press, 1989), pp. 51–85.

38. André Vauchez, *La sainteté en Occident aux derniers siècles du Moyen Âge, d'après les procès de canonisation et les documents hagiographiques* (Rome: École française de Rome, 1981), pp. 619–620; Benedicta Ward, *Miracles and the Medieval Mind: Theory, Record, and Event, 1100–1215* (Philadelphia: University of Pennsylvania Press, 1982), pp. 168–182.

39. On the increasing unity in the attribution of saints' names in twelfth- and thirteenth-century Europe, see Robert Bartlett, *The Making of Europe: Conquest, Colonization, and Cultural Change, 950–1350*, 2nd ed. (Princeton: Princeton University Press, 1994), pp. 270–280.

10. Francis of Assisi, a Joyful Ascetic

1. Christine Thouzellier, *Catharisme et valdéisme en Languedoc à la fin du XIIe et au début du XIIIe siècle* (Louvain: Nauwelaerts, 1969), pp. 30–36; Kurt-Victor Selge, *Die ersten Waldenser*, 2 vols. (Berlin: De Gruyter, 1967), 1:25–35.

2. On the Christian tradition of imitating Jesus, see Giles Constable, "The Imitation of the Body of Christ," in *Three Studies in Medieval Religion and Social Thought* (New York: Cambridge University Press, 1995), pp. 194–217.

3. Thomas de Celano, *Vita prima S. Francisci* 2.3.94–96.

4. E. Menestó and S. Brufani, eds., *Fontes Franciscani* (Assisi: Porziuncola, 1995), p. 254. Even in the Middle Ages, many doubted the stigmatization and the Franciscan claims based on it. See André Vauchez, "Les stigmates de saint François et leurs détracteurs," *Mélanges d'archéologie et d'histoire: École française de Rome* 80 (1968): 595–625.

5. Johannes M. Hocht, *Träger der Wundmale Christi*, ed. and completed by A. Guillet (Stein am Rhein, 1986); Chiara Frugoni, *Francesco e l'invenzione delle stimmate: Una storia per e immagini e parole fino a Bonaventura ed a Giotto* (Turin: Einaudi, 1993); Frugoni, *Saint François d'Assise: La vie d'un homme* (Paris: Noësis, 1997), pp. 143–171; H. W. van Os, "St. Francis of Assisi as a Second Christ in Early Italian Paintings," *Simiolus* 7 (1974): 3–20; Ruth Wolff, *Der Heilige Franziskus in Schriften und Bildern des 13. Jahrhunderts* (Berlin: Gebr. Mann Verlag, 1996).

6. Kajaetan Esser, ed., *Die "Opuscula" der hl. Franziskus von Assisi* (Grottaferrata: Editiones Collegii S. Bonaventurae ad Claras Aquas, 1976), pp. 444–445.

7. C. H. Lawrence, *The Friars: The Impact of the Early Mendicant Movement on Western Europe* (London: Longman, 1994), pp. 26–64; John Moorman, *A History of the Franciscan Order* (Oxford: Clarendon Press, 1968); Lazaro de Aspurz, *Franciscan History: The Three Orders of St. Francis of Assisi*, trans. P. Ross (Chicago: Franciscan Herald Press, 1983); Duncan Nimmo, *Reform and Division in the Medieval Franciscan Order: From St. Francis to the Foundation of the Capuchins* (Rome: Capuchin Historical Institute, 1987); Malcolm D. Lambert, *Franciscan Poverty* (London, 1961); Jacques Le Goff, *Saint François d'Assise* (Paris: Gallimard, 1999), esp. chaps. 1 and 2.

8. On Joachim and the Franciscans, see Marjorie Reeves, *The Influence of Prophecy in the Later Middle Ages* (Oxford: University of Notre Dame Press, 1969); Delno C. West and S. Zimdras-Swartz, *Joachim of Fiore: A Study in Spiritual Perception and History* (Bloomington: Indiana University Press, 1983).

9. Referring to the abandonment of the profane world, of course.

10. Aviad Kleinberg, *Prophets in Their Own Country: Living Saints and the Making of Sainthood in the Later Middle Ages* (Chicago: University of Chicago Press, 1992), pp. 126–148; E. Randolph Daniel, *The Franciscan Concept of Mission in the High Middle Ages* (Lexington: University Press of Kentucky, 1975), pp. 37–54.

11. *Scripta Leonis, Rufini et Angeli Sociorum S. Francisci*, ed. Marino Bigaroni, in *"Compilatio Assisiensis" dagli scritti di fr. Leone e compagni su S. Francesco d'Assisi* (Assisi, 1975); Felice Accroca, *Franceso e le sue immagini: Momenti della evoluzione della coscienza storica dei frati minori (secolo XIII–XIV)* (Padua: Centro di studi antoniani, 1997), pp. 57–92; Raoul Manselli, *Francesco e i suoi compagni* (Rome: Istituto storico dei cappuccini, 1995).

12. *Tractatus de miraculis beati Francisci*, in *Analecta franciscana* 10 (1926–1941): 269–331.

13. The chapter numbers are from Rosalind B. Brooke, ed. and trans., *Scripta Leonis, Rufini et Angeli Sociorum S. Francisci* (Oxford: Clarendon Press, 1970).

14. Hester Goodenough Gelber, "A Theater of Virtue: The Exemplary World of

St. Francis of Assisi," in *Saints and Virtues*, ed. John Stratton Hawley (Berkeley: University of California Press, 1987), pp. 15–35.

15. Jacques Dalarun, "La mort des saints fondateurs: De Martin à François," in *Les fonctions des saints dans le monde occidental (du IIIe au XIIIe siècle)* (Rome: École française de Rome, 1991), pp. 193–215. On the development of depictions of saints' deaths in the early Middle Ages, see Otmar Kampert, *Das Sterben der Heiligen: Sterbeberichte unblutiger Märtyrer in der lateinischen Hagiographie des vierten bis sechsten Jahrhunderts* (Altenberge: Oros Verlag, 1998), esp. pp. 229–362.

11. Fra Ginepro, the Holy Fool

1. *Vita S. Clarae* 45, in *Fontes Franciscani*, ed. E. Menestó and S. Brufani (Assisi: Porziuncola, 1995), pp. 2415–50.

2. *Speculum perfectionis* 5.85.

3. *Chronica XXIV generalium*, in *Analecta Franciscana* 3 (1897): 54–64.

4. For the scholarly edition of Fra Ginepro's Life in Latin and Italian, see Giorgio Petrocchi, ed., *La vita di frate Ginepro* (Bologna: Commissione per i testi di lingua, 1960).

5. See Riccardo Pratesi and G. Sabatelli, eds., *I fioretti di S. Francesco* (Rome, 1961).

6. Petrocchi summarizes what little information we have on Fra Ginepro (*La vita di frate Ginepro*, p. xii, n. 2). He was born in the late twelfth century, probably joined the order in 1210 when it was founded, and died in Rome in 1258. His grave is in the church of Santa Maria in Aracoeli, on the Capitoline Hill.

7. On the holy fool in the Christian tradition, see Derek Krueger, *Symeon the Holy Fool: Leontius's Life and the Late Antique City* (Berkeley: University of California Press, 1996), pp. 57–71; John Saward, *Perfect Fools: Folly for Christ's Sake in Catholic and Orthodox Spirituality* (Oxford: Oxford University Press, 1980); Lennart Rydén, ed. and trans., *The Life of St. Andrew the Fool*, 2 vols. (Uppsala: Uppsala University, 1995).

8. From chap. 85, Rosalind B. Brooke, ed. and trans., *Scripta Leonis, Rufini et Angeli Sociorum S. Francisci* (Oxford: Clarendon Press, 1970).

9. "How Brother Juniper Cut Off a Pig's Foot Just to Give It to a Sick Man," in *The Little Flowers of St. Francis*, ed. Raphael Brown [pseud.] (Garden City, N.Y.: Image Books, 1958), pp. 219–222.

10. Ibid., p. 227.

11. Petrocchi, *La vita di frate Ginepro*, pp. 50–51.

12. Ibid., p. 50.

13. That motif is further developed in chapter 8 of the *Little Flowers*. Francis describes in detail a scene of humiliation and violence from which the Franciscan monk will draw "perfect joy" if only he can overcome it willingly.

14. *Little Flowers of St. Francis*, pp. 235–236.

15. Ibid., pp. 227–229.
16. Ibid., p. 234.

12. The Golden Legend

1. The most important work on *The Golden Legend* is still Alain Boureau's *Légende dorée: Le système narratif de Jacques de Voragine († 1298)* (Paris: Éditions du Cerf, 1984). Boureau undertakes what is essentially a structuralist analysis of the *Legend*, based on the hypothesis that, for the most part, it was a theological treatise disguised as a collection of stories and that the narrative almost disappears at times under a jumble of theological messages. Although it is true that Jacobus tries to convey theological messages, in general it is the narrative (after all the cuts that have been made to it) that takes precedence. Few people take *The Golden Legend* for a theological essay. The second part of Boureau's book, which deals with the components of the narration (pp. 190–204), is particularly rich. See also Maria von Nagy and Christoph de Nagy, *Die Legenda Aurea und ihr Verfasser Jacobus de Voragine* (Bern: Francke, 1971); Sherry L. Reames, *The Legenda Aurea: A Reexamination of Its Paradoxical History* (Madison: University of Wisconsin Press, 1985). On Jacobus, see Gabriella Airaldi, *Jacopo da Varagine: Tra santi e mercanti* (Milan: Camunia, 1988); *Legenda Aurea*, trans. Alessandro Vitale Brovarone and Lucetta Vitale Brovarone (Turin: Einaudi, 1995), pp. xii–xix; Regalinde Rhein, *Die Legenda Aurea des Jacobus de Voragine: Die Entfaltung von Heiligkeit in "Historia" und "Doctrine"* (Cologne, 1995), pp. 5–15; Stefania Bertini Guidetti, *I "sermones" di Jacopo da Varazze: Il potere delle immagini nel Duecento* (Florence: Edizioni del Galluzo, 1998), pp. 17–40.

2. For the list of Jacobus' sources, see the recent scholarly edition, Giovanni Paolo Maggioni, ed., *Die Legenda Aurea*, 2 vols. (Tavarnuzze: Edizioni del Galluzzo, 1998), 1:xii–xxv; Rhein, *Die Legenda Aurea*, pp. 21–43; as well as Alain Boureau's introduction in his recent edition (Paris: Gallimard, Bibliothèque de la Pléiade, 2004), pp. xv–xlviii.

3. On the creation of the corpus of saints' narratives in the thirteenth century, see the preface by Antoine Dondaine in his French translation of Jean de Mailly, *Abrégé des gestes et de miracles des saints* (Paris, 1947).

4. On the historical and conceptual background behind the compilation of *The Golden Legend*, see Alain Boureau, "Le grand légendier chrétien," in *L'événment sans fin: Récit et christianisme au Moyen Âge* (Paris: Les Belles Lettres, 1993), pp. 15–37, and his aforementioned introduction to the Pléiade edition.

5. Boureau, *La légende dorée*, pp. 21–25.

6. Maggioni's scholarly edition arrived too late for me to be able to use it. I am not sure, however, that it was a sound decision on the editor's part to favor the text reflecting Jacobus' definitive opinion (Jacobus continued to edit his collection) and

not the more widespread versions. I have based my discussion on the third edition of Theodor Graesse's *Legenda Aurea* (Dresden, 1890; reprint, Osnabrück: O. Zeller, 1969), and on Boureau's edition.

7. On Mary, see Susan Haskins, *Mary Magdalen: Myth and Metaphor* (Orlando, Fla.: Harcourt, 1994); Victor Saxer, *Le culte de Marie Madeleine en Occident des origines à la fin du Moyen Âge* (Auxerre: Publications de la société des fouilles archéologiques et des monuments historiques de l'Yonne, 1959).

8. Jacobus collected and reformulated more than he invented. But he played a critical role in diffusing and popularizing materials which were little known before his collection was compiled.

9. See Victor Saxer, *Le dossier vézelien de Marie-Madeleine: Invention et translation des reliques en 1265–1267* (Brussels: Société des bollandistes, 1975).

10. See Haskins, *Mary Magdalen*, pp. 98–133. On forgeries and fictive transfers in the Middle Ages, see Patrick J. Geary, *Furta Sacra: Thefts of Relics in the Central Middle Ages* (Princeton: Princeton University Press, 1978), pp. 74–78.

11. Katherine Ludwig Jansen, "Maria Magdalena: Apostolorum Apostola," in *Women Preachers and Prophets: Through Two Millennia of Christianity*, ed. B. Mayne Kienzle and P. J. Walker (Berkeley: University of California Press, 1998), pp. 57–96; Nicole Bériou, "La Madeleine dans les sermons Parisiens du XIIIe siècle," in *Modern Questions about Medieval Sermons*, ed. N. Bériou and D. L. D'Avray (Spoleto: Centro italiano di studi sull'Alto medioevo, 1994), pp. 323–399.

12. Jacobus de Voragine, *The Golden Legend: Readings on the Saints*, trans. William Granger Ryan, 2 vols. (Princeton: Princeton University Press, 1993), 1:377.

13. Ibid.

14. Ibid., p. 379.

15. Ibid.

16. Ibid.

17. Mary Magdalene's story appropriates elements from the story of another Mary, Mary the Egyptian, a repentant harlot who lived many years in the desert practicing rigorous asceticism.

18. Jacobus de Voragine, *The Golden Legend*, 1:382.

19. In the East, the dragon first appears in images of the saint in the early eleventh century. See Kenneth M. Setton, "St. George's Head," *Speculum* 48 (1973): 2.

20. Georges Didi-Huberman et al., *Saint Georges et le dragon: Versions d'une légende* (Paris: A. Biro, 1994), pp. 42–44; C. Bremond and C. Velay-Valentin, *Formes médiévales du conte merveilleux* (Paris: Stock, 1989), pp. 24–29.

21. Jean de Mailly, *Abrégé des gestes et miracles des saints*, pp. 170–172.

22. Odo of Cluny, *Vita S. Geraldi*, in *PL*, vol. 133, cols. 639–704; Georges Duby, *Le Moyen Âge, 987–1460* (Paris: Hachette, 1987), pp. 32–34.

23. Hippolyte Delehaye, *Les légendes grecques des saints militaires* (Paris: Picard, 1909), pp. 45–76.

24. Franz Cumont, "La plus ancienne légende de S. Georges," *Revue de l'histoire des religions* 114 (1936): 5–51.

25. Herbert Thurston, "St. George," *The Month* 61 (1892): 27–32.

26. Jonathan Riley-Smith, *The First Crusade and the Idea of Crusading* (Philadelphia: University of Pennsylvania Press, 1986), p. 105. Jacobus sets the vision in Jerusalem. According to Karl Erdmann, George's first appearance as a knight leading Christian troops on horseback is in 1068, in a battle near Cerami, Sicily. Karl Erdmann, *The Origin of the Idea of Crusade*, trans. M. W. Baldwin and W. Goffart (Princeton: Princeton University Press, 1977), pp. 134–135.

27. Ron Barkay, "Myths and Their Role in Spanish Historiography of the Middle Ages and the Modern Period" (in Hebrew), in *Science, Magic, and Mythology in the Middle Ages* (Jerusalem, 1987), pp. 85–88; see also William Melczer, *The Pilgrim's Guide to Santiago de Compostela* (New York: Italica Press, 1993), pp. 65–66.

28. On the introduction of the military term *miles Christi* into religious discourse, see Franco Cardini, *Alle radici della cavalleria medievale* (Florence: La nuova Italia, 1981), pp. 178–183.

29. Jacobus de Voragine, *The Golden Legend*, 1:239.

30. Baudouin de Gaiffier, "La mort par le glaive dans les passions des martyrs," in *Recherches d'hagiographie latine* (Brussels: Subsidia Hagiographica, 1971), pp. 70–76.

31. Hans Friedrich Rosenfeld, *Der heilige Christophorus, seine Verehrung und seine Legende* (Leipzig: Kommissionsverlag O. Harrassowitz, 1937), pp. 8–14.

32. Jacobus de Voragine, *The Golden Legend*, 2:11.

33. Ibid.

34. Rosenfeld, *Der heilige Christophorus*, pp. 473–498.

35. Jacobus de Voragine, *The Golden Legend*, 1:127–128. [Translation modified by the author.]

36. On the manuscript tradition, see Margarete Rösler, *Die Fassungen der Alexius Legende* (Vienna: W. Braumüller, 1905), pp. 23–25. A previous version of this discussion was published in English: Aviad Kleinberg, "The Prodigal Son: St. Alexis and the Role of Saintly Myths in Medieval Culture," *Tel Aviver Jahrbuch für deutsche Geschichte* 22 (1993): 43–57.

37. An English translation of the Syriac and Greek versions and a study of the sources can be found in Carl J. Odenkirchen, *The Life of St. Alexius* (Brookline, Mass.: Classical Folia Edition, 1978). The translated Syriac legend appears on pp. 13–20. See also Han J. W. Drijvers, "Die Legenda des heilige Alexius und der Typus des Gottesmannes in syrischen Christentums," in *Typus, Symbol, Allegorie bei dem Öostlischen Vätern und ihren Parallelen im Mittelalter*, ed. M. Schmidt and C. F. Geyer (Regensburg: Pustet, 1982), pp. 187–217; Ulrich Melk, "Saint Alexis et son épouse dans la légende latine et la première chanson française," in *Love and Marriage in the Twelfth Century*, ed. W. van Hoecke and A. Welkenhuysen (Louvain: Mediaevelia Lovaniensia, 1981), pp. 162–170.

38. Odenkirchen, *Life of St. Alexius*, pp. 20–28.

39. *MGH, SS* 6.477. See also Brian Stock, *Listening for the Text: On the Uses of the Past* (Baltimore: Johns Hopkins University Press, 1990), pp. 24–28. On the influence of the story of Alexis, see Dyan Elliott, *Spiritual Marriage: Sexual Abstinence in Medieval Wedlock* (Princeton: Princeton University Press, 1993), pp. 104–113.

40. Christopher Storey, ed., *La vie de saint Alexis* 12.56–60 (Oxford: Blackwell, 1968), pp. 95–96. For the version based on a different manuscript, see T. D. Hemmings, ed., *La vie de saint Alexis* (Exeter, U.K., 1994).

41. *Li roumans de saint Alessin* 11.169–172, in Alison Goddard Elliott, *The "Vie de saint Alexis" in the Twelfth and Thirteenth Centuries: An Edition and a Commentary* (Chapel Hill: University of North Carolina Press, 1983), pp. 28–43. For a comparison between the Latin and French versions, see Charles E. Stebbins, *A Critical Edition of the 13th and 14th Centuries Old French Poem Versions of the "Vie de Saint Alexis"* (Tübingen: M. Niemeyer, 1974), pp. 71–83. The French version waters down the Latin text a great deal.

42. Baudouin de Gaiffier, "*Intactam sponsam reliquens:* À propos de la vie de S. Alexis," *Analecta Bollandiana* 65 (1947): 157–195.

43. Aleksander Gieysztor, "*Pauper sum et peregrinus*. La légende de saint Alexis en Occident: Un idéal de pauvreté," in *Études sur l'histoire de la pauvreté*, ed. Michel Mollat, 8 vols. (Paris: Publications de la Sorbonne, 1974), 1:125–139.

44. Jacobus de Voragine, *The Golden Legend*, 1:372.

45. Ibid.

46. Ibid. [Translation modified by the author.]

47. Ibid., 1:373.

48. Ibid.

49. Mary Clayton and Hugh Magennis, *The Old English Lives of St. Margaret* (New York: Cambridge University Press, 1994), pp. 1–34. On the story of Margaret, see also Elizabeth A. Petroff, "Transforming the World: The Serpent-Dragon and the Virgin Saint," in *Body and Soul: Essays on Medieval Women and Mysticism* (New York: Oxford University Press, 1994), pp. 97–109.

50. David H. Farmer, "Fourteen Holy Helpers," in *Oxford Dictionary of Saints*, 3rd ed. (New York: Oxford University Press, 1992), p. 185.

51. J. P. Kirsch, *Die heilige Cäcilia in der römischen Kirche des Altertums* (Paderborn: Studien zur Geschichte und Kultur des Altertums, 1910), pp. 8–14, 58–74; Hippolyte Delehaye, *Étude sur le légendier romain: Les saints de novembre et de décembre* (Brussels: Subsidia Hagiographica, 1936), pp. 73–96; Elliott, *Spiritual Marriage*, pp. 67–73.

52. *Calendarium romanum* (Vatican City, 1969), pp. 68–69.

53. Jacobus de Voragine, *The Golden Legend*, 2:319.

54. "Dearer" in the English translation. Ibid., pp. 319–320.

55. Ibid., p. 320.

56. Ibid., p. 322.

57. Ibid., 1:369.

58. Ibid.

59. Ibid., 2:337.

60. Elizabeth Robertson, "The Corporeality of Female Sanctity in *The Life of Saint Margaret*," in *Images of Sainthood in Medieval Europe*, ed. R. Blumenfeld-Kosinski and T. Szell (Ithaca: Cornell University Press, 1991), pp. 268–287. For another legend in which sexual combat occupies a central place, see Shari Horner, "Spiritual Truth and Sexual Violence: The Old English *Juliana*, Anglo-Saxon Nuns, and the Discourse of Female Monastic Enclosure," *Signs* 19, no. 3 (1994): 649–675. On how Jacobus de Voragine conceives of sexuality, see Guidetti, *I "sermones" di Jacopo da Varazze*, pp. 83–102.

61. Jacobus de Voragine, *The Golden Legend*, 1:369.

Concluding Reflections

1. This expression is drawn from Michel de Certeau's brilliant introduction to his *Invention du quotidien* (Paris: Gallimard, 1990), pp. xxxvi–lx. The rest of the book does not keep the introduction's promise and becomes in great part a scholastic exercise of the very sort it is criticizing.

2. Jacobus de Voragine, *The Golden Legend: Readings on the Saints*, trans. William Granger Ryan, 2 vols. (Princeton: Princeton University Press, 1993), 1:25.

3. Jerome Bruner shows how a reader of James Joyce's short story "Clay" creates a "virtual" text from the written text. See his "Two Modes of Thought," in *Actual Minds, Possible Worlds* (Cambridge, Mass.: Harvard University Press, 1986), pp. 11–43, 161–171. We may assume that the process is even more creative in the case of an unwritten text, heard only once in its entirety under fluctuating conditions of attention and external disturbances. On the relation between what is heard and what is written, see John McNamara, "Problems in Contextualizing Oral Circulation of Early Medieval Saints' Legends," in *Telling Tales: Medieval Narrative and the Folk Tradition*, ed. F. Canadé Sautman et al. (New York: St. Martin's Press, 1998), pp. 21–36.

4. See Richard Southern's brilliant analysis of the collapse of papal power in the Middle Ages. He attributes it to the fact that the system of ecclesiastical authority had become complicated and dependent on a large group of local agents. The gap between stunning declarations and a truth full of holes destabilized the entire structure of ecclesiastical power. See Richard Southern, *Western Society and the Church in the Middle Ages* (Harmondsworth: Penguin, 1990), pp. 91–169.

5. James Scott's books describe the price that totalitarian societies are willing to pay to maintain the appearance of power. On this particularly important debate, see his *Domination and the Arts of Resistance: Hidden Transcripts* (New Haven: Yale University Press, 1990), pp. 45–69.

6. In a series of interviews with Catherine Darbo-Peschanski, Paul Veyne deals with the question of the nonideological nature of religion consumers' activities and

the broader repercussions of that phenomenon of "everydayness." Like Southern, Veyne also notes the importance of the "little reasons," often neglected by historians, in triggering historical processes. See Paul Veyne, *Le quotidien et l'intéressant: Entretiens avec Catherine Darbo-Peschanski* (Paris: Albin Michel, 1995), pp. 147–190.

7. Sherry Reames shows that the learned attacks on *The Golden Legend* began in the late fourteenth century in humanist circles and that a certain decline in its diffusion can be observed in the late fifteenth century, following constant criticism by humanists. See Sherry L. Reames, *The Legenda Aurea: A Reexamination of Its Paradoxical History* (Madison: University of Wisconsin Press, 1985), pp. 27–70.

8. Innocent IV, *Commentaria in quinque libros decretalium* 1.1, s.v. *firmiter* (Frankfurt, 1570).

9. See Emmanuel Le Roy Ladurie, *Montaillou, village occitan de 1294 à 1324* (Paris: Gallimard, 1975).

10. Jean-Claude Schmitt, *Le saint lévrier: Guinefort, guérisseur d'enfants depuis le XIIIe siècle* (Paris: Flammarion, 1979).

11. An eloquent example of the major difference between dogma and its practical application in Judaism can be found in Ruth Lamdan's work, which deals with the question of the attitude of the halacha toward women in Palestine, Syria, and Egypt in the sixteenth century. The implicit theology underlying concrete halachic decisions is very different from the theological notions found in books, which are supposed to serve as a source for those promulgating the decisions. See Ruth Lamdan, *A People in Itself: Jewish Women in Palestine, Syria, and Egypt in the Sixteenth Century* (in Hebrew) (Tel Aviv, 1996).

12. Although ideological questions do not interest him, it is worth mentioning here the pioneering work of Erving Goffman, who also influenced James Scott and Michel de Certeau. Goffman examines how apparently powerless people jam the system in which they find themselves, and he shows how even acts that were not designed to be harmful can contribute toward undermining an authoritarian system. See Erving Goffman, *Asylums: Essays on the Social Situation of Mental Patients and Other Inmates* (1961; reprint, Harmondsworth: Anchor Books, 1968), pp. 187–266.

INDEX

Asceticism (*continued*)

101, 109, 115, 149–150, 170–171, 174–176, 221–223, 270–271; social meaning of, 85–86, 87–88, 90, 99–101, 110, 119, 121–127, 132–133, 136–141, 149–150; ideological or theological foundation of, 86–87; and salvation, 86–87, 90, 98, 99, 100, 122–123, 188; and surplus of suffering or virtue, 86–87, 100, 123, 125, 188; power of ascetics, 87, 122–123, 126, 132, 133–134, 136–137, 172–176, 178–180, 214–215, 216; skepticism regarding, 88, 136–137; in Egyptian desert, 89, 111–112; and Stoicism, 92–95, 96–98, 99, 112, 113, 227; and Cynicism, 95–96, 98, 227; as athletic contest or battle, 96, 104, 111; Christian as opposed to Stoic, 96–98, 99; attitudes of church hierarchy toward, 99–101, 127–133, 141–142, 150; charisma of ascetics, 101, 109, 128–134, 198, 199, 213, 216, 217; as reform movement, 101–102; master-disciple relationship, 113–114, 142–145; and sanctity, 118–119; veneration of ascetics, 118–119, 124–127, 129, 130; ascetics as liminal figures, 121–127, 133–134, 138, 148, 179–180, 243; eremitic communities, 142–144, 146–150; cenobitic communities, 144–150, 165; in Jacobus de Voragine's *Golden Legend*, 242, 250, 263–264, 265–267, 272, 283. *See also* Antony, St.; Cult of saints; Monasticism; Simeon Stylites, St.

Athanasius' *Life of Saint Antony. See* Antony, St.

Augustine, St., 55, 72; on cult of saints, 48–49, 51–52, 190–191; *City of God,*

98; on Donatists, 115; *Confessions,* 190–191; and Augustinian rule, 198

Augustine of Canterbury, 51–52

Augustinians, 198, 199

Austin, J. L., on performatives, 126

Babylas, St., 45

Babylonian Talmud: Avodah Zarah 18a, 18–19; Rabbi Yose Ben Kisma and Rabbi Chanina Ben Teradyon in, 18–19, 157; *Sanhedrin* 96b, 23; Zechariah's blood, 23; Rabbi Shimon bar Yochai and son, 135–136; *Shabbos* 33b, 135–136, 157

Balaam, prophecy of, 114

Bar Kochba revolt, 18

Barnabas, 38

Bartholomew (apostle), martyrdom of, 20

Bartholomew of Trent, 251; *Liber epilogorum in gesta sanctorum,* 240

Basil of Caesarea, St., 145

Becket, St. Thomas, 240

Benedict of Nursia, St., 256; and monasticism, 145–146, 184, 186–189, 190, 194, 197, 198, 202

Bernard of Clairvaux, St., 240

Biblical passages: Amos 7:10–17, 4; Matt. 11:3–5, 9; Mark 1:22, 10; Mark 2:7–11, 10; Mark 3:21–22, 10; Matt. 13:35, 10; Mark 6:2–6, 10–11; Luke 6:20–26, 11–12; Isaiah 53:3–11, 13–14; John 18:36, 32; Rom. 13:1–2, 32; Acts 34–41, 37; Gen. 28:12–15, 65; Matt. 18:12–13, 67; Ps. 23, 67; Matt. 7:23, 80; Matt. 11:18–19, 90; Luke 6:24–25, 97; 2 Cor. 3:6, 105; Matt. 6:34, 107, 108; Matt. 19:21–22, 107, 108; Isaiah 35:1, 114; Num. 24:5–6, 114; Luke 14:26, 133; Luke 14:33,